Systematic Approach to
ADVERTISING CREATIVITY

BOOKS BY THE AUTHOR

Advertising Layout and Art Direction

Visual Persuasion: The Effect of Pictures
on the Subconscious

How to Live with a Neurotic Dog

How to Play Golf in the Low 120's

How to Live with a Neurotic Wife

How to Live with a Neurotic Husband

How to Look Like Somebody in Business
without Being Anybody

How to Be Analyzed by a
Neurotic Psychoanalyst

Games Dogs Play

Systematic Approach to
Advertising Creativity

How to Get a Better-paying Job—without
Asking for It

Motorist Guide to New York

Pictionary

My First Crossword Puzzle

Systematic Approach to ADVERTISING CREATIVITY

Written and designed by

STEPHEN BAKER

McGraw-Hill Book Company

New York   St. Louis   San Francisco   Auckland   Bogotá
Düsseldorf   Johannesburg   London   Madrid   Mexico   Montreal
New Delhi   Panama   São Paulo   Singapore   Sydney   Tokyo   Toronto

All ideas begin with information

Library of Congress Cataloging in Publication Data

Baker, Stephen, date.
 Systematic approach to advertising creativity.

 Includes index.
 1. Advertising. 2. Creative ability in business.
I. Title.
HF5823.B254   659.1   78-23814
ISBN 0-07-003352-8

7890   HDHD   865

The editors for this book were W. Hodson Mogan and Tobia L. Worth,
the art editor was Richard A. Roth, and the production supervisor
was Teresa F. Leaden. It was set in Times Roman
by The Clarinda Company.

Printed and bound by Halliday Lithograph.

Contents

Preface

This is a different kind of book, one that may cause a few raised eyebrows among diehard academicians. The traditional piecemeal approach to advertising, which deals with media, art, copy, marketing, and other departments as separate subjects, is set aside. Instead, advertising is treated as a whole, with the *creative* as the pivotal force.

There is a reason for having taken this approach. For too long a time various advertising functions have been treated as if they were isolated entities, each moving in its self-imposed orbit. This just is not so. All parts in advertising are closely interwoven. Therefore, no one working in the field, regardless of job title, can afford to have details obscure his or her vision of the end product, the advertising campaign. More and more people in the field are beginning to find that out. This is why today so many art directors are writing headlines, copywriters drawing pictures, creative directors working on marketing plans, and even agency presidents scribbling on yellow pads thoughts that serve as a springboard to print and television campaigns. The barriers between departments have come tumbling down.

That being the case, we hope that this book has something to offer to everyone in advertising—something to the art director or copywriter who wishes to find out more about the business side of his or her job, the account executive who is eager to solidify his or her relationship with the creative department, and even the advertiser who tries to make sense out of the advertising agency.

Moreover, this book implies that the differences between *creative* and *noncreative* are not nearly so sharp as they are reputed to be. This contention, too, may be challenged by those who feel that their territorial prerogatives are encroached upon. To them, we have this to say: lately behavioral psychologists have raised important questions about the inviolability of creativity—about whether that trait is genetic. There is growing evidence that, much like an individual's intelligence quotient, creative performance too changes with the environment.

The fact is that creativity, visceral as it may "feel," is as much of an intellectual process as it is an emotional one. As in mathematics, the steps involved in problem solving follow an orderly sequence. The basic formula is much the same every time. Information gathering comes first; analysis follows. And finally—eureka!—the idea "occurs."

The pyramid principle proposed in this book is one adman's grandiose attempt to illustrate *creative logic*. No doubt, others would have found another, perhaps a better, way to describe the process. For our purpose, the pyramid principle will have to do. It describes fairly what we are talking about.

There is really nothing elusive or mysterious about creativity. Anyone who can talk is able to write. Anyone who can see is able to visualize. *And anyone who can think is able to have ideas*.

So welcome, you new breed of all-around advertising professionals, the creative generalists.

**Stephen Baker
New York, New York**

Acknowledgments

It takes time and effort to put together a book like this. To the hundreds of professionals who so willingly lent a hand, the author can only say, "Thank you very much, all of you." It would be an impossible task to mention everyone who helped in making this book a reality. Here is an attempt:

Shirley Simkin, Robert Steigman, and George Watts (Young & Rubicam International Inc.); William E. Robertson (U.S. News & World Report); Alan Purver (Bubble & Squeak Productions, Ltd.); Steve Erenberg (Don Smolev Advertising & Graphics, Inc.); Bert R. Briller (Television Information Service); Robert Javits (Volkswagen); D. C. Austin (B. F. Goodrich Co.); Cathy Grandjean and Bob Berenson (Grey Advertising Inc.); Mervyn G. Oakner (Anderson McConnel Oakner Inc.); Art Meramus, Ron Howell, Richard Shintaku, and Tony Chevins (Cunningham & Walsh Inc.); Gordon Horsburgh (Cadillac Motor Car Division); J. Mandracchia (Kenyon & Eckhardt Inc.); L. Claypool (Pabst Blue Ribbon); Edwin Lewis and Nat Bukar (Lewis Levine Advertising); James Himonas and Dan Cohen (Rosenfeld, Sirowitz, Lawson & West, Inc.); Don Carlos (Bozell & Jacobs, Inc.); Thomas W. Laughlin and Jan Ponchalek (Clinton E. Frank, Inc.); Edward I. Barz (W. R. Simmons & Associates Research); Marie D. Agnitch and W. A. Armbruster (D'Arcy-MacManus & Masius, Inc.); David A. Bortner (David A. Bortner, Inc.); Phil Wasserman (Solters & Roskin, Inc.); Frank Cowan (Frank Cowan Photography); Molly A. Hudson (Campbell-Ewald Co.); Stan Levy (WNBC-TV); Albert Warren (Television Digest); Howard G. Mitchell (Fairburn System, Mitchell Press Limited); George Lois (Lois Holland Callaway Inc.); H. Allen Carrol, Dan Hutchins, Sue Sawyer, Emery Westfall, and Susan Farell (AT&T); Burns W. Roper (The Roper Organization, Inc.); Marylin M. Bockman (American Association of Advertising Agencies); David H. Polinger and Christina Parham (WSNL-TV); Susan D. Sanders (Friedlich, Fearon & Strohmeier Inc.); Carl Ally, Gerald Shapiro, and David May (Carl Ally Inc.); Robert H. Levenson, Helmut Krone, Nat Waterson, John Leonard, Bill Abrams, Ruth Ziff, Marvin Honig, Bert Steinhauser, Jerry Genteel, Glenn Phillips, and many others (Doyle Dane Bernbach Inc.); John E. Tuthill (Commercial Credit Company); Jack Cantwell (Jack Cantwell, Inc.); David Deutsch (David Deutsch Associates, Inc.); Ben Somoroff (Ben Somoroff Photography); Zal Venet (Venet Advertising); Russel K. Shaffer (Richard K. Manoff Inc.); Zach Baym (Paradigm Advertising, Inc.); Randy Barket (Long, Haymes & Carr, Incorporated); S. Kent Wall (Beautymist Brand, Hanes Hosiery, Inc.); Donald G. Hileman (University of Tennessee); Robert Bach, Agi Clarke, and Jerry Siano (N. W. Ayer & Co.); Nat B. Eisenberg (Nat B. Eisenberg Production); Raymond and Eleanor Jacobs (Earth Shoes, Kalso Systemet, Inc.); Dr. Louis N. Baker and Larry Chilnick (New York–New Jersey Regional Transplant); Edith Munger and Joe Grazzianio (Chapel Hill Memorial Home); Howard Zieff (film director); George Doubrava (Earle & Jones, Inc.); Norman Rinehart (Movielab, Inc.); Kenneth L. Roper, Jr. (Eva Gabor International); Charlette Thompson, Joe Hannon, Al Hamlin, Beverly Fitzsimmons, Jim Caroll, and Al Bensusen (Benton & Bowles, Inc.); Gene Federico and Dick Lord (Lord, Geller, Federico & Partners Inc.); Peter Greer (Greer, DuBois & Co., Inc.); Lou Dorfsman (CBS); Tom Dale and Sid Shapiro (Penthouse U.); Sam Vitt and Mike La Terra (Vitt Media International); Elies Getz and Arnold Arlow (Martin Landey, Arlow Advertising, Inc.); Alan Stanley (Dolphin Productions, Inc.); Melvin Gray (Bettmann Archive, Inc.); Clarence H. Baylis (The Type Group Inc.); Tim Boxer (Manhattan Magazine); Richard Weiner (Richard Weiner, Inc.); Milton Glazer (New York Magazine); Chris Samuels (Information System); George Schmidt (Industrial Motivation, Inc.); Karen Gregory, Jeremy Ritzer, and Raymond A. League (Zebra Advertising); Peter Fallon (Modern Talking Picture Service, Inc.); William Leonard (LCP Design, Inc.); Don Adler (Filmplace, Inc.); Thomas J. McGoldrick and George Huntington (Television Bureau); Ed Tricomi (IF Studios); Kathy Spellman and Bill Berta (Bloomingdale's); Paul Hoffman and Paul Fredrics (Funnyface); Evin C. Varner (Shotwell, Craven, Varner, Inc.); H. Hamburger (Visual Promotions, Inc.); Caroll Stettner (A-Tee-Shirt); Art Jacks (Anaforms, Inc.); Tom Hechts, Joe Schindelman, and Ray Myers (Wells, Rich, Greene, Inc.); Tom Nathan and Mike Drazen (Scali, McCabe, Sloves, Inc.); Bob Brown (Batten, Barton, Durstine & Osborn, Inc.); Nick Pappas (Ted Bates & Co., Inc.); Paul E. Gershald and Peter Case (Advertising Research Foundation); Tony Molocon (Douglas Leigh, Inc.); Jerry Taylor (Harper's Bazaar); Bill Tate (The New York Times); Pat Dawson and Richard Neer (WNEW); Dick Levsky (Music House, Inc.); Jay Maisel (photographer); Irving Penn (Photographer); Robert Palmer and Ernie Potischman (Kelly, Nason, Inc.); Douglas Leigh Transit Advertising; Bill Stettner (photographer); Warren Pfaff (Warren Pfaff, Inc.); John Claunts (Bartlett-Collins Co.); Doris Shaw and Jerry Bennett (Saks Fifth Avenue); Betty Dornheim and Jane Kinne (photo researchers); Susan Swimmer (Viacom); Bill Evans (Clio); Don Turner and Pat Elis (Doubleday Advertising); Ira Weinblatt and Susan A. Irwin (Dancer Fitzgerald Sample, Inc.); Luisa Bacchiani, Claire Mangers, Margie Schiff, Sidney Koblenz, and Gene Schwartz (Megaman, Inc.); Michael Smith (Unification Church); Herb Valen (Valen Associates); Walter F. Higgins (Hecht Higgins & Petterson); Meryl Joseph and William R. Behannia (A. C. Nielsen Company); Chuck Philpott (Ad Man Company, Inc.); Richard Lebenson (Pratt Institute); Leonard Kalcheim (Paramount Pictures Corporation); Maxwell J. Gosling (J. Walter Thompson Company); Nancy Lee Fuller (Norcross Inc.); Brian Harrod and Allan Kazmer (McCann-Erickson, Toronto); Madeleine Morrissey (Dana Perfumes Corporation); and Donald G. Conant (Eastman Kodak Company).

Special gratitude should go to several close friends who were there when needed (if they were not close friends at the beginning of writing this book, they became so when we finished). To mention a few: Janice Holling, a writer who can type; Lynn Clayton, a staunch defender of the English language; Mike Drexler, head of the media department at Doyle Dane Bernbach and foremost expert in his field; Tobia L. Worth and Richard A. Roth, at McGraw-Hill, involved in the day-to-day production of this book, and, finally, William Mogan, in charge of keeping wandering authors from wandering too far.

I thank all of you.

Systematic Approach to ADVERTISING CREATIVITY

Chapter One

Creativity Is a State of Mind

Many people, perhaps most, think that ideas fall from heaven like manna: all one has to do is look up and pray. Unfortunately, creativity does not work quite that way. Ideas rarely happen as if by divine revelation. More often than not, they are the end product of arduous and well-organized intellectual activity. The final thought, referred to here as the *idea,* is the result.

Once you are willing to concede that creativity is not a haphazard but a purposeful exercise, things fall into line with surprising ease. Remember that logic encourages, *not* discourages, inspiration. Use it and you will never again experience a paucity of ideas.

The Pyramid Principle

To illustrate our point, we have chosen as a symbol one of man's most extraordinary achievements, the pyramid. This structure rests on a wide base. Reaching for the sky, it tapers upward until it comes to a point. In that it bears a close re-

semblance to systematic problem solving.

Now let us divide the pyramid into three parts and examine each part a little more closely.

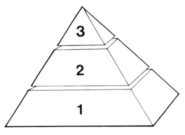

Part 1 The foundation of the pyramid, Part 1, is the equivalent of the beginning of the creative thought process, the gathering of *information*. Without it, the structure would have no more solidity than a house of cards.

Part 2 Part 2 represents the next phase, *analysis,* which includes a wide variety of activities. Fortunately, the human brain is eminently flexible. It can stretch, dissect, combine, compare, backtrack, and juggle thought components with amazing facility. When it comes to reasoning, the brain surpasses even the largest computers, which admit-

tedly can ingest several billion bits of information but, unless told what to do with all that fodder, produce nothing of value.

Part 3 This part is the culmination of all the effort, the *idea*.

Conscious versus Subconscious

There are those who reject the notion that creativity is merely a form of discipline. Most of the nonbelievers come from three groups.

Members of the first group are adherents of mystic cults that advocate "total relaxation" as a shortcut method of making creative discoveries rather than taxing one's energies. They offer "scientific evidence" that staring blankly into space produces significant physiological changes in the brain, the heart, the stomach, and even the skin to herald the arrival of new and profound discoveries. The goal is a state of no-thought tranquillity. Since the purpose of this book is to nourish the mind and not to "purify" it, we shall touch only lightly and somewhat skeptically on this form of creativity in Chapter 6.

The second group consists of those who seek creative stimulation through the ingestion of drugs (almost 1 out of 5 adults in the United States has had experience with marijuana) or alcohol (an estimated 75 million people habitually pour themselves a drink or two for moral support). Unfortunately, nothing much happens in the way of inspiration by using this method. While it is true that on some occasions (mostly social), any of these feel-good staples does possess a certain therapeutic value, it is hardly a substitute for sound thinking. Few good ideas occur in the vacuous existence of various "highs."

The third group that dislikes a systematic approach to creativity is the most knowledgeable sector of all: the creative professionals. Among them are writers, art directors, illustrators, photographers, television directors, creative directors, advertising executives, and others whose job it is to create. Many of these people feel strongly that creativity is a God-given talent, not a self-taught skill. And since they are supposed to be experts on the subject, their protestations cannot be dismissed with a shrug of the shoulders.

Actually, if members of this elite group would only probe deeper into their thought processes, they would find that they, too, follow the information-cogitation-idea formula based on the pyramid principle. Since they have followed the same routine for many years, however, this thought process has become nothing more than a reflex action. The fact is that creativity calls for a conscious effort, just as do the recitation of a poem, the execution of a golf swing, the preparation of a meal. As such, it can be learned by anyone.

Creativity versus Talent

It is important and reassuring to know that the ability to create something tangible (a picture, a book, a play, or a headline) is hardly the sole

criterion of being creative. Such an accomplishment merely suggests the presence of a certain *talent;* it qualifies the individual as an expert in a field. However, it is possible to be creative yet not to profess technical virtuosity in any one area. We all know of people who manage large and complex corporations, teach at universities, organize municipalities, and send rockets into orbit, all in the conspicuous absence of a single patent or copyright to their names or even a credit line anywhere. Yet they, too, are breaking ground and can be considered as creative as anyone at the drawing table or the typewriter.

The hallmark of creative persons is their ability to initiate projects. If they lack the particular talent or training needed to implement their ideas, as is often the case, they know how to find someone who has it.

Purposeful Creativity: The Importance of Having a Goal

Setting a specific goal may inhibit those who view creativity as a prime outlet for self-expression: abstract painters, poets, jazz musicians, stand-up comedians, or others whose success depends on their spontaneous charm. Few advertising people can afford to adopt that attitude. There is not much room for vagabond minds in a business in which close deadlines, marketing platforms, stringent reproduction requirements (size, number of colors, screen, and so on) and tight budgets prevail. A great deal of money is invested in ideas in advertising, which is a $30 billion-plus-a-year industry. In fact, in an advertising agency the financial penalties for a single creative faux pas may be serious enough for the culprit to lose his or her job. There is a further point: one of the most interesting aspects of creativity is that a clear definition of purpose encourages not only better ideas but *more* of them.

You Are Creative

Advertising is a creative undertaking; the field attracts active minds. If you are in the advertising business, your mind must be one of them. So do not let anybody brainwash you and tell you that you have no creative spark. This is nonsense. If you can hold down your job, you are creative. It makes no difference in which department you work or what your job title may be; you definitely are not a mental slouch. Remember that creativity is an acquired trait. To be creative, all you must do is make up your mind that this is what you want to do.

Your attitude has as much to do with your creative potential as any talent that accompanies your job description.

It is essential, of course, that you maintain a positive image of yourself. Nothing hampers creative growth more than a lack of genuine self-confidence—the tendency to recoil at the prospect of being asked to solve a problem.

Learn to ignore certain myths that have a way of getting around. Most of them are circulated by groups of individuals for purposes of self-aggrandizement.

Myth 1: Creative Departments (Copy, Art) Have a Monopoly on Creativity For obvious reasons, writers and artists subscribe to this myth. Why shouldn't they? Their livelihood depends on keeping it alive. But what about your livelihood? The fact is that it takes creativity to tackle almost any type of assignment in advertising, not only a headline or a layout but also a media plan, a research project, a business letter, and even a friendly lunch with a client.

Myth 2: Age Determines Creative Ability This myth is a favorite contention of ambitious people who feel that their lot would vastly improve if only those past the age of 30 would see the light, concede defeat, and move over. It has yet to be demonstrated that creative ability diminishes with age. People may become less restive in their quest for new ideas as they get older, but that

3

loss is more than compensated for with judgment nurtured by experience.

Some of the most vigorous and best-known creative people in advertising have long passed their Wunderkind phase. Many are old enough to tell stories to their grandchildren. Not a single member of the Copy Hall of Fame (membership is a singular honor bestowed on an individual for outstanding creative performance) is under 40 years of age. In a survey conducted by *Ad Daily* in 1972, more than half of the "outstanding art directors and copywriters" (and an even higher percentage of creative marketing executives) voted upon by the advertising community had passed that chronological milestone. Doyle Dane Bernbach, the agency that is acknowledged to have started the creative revolution in the 1960s, lists no less than one-third of its creative stars as past the age of 50, including the most luminous of all, the still-active William Bernbach, who is—very slowly—edging into his seventies.

Myth 3: It Is More Difficult for a Woman to Be Recognized for Her Creative Ability In fact, the value put on intuitive feelings makes women particularly welcome in advertising; more than one-third of the labor force in the field is female. At least two dozen women hold the title of president. Among them is Mary Wells Lawrence, the highest-salaried advertising executive ($368,796 annually at this writing).

Many of the so-called feminine traits created by early environment and social pressures (there are such traits despite the passionate outcries of a few who feel that all distinctions between the sexes should be obliterated) make the presence of women vital in the advertising business. Among these traits are people awareness, aesthetic sensitivity, verbal fluency, and, last but not least, an intimate acquaintance with the most influential purchasing segment in the United States: women.

Myth 4: Exceptional Intelligence Acts as a Springboard to Creativity Research shows that there is a surprisingly low correlation between creativity and academic achievement; this is reflected in most standard intelligence tests. Jacob W. Getzels and P. W. Jackson, for example, found that those who scored highest in creative achievement actually averaged 22 points lower on IQ tests than the top scorers on intelligence. (Accountants, engineers, and lawyers headed the list.) Vivacity of imagination does not always show up on conventional IQ tests. For purposes of measurability, most tests must concentrate on other, more readily definable mental feats, such as memory, vocabulary, reading ability, and study skills.

Myth 5: Formal Education Is an Absolute Prerequisite of Creative Ability This statement is not necessarily true. Schools tend to concentrate on information already in existence rather than encouraging intellectual forays into unknown territory. To ease their heavy workload, most teachers favor a structured curriculum. Frank William, in summarizing his findings, reports that "approximately one-quarter to one-half of total classroom time is spent telling students what to do. Another quarter of the time is devoted to providing information, mostly administrative. Only five per cent of class time is spent on the reinforcement of student response. (Reinforcement for creative responses was almost completely lacking.)" Dr. L. I. Thurstone, another astute observer of the educational scene, concludes rather sourly that "students with high intelligence are not necessarily the ones who produce the most original ideas. To be extremely intelligent is not the same as to be gifted in creative work."

One does not have to look far in an advertising agency to find that a college diploma or even a Phi Beta Kappa key does not guarantee professional success. Some of the best writers and art directors have learned their craft not in a classroom but on the job. It appears that there is little if any difference in creative aptitude between college graduates and those who have received their education in the office. Investigations reveal merely the unstartling fact that those lucky enough to have acquired the learning habit make faster progress in their careers.

THE TEACHABILITY OF CREATIVITY

It is amazing how easy it is to turn noncreative minds into creative ones by gentle prodding. Courses given in creativity are a case in point. When Dr. Arnold Meadow and Dr. Sidney J. Parnes, two enterprising teachers, offered to more than 300 of their students a course in creativity emphasizing goal-oriented thinking and utilization of knowledge, they found that within a single semester their students had become 94 percent more creative. Another pioneer in the field, Dr. Jere W. Clark, found that the names of more than half of those who had taken his course in creativity appeared in *Who's Who in American Colleges and Universities*. Perhaps the most optimistic of all the advocates is Rhoda Kellogg, a prominent San Francisco preschool educator who studied children for some 30 years and collected more than 2 million of their drawings. She says flatly: "The idea that creativity is the gift of a special few is just not true. We are all born creative."

Corporations offer additional proof of the pliability of creative talent. *The Wall Street Journal* reports that a 2-year in-house course offered by General Electric on creativity produced an avalanche of patentable concepts—a 60 percent increase over previous averages. When Pittsburgh Plate Glass followed suit with its own brand of creative training program, it found that graduates submitted a 300 percent larger number of viable ideas than those who chose not to take the course. Thus, the company was able to recoup its original investment. At Sylvania, several thousand engineers breezed through a 40-hour program in creative problem solving. The results produced savings amounting to $20 for each $1 spent.

In all, it is estimated that nearly 1 million employees have received some form of education in creativity in the last 10 years. Increasing numbers of courses are being conducted by business organizations. In addition, intramural instruction is offered by scores of federal agencies, adult education universities, media, and, of course, advertising agencies.

PURPOSEFUL CREATIVITY: THE COMPANY EMPLOYEE

A program called BAD, short for Buck-a-Day, encouraged employees to submit cost-reducing suggestions to help their company cope with inflation. (A token coffee cup bearing the legend "I had a BAD idea" was the employee's sole reward.) Reports submitted by the 500-odd organizations that tried the program demonstrate once again that goal orientation encourages creativity even among people who see themselves as "not particularly imaginative." Participation ran between 50 and 80 percent among the rank and file, or more than twice the number afforded by the routine suggestion-box type of approach, which has become associated primarily with airing grievances. The folder shown here contains posters, booklets, flyers, stickers, and other campaign materials to encourage participation.

[Courtesy of Industrial Motivation, Inc.]

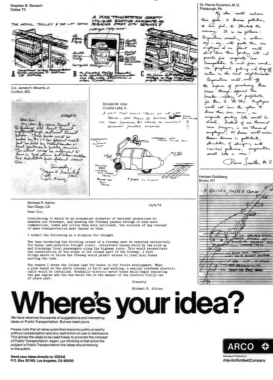

PURPOSEFUL CREATIVITY: THE PUBLIC

When Atlantic Richfield decided to launch an $8 million advertising campaign on mass-transit improvement, the response exceeded even the most optimistic expectations. In less than a year, nearly 30,000 suggestions came in, typed, handwritten, drafted, and doodled from all over the world. A sample list of ideas: a three-decker bus, a magnetic train, a government transit bond, a special tax on second cars, water streets, corporate car pools, a 200-seat zeppelin, municipal financing of jitneys, a 190-mile-an-hour (306-kilometer-an-hour) train, and a land ferry (the last two ideas were used as the basis for television commercials).

PURPOSEFUL CREATIVITY: THE ADVERTISING AGENCY

For fun and profit (first prize, $500), Al Hampel, executive vice president and director of creative services at Benton & Bowles, invited employees to demonstrate their own creativity by interpreting the agency's famous slogan "It's Not Creative Unless It Sells." Contributions came from all corners, with secretaries, receptionists, projectionists, the production manager, the casting director (who won second prize), producers, writers, and, of course, art directors all having their say.

Creator: Elizabeth Kratzman, Assistant Art Director
Small cash register with names of B&B clients on each button. When a button is punched, INCUIS flashes up in the window.

Creator: Mike Norcia, Assistant Art Director
Mobile: It's Not Creative Unless It ell.

Creator: Doug Fais, Lettering and Design
Large gilded wooden "coin" with INCUIS embossed and mounted on black velvet. Printed on the velvet: "We Coined a Phrase."

Creator: Don Blauweiss, Art Director
Framed dollar bill with INCUIS trailing from George Washington's mouth.

Creator: Charles Kornberger, Art Director
INCUIS written in toothpaste coming from a crinkled tube of Crest.

6

Creator: Eileen Vanderbilt, Receptionist
Denim overalls with red straps and a kerchief sticking out of the pocket. INCUIS done across the seat in patchwork material.

Creator: Linda Miller, Assistant Art Director
Black light box with a red button marked "Press." When lighted, the box reveals a photograph of 909 Third Avenue at night. Lights on the building spell INCUIS.

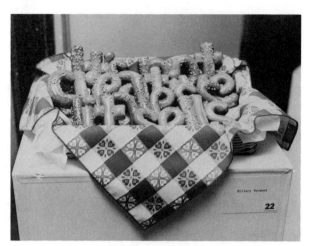

Creator: Hillary Vermont, Assistant Art Director
INCUIS baked in dough.

Creator: Bob Zeschin, Copywriter
INCUIS done in a collage of client products, plus print ads and tag lines from campaigns.

Creator: Ron Sims, Assistant Art Director
Neon sign of INCUIS.

7

1. A period of intensive soul searching came first. Oleda was sowing her creative oats to discover what would best satisfy her desires. She tried her hand at (*a*) designing jewelry, (*b*) making decoupage boxes, and (*c*), undaunted by her lack of formal art training, painting in oils. None of these experiments seemed to give her the fulfillment she was looking for; she wanted something uniquely her own.

PURPOSEFUL CREATIVITY: THE INDIVIDUAL

Weary of her modeling career, Oleda Baker, the author's wife, made a resolution on her fortieth birthday: to find a new career. She wanted one that would offer her both intellectual stimulation and financial rewards.

2. The idea for a book, *The Models' Way to Beauty, Slenderness, and Glowing Health,* occurred to Oleda after many months of trial and error. Intrigued by the subject of the book, the publisher agreed to a contract after seeing a one-page outline. Since this was Oleda's first attempt at book writing, she enlisted writer Bill Gale and photographer Richard Hochman to help her with the assignment.

3. An extensive direct-response campaign helped boost book sales. In its first year, *Models' Way* sold more than 150,000 copies. Encouraged by the response, Oleda now felt that she was on her way to positioning herself in the marketplace as a beauty expert. Still, something was missing; there were many other women like her who were successfully capitalizing on their good looks.

8

4. Two other books, put together with the assistance of a secretary, were published soon after the first. Combined sales of *The I Hate to Make Up Book* and *Be a Woman* exceeded 250,000 copies. Oleda's innate marketing savvy was now beginning to pay off. She recognized that she had found a unique selling point in a crowded marketplace, one few other beauty experts could fill, that is, a very youthful appearance at 40-plus. Both in advertising and in her publicity stories, she decided that giving away her age (in years, months, and days) was more practical than it was painful.

5. Other projects followed: a monthly column in *Model's Circle*, booklets on beauty tips (*Oleda Baker's Face-Savers* and *Oleda Baker's Hair Savers*), *Confidential Report on the "Age-Less Diet,"* TV appearances, and, finally, a line of forty-five new beauty products promoted through an "age-less" catalog. Today, Oleda is president of her own beauty products company, Oleda Unlimited, Inc. Her slogan: "Every Woman Has the Right to Be Beautiful!"

Yes **No**

Are you positive in your outlook? Do you look for reasons to do a job as opposed to not doing it?

Are you killing ideas (your own and those of others) by being overly critical? Too much analysis can slow you down. You should learn to ignore some of the obstacles. There always will be a few.

Are you willing to stay with the project? Many good ideas fall by the wayside for lack of adequate follow-through. How many articles, stories, books, or advertising campaigns do you have filed away in your desk drawer or some crevice of your mind, on which you have given up hope forever? How many more have you been thinking about but have never quite got around to undertaking? How long has it been since you presented your ideas to someone in a position to buy them? Or have you excused yourself from the open marketplace for fear that corporations will appropriate your ideas and leave you in limbo? (Few

Yes **No**

do so.) How persistent are you in marketing ideas? Are you the type that becomes discouraged too soon—a creative wallflower?

Are you open-minded in your approach to life? How fixed are your opinions and attitudes regarding politics, religion, sex, the upbringing of children, marriage, books and movies, and the upcoming generation? Social and professional flexibility usually go hand in hand; creative people see new marketing opportunities in changing life-styles.

Are you confusing lack of professional success with personal failure? Competition is keen in the idea market. For every idea that survives, many die a slow death. All ideas encounter opposition. Yours is no exception.

Do you have an inquisitive mind? All original thinkers do. (There is more on this subject in Chapter 5.) It is true that curiosity may kill the cat, but never a creative person.

Chapter Two
Defining the Problem: The Big Picture

Many advertising ideas, brilliant as they may seem at their inception, prove to be of little or no value because, quite simply, they fail to solve the specific problem at hand. This is a common dilemma and one that even veteran problem solvers are familiar with.

One cause of ill-conceived ideas is the understandable human tendency to want to produce in a hurry. Our action-oriented and pragmatic society encourages this attitude. A tangible product, such as a layout or a headline, is considered proof that an effort has been made. On the other hand, the act of contemplation, of mulling over a problem, shows only good intentions.

We must first accept the notion that thinking is an active undertaking, even though sitting and gazing at the ceiling may seem passive. It is not. Planning requires effort. In systematic problem solving, planning may be the most important activity of all.

The Upside-down Pyramid Syndrome: Bane of the Creative

Do you remember our pyramid? This is the way it looked:

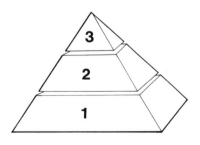

On the bottom is information. This is followed by analysis. The idea, the end product, is on top. Now,

here is the same pyramid but in a very different position:

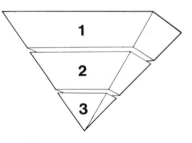

Everything has been turned around. The idea is at the bottom, "supporting" the rest of the pyramid. A ridiculous premise? Maybe so. Yet this is an all-too-familiar phenomenon in any idea business, and most particularly in advertising.

Campaign themes fabricated in this way usually rest on as wobbly a foundation as does our upside-down structure. The idea may be so flimsy that it can hardly be called a selling concept. Often it is not much more than a new way to execute an old idea—a gimmick. A twist on words in a headline, the use of white space, and a different typeface are the kinds of ideas that may fall into this I-have-the-solution-now-let's-find-the-problem-that-will-fit-it category.

Keeping the Big Picture in Mind

One way to avoid the upside-down–pyramid syndrome is to make sure that we see not only part of the problem but all of it. Typically, the person at the receiving end, the ultimate consumer, always comprehends advertising in its totality. Bombarded by some 590 advertising messages a day (a conservative estimate by Batten, Barton, Durstine & Osborn (BBDO), the consumer usually has neither the time nor the inclination to examine closely the fine points of implementation. More than anything, he or she is interested in the *substance* of the message.

Different People See the Big Picture Differently

To put things in the right perspective, it also helps to keep in mind that even before the advertising message reaches the consumer, reactions to it will vary with the point of view of the approver. Profits may be foremost in the mind of the financial executive, but someone else may look at the same campaign differently, using sales forecasts as the major criterion. Still others may be interested only in production costs. And then, of course, there are those who become intrigued by graphic and verbal minutiae and think in terms of execution, so it is no wonder that in

a large corporation it often takes weeks or even months to get final approvals on a single idea.

A Quick Overview: The Evolution of an Advertising Campaign

Here are the various aspects of an advertising campaign perceived by different individuals as it is channeled through various approval stages.

1. *Cost of advertising*. There must be a reasonable chance that advertising will pay off in increased sales.

2. *Market analysis*. The problem is defined on the basis of the target. Market analysis always precedes the creation of an advertising campaign.

3. *Selling strategy*. A number of factors, including many that may or may not have much to do with advertising, are considered. Among them are production capabilities, inventory problems, channels of distribution, product experience, competition, pricing, retail cooperation, the ability of the sales force, and legal ramifications.

Up to this point, decisions rest largely with the client (the president, marketing and sales heads, and advertising manager). Now gradually the focus shifts to the advertising agency, which is given an increasingly active role in the decision-making process.

4. *Media planning*. Various vehicles are available to the advertiser to communicate with the audience: magazines, newspapers, television, posters, direct mail, and others (see Chapter 9). Finding the right media mix requires the participation of experts, usually working for advertising agencies or for independent media services.

5. *Preparation of a creative platform*. On the basis of the marketing information, it is now possible to decide on a campaign theme on which individual ads, graphics, and copy can be built. To assure continuity of the campaign, it is impera-

tive that the creative platform be well defined and thoroughly understood by everyone.

6. *Writing copy*. The next step involves committing the selling message to words. To be effective, the copywriter must be familiar with the product, the audience, and the nature of the media.

7. *Visualizing the advertisement*. This is the responsibility of the art director. However, as mentioned before, lines of demarcation between job responsibilities are becoming thinner than ever. Ads are usually the result of a cooperative effort of artist-writer creative teams.

8. *Mechanical reproduction*. After the copy and the layout have been approved by the client, the advertisement goes into production. A print ad (for a newspaper, magazine, poster, or the like) usually calls for a finished paste-up or a mechanical with type, illustration, and other elements in place. For television, the commercial is put on film or tape. Radio spots are either cut on tape or broadcast live.

9. *Evaluating effectiveness*. Various research methods help the advertiser to check advertising effectiveness. Ads can be tested either before they appear (as in copy testing) or after (as in measuring the recall of a television commercial or the readership of a print ad).

In summary, first the market is defined; second, the media which cover it are found; third, the creative platform is determined; and fourth, the ideas are implemented by writers, artists, and production people, with research providing input along the way. This sequence of events is required for any sound marketing-advertising campaign. Typically, it, too, is based upon the pyramid principle. Tamper with it, and the structure will crumble to the ground.

The Importance of Keeping Up the Dialogue

The foregoing suggests that a large number of people, representing a wide variety of opinions, are involved in the preparation of advertising. That is usually the case. To avoid overlapping responsibilities and traffic jams, it is imperative that lines of communication be kept open between organizations, departments and individuals.

Within the advertising agency, information must flow freely between marketing and creative departments. Both should be apprised of new developments; neither should be overly chauvinistic in its approach.

There also must be a free flow of information between the advertiser and the advertising agency. Thinking of the agency primarily as an organization of specialists, many clients tend to confine information to what, in their opinion, falls within the limited purview of communication. This approach has product intelligence staying with engineers who feel that they must guard company trade secrets, sales results with product and sales managers, overall corporate policy with top management, and fiscal data with the comptroller. Needless to say, this close-mouthed corporate attitude helps no one, least of all the corporation. To make sound business judgments, the advertising agency must have adequate information on:

The product
The market
Sales policy
Sales results
Sales/advertising (S/A) ratio
Trade reaction to the advertising campaign
Trade customs
Competition
Profitability of the advertising campaign from the advertiser's point of view
Corporate history
Past selling experience
Management policies
Future plans

Among the explanations offered for lost accounts, which total about $500 million worth of billings every year, the favorite cop-out phrase is "differences of opinion." This term frequently appears in trade announcements as an official explanation.

Improved lines of communication might have prevented many of these breakups between client and advertising agency.

Where It All Begins: Advertising Strategy for Nice 'n Easy Hair Coloring

(Courtesy of Doyle Dane Bernbach)

1. *The most compelling reason why women prefer a brand of hair coloring is the naturalness of the results.* Because of the educational efforts of New Dawn and Nice 'n Easy and the flurry of later entries in the shampoo-in field, ease of application can almost be taken for granted.

2. *Among young people today, naturalness seems to be the key.* This makes sense, in view of young people's passionate demand for honesty and naturalness in all areas of life. That the naturalness idea can sell goods to young people is vividly demonstrated by the brilliant success of the un-made-up look in makeup and the attraction "Innocent Color" has for young people.

3. *There is evidence that while we are retaining our more mature users, we are not attracting younger people to the brand.*

4. *Nice 'n Easy is still the largest seller in shampoo-ins.* However apprehensive we may be about the weakening of the brand's position, the blunt fact of Nice 'n Easy's leadership is impressive evidence to the consumer that this brand must be delivering natural color, since women know that is what other women look for too.

5. *We propose that the selling strategy of naturalness not be changed but be reinterpreted and updated.*

6. *We also propose that we link the brand's leadership with naturalness.*

7. *By drawing a parallel between the natural look in makeup and the natural look achieved with Nice 'n Easy, we hope further to emphasize natural results and particularly to attract and reassure new users.*

Selling Strategy We will continue our successful strategy of convincing women that Nice 'n Easy is *the* natural-looking hair color, the one that never makes a woman feel overdone or the slightest bit phony-looking. This appeal is relevant to a very broad spectrum of women who desire to improve their appearance and will use artificial aids to do so but want a natural effect. The appeal is to a woman's desire to be confident of her appearance, to be free to project her own self-image. This allows her to be spontaneous and carefree.

Target Group Advertising will continue to be targeted primarily to the broad national potential audience of all women between 25 and 34 years old. A separate advertising effort designed to expand the brand's user base will be directed toward young adult women, aged 18 to 24, who are nonusers of hair coloring.

Executional Strategy: Basic Plan In television, we will preserve our strategy of depicting the Nice 'n Easy young woman engaged in activities with a man in which her natural spunkiness can be projected. Thus at the climax of each spot, on the theme line "It lets me be me," a single gesture from the young woman will express her impulsive, free, even irrepressible nature. The commercials will have the qualities of honesty and naturalness. As in the past, print will be an extension of the TV campaign and, as such, will attempt to capture the Nice 'n Easy young woman's exuberant personality as she relates to a man.

Chapter Three

Defining the Problem: The Not-So-Big Picture

Information is vital to problem solving; as we have said, it is the base of our pyramid. However, too much information can be just as bewildering as too little. And how easy it is to gather a surplus of information in an attempt to solve a problem!

If this sounds like a moot point, consider the answer to this question: How often have you acquired a piece of information so intriguing that you just could not let it go? It has happened to this author many times. Fred L. Worth compiled more than 8000 such randomly picked facts in *The Trivia Encyclopedia,* which he admits "could have been called an encyclopedia of chaos." The book is filled with delightful tidbits of information, most of which are admittedly mentioned mostly for the sake of enjoyment. Here is a sample list: Idaho is the only state in the United States over which no foreign flag has ever flown; the names of the seven woodland companions of Snow White are Bashful, Doc, Dopey, Grumpy, Happy, Sleepy, and Sneezy; and the distance between two bases on a baseball field is 90 feet (27.4 meters).

Often, so much effort and money are spent in gleaning information—pouring over stacks of magazines, newspapers, and books, interviewing people, and visiting places—that it is only human to want to get maximum use out of it. The compulsion to cover everything fully is so great that it can, and often does, obscure the message. It is probably one of the major causes for so much obesity in marketing plans, new-business presentations, advertising copy, and yes, even textbooks.

Easy access to information in this day and age makes intellectual ostentation all the more tempting. "Information explosion" is no empty catch phrase; it is an integral part of modern civilization. Look at the traffic: More than 11,000 dailies and weeklies are published in the United States (aggregating more than 60 million copies). Almost half of the 90 million households today have not one but two television sets holding forth more than 6 hours a day on the average, and there are more than 3 times as many radios as there are television sets. Add to this maze of information exchange the office memos and letters sent back and forth, various forms, magnetic tapes, about 500 million telephone calls every day, and ordinary conversations, and you have today's version of the Tower of Babel.

Remember the Pyramid: It Narrows toward the Top

Apparently, the ability to *reject* information is as important a business asset as is the ability to *accept* it. When attempting to focus on a problem, creative people perhaps could learn something from their mathematically minded colleagues in marketing and research. To reach some workable segment, these colleagues use regression analysis, literally backing into a solution by eliminating the variables.

As Arthur Herzog wrote in his waggish but perceptive book, *The B.S. Factor,* "A Problem Problem arises when something is identified as *the* problem which is not the problem or is only part of a problem. Problem Problems generate more problems than existed before."

Right to the point, too, is the comment made by Bernard Lipsky, a top research executive at Foote, Cone & Belding: "Forget the all-encompassing urge to answer every problem, and design a program on just what is necessary."

How to Make Your Problem Less Complicated

Once the problem has been defined, the next step is relatively simple. It is to classify information in the order of its importance:

$$\text{INFORMATION} \begin{cases} \text{NONESSENTIAL} \\ \text{ESSENTIAL} \\ \text{VERY ESSENTIAL} \end{cases}$$

Nonessential information can be relegated summarily to the nearest wastebasket. *Essential* information, including articles, statistical tables, reports, and competitive advertising, may be filed for future reference. *Very essential* information should be kept right at our fingertips, ready for use at short notice.

Know What You Are Looking For

Hundreds of creative assignments are pushed through advertising agencies every day. Some of these assignments are so burdened with irrelevancies that the cruxes of the problems all but disappear, particularly after they have been worked over by someone who is confused about the basic problem. In trying to make order out of this can't-see-the-forest-for-the-trees chaos, perhaps it is well to remember that all creative assignments fall basically into one of four problem areas:

1. *Assignment to create a product.* Design of a new product, modification of an old one, change in package suggesting new applications.

2. *Assignment to devise a marketing plan.* Use of new media, new approach to positioning in the marketplace, opening new retail outlets, geographical or demographic segmentation, change in emphasis on advertising.

3. *Assignment to create an advertising campaign.* New creative approach, use of a new copy appeal, change in headline, slogan, layout, illustration.

4. *Assignment that combines several factors.* A new package design, cooperative advertising, audiovideo presentation, special promotions, publicity campaign.

Granted, this may seem to be an oversimplified approach to the assortment of creative assignments which ricochet between the departments of an advertising agency. It is not. Most of the work done by creative people fits into the categories listed here.

Marketing versus Advertising Problems

Sometimes the close relationship between marketing and advertising obscures differences between the two functions. To avoid confusion, a distinction should be made. A layout, for example, is primarily an advertising problem, and it is of greatest concern to an art director. On the other hand, an art director's interest in marketing may be only peripheral. Establishing new retail outlets, to use another example, is more a marketing than an advertising problem and requires the expertise of a marketer.

To put the distinction in another way, advertising concerns itself basically with the needs of the *consumer,* his or her motivation to buy, attitudes, interests, opinions, and relationship with the product. Marketing, on the other hand, concerns itself basically with the needs of the *manufacturer.*

Advertising versus Publicity

Equally vague may be the demarcation between advertising and public-

ity. There is a tendency, particularly among advertisers who are relatively less familiar with trade jargon, to consider both functions pretty much one and the same and to lump them under the public relations category. Actually, advertising and publicity should be considered distant cousins at best. A press release is by no means the same as a piece of advertising copy.

It is the end use to which the material is put that dictates different creative approaches.

Advertising is designed to run in paid space or time, giving the media practically no jurisdiction over content; its placement is virtually guaranteed.

With publicity material, the editor is the final arbiter of what is used and what is not. To split hairs even further, the prime function of advertising is to *persuade* and of publicity to *provide news.*

Publicity versus Public Relations

Even more subtle are the differences between publicity and public relations. The two functions often overlap. Both concern themselves with the dissemination of news. Both may take advantage of the same type of specialized outside suppliers (such as monitoring and mailing services) or use the same outlets (such as television stations and press associations) to get the news to the public. However, here the similarities end.

Publicity entails a more aggressive posture; the ability of publicity agents is often gauged by their success in gaining exposure in print and broadcast. Thus, they will actively seek placements through their personal and business contacts. The role of public relations practitioners is a little more subtle; much of the news they deal with is supplied by people other than themselves (for example, a newscaster or a reporter). In many ways, they act as official spokespersons, or toastmasters, for the corporation.

THE EVOLUTION OF AN IDEA FOR A NEW TYPE OF INSURANCE POLICY BASED ON PROBLEM DEFINITION

Development of the Product The assignment is to create a new type of insurance program with a demonstrable product difference. The program should have broad consumer appeal so that the product can be sold in mass media via direct-response advertising.

NONESSENTIAL DATA	ESSENTIAL DATA	VERY ESSENTIAL DATA
1. National income	1. Types of coverage	1. Universality of appeal
2. Qualifications of an insurance agent	2. Average cost of premiums	2. Timeliness of the product
3. Aggregate value of policies in force	3. Ratio of premiums to disposable income	3. Number of users
4. Data processing facilities	4. Surrender values	4. Consumer data
5. National health expenditures	5. Method of making payments	5. Cost of hospitalization and medical care
6. Number of insurance companies	6. Annuity considerations	6. Pricing
7. Number of policies in force	7. Termination rate	7. Federal and state regulations affecting the product
8. Inderdepartmental conflicts	8. Reasons for policy lapse	8. Legal aspects affecting the product
	9. Commission structure	
	10. Underwriting leverage	

Development of Marketing Plan The assignment is to test the product's effectiveness in a limited regional area to provide information for a roll-out test. Define the target audience and find the most efficient way of reaching prime prospects. Develop a media strategy, including data on reach, frequency, and schedule. Make first-year budgetary recommendations with a breakdown of media and production costs.

NONESSENTIAL DATA	ESSENTIAL DATA	VERY ESSENTIAL DATA
1. Potential profits to the advertising agency	1. Company's financial stability	1. Geographical data
	2. Corporate experience in selling insurance through the mail	2. Demographic data
	3. Agent resistance to direct selling	3. Psychographic data
	4. Advertising/selling	4. Type of media available
	5. Consumers' disposable income	5. Media reach and cost/efficiency (RMP) data
	6. Persistence rate, that is, perceived risk in buying insurance through the mail	6. Method of pretesting
	7. Availability of mailing lists	7. Competitive activity
		8. Long-range financial projection

Development of an Advertising Campaign The assignment is to decide on copy and graphic approaches. Test various incentives as an opening gambit. Examine use of third-party testimonials. Recommend an advertising slogan on which to build a viable advertising theme.

NONESSENTIAL DATA	ESSENTIAL DATA	VERY ESSENTIAL DATA
1. Information on prospects over 6 feet 4 inches and under 5 feet (statistically insignificant).	1. Past performance of third-party approach in insurance advertising	1. Name of product
	2. Long copy versus short copy in selling insurance by mail	2. Type of media in which advertising will appear
	3. Qualitative marketing data	3. Type of initial offer
		4. Copy claims

The answers to these questions helped to pinpoint the problem: to learn about the marketplace, to define a need, and, finally, to have the idea for a new insurance program evolve from working with the facts. Basically, the program is based upon the well-known actuarial truism that fat people die younger than thin people do. With group A constituting more than 60 percent of the United States population, it became economically feasible to use mass-media advertising.

Advertising Age

® Entire contents copyright 1973 by Crain Communications Inc.

35¢ a Copy; $10 a Year   *The National Newspaper of Marketing*   April 30, 1973

ASR to push
new Double I...
raz...

Introducing *Personna* DOUBLE II

Wants 10 ca...

...rectors:
...e cases

By ...

NEW Y...
fort to o...
and War...
twin-blad...
Safety R...
with the ...
first cart...
with "twin...

The Dou...
ing shipped...
available in...
as next mo...
tribution ta...

According...
who recently...
Personna bra...
national sale...
Morris USA...
vest $1,000,00...
offer and $1,7...
over a six-...
period. Spots ...
on major le...
also will air o...
casts and netw...

Commercials...
Burnett Co., C...
Trac II, Super...
razors being he...
the fingers of ...

Texiz...
Greas...

By RANCE...

ATLANTA, Apr...
Products Inc., a ...
formed by the fath...
Jack and Dick Gree...
ing Grease Relief, ...
greaser" that com...
capsule container.

Intex plans to s...
$4,500,000 and $5,00...
tional rollout of the ...
initial distribution (...
in Georgia, the Ca...
metro Jacksonville,...
agency almost as new...
pany itself, Weltin ...
here, is handling the ...

If the Greer name ...
miliar, it's because J...
started Texize Chemi...
1945, and his eldest son...
currently president of...
now a division of M...
wich, Dick, the third n...
the family, is Intex's 2...
vp of marketing and sal...

Key members of the ...
uct effort—Dick Gree...
Weltin, ex-Needham, H...
Steers account exec who...
Henderson Advertising ...
Atlanta office (Henders...
longtime Texize agency...
Hemsley, vp-director of...
service of Weltin (out ...
and Henderson); Lou Ka...
ski, vp-creative director a...
and also a Henderson al...
and Everett M Nelson, W...
vp-media director—talked ...
advertising and marketing ...
gy for Grease Relief at W...

Adman Baker's idea in test:
Slims earn insurance break

NEW YORK, Oct. 17—"I'm a 6-ft.-4-in. adman who weighs 180 lbs., and felt I should get a break on my life insurance!"

That beef led tall, lean Stephen Baker, president of Baker & Hartel, to confront the principals of Liberty Life Insurance Co., Greenville, S.C.

Results? He's test marketing an ad campaign for his own innovation called TRIMsurance to promote health and life insurance for men and women who will pay premiums appropriate to their weight and physical fitness. The slogan tells the story: "The *less* you weigh, the *less* you pay."

Other insurance companies similarly have promoted lower insurance rates for specially qualified customers. These concepts include lower auto insurance costs for drivers over age 50, motorists whose cars have special shock absorbing bumpers, and non-drinkers as well as non-smokers.

■ Liberty Life's approach is summed up in its page ad headlined "Why should you pay as much for insurance as a fat person?"

One direct mail campaign is currently under way, and on Oct. 14 the company started newspaper and mailing campaigns in one test market state on the West Coast and in six states in the Midwest. On Oct. 23, about 1,000,000 six-page inserts, with mail reply cards, will be distributed through newspapers in three states.

Although all ads will be direct response from advertiser to the customer, who will then reply by sending back a newspaper coupon or a postage paid card, Liberty Life also uses agents and believes in their importance. In this case, the company's ads will encourage potential insurance buyers who seek more details to make collect telephone calls to an agent who specializes in TRIMsurance.

Ad tests also will include split runs to determine the relative marketing merits of (1) use of an endorser, such as Jack LaLanne, physical fitness promoter and Liberty Life consultant, vs. no endorser; (2) different price packages; (3) advisability of a bonus payment offer vs. none; (4) relative response to health insurance vs. life insurance policies, and (5) media effectiveness. #

Reprinted with permission from the October 22, 1973, issue of Advertising Age.

Copyright 1973 by Crain Communications Inc.

...vertisers. But critics now
... in recent months there
... neither numbers nor
... cases, and that the
... particularly apparent
...ct to regional ads where
...mply stopped perform-
...no other local regula-
... has moved in.

...no to regional direc-
...he new crackdown on
...vertisers is "a special
... project." It is
...lfred Cortese Jr., as-
...utive director for le-
...tion. It says regional
...expect visits during
...th by himself or by
...ppard (his deputy)
...dleman, an assistant
...he bureau of con-
...ued on Page 8)

Avco to
buy
system

...April 27—If the
...co Broadcasting
...ocedure for spot
...s on, a compli-
...k beset business
...ost as simple as
...to go.

...year test plan
... yesterday by
...Avco president,
...oslow, vp-mar-
...stol-Myers, the
...a schedule by
...t weight, start
...co will send
... showing not
...down of the
...the product
...unt due.
...the haggling
...the running
... spots, Mr.
...pengler, di-
...vices at B-
...st Avco to
...its stations
...us, Dayton
...re the test
...estimated
...goes into
...M.

...Koslow
...they will
...n usual
...experi-
...ould be
... plan to
...o-owned
...er sta-
...gencies
...ommis-
...Avco Radio Television
...Sales will be the liaison between
...the client and the broadcaster for
...this initial test. The agency is
...B-M's own unit, Boclaro. #

(Additional news flashes on Page 77)

Once the information is available, ideas will flow more easily, feeding upon one another. Shown on this page are a few of the many creative by-products of TRIMsurance: a hospital indemnity program based on weight classification, the selling of the program through insurance agents, a measuring tape (marked in metric measurements on one side) to be used as a giveaway.

Focusing on the Problem: The Drawing-up of the Blueprint

Many seemingly routine questions have a way of cropping up in the early planning stage of an advertising campaign. Wise is the art director or copywriter who has these questions answered before he tackles his or her creative assignment, with time and energy invested in the pursuit of solutions. Nitty-gritty as some of these questions may be, they nevertheless have an important bearing on the success of the campaign.

Described on the following few pages are some of the questions that should be answered before taking to the drawing board or the typewriter.

Who?

Seldom, if ever, is the customer "everybody." In today's markets, the customer is almost always someone special.

Almost all advertising today is planned to reach "target audiences."

How Many?

Generally, the larger the market, the more money is available for advertising, both for media (reach, frequency, size of ad) and for production (print or broadcast).

Where?

Geographical factors, which are determined largely by distribution patterns, play an important part in deciding which appeal will prove to be most effective in advertising. People in different parts of the country think, feel, and act differently; certain regions have strong ethnic strains; cities, suburbs, and rural communities each have their own characteristic life-styles.

THE TELEVISION COMMERCIAL: SIZE, LENGTH, AND USE

ACADEMY FIELD   10 FIELD

TV PICT SAFETY

TITLE SAFETY

THE ART OF PLANNING A 10-SECOND TV COMMERCIAL: FEW WORDS, COMPELLING PICTURE

ANNOUNCER: "Utica Club now comes in aluminum cans. Aluminum tastes better, chills faster, and weighs less than tin."

How?

The way the ad is going to be used naturally affects the way it is going to look.

Both the art director and the copywriter must be thoroughly familiar with the physical requirements such as the size of the ad, the length of the commercial, the choice of reproduction (type of engraving, halftone screen, color, stock, printing method, typesetting, and folding technique). Also affecting the quality of the campaign is the media vehicle in which the ad is going to appear.

20

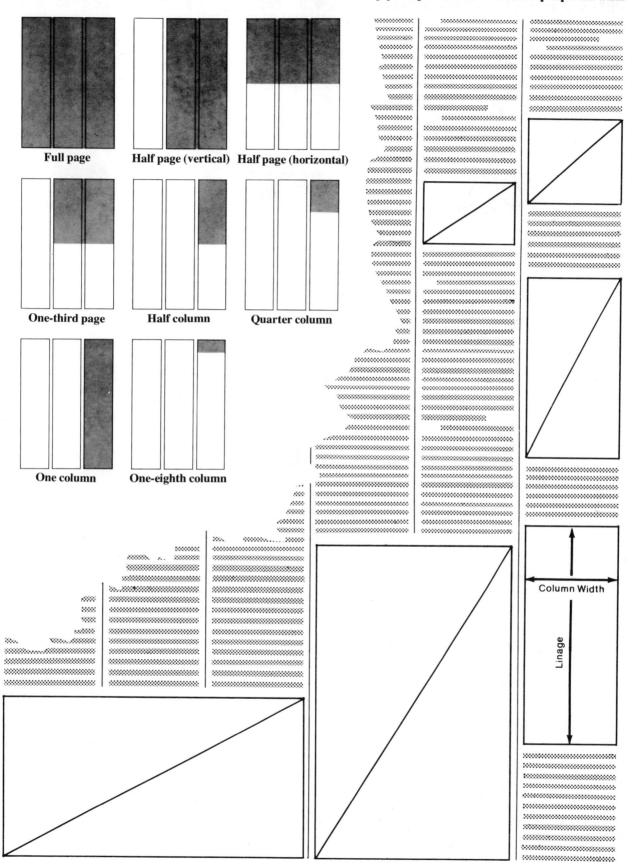

Full page   **Half page (vertical)**   **Half page (horizontal)**

One-third page   **Half column**   **Quarter column**

One column   **One-eighth column**

Column Width

Linage

Every halftone must be screened (the continuous tone broken into small dots) for reproduction. Newspapers and mass-market paperbacks use 55- to 65-line screen to make the printed matter suitable for newsprint stock on high-speed press runs.

Most magazines use 85- to 100-line screen for black-and-white or color reproduction. The finer the screen, the greater the fidelity to details. This screen is used on book papers, both coated (glossy finish) and uncoated (toothier surface).

The 120- to 133-line screen is used only on supercalendered paper. Unabsorbed ink gives added brilliance to the printed image. Screens as fine as 400-line are available. (Illustrations in this book are reproduced in 133-line screen.)

A *square halftone* is the simplest and least expensive form of halftone. The sides are straight and rectangular, and they can be cut mechanically. If the tones are highlighted by dropping out the screened dots, the halftone is called a *dropout*.

When the halftone dots are removed from the background, the plate becomes a *silhouette,* or *outline halftone*. Since most of the work is done by hand, silhouette halftones can be expensive, especially in color.

A solid line (in this case, the numbers) applied over the screen produces a *combination line and halftone*. The strength of the black printed material remains intact instead of being broken up by a screen. The process is relatively costly.

A *vignette* differs from a silhouette halftone in that its outline (or part of it) is not sharply defined; rather, there is a graduating tonal effect. Fine screen and stock are preferable; printing on newsprint may result in a hard unsightly edge.

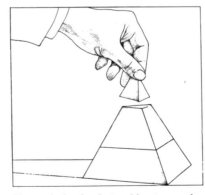

Line art is the simplest and least expensive plate to reproduce. There is no cost difference between a silhouetted and a squared-off line cut. A benday screen (dots) can be applied by an artist or engraver to simulate a halftone effect.

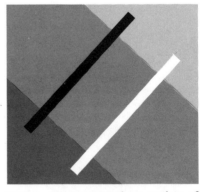

Benday screens come in a variety of shades. They can be laid over the art on the mechanical or stripped in by the engraver. In simulation of a halftone, dots can be reproduced on a line plate.

Ink on paper. **Ink on raised surface.**

Ink on paper. **Ink below printing surface.**

Ink on paper. **Ink on plane surface.**

All printing plates have one thing in common: the area to be printed must be separated from that not to be printed. In *letterpress*, or *relief*, printing, the area to be printed is raised and only the inked surface touches the paper.

Gravure is a commercial application of intaglio printing. Here the image is cut or etched into the surface of the plate. Under pressure, the paper absorbs the ink from the etched areas, leaving an impression. All copy (including type) is screened.

Offset lithography, or simple *offset*, is essentially a chemical process. There are no raised surfaces. The plate is first covered with a chemical solution. The image area rejects this solution but accepts ink. The image is then transferred to the paper.

SPACE GUIDE

Creativity

TOUCHING

Creativity

TIGHT

Creativity

NORMAL

Creativity

SPACED

Phototypesetting, affording the designer a far wider range of type choices, is the newest and perhaps most significant development in the typesetting field. Letters can be exposed directly on photosensitive film paper, and therefore it is possible to project them touching, overlapping (impossible with metal type), or spaced out.

Creativity

CONDENSED 25%

Creativity

CONDENSED 20%

Creativity

CONDENSED 15%

Creativity

EXPANDED 25%

Creativity

OBLIQUE

In phototypesetting, letters can be slanted, condensed, or extended by using prisms.

Century expanded.
Type is supposed to look beautiful, lend ambience to the advertisement, keep company with illustrations, and brighten the art director's day. Most of all, it is there to be read.

Helvetica medium.
Type is supposed to look beautiful, lend ambience to the advertisement, keep company with illustrations, and brighten the art director's day. Most of all, it is there to be read.

Melior Bold
Type is supposed to look beautiful, lend ambience to the advertisement, keep company with illustrations, and brighten the art director's day. Most of all, it is there to be read.

Souvenir
Type is supposed to look beautiful, lend ambience to the advertisement, keep company with illustrations, and brighten the art director's day. Most of all, it is there to be read.

These are some of the 1200 typefaces available today. Used as body text, each has a "color" of its own.

1-point leading.
Type is supposed to look beautiful, lend ambience to the advertisement, keep company with illustrations, and brighten the art director's day. Most of all, it is there to be read.

4-point leading.
Type is supposed to look beautiful, lend ambience to the advertisement, keep company with illustrations, and brighten the art director's day. Most of all, it is there to be read.

Spacing (leading) between lines is as important as it is between letters.

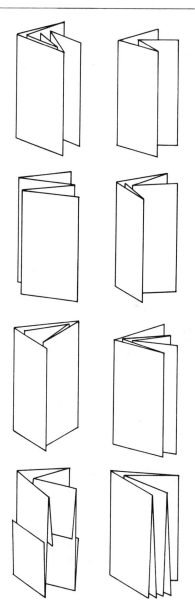

Depending on the number and direction (parallel or right-angled) of folds, a wide range of folders can be produced, ranging from four to eighty pages.

When?

Even the time of day affects the reader's or listener's receptivity to advertising messages. The typical radio listener or television viewer changes as the day progresses (see graphs on page 29). Morning newspapers are read differently from their afternoon counterparts. To create effective advertising, it pays to find out when the message is going to be seen or heard.

Selling Events in a Department Store

Clearance
Valentine's Day
Washington's Birthday
Easter
Mother's Day
Father's Day
Independence Day
Labor Day
Back to school
Election Day
Local events
White sale
Private sale
Pre-Christmas
Christmas
Post-Christmas
Graduation—spring
Graduation—summer

★ ★ ★ ★ ★ ★ ★ ★ ★

Weather conditions can exert a subtle but significant influence over sales, especially in retail. A cold spell in early November affects the sale of coats and other winter items to an even larger degree than a cold spell during subsequent weeks; hot days in the first week of July help sell more air conditioners than a later heat spell would. And as any store owner can testify, a few days of rain will put a damper on even the best-conceived promotional thrusts. Nowadays meteorologists can make 3-day forecasts with reasonable accuracy; for longer periods the batting average falls rapidly. The U.S. Weather Service keeps making predictions 30 days ahead.

A FEW OF THE MANY PROMOTIONAL DAYS, WEEKS, AND MONTHS

Air Force Day
American Art Week
American Bicycle Month
American Camp Week
American Educational Week
American Heart Month
American Home Lighting Fixture
    Month
American Red Cross fund drive
April Fool's Day
Aviation Day
Be Kind to Animals Week
Bike Safety Day
Boy Scout Week
Break a Cold Month
Cereal and Milk Spring Festival
Cheese Festival
Children's Art Month
Children's Day
Child Health Day
Christmas
Christmas Seal Campaign
Citizenship Day
Cleaner Air Week

Columbus Day
Constitution Week
Dairy Month
Diabetes Week
Fall clean-up time
Fire Prevention Week
First day of spring
Flag Day
Gold Star Mothers' Day
Goodwill Week
Groundhog Day
Halloween
Hardware Week
Holidays Are Pickle Days
Home Sweet Home Month
Honey for Breakfast Week
Human Rights Week
Humane Sunday
Inauguration Day
Independence Day
International Character Day
International Credit Union Day
Jaycee Week
Jewish Music Festival

Jewish New Year
Jewish Passover
Jewish Youth Week
Junior Clubs International Day
Know Your America Week
Lessons in Truth Week
Let's All Play Ball Week
Let's Go Hunting Month
Loyalty Day
March of Dimes
Mental Health Week
National Allergy Month
National Beauty Salon Week
National Bible Week
National Bow Tie Week
National Cat Week
National Cherry Blossom Festival
National Contact Lens Month
National Coin Week
National Cotton Week
National Crime Prevention Week
National Day of Prayer
National Dog Week
National Domestic Rabbit Week

National Egg Month
National Expectant Fathers' Day
National Family Week
National Flag Week
National Frozen Food Week
National Fur Care Week
National Garden Week
National Hobby Month
National Horse Radish Week
National Hospital Week
National Humor Week
National Iced Tea Time
National Industrial Vision Week
National Interior Design Month
National Invest-in-America Week
National Latin America Week
National Letter-writing Week
National Library Week
National Macaroni Week
National Maritime Day
National Pickle Week
National Popcorn Week
National Pretzel Week
National Ragweed Control Month
National Sandwich Month
National School Lunch Week
National Softball Week
National Sunday School Week
National Tavern Month
National Thrift Week
National Tie Week
National Wallpaper Month
National Wildlife Week
Old Maids' Day
Palm Sunday
Pan American Day
Pizza festival time
Poetry Day
Red Cross Month
Restaurant Month
Return the Borrowed Books Week
Rug Cleaning Month
Rye Bread Sales Month
Save Your Vision Week
Secretaries' Week
Sweetest Day
United Community Campaign of
    America
United Nations Day and Week
Universal Bible Week
Wheat Bread Sales Month
World Community Day
World Day of Prayer
World Peace Day
World Poetry Day
World Religion Day
World Trade Week
Worldwide Bible Reading
YMCA World Fellowship Day
Yom Kippur
Youth Week
Youth Appreciation Week
Youth Temperance Education
    Week

Invent your own promotions. This full-page newspaper ad for Johnny Walker Black Label Scotch celebrates a new high set by the Dow Jones Industrial Average. Grandmother's Day was originated by the author to stimulate the sale of silver and jewelry at the Fortunoff stores in the fall.

There is something special about every day of the month if you look hard and long enough. Promotional calendars like this are issued regularly by Metro Associated Service for distribution to its member retail stores.

TUESDAY	WEDNESDAY	THURSDAY	FRIDAY	SATURDAY
1 June is Dairy Month, Recreation Month, National Rose Month, Cat and Kitten Month, and National Ragweed Control Month. Kentucky joined Union, 1792. Tennessee joined Union, 1796.	**2** Time to emphasize summer conveniences: air conditioning, parking facilities, evening hours for cooler shopping. Continued from May: Senior Citizens Month, MS Hope Chest Campaign, through June 30.	**3** Memorial Day, Arkansas; Confederate Memorial Day, Kentucky, Louisiana, Tennessee. Jefferson Davis's birthday (1808), legal holiday in Florida, Georgia, Kentucky, Louisiana, Mississippi, South Carolina, and Tennessee.	**4** Dairy Month ads focus on light, nutritious summer meals: "Yogurt is cool." "Cottage cheese—a meal in a minute." Institutionals honor dairy farmers. Philippine Independence Day, 1946. First day of Shabuoth.	**5** Adam Smith born, 1723; Jefferson Davis Day, Alabama; NADL markets, New York City.
6 Sew what? Something lightweight, gauzy, and simply smashing for summer. Specials in fabrics, trimmings, and notions go well now. D-Day in Normandy, 1944.	**7** George (Beau) Brummell born, 1778, International Society of Weekly Newspaper Editors meets in Oregon, through June 10.	**8** Travel bug buzzing? Check luggage stores for specials, travel agents for arrangements, fashion boutiques for clearance sales, and your friendly local bank for a handy vacation loan. Frank Lloyd Wright born, 1869.	**9** Special sales honor the anniversary of the first copyrighted book, *The Philadelphia Spelling Book*, by John Barry, 1790.	**10** Wedding daze continues all month with gifts for newlyweds and their homes: furniture, appliances, silver, crystal, china, trousseau items. Caterers, photographers, and real estate agents tie in.	**11** Honor thy father with dinner at a topnotch restaurant. Make reservations now. Kamehameha Day in Hawaii.	**12** Simply ridiculous! Outdoor furniture, summer clothing, and linen and bedding clearances. Ridiculous days, moonlight sales, and sidewalk sales offer warm-weather bargains.
13 Race Unity Day sparks institutionals, community campaigns. Children's Sunday. Flag Week, through June 19.	**14** Three cheers for the Red, White, and Blue! Patriotic institutionals honor Old Glory on Flag Day, Little League Baseball Week, through June 19, features sporting-goods specials. National Ragtime Week in St. Louis, through June 19.	**15** Arkansas joined Union, 1836. Pioneer Day, Ohio.	**16** Do-it-yourself gets a shot in the arm as fabric ads celebrate the anniversary of the first cloth pattern made by Butterick, 1863. Stock-in specials push picnic and cookout supplies. Camp and cottage needs featured in hardware promotions.	**17** Just 3 shopping days to Father's Day. Time for last-minute specials, small gift items. National Newspaper Association annual meeting in Philadelphia, through June 19, Bunker Hill Day, Boston, Memorial Day, Guam.	**18** "Fun in the Sun" sparks ads for all sorts of outdoor goodies: swim wear, garden tools, soft drinks, picnic supplies, sporting goods, patio furniture, and beach and poolside equipment. Pharmacies emphasize hot-weather needs.	**19** Think ahead to July Fourth. Reserve hotel space now. Special holiday rates advertised. Summer fashion sales begin. Travel luggage goes fast.
20 It's Father's Day! Local merchants run institutional ads. July Fourth safe-driving campaigns in the works. Preparations begin for summer sales events. Association of Newspaper Classified Advertising. West Virginia joined Union, 1863.	**21** Summer is a-coming in! Promotions focus on outdoor living, fashions, vacations, and home comfort. Flower Day; National Sweet Cherry Week, through June 27. Wimbledon tennis championships through July 3. New Hampshire joined Union, 1788.	**22** Home-improvement specials, especially pools and patios, spotlighted. Paints, wallpaper, insulation, siding, and roofing advertised. Financing offered by banks and savings and loan associations.	**23** Time to travel! Vacation specials at used-car dealers. Service stations advise summer tune-ups.	**24** Stock-in Specials arranged by food stores for the long holiday weekend. Picnic and cookout supplies promoted. Plans under way for patriotic July Fourth and bicentennial institutional ads. San Juan Day, Puerto Rico. Jean Baptiste Day, Canada.	**25** Safe-driving campaigns appear as schools close and July Fourth nears. Automobile sales, service stations tie in. Korean War began, 1950. Custer's last stand, 1876. Virginia joined Union, 1788.	**26** Preparations start for special sales events: July and August fur Sales, August furniture sales, back-to-school promotions on clothing and supplies. St. Lawrence Seaway opened, 1959.
27 National Fancy Food and Confection Show, Coliseum, New York City, through June 30. National Safe Boating Week.	**28** A furry future? Furriers push storage and fur-remodeling services now, advertise summer specials and layaways for fall. Beauty shops promote hair styles, skin care, geared to hot days ahead. Convenience items are big sellers.	**29** Blanket buys, white sales, and coat layaway values are business builders now.	**30** Supersavings now with end-of-month clearances in linens, housewares, and fashions. Last call for fur storage. Travel luggage sells fast. Food ads feature all-American values in cookout and picnic treats and supplies.	Corsage flower: Rose Birthstone: Moonstone, pearl, alexandrite	

Television audiences change during the day, and so does their receptiveness to commercial messages. Audiences are willing to listen to more of them in the daytime. As a rule, older people (over 55) and children consider commercials less intrusive than do viewers of other ages.

[*Source: Nielsen Television Index, 1976*]

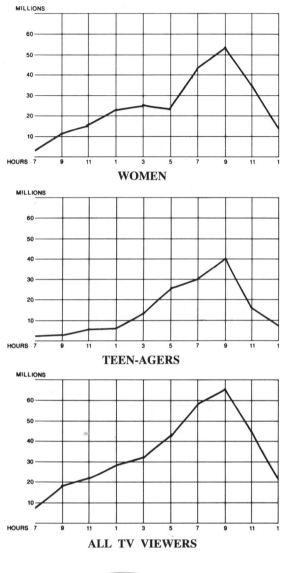

WOMEN

TEEN-AGERS

ALL TV VIEWERS

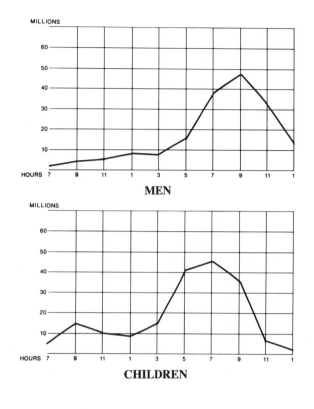

MEN

CHILDREN

Each product has its own selling cycle. Automobile sales reach their peak during the introductory months, when new models arrive, and rise with warm weather. More hard-cover books, liquor, and fragrances are sold during the holiday season (4 weeks preceding Christmas) than during all the preceding months; most are obviously bought as gifts. Retail stores do best in September through November, March, April, May, and June.

THE RESPONSE CYCLE

According to Ray Snyder and other direct-mail experts, some months bring in higher responses than others. Except for certain seasonal items such as female shaving creams, bathing suits, air conditioning units, and overcoats, the best month is January, with June at the opposite end of the scale. All in all, response to direct mail selling is on the increase as readers gain confidence in this type of impersonal selling.

Month	Comparative percentage
January	100.0
February	96.3
March	71.0
April	71.5
May	71.5
June	67.0
July	73.3
August	87.0
September	79.0
October	89.9
November	81.0
December	79.0

27

Why?

Reasons for advertising vary. In any creative assignment, the question "Why?" often crops up.

Here are some of the reasons for advertising:

To Create Immediate Sales This type of advertising is commonly referred to as *hard sell*. Advertising with a built-in direct-response device (coupon, type-in postcard, package insert, direct-mail reply card, toll-free telephone number), a special offer (10 cents off, three for the price of one, premium at cost, cash refunds, free gift, sweepstakes, contests, free sample), price ads (as in supermarket advertising), and use of a selling event, such as holidays, belong in this category.

To Build a Corporate Image The emphasis is on the corporate philosophy and policies (guarantees, warranties), reputation, goodwill (testimonials by satisfied customers), way of doing business, dependability, awards for outstanding service, and civic consciousness. The goal is not to create immediate sales but to leave a general impression with the audience. So-called advocacy advertising is a form of corporate-image building (see below).

Self-liquidating premium offer.

Free premium offer. This kind of approach is especially effective when introducing a new product.

MOBIL FINDS SPEAKING OUT PAYS

[*Courtesy of* The New York Times; *"Advertising" column by William D. Smith*]

Historically, the corporate code has been to keep a low profile on public issues unless they are as noncontroversial as apple pie and Mom.

The concomitant concept was that the job of advertising was to sell the salami, not to discuss the public issues surrounding salami sales.

Perhaps the most notable corporate maverick in recent years against these hallowed boardroom canons has been the Mobil Oil Corporation, which chose the medium of advertising to offer its views on a variety of issues, particularly those that are directly or indirectly concerned with the oil industry.

For its efforts, Mobil has been condemned by some members of the news media and politicians, praised by other members of the media and politicians, and even occasionally emulated by other corporations.

The decision to move the company into the forefront of public issue advertising was made by Rawleigh Warner, Jr., Mobil's chairman. The man chosen to implement the decision was Herbert Schmertz, vice president for public affairs.

Mr. Schmertz commented, "The problems of the industry had become very much larger, and the coverage by the press and other media was often neither accurate nor complete."

The ads have, at times, run in as many as 100 papers nationwide, but they make a weekly appearance in six papers: *The New York Times, The Wall Street Journal, The Chicago Sun Times, The Los Angeles Times, The Washington Post* and *The Boston Globe*. The ads, while frequently concerning public issues, often carry public interest or public service messages.

Mobil instituted a bimonthly advertisement called "Observations" that lists events, issues, and comments of interest that Mobil thinks are not important enough to warrant a full Op Ed page effort.

Mobil's agency is Doyle Dane Bernbach, but the ideas for some ads have been provided by clerks and secretaries, according to Mr. Schmertz. Mobil's issues ads have been criticized by some as an attempt to use corporate coffers to "brainwash" the public. To this Mr. Schmertz replies, "To say that some people should not be allowed to speak their piece on an issue sets a dangerous precedent and is inherently contrary to our form of government."

Others, some within the oil industry, have criticized Mobil's ads as a waste of time and money, and as possibly being counterproductive. An executive at another oil company commented: "When people see one of these ads their first question is, 'Why aren't they using the ad costs to find more oil?' Their second thought is that, if the oil companies are trying to convince us of something, the opposite must be true."

Mr. Schmertz commented, "We can't tell scientifically that our ads have been successful, but our impression is that they definitely have." He gave as his reasons a high awareness of what Mobil has been saying, and public opinion changes.

"I am not saying that we brought on changes in policy or public opinion. I am only saying that we contributed to the dialogue."

He further explained, "When we went into this we knew it would not have any results for four or five years. You have to stay in the market place for ideas. You can't just hop in and out."

Mr. Schmertz indicated that big business was remiss in not becoming more active in issue advertising: "Companies have a responsibility to participate in the dialogue about the future of this country and too often they don't."

This particular campaign is an outstanding example of advocacy image building, providing the public with genuinely useful information.

INDUSTRY LEADERS BUILD CORPORATE IMAGE
BY SELLING THEIR PRODUCTS GENERICALLY

Eastman Kodak sells memories.

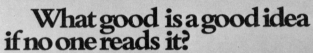

What good is a good idea if no one reads it?

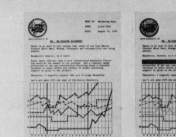

Xerox sells reproduction.

Apple Pie

Chevrolet sells America*

Think of the computer as energy. As mental energy. Power to get things done. IBM.

IBM sells thinking.

*Cheryl, age 9, from Las Vegas, Nevada, answered the question "List some customs that are found only in the United States" on a written test like this; "Baseball, hot dogs, apple pie, Chevrolet."

29

To Combine Hard and Soft Sell This phrase describes the type of advertising that speaks softly but hits hard with specific copy claims. It is worth mentioning that one type of selling does not have to cancel out the other. The two can be very successfully combined, as demonstrated later in this book.

These ads are informative and hard-hitting, yet appealing to the eye.

Tough-talking retailer talks tongue in cheek.

To Confront Competition This practice is viewed with skepticism by some advertisers, who believe that such advertising leads to needless controversy. There are indications, however, that consumers do not share this view. In fact, most of them welcome the opportunity to compare specific features of one product with those of another.

To Introduce a New Product or Service Implicit in this type of advertising is the excitement of presenting something new, accompanied by a sense of urgency.

ANNOUNCER (voice-over): Let's compare the legroom for passengers in the front seat of America's most luxurious cars. Chrysler Imperial . . . 42.8 inches.

Lincoln Continental . . . 43.3 inches.

Cadillac Eldorado . . . 43.4 inches.

Fiat 128 . . . 43.8 inches. More than the Imperial, Continental, the Eldorado. Now that's luxury.

No. 2 says he tries harder. Than who?

We wouldn't, for a minute, argue with No. 2. If he says he tries harder, we'll take him at his word.

The only thing is, a lot of people assume it's us he's trying harder than.

That's hardly the case. And we're sure that No. 2 would be the first to agree. Especially in light of the following.

A car where you need it.

The first step in renting a car is getting to the car. Hertz makes that easier for you to do than anybody else.

We're at every major airport in the United States. And at some airports that are not so major. Ever fly to Whitefish, Montana? Some people do. And have a Hertz car waiting.

No matter how small the airport you fly to, if it's served by a commercial airline, 97 chances out of 100 it's also served by Hertz or by a Hertz office within 20 minutes of it.

We also have locations throughout the down-town and suburban areas of every major city.

In all, Hertz has over 2,900 places throughout the world where you can pick up or leave a car. Nearly twice as many as No. 2.

Can't come to us? We'll come to you.

We have a direct-line telephone in most major hotels and motels in the U.S. It's marked HERTZ and it's in the lobby. Pick it up, ask for a car, and we'll deliver one to the door. You often can't get a cab as easily.

What kind of car would you like?

When you rent from Hertz, you're less likely to get stuck with a beige sedan when you want a red convertible. We have over twice as many cars as No. 2.

Not only is our fleet big, it's varied. We do our best to give you what you want. From Fords, to Mustangs, to Thunderbirds, to Lincolns and everything in between. Including the rather fantastic Shelby GT-350-H.

What kind of service will you get?

When you rent a car from us or anybody else, you expect it to be sitting there waiting, ready to go, looking like new.

On that score we claim no superiority over our competition. They goof once in awhile. We goof once in awhile.

Except when we goof it bothers us more because people don't expect the big one to goof. And to make up for it, if our service is not up to Hertz standards we give you $50 in free rentals.* Plus an apology.

No. 2 gives a quarter plus an apology. And

advertises that he "can't afford" to do more.

We feel the other way about it. We can't afford to do less.

Besides, the $50 comes out of the station manager's local operating funds. This tends to keep him very alert . . . and our service very good.

Hot line.

When you're in one city and you're flying to another city and you want to have a car waiting when you arrive and you want it confirmed before you leave, we can do it for you. Instantly. In any one of 1,038 U.S. cities. No other rent-a-car company can make that statement.

The major reason we can do it is because we recently installed one of the world's most advanced reservation systems.

After all, with the supersonic jets in sight and one hour coast to coast flights in prospect, you'll need some quick answers.

We can give them to you today.

About credit.

If you've got a national credit card with most any major company, you've got credit with us.

A businesslike way of doing business.

If you own your own firm or are instrumental in running a firm, you know what a nightmare billing can be.

Have your company rent from us and we'll help ease that nightmare. We can even tailor our

billing cycle to fit your paying cycle.

We'll bill by the rental, by the month, by division, by department, by individual, and by blood type if it'll help you.

Speak up No. 3.

Is it you that No. 2 tries harder than?

Hertz

An object lesson in comparison advertising has been the classic Avis Number Two advertising campaign. At first, Hertz, confident of its superiority, chose to ignore its competitor's claims. But as consumers began to switch loyalties, Hertz decided to fight back.

Both advertisers won in this case; the public enjoyed the fray and became more aware of car rentals in general.

Solicitation to Get New Business When based upon solid information, speculative presentations offer a rare opportunity to demonstrate creative flair; the absence of sacred cows unshackles the mind. Some of the strongest advertising campaigns make their debut as new-business presentations.

What?

Information about the product or service (product advertising still outranks service advertising by about 3 to 1, but this ratio is changing as consumers today spend more than half of their incomes on services) is the first and one of the most important steps in solving an advertising problem. Most strong advertising ideas originate with the product itself.

How Much?

All persons involved in the project (media buyers, account executives, art directors, and print and television production managers) must be made aware of the budget. If possible, all written estimates should have the client's approval before, not after, commencing the job. Generally speaking, the cost of execution depends on the following factors:

1. *Volume of work.* The larger the order, the lower the cost per job. Most suppliers will accept a package price for bulk assignments.

2. *Professional standard.* Estimates on jobs vary, depending on a number of factors. Photographs can cost anywhere from $30 to $3000 (one of Richard Avedon's photographs at the Museum of Modern Art in New York sold for $20,000), and a commercial from $500 to $50,000 (one soap company paid more than $500,000 on production to introduce its new detergent). The complexity of the assignment, the absence of close deadlines, a chance to do outstanding work (which will enhance the contributor's sample reel or a portfolio), or the need for work makes the difference.

3. *Ability to pay.* Suppliers are quick to find out (sometimes they are told) what the traffic can bear. Large advertisers may be asked to pay higher prices simply because they can afford to do so.

4. *Use of material.* Schedule (the number of times that the work will appear), coverage (local or national), and the type of medium in which the work is to appear (album cover, poster, mailing piece, newspaper, trade or general magazine, radio, television) have a great bearing on costs, possibly more than have the actual hours spent on the assignment.

5. *Size of the total budget.* The larger the advertising budget, the greater the sum that can be set aside to cover production costs, although *proportionately* there may be a decrease.

The cost of a drawing like this, prepared for retail advertising, ranges from $25 to $100, depending on its use.

ANNUAL BUDGET/PRODUCTION COSTS RATIOS ARE COMMON IN ADVERTISING

TOTAL ANNUAL ADVERTISING BUDGET	ANNUAL PRODUCTION EXPENDITURES	PERCENTAGE OF PRODUCTION EXPENDITURE IN RELATION TO TOTAL BUDGET
$ 100,000	$ 25,000–$ 35,000	25–55
300,000	45,000– 90,000	15–30
1,000,000	100,000– 250,000	10–25
2,000,000	150,000– 400,000	7.5–20
5,000,000	300,000– 750,000	6–15
10,000,000	500,000– 1,000,000	5–10

Naturally, larger advertisers can afford the luxury of juggling funds by following the robbing-from-Peter-to-pay-Paul principle. As long as there is money available somewhere, it is relatively simple to dip into the media budget (which can be as much as three-fourths of the total advertising budget) and spend it, say, on the services of a "name" photographer.

It goes without saying that the creative person should try cutting production costs wherever possible. However, it also should be borne in mind that the greatest potentials for savings lie in astute media buying. It hardly makes good business sense to pinch pennies on production—and affect the quality of the ad—and go on a spending spree in media.

Reputation and artistic flair enable well-known fashion illustrators to ask from $150 to $1000 for "quick" sketches like this.

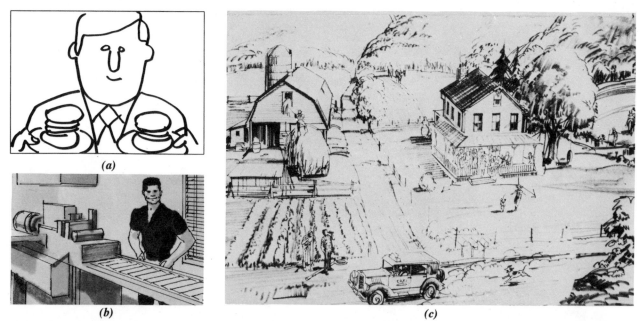

(a)

(b)

(c)

Prices for renderings have a wide range, depending on the sketch artist's technical skill and conceptual contribution. Shown in the upper-left corner *(a)* is a felt-pen indication by top art director Ralph Ammirati, with emphasis on the basic concept, not the execution. More highly polished is a sketch *(b)* prepared by a professional rendering artist ("comp man"), costing $5 to $10 per frame. The frame designed for a Coca-Cola commercial *(c)* represents the ultimate in refinement, just a short step removed from finished art. The cost of a drawing like this hovers between $25 and $75. All sketches shown here are part of complete storyboards (or *boards,* as they are called) of eight to twenty-four frames.

An illustrator's distinctive style may be so intrinsic a part of the campaign theme that he may demand $1000 or more per ad, depending on the number of assignments.

Top artists are paid for their unique talent, not complexity of the job or the hours they must spend on it. Illustrator Folon usually submits his own visual ideas, as opposed to finishing up someone else's layout. Crude as his drawing style may appear to the untrained eye, it is not that at all. This artist is able to command top prices. The same is true of the stark still-life photographs by Rudy Legname; behind his simple compositions is the exquisite taste of a fine designer. The primitive but highly sophisticated and charming drawings by cartoonist Robert Blechman represent a welcome rest for the eye of the commercial-clutter–conscious television viewer. He, too, is highly paid for his contributions.

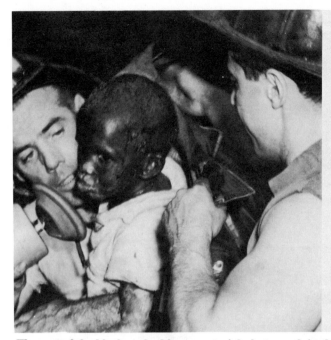

'Cause someone played with an alarm box, the engines got to the real fire too late!

¡No mande alarmas falsas!

City of New York Fire Department

The cost of the black-and-white reportorial photograph in this subway poster was on the low side. Yet it proved to be an appropriate choice for dramatizing this particular message. It is not always necessary to use an established name photographer to produce an outstanding piece of work.

The loosely executed flyer did not win awards for graphic excellence but brought Papa Chickardi's plenty of pizza orders; the informal tone of his advertising is just right for his type of establishment. As the work of old masters (in this case, Toulouse-Lautrec) comes into the public domain, it can be used at little or no charge. The same holds true of the wide variety of drawings of the past.

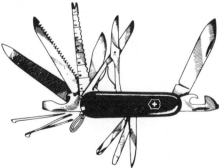

These pen-and-ink drawings show up well on even the roughest newspaper stock. Usually, they are turned out at short notice, and for as little as $10 to $25, by in-house art studios charging for their work on an hourly basis.

Meticulously executed "product pictures" like these command slightly higher prices, typically between $25 and $50 apiece. The art technique makes costs go up.

By means of adroit computer animation, Dolphin Productions transferred Bob Peak's kaleidoscopic, multi-image poster illustrations to tape, then used electronically induced optical effects to make the drawings move on the screen. Money was saved by cutting down production time.

Showing a hand but not the face in this demonstration commercial meant substantial savings to the advertiser, perhaps more than $1000 in residual payments which would have had to be paid to a *principal* per 13-week cycle.

A stand-up spokesman may command a fair amount of money, as in the case of John Houseman extolling the virtues of Volvo. However, simple production technique more than made up the difference in costs and without interfering with quality.

Cost of animation averages about $25 per foot ($82 per meter) and more if elaborate drawings and camera movements are required, as in this commercial. A 30-second film in 35-millimeter is 45 feet (13.7 meters).

"Production" commercials (with large casts and spacious settings) raise the costs, but the effect may justify the initial investment. The higher the frequency, the more quickly costs are amortized.

Basic costs:

On getting ideas: Sometimes it is more economical — and efficient — to approach problems on a project-by-project basis. This list was prepared with that in mind.

Advertising campaign idea development
Headlines & layouts for 3 to 6 print ads. $300-600
Script & rough storyboard for TV commercial . . . . $750 each
Creative platform (3 to 6 written pages) $500
(Body copy billed separately)

Presentation to acquire new business
Complete (headlines & rough layouts, creative platform, working with creative teams, if needed) . . $1500-3000
Once the account is retained, add 2.5% of first year's gross billing but only in excess of basic creative fee.
Participation (as an outside consultant) in presentation to client $50-100/hour
Legal assurance provided that no further communication will exist between consultant and advertiser without prior approval by the advertising agency.

Follow-through on print ads
Type specification, supervision of photography, art work, mechanical production $200/day

Follow-through on TV commercials
Pre-production (selection of suppliers, talent, props, creative supervision, conferences, etc. $500-2000
Participation at the shooting, location or studio. $500/day
Post-production (supervision of music, voice, mixing, prints) $1000-1500
Complete follow-through from beginning to end $1500-3500
(Per diem costs, such as traveling, room & board, etc. not included)

Radio commercials
Script $100-300
Follow-through (voice, music, mixing, recording) $100-300
Media recommendation. $100-300

Preparation of a direct mail campaign
Rough layout & copy (body copy included) $1500-3000
Follow-through (consultation on selection of lists, mechanics of mailing, production, analysis of returns, fulfillment, etc.) $1500-3000

Brochures
Copy & layout . . . . to be determined

Displays
Copy & layout . . . . to be determined

Packaging concepts
Rough layouts (3 to 6) $600-1200
Follow-through (prototype, reproduction, printing, production) $2000
Testing (supervision of pre-production research) $250
(Comprehensive layouts billed separately)

Audio-video presentation
General concept (in form of written creative platform) $1000
Preparation of audio-video material . . . . to be determined

Motion picture film (10 to 20 minutes)
Script $2000-3000
Visual presentation (storyboard) $1000-4000
Pre-production follow-through $1000-2000
Shooting (supervision) $500/day
Post-production follow-through. $2000-4000

Corporate image development
Graphic consistency, logo, letterheads, signs, etc. $750-1500

Evaluation of present advertising campaign
3 to 6 written pages $250

Working with creative teams
Conferences, exchange of ideas, thumbnail sketches, etc. $100/hour
Weekly basis (minimum 25 hours) $1000

Conferences
With marketing executives, clients, creative people, business executives $100/hour
New product development $100/hour
Ideas for books $100/hour

Prices are listed on this a la carte chart of free-lance advertising services ranging from purely creative to administrative. These prices are slightly above average.

McCANN-ERICKSON, INC.
Television Commercial Estimate

CLIENT_____ PRODUCT_____ ESTIMATE NUMBER_____
DATE_____ SUBJECT_____ STUDIO_____
TITLES & CODE #_____

GROSS TOTAL ESTIMATE

Film Production (see breakout below) $_____
Editing Only   _____
Contingency Fund   _____
Talent: *
_____On Camera . . . $_____   _____ Extra . . . . $_____
_____Voice Over . . . $_____   _____ Other . . . . $_____
_____Singer(s) . . . . $_____   _____ Wardrobe . . . . $_____
                                        _____% Pension & Welfare . . $_____
Talent Travel & Living   _____
Music Scoring (Salaries, creative/arranging fees, etc.)   _____
Stock Music   _____
Recording Charges (studio, editing, mixing, tapes, etc.)   _____
Sound Effects   _____
Art Work — Photostats — Storyboards   _____
Agency Props   _____
Stock Footage   _____
Other   _____

                                                    NET TOTAL $_____

Agency Commission_____%   _____
Employer's Tax_____%   _____
Sales Tax_____%   _____
Sales Tax_____%   _____
Agency Travel & Living**   _____
**# People_____;   # Days_____   Total Air Fare $_____
                                                    Total Per Diem $_____
WEATHER CONTINGENCY: $_____ NET PER DAY
TALENT CONTINGENCY: $_____ NET PER DAY | **GROSS TOTAL** $_____ |

NOTES:
1. Prints, Agency Commission and NY Sales Tax included; packing and shipping charges will be extra.
2. *Talent is paid minimum unit rate. No provision is made for use or reuse.

ACCOUNT SERVICE:_____
EXECUTIVE PRODUCER:_____ TV/R BUSINESS MANAGER:_____
CLIENT APPROVAL:_____ DATE:_____

PRODUCTION BID BREAKOUT

No. pre-prod. days_____ pre-light/rehearse_____
No. build/strike days_____ Hours:_____
No. Studio shoot days_____ Hours:_____
No. Location days_____ Hours:_____
Location sites:_____
_____

(L) MISCELLANEOUS
(126) Payroll &
        P&W Taxes $_____
(127) Shipping   _____
(128) Phones and Cable   _____
(129) Petty Cash   _____
(130) Messengers   _____

DIRECT COSTS TOTAL $_____
        Mark Up (_____%)   _____

PRE, POST-PRODUCTION   **PRODUCTION**
(K) Director: Prep,   (K) Director $_____   (O) Talent Expenses   _____
     Travel & Post $_____ (B) Crew   _____   (181) Insurance   _____
(C) Materials   _____   (G) Location Expense _____
(A) Crew   _____   (H) Equipment   _____   TOTAL PRODUCTION $_____
                                 (I) Raw Stock, print
SET CONSTRUCTION   & develop   _____
(D) Crew $_____   (J) Props &   **POST-PRODUCTION**
(E) Materials _____   Wardrobe   _____   See details on
(F) Studio Exp. _____   spec. sheet $_____
                                 _____   _____
                                 _____   _____   GRAND TOTAL $_____

SUBMITTED FOR:_____ BY:_____ DATE:_____
B-75 R3/74   CONTRACT NO._____

**TV commercial
estimates like this
one keep costs
under control.**

[*Courtesy of
McCann Erickson, Inc.*]

ADVERTISING PRODUCTION ESTIMATE

CLIENT ______ JOB No. ______

DESCRIPTION ______ DATE ______

ART		PRODUCTION	
LAYOUT		TYPE	
RESCALES			
ART		ENGRAVING	
PHOTOS			
		ELECTROS	
RETOUCHING			
		MATS	
LETTERING		PRINTING INSERTS	
PHOTOSTATS			
PRINTS		**TOTAL PRODUCTION**	
TOTAL ART		TOTAL ART	

TOTAL NET COST ______

AGENCY COMMISSION ______

TOTAL COST ______

NO. OF ADS ______

TOTAL FOR CAMPAIGN ______

PRINTING JOB ESTIMATE

CLIENT ______ JOB No. ______

DATE ______ DESCRIPTION ______

SIZE ______ No. OF PAGES ______

QUANTITY ______ COLOR ______ BIND ______

LAYOUT & DESIGN	
ART OR PHOTOGRAPHY	
MECHANICAL	
RETOUCHING	
PRINTS & PHOTOSTATS	
LETTERING	
TYPESETTING	
PRINTING (PLATES, INK, BINDING)	
MAILING	
ADDRESSING	
COLLATING	
POSTAGE	
PURCHASES	
SHIPPING	
COPY	
SERVICE CHARGE	
SUBTOTAL	
CONTINGENCY	
TOTAL	

ESTIMATE VALID 30 DAYS FROM ABOVE DATE

Approval forms covering every phase of production (art, engraving, typesetting, and printing) are routed through various departments in an advertising agency. Estimates are kept in legal-size manila job jackets along with other records, such as photostats of layouts, bills, and type and engravers' proofs. At the completion of each assignment, all material is filed away for safekeeping, usually for a period of 2 or 3 years.

FORM PI-4M-10-73

PRODUCTION DEPARTMENT ORDER

TYPOGRAPHER:

OPERATION	DATE OF ORDER	DUE DATE
COMPOSITION		
REVISE		
2ND REVISE		
3RD REVISE		
MAKE-UP COMPLETE		
REVISE		
REVISE		

ENGRAVER:

DATE OF ORDER ______ DUE ______

SCREEN ______

STOCK ______ PROOFS ______

STOCK ______ PROOFS ______

STOCK ______ PROOFS ______

SCREEN ______

STOCK ______ PROOFS ______

STOCK ______ PROOFS ______

STOCK ______ PROOFS ______

FINAL PROOFS

QUANTITY AND STOCK	DUE DATE

DISTRIBUTION

STANDARD ☐ OTHER ☐ (SEE REVERSE SIDE)

FOUNDRY

FORM TO: ______

BILL TYPE ______

CUT RELEASE	DUE
SENT TO:	

SPECIAL INSTRUCTIONS:

ELECTROTYPER:

TYPE OF PLATE	PUBLICATION AND ADDRESS	SHIP DATE	SHIP METHOD

FORWARDING

DATE	PUBLICATION	TYPE OF MATERIAL	FROM

SNEEZE.

Hi. I'm Joey Faye. I've been sneezing for a living since I started in vaudeville, age 14.

START SNEEZE, HOLD UNDER.

I'm going to sneeze into Kleenex. Two-ply tissue; 200 to the box.

. . . SNEEZE.

Very soft. Now I'm going to sneeze into Marcal. Two-ply tissue; 200 to the box.

SNEEZE.

Also very soft. But if you sneezed as much as I sneeze—(SNEEZE), you'd sneeze into Marcal. Because Marcal costs about 10 cents less than Kleenex. And 10 cents a box is nothing to—(SNEEZE) sneeze at.

Commercials like this 30-second spot with Joey Faye demonstrating the superiority of Marcal fluff-out facial tissues over those of Kleenex seem so simple in concept that it is hard to understand why days or even weeks had to be spent in executing them. There is more here than meets the eye, however. Casting, rehearsals, negotiations, legal clearances, and getting client's approvals all take time and effort. So do laboratory work, editing, inclusion of optical, sound mixing, and printing, and so on.

How Long?

In advertising, every job has a deadline. Closing dates lurk around the corner while the job wends its way through the creative and production departments. Generally, assignments pass through fastest in retail advertising departments (where it is possible to get quick approvals) and more fitfully in advertising agencies (where ideas are brooded upon by many creative minds).

TIME SCHEDULE OF A TYPICAL PRINT AD

Copy: 3 days ⎫ Arts and copy
Layout: 2 days ⎰ often created together
Approvals (inside): 1 day to 1 week
Legal approval: 1 day to 1 week
Approvals (client): 1 day to 1 week
Finished art: 5 days to 1 month
Typesetting: 1 day
Retouching: 2 days
Mechanical: 1 day

This does not include time spent on changes. After this stage, changes are more difficult to make.

Final approval (client): 1 day to 1 week
Black-and-white engraving: 1 day
Color engraving: 2 to 4 weeks
Printing: 1 to 4 weeks
Advance insertion requirements:
  Newspapers: 1 day
  Magazines: 1 to 8 weeks
  Mailing: 3 days

Built into this schedule is the time needed for the creation and follow-through of an average assignment. Some agencies make a special effort to give their copywriters and art directors several days or weeks to produce ideas for a campaign. They feel that the extra time spent on planning is a worthwhile luxury that will prove itself in the quality of the work.

Many timesaving and cost-cutting opportunities are available. Most publications offer typesetting and engraving facilities to the advertiser at little or no cost and can put ads to bed in less than 24 hours. Only minimal allowances can be made for checking type and engraving proofs under these circumstances, and the quality of reproduction may suffer as a result.

TIME SCHEDULE OF A TYPICAL TELEVISION COMMERCIAL

Script: 3 days
Storyboard: 2 days
Legal approvals: 1 day to 1 week
Preproduction activity prior to client's approval: 1 day
Approval (inside): 1 day
Approval (client): 1 day to 1 week

Upon the client's approval, the television storyboard is ready for production. Unlike printing, television production is highly complex, requiring from six persons (art director, writer, director-cameraman, assistant cameraman, and three-member crew) to as many as fifty people at the shooting. Nurturing the film through editing and developing are from four (editor, sound mixer, optical laboratician, effects man) to twenty or thirty technicians. Shooting ratios average 20 to 1 in television commercial film footage.

Preproduction Activity after Client's Approval

Bidding (usually inviting three competitive bids): 3 to 7 days
Evaluation and selection of production house: 2 days
Casting (exclusive of rehearsals): 2 to 5 days
Scouting for location: 1 to 6 days
Approval of demo tape: 1 day
Styling and propping: 3 days
Preparation of graphics: 1 to 7 days
Building the set: 2 to 14 days

Not all these steps are necessary for every commercial. If the commercial is to be shot on location, no

---

Procter & Gamble recommends a 9-week schedule to its advertising agencies for completion (from approval stage to air date) of a 35-millimeter 1-minute TV commercial, shot in a New York studio and utilizing standard film completion. Moreover, 2 days are added for location shooting (for search), 4 days for original music, another week for complicated opticals, 4 weeks for animation (for drawing, pencil test, and inking), and 1 week for shooting outside New York City. Any delays in approval would add a corresponding number of days to the schedule.

additional set or props may be required. If there are no performers, no casting sessions are needed. Amateur performers may need more time for rehearsals. Activities such as scouting for locations and arranging casting sessions may overlap.

Putting Together the Television Commercial

Filming: 1 to 3 days (traveling time may or may not be included)
Rushes: 1 day

Postproduction Activity (All Film)

Editing: 2 to 4 days
Approval (legal): 1 day
Approval (client): 1 day
Interpositives: 3 days
Preoptical negative: 2 days
Optical internegative: 1 day
Corrected prints: 2 days
Protection interpositive: 1 day

Reduction prints: 1 day
Final-check print: 1 day
Multiple prints: 3 to 7 days
Shipping: 1 to 4 days

Postproduction Activity (Film and Then Tape Dupes as the Distribution Medium)

Same as for all film to corrected-print stage
Transfer to tape: 2 days
Multiple prints (tape dupes): 2 days
Shipping: 1 to 2 days

Postproduction Activity (All Tape; Single Camera Used)

Shooting: 1 day
Editing: 1 day (sometimes same day)
Approval (legal): 1 day (sometimes same day)
Approval (client): 1 day (sometimes same day)
Multiple prints (tape dupes): 1 to 2 days
Shipping: 1 to 2 days

Postproduction Activity (Multiple Camera)

Shooting: 1 day
Editing: same day
Multiple prints: 1 day

These are rough time estimates. It is possible to shoot several commercials on the same day. Modern tape techniques, such as CMX editing or 1-inch (25.4-millimeter) videotape editing, save time. Kinescope distribution eliminates film transfer.

Additional time can be saved by using the production facilities of television studios, which are often made available to advertisers. This may be the fastest, and certainly is the cheapest, method of producing a television commercial. However, production shortcuts may weaken the impact of the final product.

Chapter Four

Meet Your Customer

To an advertising professional, the consumer must be a close acquaintance. As a *marketer,* the professional must know the customer's income, marital status, occupation, family size, education, age, lifestyle, hobbies, and others like him or her living in the same market area and media reach. As a *media planner,* the professional must know the customer's reading, listening, and viewing habits, special interests, and media preferences. As a *creative person,* the professional must know much of the foregoing as well as what goes on inside the customer's head: his or her motivations, opinions, aspirations, biases, and, sometimes, neuroses.

Armed with this information, the advertising professional is in a position to examine and understand the subtle reciprocal relationships between:

The consumer and the product
The consumer and the media
The consumer and the advertising
The consumer and the elements of advertising such as pictures, words, and layout

Unless these relationships are understood, the advertising professional is working in limbo. This topic will be touched upon in subsequent chapters. Suffice it to say at this point that to an advertiser the consumer represents more than just "a name and serial number." He or she is an individual and, most important, a prospect.

Computers can supply much information about consumers, but only on an impersonal level. Technology, advanced as it may be, cannot cope effectively with the vast and complex spectrum of human emotions. Only people are qualified to understand people.

When Consumers Differ and When They Do Not

Before we discuss the differences among consumers, a quick look at the resemblances may be in order. In these days of relentless market segmentation, it is wise to bear in mind, when looking for the right appeal, that rich or poor, conservative or liberal, married or unmarried, tall or short, *human beings still comprise a race of kindred spirits*. We all have the same basic needs for our physical and emotional well-being. Some of these needs have been passed down to us from our ancestors living in caves. While it is true that today we express our feelings more subtly, we still have them and probably always will.

We all crave:

Love
Recognition
Pleasure
Health
Success
Security
Positive self-image
Social acceptance
Comfort
Freedom

And we all try to avoid:

Conflict
Pain
Sickness
Poverty
Uncertainty
Trouble
Loneliness
Death

These feelings are so nearly universal that they transcend any and all demographic barriers.

And Now for the Differences: Market Segmentation

In spite of the foregoing similarities, it is becoming increasingly obvious that from a marketing point of view the so-called average customer is an endangered species in today's society. The rarer such a customer becomes, the more it costs to reach him or her. In fact, it takes an enormous amount of investment capital to enter today's market successfully with a generic, all-embracing mass product, such as a toothpaste, a pain reliever, or an electric light bulb.

This is why modern advertisers try focusing on the differences between customers rather than on the resemblances. This approach, the basis for *market segmentation,* makes it possible to splinter a huge marketplace into more manageable units and to design products as well as advertising around specific needs.

The three basic methods used in market segmentation are geographic, demographic, and psychological. They will be explained in detail in the following pages.

It goes without saying that segmentation as a marketing total must be handled with expert care. A combination of factors is always present. One factor in itself hardly ever serves as the sole criterion on which to build a marketing plan. Here are a few illustrations. Living side by side in the same trading area (a geographical characteristic) may be several different ethnic groups (a demographic characteristic), each with a tradition of its own (a psychological characteristic). Based upon their incomes, truck drivers and college professors belong in the same demographic classification, yet they have different interests. Surrounding every metropolis are suburbs whose inhabitants, for the sake of statistical expedience, may be lumped together with city apartment dwellers pursuing a variety of lifestyles.

A SIMPLE LESSON IN DEMOGRAPHIC SEGMENTATION: THE REMARKABLE 80-20 PERCENT RULE

A basic yet effective approach to segmentation is to divide the entire United States population into two parts on the basis of income, one part being about 4 times as large as the other.

"The one beer to have when you're having more than one" campaign for the Schaefer brewery once again brought this marketing truism to the attention of the advertising community, although the same statistics had been staring marketers in the face for more than a quarter of a century. As it happened, this brewery had drifted into a comfortable but static third-place position among the local brands that dominated the huge beer market around New York City in the 1950s. It was not until 10 years later that its advertising agency, BBDO, discovered that about 20 percent of heavy beer drinkers guzzled about 80 percent of all the beer sold.

It appeared that the heavy beer drinker was happy with the way his beer tasted in the first cold glass; it was the taste of his second and third that bothered him. Each drink seemed to lose a little, not measuring up to the first. Since Schaefer's beer is less bitter, heightened enjoyment could be a genuine promise. The new advertising campaign, based upon this approach, helped to push Schaefer into the Number 1 position in New York City and near the top in its entire marketing area.

Following the Schaefer experience, other advertisers found that their prime users, too, were concentrated in a relatively small target area, covering about 20 percent of the market. AT&T discovered that 80 percent of all telephone calls were made by 20 percent of their customers. A food company simplified its product line when researchers told its officials that the average housewife, obviously a creature of habit, repeats 20 percent of the recipes 80 percent of the time. When a paint distributor learned that 20 percent of his orders were responsible for 80 percent of his business, he changed his media schedule to concentrate on his most important customers.

Several image-building campaigns, too, focus on a quintile of the market—opinion-leaders in the highest income brackets, the initiators of intellectual trends.

Figures released by the U.S. Bureau of the Census shed some light on the 80-20 percent marketing phenomenon, at least as far as the general population is concerned. It appears that for over the last two decades about half of the total United States income was received by a little more than 20 percent of American households.

Demographic studies show that the typical heavy beer drinker is male, 25 to 49 years old, a high school graduate with an income of $12,000 to $18,000 who works in a blue-collar job and glorifies sports personalities. He could readily identify himself with the rugged characters in these commercials for Schaefer beer.

Market Segmentation, Continued

What Consumers Do Is What They Buy Consumers' occupations and hobbies define their wants. Fishing enthusiasts (poor or rich, old or young, male or female, car or bicycle owner, grade school or college graduate, or whatever their demographic classification may be) buy fishing poles. Camera buffs spend part of their disposable income on photographic equipment and film, and presumably as long as they pursue their hobby, they will continue to do just that. Golfers will always need golf balls; tennis players, tennis balls; and table tennis players, table-tennis balls.

These market segments can be reached through special-interest publications, trade magazines, or selective mailing lists, the latter of which offer breakdowns of as many as 20,000 different occupations.

Where Consumers Live Is What They Buy Distribution areas may presolve geographical segmentation: supply covers demand, and vice versa. The creator of an advertisement (the art director or the copywriter) may take only a peripheral interest in this particular aspect of segmentation. Presumably, distribution is the business of the advertiser, not the advertising agency. However, since environment affects people's life-styles, the whereabouts of users may well provide important clues to the kind of appeal they are most likely to respond to.

Generally, trends start either in

New York City or on the West Coast (primarily Los Angeles and San Francisco). The latter has a slight edge, according to *Sunset* magazine. It takes an average of 2 years for a trend to permeate the entire United States population, with the Southeast usually holding out the longest.

Buying predilections vary greatly in different parts of the country, depending upon such factors as climate, employment opportunities, average income, and cultural background.

What Consumers Look Like Is What They Buy Another interesting approach to segmentation, and one that receives special attention in periods of prosperity, is to market a product according to the customer's physical appearance. In using this method, a certain kind of apparel is sold only to tall or chubby customers, moisturizers to women with dry-skin problems, toupees to balding men, bust-line–contouring devices to the small-chested (or those who would like to help nature along), bikinis to the slender-waisted, cream cover-ups to those with telltale circles under their eyes, hair straighteners to black men and women wishing to change their coiffures, and so on.

What Consumers Know Is What They Buy Sophisticated techniques make it possible today to preselect groups

of heavy, medium, or light users which then can be superimposed on geographical, demographical, or psychological clusters. In fact, the ability to help advertisers track down customers has become a much-stressed selling point with media. Networks, radio and television stations, and outdoor-poster companies all offer their own brands of buys tailored to the advertiser's specific needs. Along the same lines, many newspapers offer to split runs, some into as many as twenty-five to thirty segments. Nearly all magazines have regional issues, with several offering more than 300 different geographic or demographic advertising availabilities or both.

Such control over media coverage enables advertisers not only to reach their markets efficiently but also to create advertising copy that speaks the language of their audience.

What Consumers Need Is What They Buy Varicose-vein sufferers are the prime target for support stockings, myopic people for eyeglasses, women for douches, men for razors, and families of the bereaved for funeral arrangements. The purchase of these items, unlike those bought more or less because "they would be nice to have," is perceived by consumers as a necessity; they feel that they are entitled to have these things to maintain a decent quality of life. Thus, a rational, straightforward selling argument may be all that is needed to spur action.

What Consumers Use Is What They Buy Of all the approaches to segmentation, this is the most widely used, the easiest to apply, and, perhaps, the most simplistic in concept. Consumer acceptance is predicated upon proven buying patterns: milk drinkers are prime prospects for milk, smokers for cigarettes, pregnant women for bassinets. A modified approach to the product-use type of segmentation is the selling of products to *complement* those already owned by the consumer. Car owners are the major purchasers of automobile parts and gasoline, new homeowners of furniture, owners of refrigerators of frozen food, dog owners of dog foods, and so on.

REGIONAL DIFFERENCES: CLIMATE, ENVIRONMENT, AND SIMILARITY OF INTERESTS CREATE

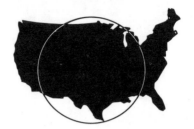

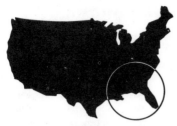

NORTHEAST (VERMONT, MASSA-CHUSETTS, NEW HAMPSHIRE, MAINE, ETC.) This region respects old values, prefers soft to hard sell. Vermont was the first state to regulate outdoor advertising. Favorite colors are blue and white. Irrepressible local citizens offer a *pièce de résistance* to high-pressure direct-mail advertisers. Even so, cents-off coupons fare well. This is a big market for flatware, especially the pistol-grip type. Canco Cartons changed its premium offer to dining utensils from terry-cloth aprons and nylon hosiery to suit local tastes. This is snow country, still buying potbelly stoves, quilts, snow tires, and, for reasons known only to the natives, cream cheese, frozen waffles, pancakes, and paper napkins. Time not being of the essence, about 10 times as much regular tea as instant is consumed.

MIDWEST AND MOUNTAIN STATES (OHIO, INDIANA, ILLINOIS, MICHI-GAN, MISSOURI, TEXAS, NEW MEXICO, UTAH, WYOMING, ETC.) People in this region have mixed feelings about progress and pursue a love-hate relationship with fast-talking Easterners. Provincialism clashes with increased interest in cultural affairs. This is macho country, where men are still men and women are women. There are no favorite colors. The region is a poor market for crabgrass killer and mayonnaise but a good one for guns, fishing poles, soft-cover books, season tickets to football games, ordinary life insurance, figurine table lamps, cake mixes, regular coffee, cottage cheese, vitamin tablets, television consoles, Caterpillars, girdles, toilet-bowl cleaners, and movies with a happy ending.

SOUTHEAST (GEORGIA, ARKANSAS, FLORIDA, THE VIRGINIAS, THE CAR-OLINAS, ETC.) This region takes pride in its traditions. Though courteous and hospitable, Southerners still tend to treat Yankees as outsiders. The most popular colors are yellow and orange. Ornamental silverware is favored over other patterns. Bourbon still ranks high on the drinking list. Women's full slips sell 3 times as briskly here as they do in New York City, at the other extreme. Stores still carry quad (AAAA) shoes for dainty feet. The Scott Paper Company changed the shape of the container of Scotkins paper napkins but retained the familiar polka-dot box in this region. Soap operas do well on Nielsens. Housewives love pancakes but not if they are frozen. Yet this is the largest market for home freezers. Pine-fragrance products are big sellers, as are mouthwash and the gold-embossed version of the family Bible.

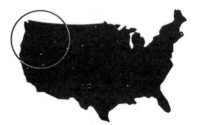

NORTHWEST (WASHINGTON, ORE-GON, IDAHO, MONTANA, ETC.) Rain, a steady drizzle for days at a time, is accepted stoically. Winters are mild, but long and gloomy. Favorite colors are blue, green, and brown. The region is a good market for boats, power house trailers, mohair rugs, mounted trophies, scrim-shawed articles, stag movies, airplane components, sleeping bags, down clothing, tents, and Japanese food with plenty of soy sauce.

NEW YORK CITY The city is a market unto itself, dynamic, cosmopolitan, and a maze of contradictions. Quite a few New Yorkers cannot afford to take vacations at all, yet more people here than anywhere else make arrangements for trips around the world. The greatest concentration of purchasing power in the world is in New York City, representing about 10 percent of the total market in the country. New York is one of the toughest and most expensive markets to crack for an advertiser. To make even the slightest impression on hard-nosed skeptics in the city, the advertiser needs about fifty to sixty 30-second television and seventy to eighty radio spots a week, a total of about 30,000 lines of advertising in newspapers, and twelve pages in regional issues of magazines for about three months . . . just for openers.

U.S. Cities Ranked on Basis of Cultural Sophistication*	1. New York City 2. San Francisco 3. The Suburbs: Greenwich Norwalk Westport The Hamptons

*Based upon hard-cover book sales, choice of television programs, and interest in cultural activities.

CULTUROLOGICAL CLUSTERS

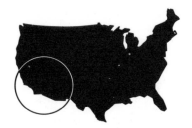

WEST COAST (CALIFORNIA) This is a region with its own plastic culture. Always looking for ways to raise their consciousness, Californians readily embrace cults and movements. People's responsiveness makes this state an ideal target for direct-mail advertisers. Favorite colors are yellow, orange, and, of all colors, pink. Willing to try anything once, West Coast inhabitants offer atypical test-market opportunities. The region is a good market for tires, suntan lotion, cameras, motorcycles, foreign cars, Mexican food, tennis balls, love beads, spray cleaners, charcoal broilers, Coca-Cola, panty girdles, tickets to the Orient, garbage-disposal units, and uppers and downers.

[*Based upon a compilation of corporate sales reports, U.S. Census figures, Sales Areas Marketing, Inc., or SAMI, data, Simmons Study of Selective Studies and the Media Reaching Them, and a survey prepared for Needham, Harper & Steers by William D. Wells*]

I lost half of myself without taking diet pills.

By Donna Walker — as told to Ruth L. McCarthy

When I weighed 278 pounds, my friends called me a Floating Island. See why?

When I was 66 inches around, and 65 inches tall, even my favorite fat lady's store had a problem. I know, because at 278 pounds I wore the largest bloomers they had. And that's the only word for them -- bloomers -- even though I'm of the generation that usually refers to ladies' panties as briefs.

Fact is, the thought of having nothing to wear made me so panicky, I said to myself: "This is it! You've got to lose weight, Donna." Not that I was unaware of my size before. There were too many embarrassing reminders in my life for me to ignore my weight. For instance, at my fullest figure, I fit so snugly into a tub that the water was dammed up behind me when I pulled the plug out in front of me. And when I stood up in a shower stall, I couldn't even bend over to pick up a bar of soap. I was trapped by my appetite.

As for dresses, I had one — to go to work in. I washed it every night and every day for one whole year because it was the only dress that fit.

I think I ought to mention that chocolate and sweets were my undoing. But ironically, candy is what really helped me lose weight. Ayds® Reducing Plan Candy. I'd read ads about it in magazines and when I learned that Ayds contains vitamins and minerals, but no drugs, I thought maybe, at last, I'd found what I needed. I knew from past experience that diet pills, weekly reducing sessions and even a psychiatrist were not the answer for me. I needed something to help curb my appetite and my eternal craving for sweets.

So, I bought a box of chocolate fudge Ayds at the drug store and started on the plan in the fall. I took one or two Ayds about 15 minutes before each meal with a hot drink and it really helped me cut down on what I ate. And I ate regular meals, nothing special.

Right from the start, I had such a positive feeling about the Ayds plan, I took on a $50 bet from my friend's husband. He'd heard me talk about

Now I'm 136 pounds, my friends in West Hartford, Conn., hardly recognize me.

losing weight for 10 years, but never saw me do anything about it. So he figured it was going to be an easy win. Was he wrong! In the end, he had to pay up, because the weight came off.

Nobody really noticed it until I'd lost more than 50 pounds. You see, I hadn't bought any new clothes, so I was hidden under a lot of baggy pants and sacky tops. Then at Easter, when I'd taken off 78 pounds on the Ayds plan, I turned out in a new lavender pantsuit and everybody was amazed. I was thrilled, and more determined than ever to stick to the Ayds plan.

I guess, though, we never see ourselves as others do. Let me tell you about a remark my nephew made while I was still losing weight. He'd seen me at his sister's wedding, wearing a size 52 beige tent. Months after I'd been on the Ayds plan, I appeared at his wedding in a size 18 dress. He was so shocked, he said: "What were you wearing the last time I saw you — your beige Volkswagen?" Funny, I knew I was fat, but not that fat.

How long did it take me to lose 142 pounds on the Ayds plan? Just about a year, and now I can do things I never could before. For the first time, believe it or not, I can cross my legs — like a lady. I can also see all of me in a mirror. And I can even climb up a pool ladder without fear of breaking it.

On the serious side, my teenage nieces and nephews are now proud to introduce me as their aunt. In fact, everybody is a lot happier with me, now that I'm only 37½ inches around. Which makes me forever grateful for the Ayds plan.

BEFORE AND AFTER MEASUREMENTS		
	Before	After
Height	5′5″	5′5″
Weight	278 lbs.	136 lbs.
Bust	49″	35¾″
Waist	45″	27″
Hips	66″	37½″
Dress	52	12

Ads like these, part of a long and successful grass-roots advertising campaign conducted by Ayds, have a greater appeal to those living outside large metropolitan areas.

Sophisticated layout and clever copy please hard-core urbanites, the audience these ads are designed to reach.

American Association of Advertising Agencies' Recommended Standard Breakdowns for Demographic Characteristics

This breakdown is designed to assist advertising agencies with comparable media and marketing data. It reflects the economic, sociological, and demographic composition of the population of the United States.

I. DATA FOR HOUSEHOLDS	MINIMUM BASIC DATA	ADDITIONAL DATA HIGHLY DESIRED
A. County size:		
	1. County size	
	2. County size	
	3. County size	
	4. County size	
B. Geographic area (as defined by Bureau of the Census)	Inside standard metropolitan statistical area	Central city; other
	Outside standard metropolitan statistical area	
	Urban	Urban
	Rural	Urbanized areas
		Central cities
		Urban fringe
		Other urban
		Places of 10,000 or more
		Places of 2500 to 10,000
		Standard metropolitan Statistical area
		4,000,000 or over
		1,000,000–3,999,999
		500,000– 999,999
		250,000– 499,999
		100,000– 249,999
		50,000– 99,999
C. Geographic region (as defined by Bureau of the Census)	Northeast	New England
	North central	Consolidated Metropolitan New York*
	South	Mid-Atlantic
	West	East Central
		Consolidated Metropolitan Chicago*
		West Central
		Southeast
		Southwest
		Pacific
		Metropolitan Los Angeles*
D. Ages of children	No child under 18	Youngest child 12–17
	Youngest child 6–17	Youngest child 6–11
	Youngest child under 6	Youngest child 2–5
		Youngest child under 2
E. Household size	1 or 2 members	
	3 or 4 members	
	5 or more members	
F. Number of children under 18	None	Number of children by household size
	1	
	More than 1	
G. Household income†	Under $5,000	$12,000–14,999
	$ 5,000– 9,999	25,000 and over
	10,000–11,999	
	12,000–14,999	
	15,000–19,999	
	20,000 and over	

DATA FOR HOUSE-HOLDS	MINIMUM BASIC DATA	ADDITIONAL DATA HIGHLY DESIRED
H. Home ownership	Own home	Residence in past 5 years prior to survey date
	Rent home	Lived in same house
		Lived in different house
		In same county
		In different county
I. Dwelling characteristics	1. Unattached house	Own home
	2. Attached house	Rent home
	3. Apartment	
	4. Mobile home or trailer	

II. DATA FOR INDIVIDUALS	MINIMUM BASIC DATA	ADDITIONAL DATA HIGHLY DESIRED
A. Age	Under 6	6–8
	6–11	12–14
	12–17	18–21‡
	18–24	35–49‡
	25–34	
	35–44	
	45–54	
	54–64	
	65 and over	
B. Sex	Male	Age School
	Female	6– 8 Grammar
C. Education	Some high school	9–11 Grammar
	Graduated high school (grades 9–12)	12–14 Junior high school
	Some college	15–17 High school
	Graduated college	
		Some postgraduate college work
D. Marital status	Married	
	Widowed	
	Divorced or separated	
	Single (never married)	
E. Occupation	Employed	
	Professional and technical	
	Managers, officials, and proprietórs, except farm	
	Clerical; sales	
	Craftsmen; foremen	
	Operatives; nonfarm laborers; service workers; private household workers	
	Farmers; farm managers; farm laborers; foremen	
	Armed services	
	Retired	
	Students	
	Housewives (not employed outside home)	
	Unemployed, looking for work	
	Other	

III. DATA FOR HOUSEHOLD HEADS	MINIMUM BASIC DATA	ADDITIONAL DATA HIGHLY DESIRED
A. Sex	Male Female	Both male and female Male only Female only
B. Age	24 and younger 25–34 35–44 45–54 55–64 65 and older	35–49
C. Education	Grade school or less (grades 1–8) Some high school Graduated high school (grades 9–12) Some college Graduated college	Some postgraduate college work
D. Occupation (as defined by Bureau of the Census)	Employed Professional and technical Managers, officials, and proprietors, except farm Clerical; sales Craftsmen; foremen Operatives; nonfarm laborers; service workers; private household workers Farmers; farm managers; farm laborers; foremen Armed services Retired Unemployed, looking for work Other	Employed Full time, 30 hours or more per week Part time, less than 30 hours per week
E. Race	White Nonwhite	
F. Principal language spoken at home	English Spanish Other	
G. Individual employment income (see I-G for definition)		

IV. DATA FOR HOUSEWIVES	MINIMUM BASIC DATA	ADDITIONAL DATA HIGHLY DESIRED
A. Age	24 and younger 25–34 35–44 45–54 55–64 65 and older	35–49
B. Education	Grade school or less (grades 1–8) Some high school Graduated high school (grades 9–12) Some college Graduated college	Some postgraduate college work
C. Employment (as defined by Bureau of the Census)	Employed outside home Employed full time (30 hours or more per week) Employed part time (less than 30 hours per week) Not employed outside home Unemployed, looking for work Other	Number of hours of working Before 6 P.M. After 6 P.M.
D. Race	White Nonwhite	
E. Principal language spoken at home	English Spanish Other	
F. Individual employment income (see I-G for definition)		

HOUSEHOLD INCOME BY QUINTILE				
	PERCENT	INCOME INTERVAL		
QUINTILE	ADULTS	LOW	HIGH	MEDIAN INCOME
1	20	. . .	$ 5,000	$ 4,300
2	20	$ 5,001	8,300	7,900
3	20	8,301	12,800	10,300
4	20	12,801	19,000	17,500
5	20	19,001	. . .	23,500

*If consideration is given to reporting metropolitan or individual local market data, unduplicated TV coverage areas are acceptable alternatives.

†Household income by quintile (see example at end of breakdown).
‡The 18–21 group is highly desired since adult life-styles change frequently in the earlier adult years. The 35–49 breakdown would be required for several years for a transition period.
Changing the adult age breakdown to 10-year increments facilitates comparison with census data. Furthermore, economic and marketing data indicate that the 50–54 group is more similar to the 35–49 group than it is to the 50–64 group with which it has been reported in the past.

HOW DEMOGRAPHIC DATA HELP SHOOTING AT THE TARGET: DIFFERENT TYPES OF VACATIONERS WANT DIFFERENT TYPES OF VACATIONS

USER'S PROFILE

INCOME LEVEL			MARITAL STATUS		SIZE OF HOUSEHOLD		TYPE OF VACATION DESIRED
HIGH	MEDIUM	LOW	SINGLE	MARRIED	NO CHILDREN	CHILDREN	
✔			✔				A
✔				✔	✔		B
✔				✔		✔	C
	✔		✔				D
	✔			✔	✔		E
	✔			✔		✔	F
		✔	✔				G
		✔		✔	✔		H
		✔		✔		✔	I

This is a vacation particularly appealing to a middle-income family with children.

The tone of this ad preselects its audience: high-income couples without the ubiquitous presence of children.

Great Gorge Hotel has a message that comes across clearly to the single set.

Other Factors That Influence Purchasing Decisions Among such factors are education (the better-educated travel more), place of residence (those living on the West Coast are more likely to go to the Orient or Hawaii), season (more people travel in summer), occupation (students, teachers, and civil service employees take longer vacations; business executives take shorter ones), cultural interests (museums, theaters, and so on), sports and entertainment preferences (tennis, golf, horseback riding, skiing, swimming, night life), car ownership (vacationers may want to travel in their own cars, as on the Autotrain), pet ownership (dog and cat fanciers must choose accommodations that will accept animals), age (by and large, young people are looking for "action" while older people tend to be more reflective), travel experience

A typical Cadillac ad—dramatic, different, and exuding class appeal. Lack of illustration and descriptive copy presupposes reader's familiarity with the product.

(those who have traveled extensively are often in the market for out-of-the-way places), penchant for luxury (money is not always the deciding factor), and, of course, size of pocketbook (wealthy clients not only spend more but tend to keep company with their peers as do many other types of groups—snobbery still lives!).

Demographics: What It Will Not Tell You

Demographic data, while revealing much pertinent statistical information about consumers, say woefully little about consumers' *feelings* toward the product and themselves. Both factors are important in judging their predisposition to buy.

To illustrate, let us take a look at the overt and underlying motives of a person about to buy a luxury automobile, in this case, a Cadillac Coupe de Ville.

Obviously, there are some very good practical reasons for purchasing a Cadillac Coupe de Ville, but, as shown here, the *psychological*

foundation for buying may be just as important, particularly in the middle to low-income group. Sales figures by R. L. Polk show just how strong these feelings can be; in New York City, nearly one-third of all Cadillacs are sold in the Harlem area. (Typically, in times of economic downturn, sales of Cadillacs drop sharply among lower-income groups, which have less of a financial cushion to fall back on. Among affluent purchasers, sales remain at approximately the same level.)

Enter Motivational Research

The first major attempt to bring the advertising writer into closer touch with the feelings of his or her customer (leaving statistics largely in the hands of statisticians) was so-called motivational research. Based on an informal in-depth interviewing technique, it was developed by Dr. Ernest Dichter, a Viennese psychologist, who shrewdly perceived its commercial application. Although this was not the first time that psychology had been applied to selling (as far back as 1920 La Salle Extension University, in its sales training course, pointed to the lack of a clear-cut rationale in the making of buying decisions), the notion that the human mind would lend itself to some kind of scientific evaluation was immediately embraced by an industry which deals basically with people.

Motivational research helped greatly in refining selling techniques. It swept aside many long-cherished beliefs. Once again, it shifted the emphasis to the psychological predilections of people: that they expressed one desire but felt another, that they clung to value judgments formed years ago in their early childhood, and that they purchased products for deep-seated psychological reasons (for example, to assert their masculinity) while always ready to offer rational arguments to cover up their motives.

As time went by, however, it be-

came increasingly apparent that, as useful a marketing tool as this type of research was, it disregarded a number of important points. In its concentration on the subconscious mind, it failed to take into account such much-needed demographic data as income, size of family, and media preferences, many of which could be less dramatic but nevertheless valid reasons for making or not making a purchase.

Equally disconcerting, at least from a marketing point of view, was the relative lack of projectability of this kind of research. The length and expense of personal interviewing made it difficult, if not impossible, to obtain reliable samples with which to launch a mass attack. This left one of the most important questions in marketing still hanging in the air: *What proportion* of people react to *which appeal?*

A New Wrinkle: Psychographics

Somewhere between where demographics leaves off and motivational research picks up is *psychographics,* a carefully designed behavioral science that deals with both the quality and the quantity of prospects. Serving the advertiser, psychographics fills the voids inherent in motivational research. It brings customers together in measurable statistical entities, based upon a number of variables, such as their attitudes (about politics, religion, youth, sex), life-styles (leisure activities, home entertainment, TV viewing habits), and personality traits (aggressive, fearful, conservative).

Moreover, psychographics delves deeply into consumer-product relationships as well. Such relationships include the variety of reasons for buying a product (decay prevention, whiteness, and taste in the case of a toothpaste), personal likes and dislikes about the product, situations in which the product may be used, the consumer's images about the competitive brand, and general advertising awareness.

HOW THE LEO BURNETT AGENCY
APPLIES LIFE-STYLE STUDIES

Life-style studies try to determine the individual's propensity to buy a certain product. Superimposed on demographics are people's *feelings about the world in general.*

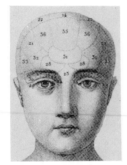

ACTIVITIES
Work
Hobbies
Social events
Vacations
Entertainment
Club membership
Community
Shopping
Sports

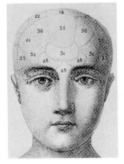

INTERESTS
Family
Home
Job
Community
Recreation
Fashion
Food
Media
Achievements

OPINIONS
Themselves
Social issues
Politics
Business
Economics
Education
Products
Future
Culture

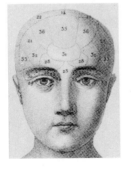

DEMOGRAPHICS
Age
Education
Income
Occupation
Family size
Dwelling
Geographic
City size
Stage of life cycle

Typical statements obtained from respondents are:
"I like gardening."
"I do not get enough sleep."
"A news magazine is more interesting than a fiction magazine."
"There should be a gun in every home."
"Instant coffee is more economical than ground coffee."
"I stay at home most evenings."
"There is a lot of love in our family."
"It is a real tragedy to see our lakes and streams dying."
"Television is a primary source of entertainment."

Each respondent is then asked about his media preferences, such as his favorite television and radio programs and the magazines he reads. The average usage of certain household products is also learned. On the basis of the information, a profile of the heavy user of a product is constructed.

The application of life-style data is most useful in the creation of advertising campaigns at the agency. It provides a more lifelike picture of the prime customer than does demographics alone. William D. Wells says in his book *Life Style and Psychographics:* "This type of data provides guidelines for the basic 'tone of voice' for the advertising. The creatives can get a sense of whether the tone of voice should be serious or humorous, authoritative or cooperative, contemporary or traditional. Moreover, it provides inferences about how the product fits into the consumer's life. If, for example, there is nothing in the portrait that indicates the consumer is convenience oriented, the inference is that the product does not perform a convenience function" (American Marketing Association, New York, 1974).

MATCHING A PRODUCT WITH PSYCHOGRAPHIC PROFILE: AN EXAMPLE OF BENEFIT SEGMENTATION

Attitude studies help in analyzing consumer-product relationships. The example below was prepared by Thomas P. Hustad and Edgar A. Pessemier of the Herman C. Krannert Graduate School of Industrial Administration, Purdue University, for the Purdue Consumer Behavior Project:

	THE SENSORY SEGMENT	THE SOCIABLES	THE WORRIERS	THE INDEPENDENT SEGMENT
Principal benefit sought	Flavor, product appearance	Brightness of teeth	Decay prevention	Price
Demographic strengths	Children	Teens, young people	Large families	Men
Special behavioral characteristics	Users of spear-mint-flavored toothpaste	Smokers	Heavy users	Heavy users
Brands disproportionately favored	Colgate, Stripe	MacLeans, Plus White, Ultra Brite	Crest	Brands on sale
Personality characteristics	High self-involvement	High sociability	High hypochondriasis	High autonomy
Life-style characteristics	Hedonistic	Active	Conservative	Value-oriented

Reprinted from William D. Wells, Life Style and Psychographics, *published by the American Marketing Association*

The segmentation model on the right was useful in finding the so-called creative consumers, those with greater self-confidence and willingness to try new products. *Holiday* magazine effectively used this tabulation to pinpoint potential travelers, fliers, drinkers, party givers, and best prospects for new products. Since income was important in this study in terms of buying power, the respondents were divided into groups earning more and less than $15,000 a year.

ACTIVITIES AND ATTITUDES OF CREATIVE AND PASSIVE CONSUMERS BY INCOME CLASS

	$10,000–15,000		$15,000 or more	
	PERCENT PASSIVE	PERCENT CREATIVE	PERCENT PASSIVE	PERCENT CREATIVE
Visited museum during past 6 months	18.5	52.8	17.3	52.9
Attended classical-music concert during past 12 months	5.4	25.8	10.2	32.9
Member or user of book rental or book club and/or record club	21.2	46.0	16.5	43.1
Read 5 or more nonfiction books in past 12 months	13.8	57.6	15.0	47.1
Have ever taken adult education courses	43.1	70.6	50.3	67.5
Believe Negroes are right about job opportunities being equal	21.5	51.5	22.4	60.4
Chance of moving up in company in next 12 months (very good or excellent chance)	30.9	49.1	34.1	48.3
Had alcoholic beverage other than beer or wine, outside home during past week	41.0	67.5	44.3	69.4

Just Who Do Customers Think They Are?

The customer's self-perception may or may not coincide with the observations made by an outsider. But then again, who is that outsider? A research organization? Media? The U.S. Bureau of the Census? The Internal Revenue Service? Spouse? Friend? Foe?

Obviously, descriptions of one person will run a wide gamut. To a marketer looking for a single and, preferably, simple answer, this can be very confusing. In this case, the marketer may take the customer's *self-image* (wants and needs as he or she perceives them to be) as a major criterion.

That may yet be the most important element in the customer's purchasing decision, more important even than his or her carefully structured, computer-approved demographic profile.

As an illustration, not all middle-income people see themselves as middle-income people; many teachers, social workers, ministers, and painters make less than $15,000 annually, but because of their social position (as they see it) they feel richer than their fellow citizens loading garbage trucks. Yet, from a demographic point of view, both groups belong in the same income category. Similarly, some students on a campus may ally themselves with various youth movements (and buy sports cars, records of their favorite rock singers) or join the establishment (and buy three-piece suits, junior memberships in country clubs); farmers may see themselves either as "workers" or as "executives"; foremen, either as "rank and file" *or* as members of "management" groups; and American Indians, either as bearers of a proud history or an abused minority group.

Perhaps it is the psychological, not the economic, affinity that encourages various professional groups to form homogeneous entities—a marketing target for the advertiser.

Cosmopolitan's advertising copy, though ostensibly written by a third party, reflects its editorial philosophy. Even though few readers (25–35-year-olds, single and married, well-educated, up-scale) could express their feelings about themselves quite as eloquently as does a "typical" Cosmo young woman, they readily identify with her beauty and wit.

White Shoulders perfume caters to women impressed by traditional social graces. To them, candlelight and black ties symbolize romance and class.

The Chanel campaign with actress Catherine Deneuve has a universal appeal, one that easily skips over demographic strata.

Graphic restraint and Pierre-François-Pascal Guerlain's confident statement please sophisticates.

One the longest-running campaigns in advertising history is the "Marlboro Man" series. Though straight out of macho land, the campaign (to the surprise even of its creators) gained new converts among women smokers.

Well aware of the importance of product positioning is Virginia Slims. The cigarette was introduced at the start of the women's liberation movement.

At first glance, it would appear that this ad would unnerve the average law-abiding citizen doing his best to satisfy the IRS. Coupon returns proved otherwise.

Slice-of-life commercials, such as this, may be a catchall for homilies, but there is evidence that housewives have a strong rapport with the characters portrayed here.

Carving out its niche in a market of more than 200 brands is Chivas Regal Scotch with advertisements such as this. The tone is just right for people who think rich.

Users versus Nonusers: Selling a Product To Those Who Do Not Want It

Most advertisers tend to focus on heavy users, and this is hardly surprising. That is where the action is or is supposed to be.

A person, for example, who purchases a new car once every 2 years justifies more than twice the advertising expenditure for someone who buys one every 5 years. From a creative point of view, the former is easier and more economical to convince. Showing that interest leads to more interest, it is worth noting that people recall advertising on the products they use nearly 3 times as often as they do on those they do not use.

Indiscriminate concentration on heavy users, however, may create a whole new set of problems. In the first place, not even the most thorough demographic information can pinpoint users with absolute accuracy. Second, people differ in the degree (weight) of product usage even if they happen to fit into the heavy-user category. Third, even a nonuser may change his or her mind when faced with product benefits that he or she has so far failed to perceive. Thus, as if by magic, a totally new market place can be created by a simple twist of advertising themes.

Marketing history is replete with success stories proving that such things can happen. Motorcycles were bought mostly by the black-leather-jacket, chrome-flashing set until the middle 1960s, when Honda decided to broaden the market via its image-changing campaign, "Nice people ride Honda." Sales doubled in the next 2 years. Most users of Chantilly perfume were women in their forties until youth-oriented packaging and advertising moved the perfume from sixth to third place in the competitive fragrance industry. Going after affluent clientele,

Eden Roc, a hotel in Miami Beach, successfully changed its image with its "Born with a silver spoon" campaign. Taking an opposite tack was Grossinger's in the Catskills, offering affordable weekends for singles only. Cutty Sark profited by moving its Scotch boldly into the growing black market while other distilleries were still sitting on the sidelines. Columbia Records sold millions of low-priced classical records to young listeners—a market which experts had predicted was virtually nonexistent. Boutiques offering contemporary maternity clothes created a whole new market for themselves almost overnight in the face of declining birthrates. And so it goes.

New Arrivals: Segmentation on Top of Segmentation

The United States population is in a constant state of flux, far more so than the population of any other country in the world. Income levels are changing (within a decade, those with earnings equivalent to $25,000 plus will outnumber all other income groups), new affluents are arriving at the top (forming a massive market with greater numbers of discretionary dollars to spend on quality lifestyle products and services), the number of suburbanites is growing, and, slowly but surely, the median age of Americans is crossing the line from the twenties to the thirties.

New homogeneous groups, bringing new interests, attitudes, and buying propensities to the fore, are appearing almost by the day. Each represents a new marketing opportunity to the alert advertiser. Among these groups are the following:

Working Teen-Agers Three out of five teen-agers earn money working through the year. One in seven students earns more than $15 a week.

College Students Enrollments in colleges and universities have passed 11 million. It is estimated that by 1985 nearly one-third of all men and women over 25 will be college-educated. Almost half of the students own cars. Approximately two-thirds have tried marijuana; more than 40 percent of them are beer drinkers. More than one-third have had sexual experience before reaching college age.

Shrinking Families The average United States household dipped below 3 persons in 1974 for the first time, and the trend is expected to continue. Not surprisingly, families headed by women are increasing.

The Spanish Market According to the Census Bureau, there are about 15 million Hispanics in the United States, and their numbers are growing faster than the national average (Hispanic Americans have a fertility rate almost twice that of other citizens). More than half of them prefer Spanish to English as the spoken language. More than 40 percent are under the age of 21.

Live-alones This group is expanding faster than any other kind of household. One out of every four apartments in New York City is occupied by only one person.

Affluent Blacks The proportion of blacks making more than $10,000 has almost tripled in recent years.

Black Students One out of every ten college students is black.

Black City Dwellers This group is on the increase. In most major cities, blacks make up more than one-third of the population; in some, more than half.

Working Women Economists predict that soon half of all American women over 16 will be in the work force. Most of them work to supplement the family income, which in almost half of the cases is less than $10,000 a year. Women's income increased by 88 percent during the last decade. More than 60 percent of women under 30 plan to combine marriage, children, and career.

Singles Comprising about 18 percent of the adult population, the unmarried, divorced, or widowed spend more than $200 billion annually. Today almost half of all women marry after age 25.

Divorcees This group is increasing in numbers. The average marriage lasts slightly more than 6 years. Divorcees constitute nearly

54

half of the entire single population. One out of four is 40 or over. About 80 percent of them will eventually remarry.

Homosexuals Homosexuals are becoming a significant marketing force. Affluent and well-educated (according to a readership study, 95 percent have taken a vacation in the last 12 months, 71 percent have spent more than $500 on clothes in the same period, 42 percent own a home, and 67 percent have served wine in the past month), they have come out of the closet. They have their own publications, associations, and lobbying groups.

Unmarried Marrieds Close to 1,500,000 people, young and old (the latter sometimes for reasons of receiving a larger social security check), share living quarters with an unrelated person of the opposite sex.

Liberated Women This group represents a state of mind as much as a demographic niche. More than one-third of the women attended college. Two-thirds are working. More than half take birth-control pills.

Executive Dropouts Yes, counterculture trends have their impact on older, professionally more successful people, too. Many of them decide to quit 9-to-5 jobs for ideological reasons. Moreover, fewer executives change jobs only for money or a faster climb. According to executive employment agencies, quality of life is becoming an increasingly important consideration.

Those over 65 Years of Age It is estimated that in the year 2030 about 17 percent of the adult population will be over 65 and that for every 100 working persons there will be 50 retired ones. Senior citizens outnumber teen-agers and are increasing almost 4 times as fast as the total population in the United States. One American in seven receives a social security check every month. Women outlive men by approximately 8 years. There are approximately one-third as many more women over 65 today as there are men, in contrast to the situation 40 years ago, when the rate was about even.

The Fat Ones More than 60 million Americans are or have been on some sort of diet. Over two-thirds of them are women. The more prosperous the economy, the closer the attention people pay to their appearance.

Health Freaks The "return to nature" trend is responsible for a growing interest in organic, unprocessed food, casual fashion, and "natural" cosmetics. Sales of vitamins have more than doubled in the last 10 years.

Moneyed Kids Children aged 6 to 11 get a total of $2.3 billion in the form of allowances from generous parents. The average tot is given almost $75 a year to spend however his or her little heart desires. Boys are more likely than girls to spend money on frivolous items, such as toys and candy.

The Sporting Set Tennis, skiing, and snowmobiling are the three fastest-growing sports in the United States, according to a national study by the A. C. Nielsen Company. The first two sports show an increase of more than 40 percent in the last 2 years. But none of these activities leads the list in overall popularity. Swimming is still first, with more than 100,000,000 enthusiasts. Jogging, tennis, bicycling, and fishing follow. Football and basketball, both popular television fares, rank only sixteenth and seventeenth respectively as participatory sports.

Spiritual and Mind-expanding Disciples According to a Gallup poll, about 12 percent of Americans are searching for inner serenity through some form of transcendental meditation, yoga, mysticism, or Oriental religion (in that order). Practitioners tend to be young adults, 18 to 24, college students, persons who are generally nonreligious in the traditional sense.

Empathy: Still the Best Way to Learn About the Customer

The sophisticated use of consumer research is one of the most significant steps forward in today's advertising. A word of caution, however. Albert Einstein was right when he said, "Imagination is more important than knowledge." Information in itself is no guarantee that good ideas will pour forth. It serves only as a starting point.

Perhaps this is the place to point out also that an alarming number of market studies have been proved a waste of time and money because of the preponderance of *useless information*. At worst, they were merely esoteric intellectual fishing trips by people who liked to collect facts mostly for their own sake. Unfortunately, this practice has happened under the noses of even the most cost-conscious advertisers. *Ad Daily* reports of one such study in which not 1 out of 154 factors measured was related to marketing issues.

All this only emphasizes that creative intuition, the so-called gut feeling, should never be completely ignored. Much information is absorbed subconsciously and should be given a chance to come out into the open. It is still the combination of facts and feelings that remains the soundest of all guides to understanding another human being.

55

Chapter Five

More about Gathering Information

These expressions are atypical among top creative professionals:

"I never watch television."

"I don't really *have* to know."

"It's a bore."

"I go to the movies once every 3 months."

"I can't waste my time wading through all that research."

"My job gives me all the training I need."

"I know all about it."

"So what?"

"There's nothing new under the sun."

Information Gathering: It Never Stops

No two days are ever the same in advertising. The pace is swift; today's facts are tomorrow's fiction. And people in advertising are often judged on the basis of their general awareness.

A quick glance at the developments in the last decade reflects the tempo of the industry. Here is a random sample list. The research-oriented marketing approach has swung to creativity and back again. The pendulum has never stopped. Creators of ads (art directors and writers) have been given celebrity status for the first time since the early days of advertising, with more and more of them moving into top-echelon positions. This newly acquired stardom

has offered them an opportunity to open their own shops on creative reputation alone, often without even enough billing to provide them with start up costs—a circumstance that would have been considered a monumental business folly not so long ago. Television has become the dominant medium, forcing magazines and even newspapers to compete on the basis of their selective marketing reach. Computerized media planning has made it all possible.

Changes in public attitudes brought with them new trends in marketing techniques. Life-style studies came to the fore. And when consumers became more critical of products and of the way they were advertised, the government responded. Advertising agencies soon acquired and greeted with mixed emotions a new member in the family: a Big Brother (the collective body of as many as seven regulatory agencies) looking over the shoulders of writers, art directors, and account executives, nodding or shaking his head.

At the same time, technological innovations rocked the industry. Taped television photography, with instant replays editable on the spot, had art directors design commercials in studios. Photocomposition led the industry into direct printing. Photoengraving on plastic made it possible to reproduce images on delicate materials. New photographic lenses and film, new kinds of printing equipment (such as dry offset),

new tools for the illustrator, transfer type, new silkscreen processes, and countless other inventions not only made production of advertising easier and faster but offered new opportunities to the many alert, restless creative professionals in the field.

Advertising Is a Composite of Many Jobs

Unlike a good many other businesses, an advertising agency is not built around a single manufactured product or even a single industry. Usually, its employees are given a broad range of assignments (large agencies may have several hundred clients on their rosters).

It is customary in advertising agencies to assign writers and art directors to work on a number of *accounts*—an average of five, according to a survey conducted by Gallagher Reports. These accounts may fall more or less in the same general area (such as banks, insurance, real estate, and securities) or different areas (such as furniture, fashion, and travel). In about 2 percent of the cases, the account may be so demanding that it requires the full attention of a single creative person, as is true of some cigarette, automobile, and food companies. But even in these instances the advertising practitioner faces new challenges every day. This is why advertising may be ulcer-producing but never is boring.

Developing a Sensory Antenna

True to form, creative persons are sensitive to their surroundings. They are avid readers, good listeners, persons who, regardless of age, background, or professional status, do not feel that showing surprise is necessarily a sign of naïveté. They know that the first step to learning is to admit to ignorance. The more they learn, of course, the more acute their thirst for knowledge becomes: they are intellectually insatiable. Their interests are broad, ranging from psychology, sociology, history, fashion, language, art, music, and theater to the practical aspects of the business they are in.

Because of their curiosity, their powers of observation are keenly developed. They have learned to use not one but all five senses—eyes, ears, nose, tongue, and fingertips— sometimes in quick succession. Their sensory observations are then telegraphed to a receptive brain that is ready to solve problems creatively. And—lo and behold!—out leaps the idea for a new advertising campaign.

Curious People Never Grow Old

There are those who say advertising is only for the young. Facts do not support this theory. A more accurate statement would be: "Advertising is only for the curious."

Lively interest is what keeps people on the go and keeps them young. Age is never a matter of chronology alone. Some men and women start their mental vegetation in their early twenties, once they have arrived at the rather startling conclusion that they know everything there is to know. Others remain intellectual *bons vivants* far into their seventies or even their nineties.

Books: A Quick Way to Get Information

If you work in advertising, your literary appetite should not be satisfied with fewer than twenty-five books a year, regardless of your job title, your schedule, or your favorite excuses. Admittedly, this is far above the national norm. The average adult American reads fewer than three books a year, and only 5 percent of Americans buy more than six books annually. But then again, there is nothing average about people in advertising.

This brings us to the point that everyone should have an adequate supply of reading matter in his or her office, preferably within easy reach. Of course, the individual's interests, account assignments, and, last but not least, pocketbook, will have something to do with the number of books he or she keeps. Not all of us can afford to turn our offices into a miniuniversity. But we can certainly try.

Listed on the following pages are books of interest to advertising professionals. At the least, they will serve as a foundation on which to build a larger, more nearly complete business library.

Dictionaries Take your pick. The main unabridged dictionaries (thumb-indexed) are *Funk & Wagnalls New Standard Dictionary of the English Language, Webster's Third New International Dictionary, The Random House Dictionary of the English Language*, and if you feel like splurging, the thirteen volume *Oxford English Dictionary*. The best known desk-type dictionaries are *Webster's New World Dictionary, Funk & Wagnalls Standard College Dictionary, The Doubleday Dictionary, American Heritage Dictionary of the English Language, Thorndike-Barnhart Comprehensive Desk Dictionary*, and two that will definitely bring you up to date, *Harper Dictionary of Contemporary Usage* and *The Barnhart Dictionary of New English since 1963*. There are many other small, compact dictionaries. One of the handiest is *The Little Oxford Dictionary of Current English*.

Advertising copy, of course, relies heavily on the vernacular. Be sure you have dictionaries edited by the more liberal-minded lexicographers, such as American Heritage's, Doubleday's, or *Webster's New World*, the last of which propitiously states in one of its ads: "To know is to grok it." (*Grok* means "to understand thoroughly," "to empathize.")

Almanacs *The U.S. Fact Book, Information Please Almanac, World Almanac*, and *Book of Facts* present a compilation of material furnished mainly by the U.S. Bureau of the Census and the Department of Commerce and based on the *Statistical Abstract of the United States*, which can also be purchased from the source. *The Official Associated Press Almanac* (formerly *The New York Times Encyclopedic Almanac*), *Reader's Digest Almanac and Yearbook, Pocket Data Book*, and possibly the *Negro Almanac* are other sources of this type of statistical data.

Standard Rate & Data Service (Standard Rate & Data Service, Inc., Skokie, Illinois) Eleven separate volumes for *Weekly Newspapers, Newspaper Circulation Analysis, Newspaper Consumer Magazine & Farm Publications, Direct Mail List Rates and Data* (27,000 business, consumer, farm, and cooperative mailing lists), *Business Publications Networks, Spot Radio* (also, *Spot Radio Small Market Edition*), *Spot Television, National Black Network, Transit Advertising Shopping Guides, Change* and the *Change Bulletin Group*. These books describe mechanical requirements for advertising rates, issue and closing dates, circulation, and other pertinent data. The same company also issues a *Consumer/Audience Profile Service* and an ideal tool for the production department, *Print Media Production Data*.

Broadcasting Yearbooks (Broadcasting Publications, Inc., Washington, D.C.) These list radio and television facilities in the United States and Canada, National Association of Broadcasters (NAB) codes and programs services, equipment and Federal Communications Commission (FCC) rules, names of representatives, executives, regional networks, government agencies, associations, societies, unions, labor groups, and attorneys.

Television Fact Book (Television Digest, Inc., Washington, D.C.) This two-volume book, which is issued annually, contains valuable data on United States and Canadian television stations, including coverage maps, circulation and rates, technical facilities, ownership, personnel, and sales representatives.

Handbook of Independent Advertising and Marketing Services (Executive Communications, Inc., New York, 1974) This book lists modular services that are available on a project basis.

The Standard Directory of Advertisers (National Register Publishing Co., Skokie, Illinois) Issued yearly and kept current by means of monthly supplements and a pocket size geographical index, this directory is a classified guide to some 17,000 corporations and includes information on sales volume, products, names of executives, advertising agency, budgets, and type of media used. It is an invaluable guide in new-business solicitations.

The Standard Directory of Advertising Agencies (National Register Publishing Co., Skokie, Illinois) Issued 3 times a year, this directory is a compilation of some 4000 agencies, 27,000 personnel by title, and 60,000 by account.

Telephone Book: White and Yellow Pages The Yellow Pages list names of many services and suppliers needed to create and execute advertising; it can be a real time-saver. The Manhattan Yellow Pages have lists of more than 1700 commercial artists and art studios, 2400 photographers, 180 photographic retouchers, 300 mailing-list sources, 2900 printers, 100 postcard makers, and 20 statistical services.

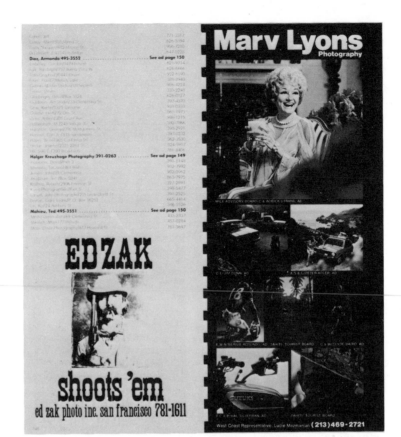

THE CREATIVE BLACK BOOK Published by Universe Books, Inc., New York, this is a 5- by 10-inch, 250-page handy reference book for finding creative talent, services, and advertising products. This book puts a few hundred portfolios, reels, catalogs, and the like at your fingertips.

THE MADISON AVENUE HANDBOOK Published by Peter Glenn Publications, Inc., New York, this book contains useful New York City telephone numbers, such as those of restaurants, art galleries, museums, institutions, transportation, theaters, and media.

Who's Who in America (also Who's Who in the East, in the South and Southwest, in Finance and Industry, in the World, of American Women) (Marquis— Who's Who Books, Chicago) These books, which are updated yearly, are works to turn to when looking for decision makers. They include vital personal statistics on leaders in various industries.

Who's Who in Advertising (Edited by Robert S. Morgan, Rye, New York) This is a compilation of outstanding figures in advertising with short biographies.

New York in Flashmaps (Flashmaps, Inc., Chappaqua, New York) This is a quick guide to everywhere in Manhattan: places to eat, entertain, relax, and so on. If you work in New York and often find yourself on the phone making luncheon appointments with clients, keep this booklet in your desk drawer.

Mager's Office Encyclopedia This book helps secretary and boss do the job.

Other General Reference Books Books worth having include the following:

Advertising Age Editorial Index (Advertising Age, Chicago; reprints of 12,000 to 15,000 articles published every year)

Advertising Campaigns: Formulation and Tactics (Gid, Columbus, Ohio)

Advertising Media Planning (Crain Books, Chicago)

All-in-One Directory of Public Relations (Gebbie Press, New Paltz, New York)

Ayer Directory of Publications (Ayer Press, Philadelphia)

Ayer Glossary of Advertising and Related Terms (Ayer Press, Philadelphia)

Roger Barton: *Handbook of Advertising Management* (McGraw-Hill Book Company, New York)

———: *Media in Advertising* (McGraw-Hill Book Company, New York)

Better and Faster Marketing Decisions (Association of National Advertisers, New York)

Books in Print (R. R. Bowker Company, New York)

Broadcast Self-Regulation (National Association of Broadcasters, New York)

Broadcasting Cable Sourcebook (Broadcasting Publications, Inc., Washington)

Victor P. Buell: *Handbook of Modern Marketing* (McGraw-Hill Book Company, New York)

J. D. Barke: *Advertising in the Marketplace* (McGraw-Hill Book Company, New York)

Business Books in Print (R. R. Bowker Company, New York)

CATV Systems: Directory, Map Service and Handbook (Communications Publishing Annual, Englewood, Colorado)

Directory of Specialized Media (Ted Bates & Co., Inc., New York)

Charles J. Dirkson and Arthur Kroeger: *Advertising Principles and Problems* (Richard D. Irwin, Inc., Homewood, Illinois)

Do's and Don'ts in Advertising Copy (Council of Better Business Bureaus, Inc., New York)

S. W. Dunn and A. Barban: *Advertising: Its Role in Modern Marketing* (The Dryden Press, Inc., Hinsdale, Illinois)

Editor & Publisher Marketing Guide (Editor & Publisher, New York; guide to newspapers)

Editor & Publisher Yearbook (Editor & Publisher, New York)

Essentials of Media Planning: A Marketing Viewpoint (Crain Books, Chicago)

Margaret Fisk (Editor): *Encyclopedia of Associations* (Gale Research Company, Detroit)

Leon Gary (Editor): *The Standard Periodical Directory* (Oxbridge Publishing Co., New York)

Guide to American Directories (Gale Research Company, Detroit; directory of more than 5000 directories)

A Handbook for the Advertising Agency Account Executive (Addison-Wesley Publishing Company, Inc., Reading, Massachusetts)

Handbook of Independent Advertising and Marketing Services (Executive Communications, Inc., New York)

Richard Hodgson: *Direct Mail and Mail Order Handbook* (The Dartnell Corporation, Chicago; more than 1500 pages of useful information)

How to Plan Media (Media Decisions, New York)

Earl W. Kintner: *A Primer on the Law of Deceptive Practices* (The Macmillan Company, New York)

Otto Kleppner and Stephen Greyser: *Advertising Procedure* (Prentice-Hall, Inc., Englewood Cliffs, New Jersey)

Legal and Business Problems of the Advertising Industry (Practising Law Institute, New York)

Levy's Public Relations Handbook (Prentice-Hall, Inc., Englewood Cliffs, New Jersey)

Marianna O. Lewis (Editor): *Foundation Directory* (Columbia University Press, New York)

Maurice I. Mandell: *Advertising* (Prentice-Hall, Inc., Englewood Cliffs, New Jersey)

Media Market Guide (New York; 100 top marketing areas)

Middle Market Directory (Dun and Bradstreet Publications, Inc., New York)

Million Dollar Directory (Dun and Bradstreet Publications, Inc., New York)

National Directory of Newsletters and Reporting Services (Gale Research Company, Detroit)

National Rate Book and College Newspaper Directory (CASS Student Advertising, Inc., New York)

F. Nicosia: *Advertising, Management, and Society* (McGraw-Hill Book Company, New York)

Poor's Register of Corporations, Directors and Executives (Standard & Poor's Corporation, New York)

Readers' Guide to Periodical Literature (The H. W. Wilson Company, New York)

M. Roman: *Telephone Marketing: How to Build Business by Telephone* (McGraw-Hill Book Company, New York)

Rosden & Rosden: *The Law of Advertising* (Matthew Bender & Co., Inc., New York)

R. Schiller: *M.A.M.E. Market and Media Evaluation: The AIA Handbook of Advertising to Business, Industry, Government, and the Profession* (The Macmillan Company, New York)

Julian L. Simon: *The Management of Advertising* (Prentice-Hall, Inc., Englewood Cliffs, New Jersey)

Richard Stansfield: *Advertising Manager's Handbook* (The Dartnell Corporation, Chicago)

———: *Sales Manager's Handbook* (The Dartnell Corporation, Chicago)

Bob Stone: *Successful Direct Marketing Methods* (Crain Books, Chicago)

Stephen J. Stuart (Editor): *Couponing and Sampling Services Directory* (Promotional Marketing Institute, Elnora, New York)

Survey of Industrial Buying Power (Sales and Marketing Management Magazine, New York)

Television Almanac (Quigley Publishing Co., New York)

Test Marketing (Dancer Fitzgerald Sample, Inc., New York)

This Is Advertising: The Ayer Book on What Advertising Is All About, Who Does What, and How to Get a Job in It (Ayer Press, Philadelphia)

Thomas Register of American Manufacturers Product Encyclopedia, Product Design & Development (Chilton Book Company, Philadelphia)

U.S. Department of Commerce: *National Associations of the United States* (Washington) About 17,000 organizations, classified by type and industry.

Richard Weiner: *Professional Guide to*

Public Relations Services (Richard Weiner, Inc., New York) A particularly excellent book, full of practical advice and sources of services.

Government Printing Office (Superintendent of Documents, Washington, D.C. 20025) The GPO is a prolific dispenser of valuable marketing information. It is easily the world's largest "bookstore." Its publications are inexpensive and readily available. One of the richest sources for data is the U.S. Bureau of the Census. Dividing the country into 23,000 census tracts, this bureau has published sixty-two different types of socioeconomic data, with separate reports on population, housing, manufacturers, business, wholesale trade, selected services, agriculture, countries and cities, transportation, and so on. A monthly *Federal Reserve Bulletin* reports on financial and business developments in the United States, including department store sales, consumer credit estimates, production indices for an extensive list of industries, prices for many products, and interest rates. Information is superimposed on the nation's 36,000 residential areas.

Zips (U.S. Postal Service) The *National Zip Code Directory* offers more than 100 types of data on consumers, supplementing information by commercial services (for example, a breakdown of the nation's 3900 zip codes according to taxpayer income).

Department of Commerce: U.S. Bureau of the Census The Census Bureau has population, employment, personal-income, and earnings data for more than 170 economic areas (areas that include at least one major city of 50,000 or more inhabitants)

and publishes information on standard metropolitan statistical areas (SMSA), standard metropolitan country areas (SMCA), and standard consolidated statistical areas (SCSA). It also reports up-to-date population shifts, broken down by states. Since it usually takes the government several years to process census information, the information on population shifts can be especially useful to the marketer who wishes to stay current.

Other Services The same kind of service is available from the National Planning Association, which has 230 metropolitan trading areas, the various state and local governments, and the chamber of commerce. One of the most popular single-figure geographic market indicators is the Buying Power Index (BPI), issued annually by *Sales Management*. This is an up-to-date study of population movements, households, spending power, retail sales, distribution, and product volume. Rating services such as Arbitron and Nielsen include demographic information on local markets in their audience-measurement reports, as do various retail-index auditors, syndicated print and broadcast rating and readership services, trade associations, and, of course, media companies.

Maps There are several business maps especially designed for market research, such as *Rating Guides* by Rand McNally & Company, the American Map Company, and the National Demographic Research Corporation (two volumes), which offer sectional maps, broken down by states, counties, cities, and postal regions on the basis of population, demographic data, trading

value, and other essential information.

Publishers Among the most authoritative books published on buying trends are those by the American Marketing Association, Crain Communications, Inc. (in cooperation with *Advertising Age*, Chicago), McGraw-Hill Book Company (including reports issued by its own Economics Department), Prentice-Hall, Inc., Fairchild Publications, Inc., Hastings House, Publishers, Inc., Doubleday & Company, Inc., Dow Jones Books, Litton Educational Publishing International, Melville Publishing Company, National Bureau of Economic Research, Inc., Random House, Inc., Simon & Schuster, Inc., Harper & Row, Publishers, Incorporated, Harcourt Brace Jovanovich, Inc., Harvard University Press, the Reuben H. Donnelley Corp., F. W. Dodge Company, Sales Management, Inc., and Industrial Marketing, Inc.

Other Sources For further information each year, *Advertising Age* has a list of available market data issued by various organizations (usually more than 1500). *Marketing Information Guide,* issued by the Department of Commerce, offers essentially the same kind of data. The Government Printing Office also provides comprehensive bibliographies of publications such as the *Monthly Catalog of United States Government Publications, Selected U.S. Government Publications, and Price Lists of Government Publications.* Another quick reference work on available sources is Linda C. Pohle's *A Guide to Popular Government Publications* (Libraries Unlimited, Inc., Littleton, Colorado).

FOR WRITERS

So much is being published about products, services, consumers, suppliers, and so on (some material by the corporations themselves) that it would be impossible even to skim the material here. Depending on their subjects of interest, writers must use their own reference sources. For a start, we recommend the following, in addition to the most important book of all, a standard dictionary.

Roget's International Thesaurus (Thomas Y. Crowell Company, New York). More than 1000 categories. As useful as a standard dictionary and, when groping for the

right expression, even more so.

Eric Partridge: *A Dictionary of Slang and Unconventional English* (The Macmillan Company, New York). A standard reference work

on slang, containing more than 100,000 words given short shrift by other lexicographers.

Lester V. Berry and Melvin Van Den Bark: *The American Thesaurus* of Slang (Thomas Y. Crowell Company, New York). Another and even more comprehensive study of the vernacular.

Theodore M. Bernstein: *Reverse Dictionary* (Quadrangle Books, Inc./ The New York Times Company). Words discovered by way of their meanings; for example, "late-blossoming": serotinous.

John Bartlett: *Familiar Quotations* (Little, Brown and Company, Boston). With emphasis on sayings by English and American authors and other notables. An index of more than 500 pages of key words to help the reader find anything that he or she wants.

Charles Noel Douglas: *40,000 Quotations* (Halcyon House, Garden City Books, New York). Prose and poetry.

William Laughlin: *Fact Finder* (Parker Publishing Co., West Nyack, New York). People, places, things, and events neatly organized. Great for bedtime reading.

Evan Esar: *20,000 Quips and Quotes* (Doubleday & Company, Inc., Garden City, New York). Includes wisecracks.

Eugene E. Landy: *The Underground Dictionary* (Simon & Schuster, New York). Where language gets to be.

E. B. White: *The Elements of Style* (The Macmillan Company, New York). All about linguistic amenities. A perennial best-seller. Another favorite: *A Manual of Style* (The University of Chicago Press, Chicago).

Frederick T. Wood: *English Colloquial Idioms* (The Macmillan Company St. Martin's Press, New York). Words used as some copywriters use them.

The Sears, Roebuck Catalogue (Chelsea House Publishers, New York). Just what mainstream Americans always wanted. Caption writing at its succinct best.

Single-volume *Columbia Encyclopedia* (Columbia University Press, New York). Containing 10¹/₂ pounds (4 ³/₄ kilograms) of solidly packed information. For those with more money and space, the thirty volumes of the *Encyclopaedia Britannica* (with a magnificent index system) are worth having. *The New Columbia Encyclopedia*, with more than 50,000 entries, is a valuable one-volume work.

Eric Partridge: *Dictionary of Clichés* (E. P. Dutton & Co., Inc., New York). Collection of clichés. An illustrated work of the same genre is *The Great American Cliché* by Lawrence Paros (Workman Publishing Co., Inc., New York).

For additional stimulation, browse through the bookshelves of the art director in the office next door (and vice versa).

FOR ART DIRECTORS

Not surprisingly, art directors have a penchant for pictures accompanied by the fewest possible words. Here are some of the standard reference books, designed to please the eye.

The One Show (Watson-Guptill Publications, Inc., New York). Features the best-designed ads of the year. Contains more than 1000 pieces of print, TV, radio, editorial, sales promotion, and point-of-sale advertising selected from some 10,000 entries by experts from all over the world. Credit is given to the writers, art directors, illustrators, photographers, advertisers, and publishers responsible for the work.

Art/Direction/Creativity (Advertising Trade Publications, Inc., New York). A knowing look at the field each year.

Graphis (distribution through Hastings House, Publishers, Inc., New York). Publishes its art collectanea not only in magazines but also in books. Among the latter are Walter Herdeg's *Graphis Annual, Graphis Annual Reports, Graphis Posters, Film & TV Graphics, Graphis-Record Covers, Graphis Packaging, Graphis-Diagrams*, and *Graphis Photographic Television Photography*, all very handsomely put together.

Illustrator's Annuals (Visual Communications Books/Hastings House). One of the most comprehensive surveys of contemporary illustration. Entries usually number about 500, some shown in glorious color. Caught up in advertising's never-ending seesaw battle between photography and illustration, the art director may come to favor the latter after perusing these volumes.

Advertising Directions (Art Directions Book Company, New York). Prints many valuable references on graphic arts, including the latest on photography, reproduction techniques, printing, typography, and illustration. For a listing, see couponed "bookshelf" page appearing in *Art Direction* magazine and *Advertising Techniques*.

Graphic Arts Manual. Comprehensive guide to creating, producing, and purchasing printed material. Included in its directory are firms, associations, schools, competitions, and awards.

Pocket Pal: A Graphic Arts Production Handbook (International Paper Company, New York). Everything you always wanted to know about advertising print production. A small, handy volume.

Art Directors' Index to Photographers (Camera/Graphic Press, Ltd., New York). A 400-plus-page reference work to help find topnotch photographers everywhere. Published periodically.

Celestine G. Frankenberg: *Picture Sources* (Special Libraries Association, New York). Contains picture collections, names of photograph research companies, and other groups in the United States of interest to professionals in research, business, and the arts.

Art Directors' Index to Photographers (Art Directions Book Company, New York). Published every year or so and showing nearly 300 photographs, most of them in color, by professionals from all over the world.

Photography Yearbook (Fountain Press, Harrison, New York). Shows the work of amateur photographers as well, proving that professional quality can be achieved without monetary incentive.

Tom Cardamone: *Advertising Agency & Studio Skills* (Watson-Guptill Publications, Inc., New York). Preparation of art and mechanicals. A handy little book for denizens of the bullpen.

James Craig: *Production for the Graphic Designer* (Watson-Guptill Publications, Inc., New York). One of the best books on advertising print production now available. Another fine reference work, by Bernard Stone & Arthur Eckstein, *Preparing Art for Printing* (Van Nostrand Reinhold Company, New York), is bigger and more expensive.

Stephen Baker: *Advertising Layout and Art Direction* (McGraw-Hill Book Company, New York). Deals with the art director's role, both as a creative designer and as a hard-headed advertising executive. Written and designed by the author.

John Snyder: *Commercial Artist's Handbook* (Watson-Guptill Publications, Inc., New York). No-nonsense reference book, describing more than 400 materials and uses.

Edited by the type-expert and former editor of *Art Direction,* Edward M. Gottschall, is *The A/D Copyfitter.* In addition to displaying some 2000 typefaces, this 24-page book has a plastic gauge in it which enables the art director to quickly determine character counts for lines up to 55 picas and for every typeface up to 24 point.

George Lois and Bill Pitts: *The Art of Advertising* (Harry N. Abrams Inc., New York). This is a spectacular, can't-put-it-down magnum opus showing the work of one of the most dynamic art directors today, George Lois. It should particularly inspire those who feel intimidated by clients. The book is gung-ho all the way through. Says the art director/author, not too modestly: "I say that you never did the job if you didn't sell it to the client. Every piece reproduced in this volume has seen the light of day, has been used, has run, has been exposed to mass audience. The accurate measure of a human being is what he actually gets done."

Two excellent volumes on abstract design have been compiled by Yasaburo Kuwayama: *Trade Marks and Symbols* (Van Nostrand Reinhold Company, New York). They include 1500 trademarks from all over the world, reproduced handsomely.

Several pictorial archives are published for those who want a backward glimpse for visual inspiration. Some of the books come with full reproduction rights to illustrations. More than 100 such books are available today. One of the best is the series by Dover Pictorial Archive, ranging in subject matter from calligraphy to gravestone designs and costing from $1.50 to approximately $30. Even more ambitious are five other copyright-free books: the two-volume *Diderot Pictorial Encyclopedia of Trades and Industry* (Art Directions Book Company, New York); *The Encyclopedia of Source Illustrations* (Morgan & Morgan, Inc. Dobbs Ferry, New York); Dick Sutphen's *The Encyclopedia of Small Spot Engravings* (Valley of the Sun Publishing Company, Phoenix Arizona). *The Bettmann Portable Archive* (Picture House Press, Inc., New York), has 3669 sample prints culled from one of the most remarkable million-plus graphic collections, hand-picked by an expert staff under the leadership of the venerable Otto L. Bettmann.

Fine Art Reproductions: Old and Modern Masters (New York Graphic Society Ltd., New York). This is one of the most comprehensive single-volume catalogs available of fine art through the ages. All the masterpieces—well over 2000—are reproduced in color. The book is a godsend for artists and art directors looking for noncommercial art samples. Most of the paintings have become public domain.

A wide range of type specimen books are available for the art director in pursuit of the right typeface (one that suits his or her taste) from more than 1000 specimens currently available. Four of the most comprehensive are the *Encyclopedia of Comparative Letterforms* (Art Directions Book Company, New York), the *Art Directors' Book of Type Faces* by J. I. Biegeleisen (Arco Publishing Company, New York), *Designing with Type* by James Craig (Watson-Guptill Publications, Inc., New York), and *Visual Alphabet Library* (Art Directions Book Company). Nearly all type books on the market are impressive but rarely are inexpensive. With cost in mind, it is fair to mention that type houses and photolettering houses publish their own catalogs, and these are as comprehensive as most type books. They can be yours free of charge, provided you are or could be a paying customer. (Four of the finest catalogs are issued by Typographic Innovations, Inc., Visual Graphics Corporation, M. J. Baumwell, Typography, and Photo Lettering, Inc., all in New York.) The same is true of lithographers, engravers, printers, bookbinders, and others, all of whom are eager to serve you. These houses will supply you with standard ink color swatchbooks (the one created by Pantone, Inc., of Moonachis, New Jersy, is outstanding), sample sheets of various printing processes, paper dummies made up to your specifications, and other information you need in production planning.

For art directors interested in developing their skills in indicating figures, two books bear mentioning: the three volumes offered by the Famous Artists School in Westport, Connecticut, and the books by *The Fairborn System of Visual References* (Fairborn System, Elk Grove Village, Illinois). The latter, which contains a unique series of 7217 photographs taken of the human figure in action from twenty-four different angles, including heads, facial expressions, and hands, is a real time-saver.

There are numerous publishers that specialize in art books. Four of the largest ones are Hastings House, Publishers, Inc., Watson-Guptill Publications, Harry N. Abrams, Inc., and Visual Communication Books, all in New York. Two publisher–distributors that can get almost any books you want or can tell you where to find them are Museum Books, Inc., and Art Directions Book Company, also in New York. Or ask your nearest art supply store for information.

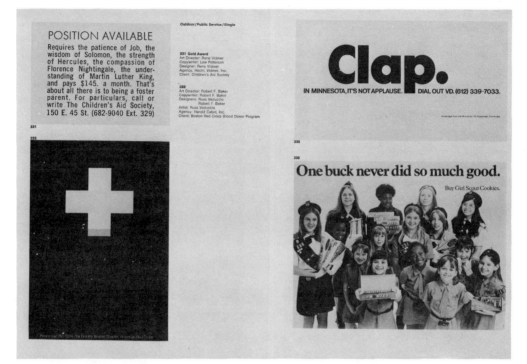

Two facing pages from the art directors' annual, *The One Show*.

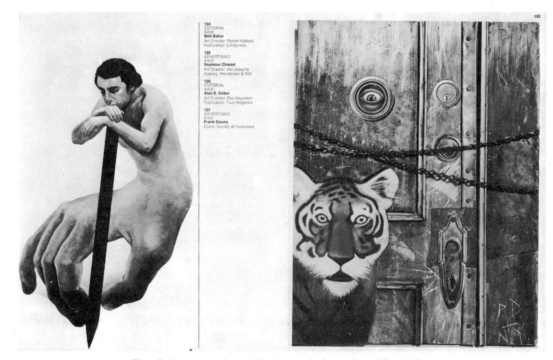

Two facing pages from *The Annual of American Illustration*.

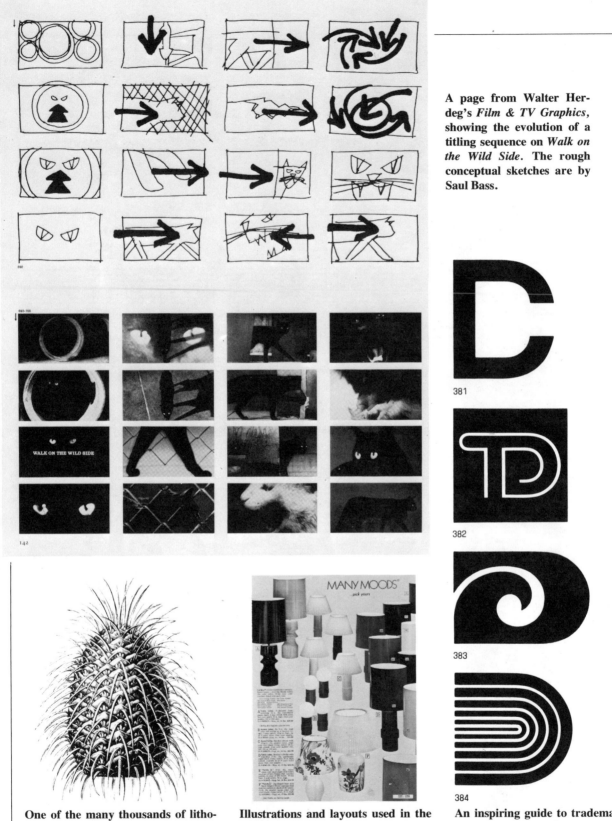

A page from Walter Herdeg's *Film & TV Graphics*, showing the evolution of a titling sequence on *Walk on the Wild Side*. The rough conceptual sketches are by Saul Bass.

381

382

383

384

One of the many thousands of lithographic plates reproduced in Dover Publications' Pictorial Art Series. Purchasers are authorized to reproduce up to ten illustrations without payment.

Illustrations and layouts used in the 1500-plus-page catalogs of Sears, Roebuck & Company are unlikely candidates for an art director's gold medal but nevertheless convey the message.

An inspiring guide to trademark designs is Yasaburo Kuwayama's two volume *Trade Marks and Symbols*. Shown here are versions of the letter form *D*.

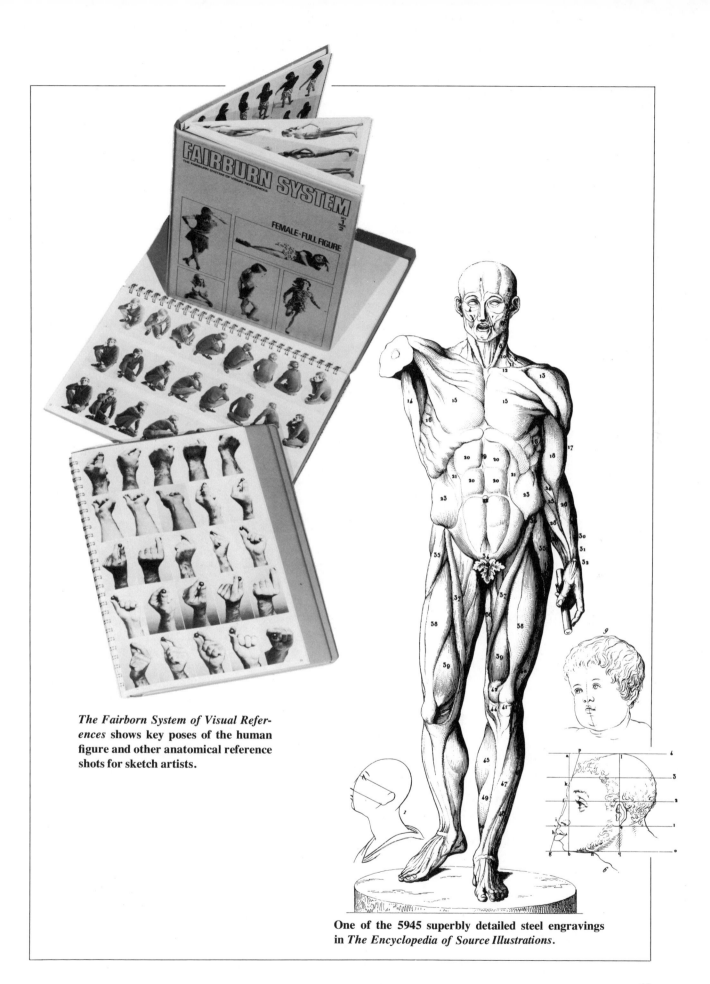

The Fairborn System of Visual References shows key poses of the human figure and other anatomical reference shots for sketch artists.

One of the 5945 superbly detailed steel engravings in *The Encyclopedia of Source Illustrations*.

The Dutch Masters Masters: Jaime Moscoso

Here in the Caribbean,

Jaime Moscoso, a master of the soil, breeds tobacco for Dutch Masters cigars.

Today he must select the best plants so their flowers can be bagged to protect the purity of their seed.

Bagging is a master's way to be sure the great taste of Dutch Masters doesn't change.

Now you see why a Dutch Masters like our

Panetela is worth more.
There really are masters at Dutch Masters.

K

Key—Main source of light

Key numbers—Identifying numbers marked along the edge of film.

Kicker light—Light from behind and to the side of a subject.

Kill—To take out of operation.

Kine—Pronounced kinny, it is the shortened version of kinescope; filming of a television program from a monitor.

L

LS—Long shot.

Lapel michrophone—Michrophone attached to lapel.

Lavaliere—Microphone worn on string around the neck.

Leader—Portion of film, blank, that allows for threading and cuing.

Leko—A light used to create background effects.

Lens—Glass ground and shaped to arrange and direct light rays.

Lens turret—A rotating disc mounted on the front of a camera with two or more lenses attached. Lens can be changed by rotating the disc.

Level—The intensity of an audio or video signal.

Limbo—Camera shot where subject has no frame of reference.

Lip sync—When the spoken word and lip action agree, or moving lips coincide with pre-recorded sound track.

Live—Transmission of program at the time of shooting.

Live copy—Copy read by announcer at time it is aired.

Live feed—A network feeding its affiliates a program while it is being aired.

Live tag—Short message added to commercial at time of broadcast by announcer.

Local advertiser—Advertiser whose business and advertising are on television in only one market.

Log—Breakdown of the day's broadcasting into seconds.

Logo—Identifying symbol.

Shown above is a sample page from a pocket glossary published by the Television Bureau of Advertising. Booklets like these are available free of charge to the curious. On the left is a typical storyboard reproduced from a filmstrip. In color or black-and-white, storyboards can be obtained from advertisers or their agencies.

Irv: I saw it first. It was kinda glidin' up through that arroyo. At first I thought it was a motorcycle, but it was real quiet. You'd have a heck of a time gettin' a mule up through there let alone a motorcycle. I don't think you could get a mule up through there. What do you think, Al?

Al: I think it should be reported to the Air Force.

Anncr.: It's like no other motorcycle you've ever seen. The Cat. From Yamaha.

To write believable TV copy, the writer must have a good ear for *spoken* language. Yamaha's announcement not only looks good; it sounds right.

The preparation and execution of a television commercial encompasses a wide spectrum of activities, each requiring its own particular expertise. There are books on lighting, cinema techniques, makeup, acting, colorcasting, camera movements, sound reproduction, special effects, animation, TV graphics, and other subjects. Some of the most important sources for reference follow.

Robert L. Hilliard (editor): *Understanding Television* (Hastings House Publishers, Inc., New York). Magnum opus written by top experts in the field.

Howard P. Abrahams: *Making TV Pay Off* (Fairchild Publications, New York). Practical, easy-to-understand reference book designed specifically for retailers who use or are about to use television.

Harry Wayne McMahan: *Television Production* (Hastings House Publishers, Inc., New York). Still one of the best handbooks by one of the most astute and articulate observers of the TV commercial scene.

Charles Anthony Wainwright: *Television Commercials* (Hastings House, Publishers, Inc., New York). Written by a professional television writer and representing a writer's point of view.

Arthur Ballaire: *The TV Commercial Cost Control Handbook* (Crain Communications, Chicago). Nitty-gritty survey of the business side of television commercial production, written by a professional who has a reputation for spending his clients' money prudently.

Kenneth H. Roberts and Win Sharples, Jr.: *A Primer for Film-Making* (Pegasus, division of the Bobbs-Merrill Company, Indianapolis). One of the best and certainly a most thorough guide to 16-millimeter and 35-millimeter film production.

Motion Picture, TV and Theatre Directory (Motion Picture Enterprises Publications, Inc., Tarrytown, New York). Detailed index of products, services, and supplier sources on a nationwide basis. *Audio-visual Source Directory,* issued by the same publisher, is another handy reference work. Both are published semiannually.

Back Stage: TV/Industrial Film & Tape Directory (Back Stage Publications, Inc., New York). Listings of major television and film centers in the United States and Canada, equipment, services, facilities distributors, and TV syndicators; updated annually.

Martin Mayer: *About Television* (Harper & Row, Publishers, Incorporated). Written for the benefit of television viewers but containing useful information for professionals as well. Bird's-eye view of the field.

Visit Your Favorite Bookstore: If You Do Not Buy, Browse

Most books, and particularly nonfiction, which constitutes more than 80 percent of the market, are published by popular demand and tell the public what it wants to hear. For example, more than 200 books on needlepoint were published when interest in the handicraft was at its peak. About 1500 titles on physical fitness reflect another national preoccupation. While transcendental meditation reigned, not one but two books on the subject made the bestseller list in a single month.

Fiction, too, reflects public opinion. Since novelists are very deeply involved in the fine points of the English language, their books offer a quick refresher course to copywriters who wish to keep their style up to date.

Most novelists have a trained ear for the verbacular or, to use Eric Partridge's phrase, "such Americanisms as have been naturalized."

The terse, tough-talk business jargon in this house ad for Clinton E. Frank, Inc., published in advertising trade journals, strikes a familiar note with its audience, clients looking for an advertising agency.

Periodicals: An Even Quicker Way to Get Information

Although modern technology permits the production of instant books (the record is 40 hours), magazines and newspapers are still ahead in this respect (newspapers can be produced in 5 to 8 hours). So periodicals more faithfully mirror the present moment.

Wise is the advertising executive who subscribes to at least ten to twenty magazines to keep abreast of the times. This is not to suggest that he or she read every page in every publication from top to bottom. That would leave little time to do anything else. At the least, however, the executive should go through the issues quickly and look for the highlights. The following are publications without which no list is complete:

Esquire
Reader's Digest
Ladies Home Journal, McCall's, Woman's Day, Family Circle, Good Housekeeping
Redbook
The New Yorker
National Geographic

Shifts in public taste are apparent in these magazines:

Glamour, Mademoiselle
Vogue, Harper's Bazaar
Better Homes & Gardens, House & Garden, House Beautiful
Gentlemen's Quarterly
Clothes
Holiday
Seventeen
Women's Wear Daily

To keep up with more subtle sociological and psychological changes, these are helpful:

Psychology Today
New Times
Sports Illustrated
People
Playboy, Penthouse or others of the same genre
Ebony, Essence, Jet
Apartment Living
New York
Cosmopolitan
Town & Country
High Times
True Confessions

Money
Saturday Review
Human Behavior
Ms.
National Lampoon
Cue
Rolling Stone, Crawdaddy, High Times
Backstage
Variety
Billboard
Law Journal
Village Voice
The Mother Earth News

Editors of these publications have a nose for business news:

Business Week, Newsweek, Nation's Business
Time
Dun's Review, Forbes
Fortune
Kiplinger's Washington Letter
Barron's

The advertising executive must, of course, be alert to everything that happens in his or her own field. These weeklies and monthlies will bring him or her up to date:

Marketing and Advertising

Advertising Age
Anny's
Ad Daily
Ad/Day USA
Madison Avenue
Journal of Marketing
Journal of Advertising
The Gallagher Report
Journal of Marketing Research
Market Digest
Journal of Retailing
Consumer Reports
Consumer Bulletin
The International Advertiser
Chain Store Age
Marketing News
Sales Management
Marketing/Communications
Advertising & Sales Promotion
Editor & Publisher
Industrial Marketing
Premium/Incentive Business
Direct Marketing
Management Review
MBA Magazine
Public Relations Quarterly

Media

Broadcasting
Media Decisions
Medical Marketing & Media
Spot Television Rates and Media
Variety
Inside Radio
Media & Methods

Television/Radio Age
Media/Scope
Media Records
More
MIN: Media Industry Newsletter
Client/Media News
Media Law Reporter

Research

Journal of Advertising Research
Journal of Marketing Research

Visual and Verbal Communications

Art Direction
Advertising Techniques
Art in America
Art News
Graphic Arts Monthly
Industrial Design
Print
Folio
Popular Photography
Designer
Modern Photography (Eastman Kodak)
Inspirations (Westwaco)
Impressions (Mead Paper Company)
American Artist
Communication Arts
Graphics, USA
Industrial Art Methods

In addition, there are approximately 4000 industry, business, and trade publications such as Women's Wear Daily, Home Furnishings Daily, and Daily Pacific Builder. Distributed monthly, weekly, or daily, they cater to special professional interests.

Magazines Are for More Than Just Reading

For business reasons, magazines tend to be published for target audiences. This is why when it comes to material, magazines cover a wide range of special interests, more than any other media.

There is no quicker way to get inside the heads of certain people than to read "their" publications analytically. These publications accurately reflect the life-styles, opinions, and feelings of their audience. The media spend considerable effort to find out exactly who their readers are; it is the hallmark of a good editor to be able to give the readers what they need to hear.

Magazines Know Their Audience

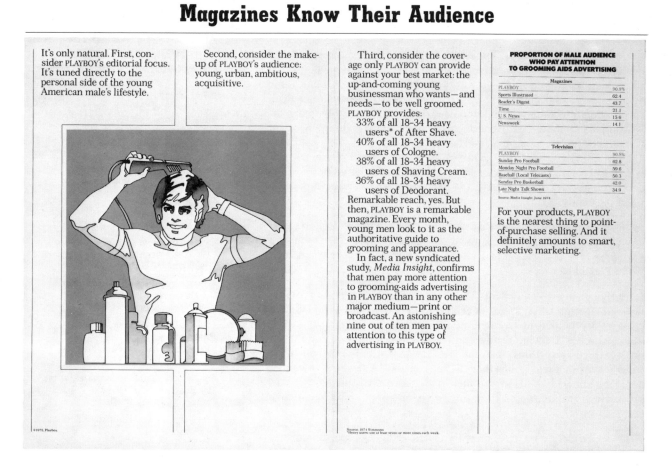

It's only natural. First, consider PLAYBOY's editorial focus. It's tuned directly to the personal side of the young American male's lifestyle.

Second, consider the make-up of PLAYBOY's audience: young, urban, ambitious, acquisitive.

Third, consider the coverage only PLAYBOY can provide against your best market: the up-and-coming young businessman who wants—and needs—to be well groomed. PLAYBOY provides:

33% of all 18–34 heavy users* of After Shave.
40% of all 18–34 heavy users of Cologne.
38% of all 18–34 heavy users of Shaving Cream.
36% of all 18–34 heavy users of Deodorant.

Remarkable reach, yes. But then, PLAYBOY is a remarkable magazine. Every month, young men look to it as the authoritative guide to grooming and appearance.

In fact, a new syndicated study, *Media Insight*, confirms that men pay more attention to grooming-aids advertising in PLAYBOY than in any other major medium—print or broadcast. An astonishing nine out of ten men pay attention to this type of advertising in PLAYBOY.

Source: 1974 Simmons
*Heavy users: use at least seven or more times each week.

PROPORTION OF MALE AUDIENCE WHO PAY ATTENTION TO GROOMING AIDS ADVERTISING

Magazines	
PLAYBOY	90.8%
Sports Illustrated	62.4
Reader's Digest	43.7
Time	21.1
U.S. News	15.6
Newsweek	14.1

Television	
PLAYBOY	90.8%
Sunday Pro Football	62.8
Monday Night Pro Football	59.6
Baseball (Local Telecasts)	50.3
Sunday Pro Basketball	42.0
Late Night Talk Shows	34.9

Source: Media Insight, June 1974

For your products, PLAYBOY is the nearest thing to point-of-purchase selling. And it definitely amounts to smart, selective marketing.

©1975, Playboy.

In addition to syndicated media research (W. R. Simmons, Target Group Index (TGI), ABC, BPA, Pulse, TAB, Major Market Index, BAR, PIB, National Arbitron, Nielsen, and so on), individual publishers, too, have in-depth and usually primary information on their audience profiles. Such profiles include demographic and psychological data as well as buying propensities. This information, along with the medium's own computerized interpretations of syndicated data, is made available to advertisers wishing to find out more about their audience.

"How Do You Feel About Being a Woman?" In its October 1974 issue, *Redbook* magazine asked its female readers 100 questions about their sexual attitudes. Here are some typical excerpts from a 28-page report:

"Further, we think that these women indicate the direction that many American women will take in the future. They are, of course, by no means unanimous in their attitudes toward women's roles, but recognizable trends can be discerned in their answers. Many of them express opinions and reflect experiences that sharply separate them from their mothers' generation, and there are indications that the values they transmit to their children will be based on the principle of sexual equality."

The increased awareness of discrimination is a striking fact of the *Redbook* survey: Among full-time workers who replied to the questionnaire, a startling 40 per cent report that they are earning less than they deserve, and 30 per cent say that they have been discriminated against in hiring and promotions. Such reports were especially true for women in positions that are male-dominated—managers, administrators, skilled technicians.

Many *Redbook* readers agree that women are subjected to another, subtler form of discrimination: Some men treat women not as whole persons but as sex objects. Half the married respondents agreed that: "I have often felt that men are more interested in my body than in me as a person." More than seven out of ten single and divorced women endorsed this statement, suggesting that the matter of male sexism is either more immediate in their lives or that they are more aware of it. Further, four wives in ten (and half the single women) reported discrimination in "the way men react to you when you are discussing things about which you have knowledge." . . .

There is no simple answer. For example, when we asked respondents how they felt about the routine tasks of keeping house—doing the dishes, laundry and cleaning—fewer than one in three finds it enjoyable and only one in four finds it unpleasant. About half say they are neutral, accepting daily chores with indifference. But they thoroughly enjoy the less-routine and more-creative aspects of homemaking. Ninety-three per cent find home decorating and entertaining their friends to be "gratifying or fun"; 70 per cent derive a good deal of pleasure from sewing clothes for themselves and their family; about the same number enjoy most aspects of child care; and a majority (54 per cent) even like everyday cooking for the family. . . .

Although a clear majority of *Redbook* readers were happy to stop working with the advent of children, about half these women view mothering as a temporary occupation and intend to return to careers when their children are older. . . .

Even though many respondents said that full-time motherhood provides many satisfactions, they were not at all certain that the housewife-mother role is totally fulfilling in itself. *Fewer than two per cent* think that: "Most women can best develop their potential by being good wives and mothers." Instead they think that the best route to self-development is through work that will "fulfill them as individuals." They believe women should be allowed to determine their own sources of satisfaction, and they strongly oppose anyone's trying to channel them into a particular role. . . .

Redbook readers who are unhappily married and who are dissatisfied with their housekeeping tasks have lower feelings of self-esteem than happily married women. That is, they tend to feel that they have more bad luck than good luck, that it is no use trying to plan ahead, that they do not feel in control of their lives. If employed, they want better jobs; if unemployed, they want to work. . . .

But what about the minority? One wife in three says her husband wants sex more often than she does; one in ten wishes her husband were more amorous. One in five achieves orgasm "infrequently or never," and these wives, as we would expect, are less happy with their marriages and more resentful of men. . . .

Menstruation is the least worrisome event for *Redbook* readers. Long gone are the days of "the curse," to say nothing of the days when women stayed in bed and were afraid to be active. More than seven respondents in ten said they do not think about menstruation much; "It's just there." To be sure, fewer than one in ten feels that it is an affirmation of womanhood; but only two in ten are irritated by menstruation or resentful that "men don't have a similar unpleasant experience." . . .

Women who put considerable emotional investment in children are, logically, more likely to believe that being a wife and mother is a full-time occupation. They are happier with the routine work in housekeeping and childcare. But we found a significant factor of their contentment with marriage and children was a prior knowledge of, and planning for, this role. Women who had no clear expectations about marriage (or whose expectations were not met) and who were not able to plan their children, are much less happy than women who had planned their roles. They are dissatisfied with the role of wife, and less positive about their experiences with pregnancy and childbirth.

70

ADVERTISING, MARKETING, AND MEDIA ASSOCIATIONS PROVIDING INFORMATION

Advertising & Marketing
International Network (AMIN)
1133 Fifteenth Street N.W.
Washington, D.C. 20005

Advertising Checking Bureau, Inc.
353 Park Avenue, South
New York, New York 10010

Advertising Council
825 Third Avenue
New York, New York 10022

Advertising Research Foundation
3 East 54th Street
New York, New York 10022

Advertising Woman of New York
153 East 57th Street
New York, New York 10022

Affiliated Advertising Agencies
International
13693 East Iliff Avenue
Denver, Colorado 80232

Agricultural Publishers Association
111 East Wacker Drive
Chicago, Illinois 60601

American Association of Advertising
Agencies
200 Park Avenue
New York, New York 10017

American Institute of Management
125 East 38th Street
New York, New York 10016

Associated Business Press, Inc. 205
East 42d Street
New York, New York 10017

Association of Direct Marketing
Agencies
527 Madison Avenue
New York, New York 10022

Audit Bureau of Circulations
123 North Wacker Drive
Chicago, Illinois 60606

Business Publications Audit of
Circulation, Inc.
360 Park Avenue South
New York, New York 10010

Canadian Association of
Broadcasters
85 Sparks Street
Ottawa 4, Ontario, Canada

Canadian Circulations Audit Board
165 Bloor Street East
Toronto 5, Ontario, Canada

Canadian Daily Newspaper
Publishers Association
250 Bloor Street East
Toronto 5, Ontario, Canada

Council of Better Business Bureaus,
Inc.
Department of Information and
  Editorial Services
1150 17th Street N.W.
Washington, D.C. 20036

Direct Mail Marketing Agency, Inc.
733 Summer Street
Stamford, Connecticut 06901

Direct Mail/Marketing Association
6 East 43rd Street
New York, New York 10017

European Association of Advertising
Agencies
19 Avenue Ernest Cambier
Brussels, Belgium

Farm Publication Reports, Inc.
111 East Wacker Drive
Chicago, Illinois 60601

First Advertising Agency Network
P.O. Box 1275
Sun City, Arizona 85351

Gesellschaft Werbeagenturen
Friedensstrasse 11
6 Frankfurt am Main, West
  Germany

Institute of Canadian Advertisers
Suite 401
8 King Street East
Toronto 5, Ontario, Canada

Intermarket Association of
  Advertising Agencies
1605 North Main Street
Dayton, Ohio 45405

International Advertising Association
475 Fifth Avenue
New York, New York 10017

International Chain of Industrial &
  Technical Advertising Agencies
2700 Route 22
Union, New Jersey 07083

Leading National Advertisers, Inc.
347 Madison Avenue
New York, New York 10017

League of Advertising Agencies, Inc.
205 West 89th Street
New York, New York 10024

Magazine Publishers Association
575 Lexington Avenue
New York, New York 10022

Mutual Advertising Agency Network
5001 West 80th St.
Minneapolis, Minnesota 55437

National Advertising Agency
  Network
420 Lexington Avenue
New York, New York 10017

National Association of Broadcasters
477 Madison Avenue
New York, New York 10022

National Radio Broadcasters
Association
1705 De Sales Street N.W.
Washington, D.C. 20036

New York City Transit Authority
  (Bus Posters)
370 Jay Street
Brooklyn, New York 11201

New York Subways Advertising
Company
750 Third Avenue
New York, New York 10017

Newspaper Advertising Bureau
485 Lexington Avenue
New York, New York 10017

Outdoor Advertising Association of
America
625 Madison Avenue
New York, New York 10022

Outdoor Advertising Association of
Canada
250 Bloor Street East
Toronto 5, Ontario, Canada

Packaging Institute USA
342 Madison Avenue
New York, New York 10017

Periodical Press Association
100 University Avenue
Toronto 1, Ontario, Canada

Point-of-Purchase Advertising
  Institute, Inc.
60 East 42nd Street
New York, New York 10017

Premium Advertising Association of
America
420 Lexington Avenue
New York, New York 10017

Publishers Information Bureau, Inc.
575 Lexington Avenue
New York, New York 10022

Radio Advertising Bureau
555 Madison Avenue
New York, New York 10022

Southwestern Association of
  Advertising Agencies
1112 Stemmons Tower West
Dallas, Texas 75207

Television Bureau of Advertising
1345 Avenue of the Americas
New York, New York 10019

Traffic Audit Bureau, Inc.
708 Third Avenue
New York, New York 10017

Transworld Advertising Agency
Network
304 Ivy Street
San Diego, California 92101

Western States Advertising Agencies
  Association, Inc.
5900 Wilshire Boulevard
Los Angeles, California 90036

What Newspapers Do You Read? What Is Your Favorite Television Show?

Everyone in advertising, no matter where his or her office is located, should make a point of reading through at least two newspapers in the morning: *The New York Times,* for news and literary style; and *The Wall Street Journal,* for in-depth reporting on business and finance. Among other things many new business leads suggest themselves in these two publications, particularly once the reader has learned to discover these leads between the lines of articles.

In addition to the metropolitan dailies there are the so-called community newspapers, reporting on their hometowns. With their editors' instinct for local news, these publications offer the reader another look at grassroots Americana, the way people live. This type of coverage is especially valuable to advertising executives huddled high in their midtown office towers who feel that they may be losing touch with their audience. Culled from one of the thousands of small-town newspapers, *The Pike Dispatch* of Milford, Pennsylvania, these headlines are typical:

Training Seminar on Citizen Advocacy
Man Killed on Route 209
Episcopal Church Lenten Programs
"Japanese Day" in Dingmans
388 Black Bears Taken by Hunters
Pa. Fish Comm. to Stock Streams
Mrs. Krause to Speak at MCC Meeting
Invitation to Count Deer Harvest Cards
Hunters Took 71,986 Bucks
Nature Study!
Weekly Lottery

The same is true of television programs. Their content and style offer additional current information about the taste of the American consumer. Program directors are well attuned to their audience, for large sums of money are spent on attracting directors able to forecast trends. Plenty of research is available. As in the case of publications, the attitudes, opinions, viewing patterns, buying habits, age, income, and other demographic data are no mystery to those responsible for deciding what Americans want. Those able to keep a finger on the pulse are highly valued—and paid—for their opinions.

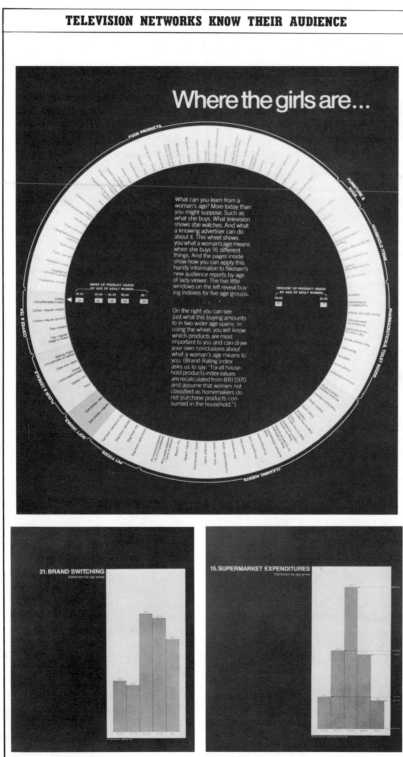

TELEVISION NETWORKS KNOW THEIR AUDIENCE

This CBS hard-cover brochure provides the advertiser with valuable clues to the buying preferences of female TV viewers of all ages.

WHO WATCHES WHAT?

According to 1970 Canadian data, women viewers may be characterized as follows on the basis of their viewing habits:

Hockey

Older

Strongly identified with traditional female role of mother, wife, and homemaker (anti-women's lib)

Active as sports participant and sports fan

Very nonpermissive about cosmetics, sex, and discipline

Not a traveler

Heavy newspaper reader

Male Singers

Lower education, slightly lower income

Pro-national brands

Brand-loyal

Strongly uncertain, distrustful, and prone to worry

Care and pride of home

Affectionate, tender, and loving

Worried about youth, drugs, and responsibility

Favoring health aids (deodorant, mouthwash, and so on)

Movies

Lower income and education

Favoring traditional conservatism such as fantasy-comedy shows

Compulsive TV viewer

Home cleanliness; care of and pride in home

Non-risk taker, very security-conscious

Homebody, not socially active

Financially dissatisfied

Price-conscious

Variety-Comedy

Very low education

Older

Lower-income

Liking cooking

Positive toward advertising

Compulsive housekeepers

Anti youth and drugs

Weight- and health-conscious

Religious, nonpermissive

Pro TV, antiprint except for *Maclean's* magazine

Conscious of fashion and personal appearance

Homebody

Security-conscious

Self-confident, self-disciplined

Believer in salvation

Desiring enjoyable, leisurely life

[*Courtesy of* Life Style and Psychographics, *published by the American Marketing Association*]

Libraries Are for Reading

Perhaps because libraries are so easily accessible and are free to use, they are often underestimated as sources of information. Yet they can be an excellent base for researchers. Even those that limit their services to professionals (fashion, fine arts, law) are usually hospitable enough to open their doors to an eager student. Most librarians are keenly aware of the role they play in disseminating information and will cooperate with the seeker of truth in any way they can.

A case in point is the central building of the New York Public Library, serving one of the largest business communities in the world. It is said that approximately 40 percent of this library's works are not available anywhere else. On its seven floors are more than 10 million books, not to mention its even larger collection of newspapers, manuscripts, maps, recordings, prints, microcopies, and other material that the library has built up through the years. Of particular interest to business executives is the Economics Division of some 30,000 books and periodicals from all over the world, with particular emphasis on such advertising-related subjects as public finance, statistics, transportation, communication techniques, marketing, and demography. For those looking for a historical perspective, a copy of every important issue of *The New York Times* published since 1851 is available. The microfilm section contains copies of more than 100,000 financial reports. Popular with artists and art directors is the library's collection of more than 8 million pictures, organized by subject matter and period. They can be borrowed for up to 30 days, photostated on the premises, or both. Visitors may bring their own typewriters to use in the typing room, or they may rent a machine. Says one of the curators who has seen his share of information seekers looking for and finding exactly what they wanted: "The library is where you go when you run out of ideas."

Not far behind in quantity and quality of business information is the Brooklyn Business Library, which maintains its own telephone reference service (212-636-3281) for callers from all over the city, nation, and world.

Some Advertising Agencies Have Their Own Libraries The library of Young & Rubicam has one of the world's largest collections. It includes subscription copies of more than 200 trade and consumer publications, several thousand government documents (including most of the Census Bureau publications), and 5000 books covering advertising and marketing as well as science, economics, social sciences, literature, art, sports, and entertainment. The material is organized in 210 vertical file drawers.

There are two special sections, the Picture Research Library and the Competitive Advertising Files. The former is designed to meet the special needs of the creative departments. It consists of more than 700 illustrated books and extensive picture files, arranged by subject and representing both print and television advertising. The latter contains all advertising of products in which the agency is involved, in one way or another, and advertisements that have been published by a professional staff trained in that area. As a member of the Special Libraries Association, this library also has access to more than 1000 special libraries in the New York metropolitan area and to many others throughout the country. Professional librarians are on hand to help with the research.

Meetings: Where Professionals Gather

Routine, everyday conversations with others in the office may be all that is needed to keep up with developments in the field. More often than not, however, there is a need to do more. The curious may want to turn to outside sources to fill in their professional voids, places such as those listed below.

Sales Conferences Formal meetings may be scheduled once, twice, or even 3 times a year by corporations primarily for the purpose of touching base with their sales force. The sessions run for 1 to 3 days at corporate headquarters or elsewhere, with New York, Chicago, Atlanta, Miami, and San Francisco leading the way as chosen sites. (Places outside the United States are also becoming popular. Air Afrique, for example, advertises "everything from small conference rooms to 2000-seat auditoriums complete with simultaneous communication facilities" to attract American-based corporations.) A change in environment is usually welcomed by sales people looking for a break in the routine.

Workshop Seminars Experts in various fields are invited to discuss their specialties, individually or on a panel. Programs can last either a few hours or as long as a week.

Most professional clubs hold symposia on a regular basis. Speakers cover a diversity of topics, including writing, design, illustration, music, acting, publishing, packaging, print and television production, film making, laws and regulations, and consumer-group activities. For instance, in a single year, the Art Directors Club in New York (any art director with 2 years of experience can join) discussed at its luncheons such eclectic subjects as "Being an Art Director in a Small Agency," "Saving Money on Typography," "Getting a Job," "Getting Better Quality in Photographic Color Prints," "Coping with the Paper Shortage," "Finding the Right Clients," "Reaching College Audiences through Video Tape Programs," and "Living Better through Astrology," often using sophisticated audio-video techniques to get various points across to its communications-conscious audience.

Presentations made by the media. Magazine and newspaper publishers and radio and television stations also make it a point to dramatize

LIST OF UPCOMING CONVENTIONS AS ANNOUNCED IN ADVERTISING AGE
(THIS COLUMN APPEARS ABOUT TWELVE TIMES A YEAR)

Advertising Age, Account Management Workshops, Hyatt Regency, Chicago, Nov. 5–6; Waldorf Astoria, New York, Nov. 12–13.

Advertising Age, Media Workshop, Continental Plaza, Chicago, Dec. 1–4.

Advertising Age, 100 Best TV Commercials of 1975, Hotel Roosevelt, New York, Feb. 10; Prudential Auditorium, Chicago, Feb. 11; Directors Guild Theatre, Hollywood, Cal., Feb. 17; Hyatt Union Square, San Francisco, Feb. 19.

Advertising Age, Political Communications Seminar, Mayflower Hotel, Washington, D.C., Oct. 8–9.

Advertising Research Foundation, annual conference, New York Hilton, Nov. 9–11.

American Advertising Federation, western region, Washington Plaza Hotel, Seattle, Nov. 6–9.

American Assn. of Advertising Agencies, account executive seminar, Marriott Hotel, Philadelphia, Oct. 2–3; western region convention, Maui Surf Hotel, Hawaii, Oct. 12–15; central region annual meeting, Continental Plaza, Chicago, Nov. 6–7, eastern annual conference, Waldorf Astoria, New York, Nov. 18–19; agency management seminar, Hyatt Regency, San Francisco, Dec. 4–5.

American Management Assn. and others, National Packaging Week, Americana Hotel, New York, Oct. 27–31.

American Marketing Assn., marketing educators' conference, ag-chem conference, Stouffer Inn, Washington, D.C., Oct. 26–28; industrial conference, Roosevelt Hotel, New York, Feb. 4; attitude research conference, Hilton Head Inn, Hilton Head Island, S.C., Feb. 11–15; marketing management conference, Carefree Inn, Carefree, Ariz., Feb. 24–28.

Assn. for Consumer Research, sixth annual conference, Stouffer's Inn, Cincinnati, Oct. 30–Nov. 2.

Assn. of Independent Television Stations, annual convention, Century Plaza Hotel, Los Angeles, Jan. 11–13.

Assn. of National Advertisers, 66th annual meeting, The Breakers Hotel, Palm Beach, Fla., Nov. 30–Dec. 3.

Assn. of Second Class Mail Publications, new ideas seminar, Essex House, New York, Oct. 8.

Audit Bureau of Circulations, 61st annual meeting, Royal York Hotel, Toronto, Oct. 22–23.

Direct Mail/Marketing Assn., 58th annual conference and trade show, MGM Hotel, Las Vegas, Oct. 19–22.

Exhibit Designers & Producers Assn., 21st annual convention, Sheraton Harbor Island, San Diego, Dec. 2–7.

First Advertising Agency Network, annual workshop, Kansas City Club, Kansas City, Mo., Nov. 5–8.

Incentive Travel & Meetings Exposition, McCormick Place, Chicago, Sept. 29–Oct. 2.

Inland Daily Press Assn., annual meeting, Drake Hotel, Chicago, Oct. 18–21; spring meeting, Williamsburg Conference Center, Williamsburg, Va., Feb. 21–24.

International Newspaper Advertising Executives, winter sales conference, Marriott Hotel, New Orleans, Jan. 25–28.

Magazine Publishers Assn., Bicentennial communications conference, Colonial Williamsburg, Williamsburg, Va., Oct. 19–22.

Mutual Advertising Agency Network, bi-annual meeting, Copley Plaza, Boston, Oct. 5–8.

National Advertising Agency Network, annual staff conference, Marquette Inn, Minneapolis, Oct. 9–11.

National Assn. of Display Industries, spring display market, Visual Merchandising Center, New York, Dec. 6–9.

National Automatic Merchandising Assn., annual convention and exhibit, The Rivergate, New Orleans, Oct. 16–19.

National Decorating Products Assn., 28th annual convention, workshop and trade show, McCormick Place, Chicago, No. 21–23.

National Newspaper Assn., annual convention and trade show, Hotel Sahara, Las Vegas, Oct. 15–18.

National Packaging Week, Americana Hotel, New York, Oct. 27–31.

National Premium Show, McCormick Place, Chicago, Sept. 29–Oct. 2.

Northeast Classified Advertising Managers Assn., annual conference, Shoreham Hotel, Washington, D.C., Jan. 18–21.

Outdoor Advertising Assn., annual convention, Hyatt-Regency, Houston, Nov. 22–25.

Point-of-Purchase Advertising Institute, 29th annual exhibit and 16th annual awards contest, McCormick Place, Chicago, Sept. 29–Oct. 1.

Premium Advertising Assn. of America, fall conference, McCormick Inn, Chicago, Sept. 30 (held in conjunction with the National Premium Show).

Southern Newspaper Publishers Assn., 72nd annual convention, Boca Raton Hotel, Boca Raton, Fla., Nov. 16–19.

Southwestern Assn. of Advertising Agencies, 5th annual educational seminar, Southern Methodist University and Hilton Inn, Dallas, Nov. 8.

Television Bureau of Advertising, 21st annual meeting, Americana Hotel, New York, Nov. 18–20.

CALENDAR OF EVENTS IN NEW YORK'S LOCAL ADVERTISING JOURNAL, ANNY'S

April 7—Advertising Club of Westchester's third annual Westchester Advertising Trade Show, rescheduled after being snowed out. Free admission to exhibits, open from 10 am to 8 pm at the Westchester Ballroom of the Rye Town Hilton Hotel, off Exit 10 of the Cross Westchester Expressway. Lunch, with speaker Albert Heck, VP-national sales, Radio Advertising Bureau, $12.50 each for advance registration; $15 at door.

April 9–12—National Association of Broadcasters' annual convention, Las Vegas Convention Center.

April 10—Business/Professional Advertising Association's New York chapter's annual BestTeller Awards Program at the Summit Hotel. Luncheon begins at 11:30 am. For additional information, contact Hank Walshak at (212) 752-8610.

April 11—Mort Barish Associates' fourth Roundtable, with 100 business leaders participating. Princeton, N.J. For details, call (609) 924-7500.

April 11—Advertising Women of New York industry luncheon at the Hotel Pierre. Discussion of "Why should we love New York?" Guest speakers, Carol Bellamy and Ellen Fleysher. Members, $16; non-members, $18. Cocktails, 11:45; lunch, 12:15. For details, call (212) 593-1950.

April 12—American Society of Magazine Editors' 13th annual National Magazine Awards presentation and luncheon. Luncheon will be in the Grand Ballroom of The Pierre. $30 per person. Reservations to Peg Fogarty, Magazine Publishers Association, 575 Lexington Ave., New York, N.Y. 10022.

April 12—Advertising Club of New York sponsors Al Ries' Marketing warfare program at its monthly meeting for members and non-members. Social hour starts at 11:30; lunch at 12:30. At Club headquarters at 3 W. 51 St.

April 12—Television and Radio Advertising Club of Philadelphia's last seminar this season. Alvin A. Achenbaum speaks on how to overcome the rising costs of media, particularly tv. Poor Richard Club, 6 p.m. $5 fee includes dinner. For reservations, call Mary Connors at (215) LO8-6700.

April 12—American Women in Radio and Television's New York City chapter holds its last Ad Hoc luncheon this season, with Dorothy Sarnoff addressing the group on public speaking. By reservation only. $5 fee includes sandwiches and coffee. Dudley-Anderson-Yutzy, 40 W. 57 St., 19th floor, 12–2 p.m.

April 14–15—New York Women in Communications' 1978 regional meeting. Annual Matrix awards; Marlo Thomas speaks. Theme: "Making It. . . . Now." Waldorf-Astoria. For details, contact Nancy Tschirhart, Benton & Bowles, at (212) 758-6200.

April 15—American Marketing Association's New York Chapter's third annual college career conference on "Career Encounters of the Best Kind," Tisch Hall, NYU Campus, 40 W. 4 St., New York City, $6, including lunch. For additional information, call (212) 687-3280.

April 18—Television and Radio Advertising Club of Philadelphia's last TRAC luncheon of season. Chuck Bednarik talks on the Eagles. Ben Franklin Hotel, noon, $9.50. For reservations, call Mary Connors at (215) LO 8-6700.

---

their story to the business community, usually during breakfast and lunch hours.

Shows The prime purpose of exhibits is to raise professional standards. Winners are chosen from various categories among as many as 15,000 entries. The jury consists of experts in the field; in the case of the New York Art Directors Club's national competition, as many as seventy-five judges spend weeks at secret voting sessions. The selected print and TV ads are then displayed at one or more exhibits (usually upon payment of a self-liquidating hanging fee) and are reproduced on the pages of one of the several annuals issued every year.

Among the principal exhibits are the One Show of the Art Directors Club (open to both art directors and copywriters), the Society of Illustrators Annual Exhibition, the Advertising Club of New York Award of Excellence, the award of the American Institute of Graphic Arts (AIGA), the Clio Award Festivals, the International Broadcasting Award, and the Art Directions Creativity Show. Many others are sponsored by industries, associations, media, and some 300 local clubs all over the country, proving once again that New York has no exclusive claim on talent.

Trade exhibits In addition to advertising shows, there are exhibits representing a variety of product lines: jewelry, shoes and handbags, furniture, appliances, gift items, health foods, business machines, recreation, cars, boats, and so on. Most are held for the benefit of buyers and to promote interest within the trade, but almost anyone who really wants to get in can be a successful gate-crasher.

Through June 19: Type Directors Club show in AIGA Gallery, 1059 Third Ave., NYC.

Through June 29: "The Nude in American Art" showing at the New York Cultural Center, 2 Columbus Circle, NYC. Works include paintings by Benjamin West and John Singleton Copley, and range through to modern artists including Philip Pearlstein and Tom Wesselman.

Through July 3: "Portrait of a New York Art Director"—a composite portrait executed by Kit Hinrichs, who has prepared a questionnaire sent out to hundreds of ADs, and will display his results at the Art Directors Club, 488 Madison Ave., NYC.

Through July 6: "Appalachian Corridors Biennial 4" is a design show open to residents of any of the 13 Appalachian regional states. It includes categories in painting, sculpture, graphics, photography, crafts and folk art.

Through July 13: Yaacov Agam: Selected Suites—first New York showing by Israeli artist of five silk-screen graphics, each one reflecting the progression of each work in a suite. At the Jewish Museum, 1109 Fifth Ave., NYC.

Through June 29: The 80th Anniversary exhibition of the comic strip will be held at the Bronx Museum of the Arts, 851 Grand Concourse. Included are "Katzenjammer Kids" (Rudolph Dirks, 1917), "Mutt & Jeff," "Pogo," "Terry & The Pirates," "Lulu & Leander" (S. M. Howarth, 1906), and many others.

June 2 through July 15: Exhibition of the work of Antonio, the noted fashion illustrator, at F.I.T.'s Resources Center building on the corner of Seventh Avenue and West 27th Street.

AGENDA OF 2-DAY WORKSHOP CONDUCTED BY ADVERTISING AGE FOR ACCOUNT EXECUTIVES: "KEEP CLIENTS SATISFIED TO GET NEW BUSINESS"

First Day

A.M.

8:45 Registration

9:15 Welcome

9:30 "The Changing Role of Account Management"

10:15 "How to Service Accounts to Keep Them" ("The Account Executive's Primary Function"; "Accounts as Seen through the Eyes of an Ex-Client"; "Effective Account Handling, or How to Hold What You've Got")

P.M.

12:30 Luncheon

2:00 "How to Know If a Client Is Really Happy"

3:30 "How to Keep the Client Profitable"

5:00 Reception

5:45 Dinner ("How to Pick an Advertising Agency")

7:30 Rap sessions ("How to Keep Present Accounts and How to Get New Ones"):
Billings in excess of $20 million
Billings between $5 million and $20 million
Billings less than $5 million

Second Day

A.M.

9:00 "How to Search Out, Solicit, and Get New Clients"

11:30 Luncheon

P.M.

12:45 "Developing the Presentation Strategy and Making the Presentation"

3:45 Adjournment

Research Organizations

Most professional research organizations have their own methods of information gathering, which they have developed through the years. Generally, the data are collected through *interviews* (via telephone, on location, through focus groups), through *mailed questionnaires* (to a random or a preselected mailing list or to consumer panels on a major scale, with anywhere from 7500 to 10,000 families reporting), through a *direct-response mechanism* (degree of interest is measured by the number of coupon returns), through technological devices (TV set attachments), or through simulated selling situations (advertising in dummy magazines, on cable television, or in stores).

Research organizations are set up primarily to measure media and advertising effectiveness. In their sampling, they may include relatively large segments of the population (1000 or more persons) or small ones (a dozen housewives at a focus-group interview, typifying homogeneity or common interest). A few of the best-known research companies are listed here.

A. C. Nielsen Company The largest research organization, it operates worldwide. Its activities include Retail Index Services (syndicated and individual store audit studies), Media Research Services (mostly TV audience studies, both local and network), and Custom Research Lines (mostly interviewing via WATS lines). The company has equipped between 1150 and 1200 television sets in homes across the country (sufficient to attain an accuracy of more than 95 percent) with small electronic boxes, which, for the purpose of rating program popularity, indicate if the set is tuned in to certain programs. Information is available within 1 to 3 days or sometimes overnight. Nielsen also has compiled a demographically classified list of 2400 households that keep diaries of their TV-viewing schedules for a period of 2 weeks. This information is available within 9 days after survey completion.

Gallup & Robinson, Inc. Readership studies gave this organization an excellent background to test the effectiveness of television commercials. Through surveys conducted via telephone interviews (in which respondents are asked to reconstruct their viewing patterns in half-hour segments), the company also examines the viewers' subjective reactions to each commercial. One type of survey covers a random selection of 3000 households in the Philadelphia area; another covers twenty-four areas across the country. Verbatim playback profiles are provided. Gallup & Robinson will also develop tailor-made research projects, including in-theater testing arrangements.

Burke Marketing Research, Inc. Almost all research projects conducted by this company are custom-made, ad hoc, and based upon reaction to actual on-air television commercials. The usual sample is 200 viewers of the test program, which yields an average of 100 to 150 viewers actually watching a well-rated show. For economic reasons, the company is reluctant to check the effectiveness of commercials on low-rated shows. Interviewing times are flexible, so that advertisers can have playbacks from the type of audience which interests them most. Popular are the company's *flash scores,* reported by telephone on the morning following the test. Though computed hurriedly, these scores are accurate within 1 or 2 percentage points. They can be confirmed in about 3 days or on a Monday following a weekend test. All verbatim responses, related and unrelated, can be available within approximately 5 days following the interviews. Coded reports with summaries are completed 3 to 4 weeks from the date of the test. Burke's file on normative data, showing mean averages, is often used by agencies for making comparisons with competitive scores. Burke's testing methods are especially popular with creative people interested in qualitative data; they offer immediate and verbatim reactions of viewers to a commercial. This makes it possible to conduct interviews in selected markets and after only a single exposure to a commercial. The results can then be used to modify the creative content of the message or to take the commercial off the air.

Many advertisers feel that on the basis of this type of testing it is clearly possible to predict the success of a commercial with reasonable accuracy.

Schwerin Research Corporation This research organization believes that persuasion to purchase a product is the major criterion of success. A test situation is set up in theaters where films are interspersed with some commercials. The audience is picked at random unless the advertisers want research to use only their prime prospects. Brand preferences are subtly determined before and after the commercial is shown.

AdTel, Ltd. The technique of this company uses a dual-cable CATV system in three cities exposed to two balanced groups of 1200 each. The audience is asked to keep a weekly diary of all food, drug, and other appropriate product purchases. For purposes of testing, two different sets of commercials are cut in the same program, with the participating advertiser owning the time. Data are summarized in a 4-week report which describes in detail such factors as trial and repeat purchases, brand switching, demographics of users, attitudes, and awareness studies.

American Research Bureau, Inc. The rating service of this organization, Arbitron, measures and makes estimates of ADI markets (areas of dominant influence) 5 times a year. These include total and TV households, number of color sets, penetration, households with more than one TV set, cable subscribers, and type of available stations. Other demographic data are also available. This information is superimposed on share and rating figures, resulting in an audience profile (for example, the number of housewives from 18 to 34 in a given area watching a specific program during a specific time period).

Daniel Starch & Staff This organization is best known for its studies among consumer magazines, newspapers, and business publications. In general, it offers three ways of measuring print advertising: *noted* (degree of attention), *seen-associated* (sponsor identification), and *read-most* (percentage of readers who read 50 percent or more of the copy). Indicating the number of readers attracted by an advertisement for each dollar invested in the Readers-per-Dollar Index. The studies include television.

Inmarco Inc. Through its subsidiary, Audience Studies (ASI), this company has functioned primarily in the area of pre- and post-television-commercial testing in a theater in Los Angeles. ASI also does in-home testing of commercials and measures consumer reaction to magazine advertisements.

Other Organizations Among other organizations that conduct extensive marketing and public opinion studies are Yankelovich, Skelly and White, Inc.; National Analysts Inc.; Opinion Research Corp.; Roper Public Opinion Research Center; Market Facts, Inc., which maintains 70,000 household members divided into thirty-five separate panels; Social Research, Inc.; Benson & Benson, Inc.; Dun and Bradstreet, Inc.; Trendex, specialists in telephone surveys with 3000 interviewers covering 600 markets; and the Institute of Motivation Research (Ernest Dichter International).

THE TWENTY LARGEST MARKETING-ADVERTISING RESEARCH COMPANIES IN THE UNITED STATES

1. A. C. Nielsen Company	11. Marketing and Research Counselors, Inc.
2. I.M.S. International	12. Data Development Corp.
3. Sales Areas Marketing, Inc. (SAMI)	13. Ehrhart-Babic Associates, Inc.
4. Arbitron Co., Inc.	14. Westat, Inc.
5. Burke International Research Corp.	15. Yankelovich, Skelly and White, Inc.
6. Market Facts, Inc.,	16. NPD Research, Inc.
7. Booz, Allen & Hamilton, Inc.	17. Louis Harris & Associates, Inc.
8. Inmarco Inc.	18. Decisions Center, Inc.
9. Audits & Surveys Co., Inc.	19. Chilton Research Services
10. United States Testing Co., Inc.	20. Walker Research, Inc.

[*Reported in* Advertising Age, *April 1977*]

For an additional list of research companies, the reader may turn to the *Green Book,* a 134-page international directory published by the New York chapter of the American Marketing Association, or Stanley R. Greenfield's *National Directory of Addresses and Telephone Numbers* (Nicholas Publishing Co., Inc./Bantam Books, New York, Toronto, London).

MINIRESEARCH—GOOD ENOUGH FOR A START
Quick, inexpensive research (street interview lasting from 5 to 10 minutes by Penthouse U., Inc.,) was used to determine the validity of an idea for pet insurance developed by the author. Some 200 dog owners were shown this full-page newspaper layout. They were asked about the price they would be willing to pay for such a program and the extent of coverage they thought it should provide.

Dear Reader:

I am writing to ask for your help -- nothing more.

You see, for many years now we have been able to publish and offer a large number of very worthwhile, reasonably priced books to our Digest friends. We could do this because our subscribers have been kind enough to tell us -- in advance -- what subjects were of most interest to them. Naturally, producing only those books that we know our readers wish to own saves us money... and lets us give you greater value at lower prices.

As you will see on the following pages, we have briefly outlined six new books now in the planning stage here at Reader's Digest. Would you help us by indicating the book or books that most appeal to you? Of course, if none of the books appeal to you, please be frank and tell us so.

It will only take a few minutes of your time to answer our survey and return it to us in the self-addressed, postage-paid envelope we have provided. But I want to thank you right now for spending those few minutes with us, helping us decide which books will be of the greatest possible interest to you and other discriminating readers.

In order to make the results of this survey as complete as possible, as soon as possible, we would deeply appreciate your early reply to our questionnaire. We have used your name and address above merely for addressing purposes and your reply, of course, involves no commitment on your part at all.

Once again, our sincere thanks for your assistance in this important project. I can assure you it will help us continue to bring you what we consider to be the greatest bargains in reading pleasure on the market today.

Yours very truly,

Carolyn Davis

USING DIRECT MAIL TO TEST A NEW PRODUCT
Reader's Digest, with a circulation of more than 18 million, has compiled a mailing list of its subscribers that, for all practical purposes, serves the magazine as its own homemade consumers' panel. In one of its new-product explorations, the company made use of its audience to gather comments on a planned series of books (prior to their publication) and paintings (prior to going into mass reproduction). Summaries of the books were mailed out with an enclosed questionnaire; sample paintings were voted upon by the public at art showings.

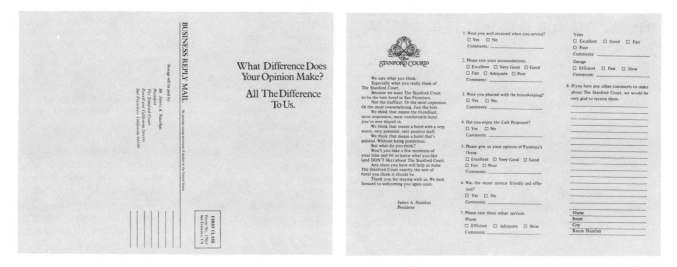

ASK THE USER: He knows better than anyone how he or she feels about the quality of service.

MUSIC/VOICE-OVER: (MALE VOICE)
Va-room . . . va-room . . . va-room . . .

Va-room . . . va-room . . . va-room . . .

Va-room . . . va-room . . . va-room . . .

MUSIC STING

MUSIC/SINGERS: Kawasaki lets the good times roll. Let the good times roll.

(FEMALE VOICE) Va-room . . . . . . va-room!

TYPICAL VERBATIM RESPONSES TO A KAWASAKI TV COMMERCIAL

The following on-air recall test was conducted by Burke Marketing Research, Inc., via telephone interviewing.

1. *a.* This fellow was in his garage like he was riding his motorcycle.
   b. He was in his night clothes and he was wearing a helmet.
   c. His wife was looking at him from the doorway like he had lost his marbles.
   d. It's a lot of fun to own a Kawasaki. So much fun that the people who own them can't wait til the next day to ride them.
2. *a.* He was sitting in the garage on his motorcycle. He was making noises like a motorcycle with his mouth.
   b. His wife watched that nut from the doorway. He was dressed in his pajamas and a helmet.
   c. That fun begins with a ride in a Kawasaki.
   d. He was sure crazy about his motorcycle. He'd like to ride it even during the night.
3. *a.* There was a guy in a garage and he was trying to ride his motorcycle right into the garage.
   b. He had a helmet on and pajamas and was barefoot. His wife thought he was nuts.
   c. Something about happy riding, that's all I can remember.

d. That the guy was so nuts about his motorcycle he couldn't sleep.
4. *a.* A woman walked out and looked in the garage and saw her husband on a Kawasaki cycle in his robe and night clothes. He was pretending to be riding the bike without even turning it on.
   b. She looked at him and laughed and he kept doing it.
   c. Don't remember any words. Kawasaki makes the good times roll.
   d. Looked to me like it was trying to strike the older people, opening up the motorcycle market to them.
   e. They try to instill the thought that you want to ride a motorcycle any time of day or night.
5. *a.* A guy sitting there on a motorcycle in his bathrobe with his helmet on going rum, rum, and he spots his wife in the rear view mirror.
   b. She was in curlers. She pulled her glasses off. The motorcycle was on stand, it was not running.
   c. All I can remember is the music Kawasaki lets the good times roll. That's all I can remember.
   d. It was trying to tell you that riding a motorcycle can be fun. I thought it was clever.
6. *a.* He was sitting out on a motorcycle and his wife was standing in the door laughing.
   b. Well, that's all I remember.
   c. Making sounds like a motorcycle like he was the motor.
   d. I don't know, I guess that it would be fun to have one.
7. *a.* The man in the garage was pantomiming the operation of a motorcycle.
   b. The wife came out and made some teasing remarks and then he went back to his playing.
   c. I heard only the noise of the motorcycle.
   d. It was a fun type vehicle. The wife does not object and lets the husband enjoy himself.
8. *a.* A guy was sitting in his garage on his motorcycle pretending he was driving it, simulating the sound of the motor. During which time his wife appeared at the garage door in her nightgown and indicated her understanding and also made the motor sound.
   b. A man, his wife, a motorcycle,

and the garage.

   c. I can't recall.

   d. The desire to have a Kawasaki and the enjoyment it gives even when not driving it. Just being with it.

9. *a.* The guy just sat on the bike and made noises.

   b. He was just making noises like he was really going and then his wife came in.

   c. I didn't hear any words.

   d. I can't say.

10. *a.* It was plain stupid. It showed an idiot riding a motorcycle in a garage.

   b. Too stupid to remember.

   c. Nothing really.

   d. None.

11. *a.* A husband was out in the garage on a motorcycle in his pajamas.

   b. I don't know.

   c. I don't know.

   d. I don't know.

12. *a.* It was pretty stupid. Most commercials are stupid. They insult the intelligence of the public. For instance last night. Where do you find a guy in his pajamas going out to the garage to ride his motorcycle. Now don't you think that's pretty stupid?

   b. No, nothing else. I just remember it was stupid.

   c. His wife said ''vroom, vroom.'' That's all.

   d. D. K.

13. *a.* N. A.

   b. A man sitting on a bike in the garage.

   c. D. K.

   d. I don't care about motorcycles. I'm 58.

14. *a.* A man was in a garage on a motorcycle in a robe with a helmet on. The motorcycle was on a stand. It was late at night.

   b. He was making a motion like driving. He turned the light on. A woman came in and he saw her out of the rear window.

   c. The woman made a noise like the roar of the motorcycle.

   d. People fascinated by motorcycles will even go out in the middle of the night to ride one.

15. *a.* The man was in the garage sitting on his motorcycle.

   b. I don't remember.

   c. I had the sound turned down.

   d. I'm not sure. I wasn't watching that close.

[Courtesy of Cunningham & Walsh]

SOMETHING NEW ON THE HORIZON: COMPUTERIZED RESEARCH

Superabundance of information in this day and age makes it almost impossible to get all the facts from a single source. To be sure, attempts are made to make this feasible, saving time and probably money for the researcher. Several companies specialize in gathering and, if needed, analyzing data tailor-made for clients. Trained personnel and modern technology are used to speed up the process.

To illustrate the point, the questions below were answered by Lockheed's dialogue information-retrieval service. This is one of the several sophisticated computer centers available to the curious for a fee and—in a very literal sense—the asking. It uses more than 5 million citations, abstracts, and other forms of business information from twenty data bases across the country, covering a wide range of topics.

Others offering similar types of services are Control Data (New York), Ayer Information Center (Philadelphia), FIND/SVP (New York), Information for Business (New York), Interel (Washington), and—the largest, busiest, and least expensive of all—the Government Printing Office (Washington).

Advertising What is the impact of advertising on children? Is direct-mail promotion effective in product-introduction campaigns? What are the effects of postal rate hikes on direct-mail advertising? What is the real benefit of point-of-sale advertising for consumer products?

Area Planning And Development Is the new-town concept dead? What are the trends in green space and density planning in planned unit developments? What are blue-collar workers' attitudes toward mass transit? Is the BART concept of San Francisco applicable to other metropolitan areas in the United States?

Banking What are the best bank-marketing techniques in times of inflation? What impact will the electronic funds transfer system (EFTS) have on bank charge cards? Is cross training of tellers effective? Should we choose career apparel for our employees? Should we consider becoming a bank-holding company? What kind of impact have automated tellers had on branching?

Economics What should a United States company know about economic planning in Canada? What impact does the Australian economy have upon the United States? Should we hire a corporate economist? What could we expect from him or her?

Finance What are the best procedures for financial budgeting in a divisionalized firm? How can we evaluate our capital-appropriations systems? What are capital-financing costs and alternatives for an industrial firm?

Insurance Captive insurance companies: Yes? No? Where? The impact of no-fault automobile insurance on court systems: Will it really save money and time? Selecting, hiring, training, and keeping the best life insurance salesperson: How do we go about it? What are the best direct marketing techniques for selling life, health, and accident insurance?

Law What has been the record of the consumer-product safety commission? Does it really work? What are states and cities doing about restricted-smoking zones in public areas? What are an employer's rights during an Equal Employment Opportunity Commission (EEOC) investigation?

Marketing How can bank marketing best use premium offers? How can we best promote oil and gas drilling ventures to the broadest possible market? The best design of a marketing information system: How do we determine its application in our firm?

Market Research Are our consumer testing parties worth the expense? Is there an adequate consumer behavioral model for our line of industrial products?

Watching the Consumer React

Reading about the consumer is one thing; seeing a live reaction is something else. Wise are the creative practitioners who make it their business to observe their audience in action, as during focus-group interviews (through a one-way mirror or direct contact), from behind a counter (as a salesperson), or in the aisles of a store.

If In Doubt, Ask the Supplier

An excellent source of information is the outside services that work closely with advertising agencies. They know a great deal about what is happening in their field. In an attempt to assist clients, they will gladly share their knowledge, as long as they feel that they are not being maneuvered into giving away confidential information. Media salesmen can be especially helpful in this respect.

Most executives try to stay in close touch with suppliers and even pay an occasional visit to their places of business. This is a good way to keep up with the latest technological developments.

These are places of particular interest to the creative advertising professional:

Television Studio or Location Shooting Producing television commercials is a complicated procedure. Find out for yourself why it takes a day or more to produce 30 seconds of film.

Recording Studio Hear how sound tracks (sometimes as many as half a dozen) are put together.

Editing and Optical Houses; Laboratories Watch "takes" being spliced into a continuous scene and finally into a television commercial.

Tape Studio Razzle-dazzle video technology in action. Editing is done on the spot electronically.

Art Studio See type proofs, artwork, photography, and other elements take shape as a print ad.

Engraver's Plant Watch pictures, type, and mechanicals gingerly cut into hard metal by a skilled technician.

Offset Lithography House Find out for yourself why this method of reproduction is gaining in popularity so rapidly.

Type Shop To keep up with typography, both artistically (new typefaces are constantly being added to existing fonts) and technologically (photocomposition is taking over old-fashioned typesetting), this is the place to go.

Printing Plant Flat color or process color—it all happens before your eyes.

Photographer's Studio See firsthand why the person behind the camera is more important than the camera.

Advertising Agency A plethora of creativity packed under one roof.

Mailing Distribution House distributing thousands of mailing pieces is not the same as mailing a postcard to the folks back home. Checking over responses, addressing envelopes, computerizing messages, and collating material call for special machinery.

If In Doubt, Ask the Client

Perhaps the client may not be as familiar with the physical nuances that go into the preparation of an ad (such as the use of white space in a layout, camera lighting techniques, and the variety of typefaces available) as some creative people would like him to be, but there is a lot he or she *does* know.

Consider the client an expert in the following areas:

1. *Product*. Application, R&D activities, and product features.

2. *Competition*. Nature of competition and its selling techniques, distribution, and market share.

3. *The company*. Experience, corporate policies, and organization.

4. *Employees*. Responsibilities, backgrounds, and record with the company.

5. *Sales*. Volume, retail markup, compensation methods, incentive plans, and type of sales force and its response to the advertising campaign.

6. *Distribution*. Geographical, retail, and wholesale channels.

7. *Consumers*. Quantity and quality.

8. *Finances*. Profit and loss, A/S ratio, and future plans.

9. *Past advertising experience*. Characteristic of the company.

PROBLEM-DETECTION TECHNIQUE AS USED BY BBDO

E. E. Norris, executive vice president of BBDO, explains the logic behind the firm's research technique this way:

> Consumers are not creative. The presumption is that they will tell you something you don't already know. They won't.
>
> What they will tell you is what you have already told them. For instance, if you ask a consumer what they want in a dandruff-remover shampoo, they will say they want a shampoo that removes dandruff. This will not make you King of R & D. . . .
>
> Thirty-five years ago, they would not have been able to tell that they wanted an automatic stick shift. But even then they could have told you that messing around with the stick shift was hard both on the car and the driver. Consumers can only tell you their problems, not the solutions. It's up to you to take it from there.

On the basis of this premise, the agency developed its own way to find out what it is the consumer really wants. The technique is called problem detection. The approach simply puts *consumer benefit* (what is in it for the consumer) ahead of *product attribute* (what is in it for the manufacturer).

Two basic steps are involved. The first is to develop a thorough list of possible consumer problems, which is then carefully checked out with prime prospects and expert marketers and against existing information. However, because the variety of marketing and technical considerations (such as manufacturing lead time and investment required, distribution, warehousing, advertising support, and impact of competition) is not always immediately apparent to laymen, not everyone's reaction is taken at face value.

The second step is to put the consumer problems in order of importance. To do that, a panel of about 150 prime prospects is asked to evaluate each problem in the following manner: (a) whether they think the problem is important, (b) whether the problem occurs frequently in their experience, and (c) whether they are aware of some existing product or service which already has solved the problem.

The answers are evaluated on the basis of importance and computed into a single number.

The larger the score, the more attractive the marketing opportunity it represents.

HOW FOOTE, CONE & BELDING ENCOURAGES ITS CREATIVE PEOPLE TO LEARN ABOUT CONSUMERS' WANTS

Periodically, in the Chicago office of Foote, Cone & Belding, artists and writers are requested to make a series of randomly selected telephone calls to consumers to conduct structured interviews. The calls start at 5 P.M. and continue until each caller has filled out his or her questionnaire. The returns are handed in the next day for expert analysis.

Reports Joe Cappo, marketing columnist in the *Chicago Daily News* about the results:

Foote Cone & Belding's Daily Survey has turned into a veritable source of information. If the account executive wants to check consumer attitudes or awareness of a competitor's advertising, he shoots the request to the manager of research services. Questions are evaluated, pre-tested, put into the questionnaires, and within two or three days, the account man then has some very fresh research.

[*Courtesy of* Madison Avenue Magazine]

GOING OUTSIDE THE IVORY TOWER: THE CLASSIC "MEN FROM CUNNINGHAM & WALSH" CAMPAIGN

The value of personal contact with the consumer has not been overlooked by Cunningham & Walsh. Historically, the agency was among the first to have its writers, artists, and account executives go out and work systematically in the field. Depending on his or her interest and job responsibility, each person had the option of choosing his or her own territory: a supermarket or an appliance, department, or fashion store. After a stint of 1 to 2 weeks, the working experience served as a basis for a written report to be circulated among the departments in the agency. Reproduced below are some of the comments made by art director, John Forzaglia.

Office Memorandum
From: John Forzaglia
Re: Man from Cunningham & Walsh
        Texaco Service Station

General: A four-pump station located on a triangular block facing Boston Post Road (a truck route), and Burke Avenue in the Bronx. Five men operate this station in two shifts from 6 A.M. to 11 P.M, daily. It is *not* a company station but one of three owned by Dan Battaglino and each is operated by partners. Dan started with The Texas Company as a truck driver twenty-three years ago. One of his stations, about half a mile from where I was, is very close to a Shell and an Esso Station, which makes competition on this truck route very keen. . . .

This station does more business than the other two. I kept busy—everything from wiping windshields to greasing my own car on my last day there. I asked many questions about cars and they answered by giving me jobs which required a bit of know-how. I *didn't* know how but they were very patient and I learned. I fixed at least 12 flats (with one tube put in backwards), assisted the mechanic by cleaning parts on brake jobs, oil changes, grease jobs, testing batteries and wrote out charge bills. All in all, I was busy and enjoyed every minute of it.

The Station has been at this location for five years. Until three months ago it was a lonely shack with an outside car lift. The winters were hard on the men. Now The Texas Company has built an enclosure and are working on a 32-foot neon sign for the top of the building. The men are pleased and take an added interest in keeping the place looking neat. A final paint job and it will look like a bright new penny.

The Men: Sal Mondello—the partner who operates this station. He knows his manuals and keeps up with all the Trade Journals. When new cars come in, he carefully studies make-up of new features and how to repair them. He also is aware of what competition is doing—probably because of Dan Battaglino who constantly talks about it and sees it daily in the Shell and Esso stations next to his. Sal makes good use of a mailing list. He sends out monthly mailing pieces featuring everything from special prices on checkups to announcements of new products. He estimates they spend 10 to 15% of their profits for local advertising.

Dominick—the master mechanic. This man is very confident in his work and, without speaking, conveys this confidence to a customer who watches him while he works. He is thorough and will go ahead with necessary repair work ignoring the cost. Sometimes this results in a customer not wanting to pay his bill for work not requested but usually the customer is made to realize that it was necessary for his safety and all turns out well.

Louis—mechanic and grease and oil man—a very friendly guy who does all repair work when Dom is off or needs help.

Harry, Toni and *Frank*—grease and oil men but mainly gas attendants. Most of their free time is spent working on old engines for practice.

Politeness is the keyword at a service station. When these men are not rushed, they are eager to spend time with a customer explaining auto problems. If a battery goes dead, they explain its make-up and methods used in testing, plus an explanation of how the testing equipment works. Would you believe that there are at least 10 different units that can be used to test a battery's strength?

The men do have a major complaint about their own appearance. It seems they do not have enough Texaco uniforms or a constant source of supply, Not knowing what kind of set-up Texaco has concerning uniforms, I told them I would look into the matter. They said they would be willing to pay for the service (if it exists) providing it's not too costly. If Texaco has such a service, I would like to inform them of it.

Charge Accounts. When the men are busy, they dislike writing out a charge bill—it takes too long and rushing can produce errors. Harry suggests a charge plate that can be inserted into a machine and stamped leaving only the amount and product to be filled out. My suggestion is to send each customer a book with a price list in it which can be filled out prior to going to a station for gas, similar to a checkbook idea. Then he gives the attendant the filled-out bill which tells at a glance how much gas the customer wants; when his tank is filled he drives off—no waiting. Also the customer has a better record in his book of what he has paid and what he owes.

Customers: Most customers with new cars ask for Hi-Test, while many old cars take regular. Yet I found that young customers with old cars asked for Hi-Test, probably for the extra power. Most, if not all, customers use the terms Hi-Test or regular. Once a customer starts using a brand of gas, he will not change if he is satisfied unless, as one Texaco customer pointed out, he was stuck near a Shell station—and even then he was reluctant to use a different gas in his tank. This leads me to believe that a good deal of advertising should be directed to young people who are about to start driving.

Most customers want to be present when any repair work is done including grease and oil changes.

Display Material: A five-foot display shelf for Gould Batteries was assembled after lying around for a month. These men don't mind intricate display pieces—in fact they love the "do-it-yourself" kits. All they require is time. So, if necessary, give them complicated pieces but send them early. Sal said that Texaco keeps him well supplied with direct mail pieces like decals, banners and folders. They have a banner up on the building supplied by the company, but, for the size of the building, it is not large enough to be impressive.

KELLY, NASON: HERE IS HOW WE DO IT (GOING TO THE SOURCE)

Rough ads like this, not concept ads, are shown to the consumer, leaving less room for subjective interpretation.

We want consumers to tell our creative people how they feel about our new product ideas or our advertising approaches before it is too late and too expensive to discard, correct, or improve them.

We want to hear their point of view directly, not filtered through a hired, "professional" interviewer who may lose the important nuances in interpretation. So we do the work ourselves. Writers, art directors, the account group, media buyers, top, middle and lower management in a give-and-take dialogue with real, live consumers.

Unlike most research organizations, we work in the homes of average, middle-class people where respondents can relax. Not in office buildings where they feel like research "subjects."

We do not use one-way mirrors. Most people have seen them on Candid Camera or Mission Impossible, anyway.

We find we get closest to the consumer's true feelings by being open and direct. People do not really buy things from "concept cards." The medium of communication between manufacturers and consumers is a form of advertising, so we show our ideas in the form of ads. Rough ads, to save time and money.

We have one of us sit at a dining room table with eight or nine consumers, and in between munching on coffee-cake, we show the ads. We get their quick instinctive reactions, lots of rejection, some approval.

The rest of us who are sitting in the room are listening. When one of us has a question, we send it in with a "runner." We're all provided with 8½ × 11 photocopies of the ads under scrutiny. We are making notes right on the ads simultaneously with the panelists' comments. If one of us gets an idea for a new ad as a result of the carnage taking place, it is quickly sketched and sent in.

After all the ads have been shown and discussed, the moderator takes the ads away, and hands out little white cards. He or she asks the panelists to jot down the things they remember from all the ads they have seen. Not "liked" or "disliked," just remembered. They are only given a moment, so it is strictly top-of-mind. They are also asked to indicate whether they are interested in buying the product in the ads, and if so, why. It is all anonymous. No respondents' names on the cards, so they are free to reject the ads or the product.

Very often the ads they "liked" are forgotten. Not newsworthy enough, perhaps, while more controversial ads have excellent recall.

The moderator probes these contradictions and obtains some additional comments.

After an hour and a half or so, it is over. We go to lunch and compare notes and reactions. Some new ideas emerge and are sketched for the afternoon panel. We spend a day or two like this every week or every other week on each project. By the time ten or twelve weeks have passed, we generally have discovered and discarded every wrong approach to selling the product.

What remains is good. It has survived the scrutiny of hundreds of consumers. It has been shaped and modified by their comments, and it has been *remembered;* people want to buy the product.

Last year, Kelly, Nason people talked to about fifteen thousand other people in this manner, in several dozen cities across the country.

It seems to work.

And as a bonus, our creative people—artists and writers assigned to the task—will gain new insights into their audience: what makes them buy or not buy.

There is a lot that people reveal in comfortable give and take situations. No written reports can ever take the place of this experience.

THE WAY IT GOES AT A TYPICAL FOCUS GROUP INTERVIEW

Conducted by Tony Wainwright of Wainwright, Spaeth & Wright, Chicago, for *Advertising Age,* March 3, 1975.

ROSE: I sat down with my husband the other night. I do not use that much sugar in baking. Most of my cookies are without sugar. Or they take half a cup of sugar.

MARVELLA: People during the holidays were complaining because of Christmas baking. They do use a tremendous amount.

LINDA: I use a little brown sugar and powdered sugar. I sat down and really thought about it, and normally my consumption of sugar, if I came down to it, even with holiday baking, is 15 lbs. a year.

WAINWRIGHT: Are you doing anything different, Sandra?

SANDRA: I think so. You know, before I would make a lot of roasts. Now you don't even think about that, except maybe once a week. Now we have more ground meat recipes.

WAINWRIGHT: You add anything to it?

EILEEN: No.

WAINWRIGHT: What's a box mix?

EILEEN: Hamburger Helper!

LINDA: You can do a lot more yourself. You pay 79¢ for noodles.

ALMA: Where I shop, they've been giving us a new cook book each week. So I've been trying some of the things in there. It's nothing you'd buy a mix for. You make it all yourself.

KATHY: Like a meatloaf.

WAINWRIGHT: How about side dishes? Anybody serving them?

ROSE: Oh, yes.

WAINWRIGHT: More or about the same?

ROSE: I'm serving less. Of course, they are very expensive so you don't save much.

WAINWRIGHT: What is there today?

We Now Buy Pop Only Once a Week

LINDA: Well, the only thing I can say is we're just eating cheaper cuts of meat. I haven't had a steak since I can't remember when. But I have two teen age sons, and it's hard to tell them: You eat this piece of meat—you don't get any more. You just can't say this to kids.

KATHY: All of a sudden you don't have the cookies and snacks in the house. Buy pop once a week instead of every time it runs out. All these things are changing.

LINDA: I've found what I've done—we get paid twice a month. So my big shopping is twice a month, and I really go in for nothing else but milk and eggs. After they have gone through what I have bought, that's it.

SANDRA: I also find I buy things on sale. If it's something I use, I will buy two, because I know when I run out it's going to be up in price.

MARVELLA: And then, don't you shop the specials of the week?

SANDRA: If it's something I use, yes.

WAINWRIGHT: What about private labels?

ALMA: A lot of them are a lot better.

LINDA: Oh, I got some Del Monte string beans the other day, and they were about half full of string beans and were about the worst tasting stuff, so I just swore off Del Monte right there.

ROSE: The only way you can beat it—is to do comparison shopping. I would suggest you look at the ads on Thursday nights and go to the A&P, go to the Jewel. You have to hit all the stores.

EILEEN: By that time, you've wasted a day.

SANDRA: That's the only way you can beat the game. Like I work. I don't have that kind of time for it. I'm better off sticking to one store.

Ground Turkey Is Cheap

MARVELLA: Make chili, Sloppy Joes. And then the macaroni.

LINDA: You can jazz up anything—a meatloaf, even.

EILEEN: I think you get tired of it, though.

SANDRA: I've been buying ground turkey because that's cheap, but I'm getting tired of that, too. I'd like a good roast.

WAINWRIGHT: How about that soy protein?

KATHY: I've used that. You know, my husband couldn't tell the difference.

MARVELLA: I'll tell you what I've done. I make my spaghetti sauce, but when I cook the soy beans I use the packaged spaghetti flavoring in the water. Then I add that into my spaghetti sauce with maybe ½ lb. of ground meat or my chili sauce and this just extends it.

REACHING THE CUSTOMER THROUGH HIS BELIEF CLUSTERS: THE D'ARCY—MACMANUS & MASIUS METHOD

On the basis of the fact that a person's feelings dictate his or her behavior, the agency developed its own unique approach to consumer research, called belief dynamics. The results are used to launch many of its campaigns.

Here is how belief dynamics works. First, users are classified by their roles (housewives, businessmen, engineers). This is followed by psychologically oriented research, enabling the agency to subdivide prospects on the basis of their belief clusters. Care is taken not to confuse superficial behavioral patterns ("He drives the car to work every morning") with more deep-seated feelings ("All Detroit cars wear out in 6 years"). The prototype emerging from the study is written up and handed over to the creative people as the definitive target. He or she is the prime user of the product.

Belief clusters are much influenced by shifts in public opinion. Some years ago, the words "Made in Japan" had a negative connotation, making Oriental imports difficult to market in the United States. However, the American disposition to forgive one's enemies (to bury the hatchet) soon changed all that. Today Sony, Datsun, Toyota, Honda, Panasonic, Kawasaki, Fuji, and other Japanese products all have achieved full acceptance in the United States.

Here a struggling car-rental company took shrewd advantage of an existing belief cluster which really had nothing to do with the product itself. With Americans always rooting for the underdog, the Avis Number Two campaign apparently struck a responsive chord among thousands of advertising watchers. The same approach probably could have failed in other parts of the world where being second best tends to be equated with admission of defeat.

Go to the Unlikely Places

Such places as:

Political fund-raising dinners, where the decision makers and takers meet.

Singles bars, where conversation flows with the drinks, and vice versa.

Discothèques, where the only sound you hear is noise.

Churches, where people go to feel good in their souls.

Hospitals, where people go to feel good in their bodies.

Revival meetings, where people go to let go.

Fashion shows, where the looks of the outfit are often more important than the one who wears it.

Porno shops, where the curious go to examine curiosa.

X-rated movies, where the audience can be more interesting than the show.

Live nude shows, where body language is eloquently spoken.

Very expensive restaurants, where people go to see and be seen.

Very inexpensive restaurants, where people go to eat but not necessarily to be seen.

Public demonstrations, where people go to hear and be heard.

Night courts, where routine is no longer routine.

Rock festivals, where the young are young.

Country clubs, where traditions are adhered to.

College campuses, where traditions are done away with.

Auctions, where salesmanship is the entertainment.

Country fairs, where the folks go to enjoy themselves.

Gambling casinos, where the only difference between losers and winners is luck.

Flea markets, where impulse buying reigns supreme.

Bus depots, where people look like the kind that would be riding buses.

Schools Are for Everybody

Schools in any large metropolitan area offer several courses in the field of advertising and marketing, such as research, media, layout, production, and writing. In addition, there are a variety of related subjects to choose from. Photography, magazine publishing, interior decorating, fashion, film making, art, literature, business law, economics, acting, dancing, music, architecture, tax accounting, and speed reading (or a more recent shortcut to omniscience, speed learning) are some of them. And there is nothing that says that advertising students must limit their interests to related subjects; the broader their interests, the better their chances to succeed in the field.

It should be emphasized here that it pays to continue one's education. Nothing should deter advertising practitioners from doing so. Least of all, the fact that they are "through" with their schooling. More than 40 million adults are back in the classrooms today. According to the American Management Association, at least 50,000 of these are executives. Another point: 1 out of 10 of the nation's 11 million college students now is at least 35 years old. Weekend colleges, which usually run from Friday evening to Sunday afternoon, are getting increasingly popular. Students' ages range from 19 to 57. "Older people are good people to teach," says Dr. Aaron Warner, dean of the School of General Studies at Columbia University. Another dean at the same institution agrees: "We find them highly motivated, very thoughtful people and usually highly intelligent. Their life experience is rich."

Some people go as far as to return to the school of their choice full time. Taking a leave of absence from one's job is one way to do it. It is good to know that several corporations support the idea of employees' taking such sabbaticals and even help them by paying part of the tuition (to mention a few, Kimberly-Clark, International Business Machines, Equitable Life Assurance Society of the United States, and Merrill Lynch, Pierce, Fenner & Smith). Clearly, they feel that on-the-job training does not offer the same learning experience as do schools and that the two work hand in hand.

Here is a partial list of colleges and universities offering full-time courses in marketing, advertising, and communications:

University of Alabama
Arizona State University
Northern Arizona University
University of Arkansas at Little Rock
Californa State University, Fresno
California State University, Fullerton
San Jose State University
University of Colorado
University of Bridgeport
Florida State University
Florida Technological University
University of Florida
University of South Florida
University of Georgia
Northern Illinois University
Northwestern University
Roosevelt University
Southern Illinois University
University of Illinois
Ball State University
Indiana University
Drake University
University of Iowa
University of Kansas
University of Kentucky
Western Kentucky University
Louisiana State University
University of Maryland
Boston University
Ferris State College
Michigan State University
Western Michigan University
University of Minnesota
University of Southern Mississippi
Lincoln University
University of Missouri
Creighton University
University of Nebraska
University of Nebraska at Omaha
University of Nevada
Fairleigh Dickinson University
Glassboro State College
New Mexico State University
City College of New York
Columbia University
Hunter College
Iona College
Long Island University — Brooklyn Center
New School of Social Research
New York University
Pace University
School of Visual Arts
Pratt Institute
St. John's University
Syracuse University
University of North Carolina
Bowling Green State University
University of Dayton
Kent State University
Ohio University

Youngstown State University
Oklahoma State University
University of Oklahoma
University of Tulsa
University of Oregon
Pennsylvania State University
University of Rhode Island
University of South Carolina
South Dakota State University
Memphis State University
University of Tennessee
East Texas State University
Texas Christian University
Texas Technological University
University of Texas
Brigham Young University
Virginia Commonwealth University
University of Washington
West Virginia University
Marquette University
University of Wisconsin
University of Wisconsin, Eau Claire
University of Wisconsin, Oshkosh

The above list is based on a booklet of colleges which teach advertising, compiled by Donald G. Hileman and Billy I. Ross. Other helpful back-to-school books are *Bricker's International Directory of University-sponsored Executive Development Programs* and James Cass and Marx Birnbaum's *Comparative Guide to American Colleges* (Harper & Row Publishers, Incorporated, New York). Several professional associations also offer courses, usually after office hours, in advertising, marketing, media, art, copy, and related subjects.

Not surprisingly, most leading schools offering adult education courses are located in major metropolitan areas such as New York, Chicago, Los Angeles, and Atlanta. The largest ones are New York University's School of Continuing Education and the New School for Social Research, both in New York City. Trailing these two giants are such eager competitors as Columbia University, Hunter College, and Marymount Manhattan College.

Several professional associations also offer courses, usually after office hours, in advertising, marketing, media, art, copy, research, and related subjects. Classes are usually conducted by executives from various fields whose knowledge comes from first-hand encounters with everyday business problems.

85

Yes, Ask Your Family and Friends

In advertising circles, the remark "His wife didn't like it" is still being bandied about as the ultimate put-down. There may be some justification in that; certainly, conclusions based upon offhand, one-person research projects are much too subjective to be taken at face value. However, this does not mean that members of one's own household should be left in the cold. Wives, children, and relatives are as well qualified to offer an opinion as anyone else is. Most products are used in the home. Moreover, the open relationship among family members and good friends usually encourages honest, straightforward give-and-take, perhaps more so than opinions collected by printed questionnaires or street interviews.

If a family member is displeased with the product or the way it is advertised, it may pay to find out what problems he or she has encountered. To paraphrase David Ogilvy's famous remark, "The wife you're talking to could be your customer."

In evaluating opinions one should carefully consider the respondent's life-style, education, income, and other variables before jumping to conclusions.

However, once the background has been accounted for, there is no reason why the feelings of those we feel closest to should not be taken seriously.

Shop a Little at Your Favorite Store

It is wise for advertising executives to stop off at their favorite supermarkets at least once a week and at a department store once a month. It is at the point of purchase that final decisions are being made. Watch closely. Do all shoppers stop and read the labels? Do they read the price codes? Are shoppers (particu-larly women in skirts) willing to bend down and look for merchandise on the lower shelves? How much are store employees able to influence purchasing decisions? Is it true that children bully their parents into buying? How do people ask for products? By name? By description? By function? How many male shoppers, as opposed to female, are in a supermarket? What type of product or which particular brand is most often rejected after a cursory examination? Do price-off promotions work? Does everyone accept trading stamps at the check-out counter? What about displays? Are they effective? Are they properly used by the store owner—the way their creators hoped they would be?

And what is going on in other types of stores? Do customers know what they want in a hardware store, or do they look to the clerk as the handyman in residence for advice? What types of women visit boutiques? Discount houses? Specialty outlets? Car and furniture showrooms? Are most automobile-purchase decisions made by singles or by couples? Who makes the final decision in buying furniture, he or she?

Particularly interesting are the differences—and they are substantial—in buying-decisions made for small-ticket package goods and big-ticket luxury items. For one thing, brand loyalty in the latter category is much lower. Purchases are seldom made impulsively or routinely as is the case with products the consumer considers more of a "necessity."

You will find that people differ greatly in their buying habits. Interesting, too, are the differences among stores, even if they display the same product line. It is the little things that give stores a unique personality.

Store owners usually have plenty to say about their stores, their selling techniques, their merchandise, and their philosophy, but their point of view is likely to be somewhat colored by the fact that they have a personal interest in their own stores. Only firsthand experience offers the type of information they need to create effective advertising.

WHAT A VISIT TO THE STORE CAN TEACH THE OBSERVER ABOUT PURCHASING DECISION-MAKING

This advertisement, featuring a glass of gusty beer, catches the eye—and sets the reader's thirsting taste buds agoing. Here, the purchasing decision-making process is a relatively uncomplicated one.

Buying a high-ticket item, such as a car, requires considerably more forethought. Rarely do people buy on impulse the first car they see in the showroom; the decision may be the result of months, and sometimes years, of careful deliberation.

Take a Bite of the Big Apple

Whatever your opinion of New York City happens to be (and you may be happy to learn that Fun City is not on the top of everyone's list; Boyden Associates, an executive recruiting firm, found that, in order of preference, San Francisco, Atlanta, Los Angeles, Boston, and Dallas were deemed more desirable by the majority of out-of-town business people), if you are in the advertising field, you owe it to yourself to spend some time in this hub of activity. More than half of all advertising agencies are located here, and 9 out of 10 are among the world's largest. Only Hollywood accommodates a larger number of film makers. The vast majority of leading publishers and network television studios are located in Manhattan, many within walking distance of each other.

Nor must a visitor to New York limit his sight-seeing to business-related events. Within a bus ride are nearly 100 theaters and major movie houses, more than 1000 churches, some 40 major colleges, universities, and professional institutes, 20 important music centers, close to 100 extensive libraries, some of the most exciting stores (large and small) in the world, more than 50 museums, approximately 600 antique dealers, and more than 300 art galleries. On any given day during the fall, winter, and spring, something like 250 exhibitions in galleries and museums in the city and surrounding areas beckon the curious. Such a variety of activities can boggle the mind and, if nothing else, stimulate it into action.

Moreover, the city is a favorite gathering place of creative people, including some of the most celebrated in the world. Of an estimated 74,000 United States advertising-agency people. 24,000 or about one-third, are employed in Manhattan. More than 1000 artists and art studios make their homes here, along with some 2000 commercial photographers and 300 theatrical and modeling agencies. This is not to suggest that all the talent in New York is top or that all top talent is in New York. It is only that, with so many luminaries lighting up the streets in a small area, the likelihood of having personal dealings with one increases proportionately.

In short, New York proves once again that nothing breeds creativity as much as more creativity. Fierce competition makes everyone work faster, harder, and probably more effectively—and perhaps more desperately at times.

This, of course, raises the philosophical question of whether the pressure of working in the big city is worth the effort. It is not within the scope of this book to discuss such a highly personal issue; suffice it to say that apparently many people find New York a major attraction while others prefer to stay as far away from it as possible. Attitudes vary as much as do people. One thing is certain, however: Even a few years of working in New York City can be an uplifting experience, one that will stay with the individual for the rest of his professional life. Or, to put it in other words, New York is the best creative bootcamp in the world.

Movies Are Not Only for Entertainment

Anybody working in the communications field, and that certainly includes advertising people, should be an inveterate movie buff. His or her diet should include two to four feature films a month. There is much to be gleaned from a movie, especially if watched through the eyes of a professional.

Generally, a good movie is really not much different from a good television commercial, transitory as the latter may seem compared with a full-length feature. Here are the basic creative ingredients to watch for in any movie:

1. *The story*. Does it have a beginning, a middle, and an end? Does the plot move toward a satisfying climax? Is it the story itself that intrigues you or the way it is being presented on the screen? (Both should be compelling.)

2. *Characters*. Do they hold your attention? Are the people believable?

3. *Acting*. Do the performers convincingly portray the characters? Are they able to display emotions honestly? This is particularly important under the the close, relentless scrutiny of the camera, as opposed to stage performances.

4. *Camera*. Are you conscious of its presence? (You should not be.) Are dramatic scenes reinforced by camera movements? Are these too static? Too active?

5. *Lighting*. Is it used to create moods? Does it look natural or artificial? (Both have their place.)

6. *Direction*. Is the quality of acting consistent throughout the film? Is the pacing? How good is the editing?

7. *Sound*. Is the background music overpowering? (It should not be.) Is it consistent with the mood of the picture?

8. *Print quality*. Is the color temperature uniform from beginning to end? (Not all scenes are shot on a single day. Weather conditions change and adjustments must be made in the development process.)

Next time you are sitting in a movie theater, close your eyes and listen to the dialogue only, especially if you happen to be a word man. Then compare an average movie script with some of the dialogue you hear on most television commercials. Sometimes, the difference between the two is quite noticeable. On the movie screen, performers are out of breath, rudely interrupt each other, grope for words, make redundant statements, leave sentences unfinished, and act as perfectly normal human beings do. Not so the performers in many a television commercial. They tend to be more precise, more articulate, and less natural. Writers of slice-of-life commercials, please take note.

Lunch Hour: Food for Thought

There are many ways to spend a lunch "hour." (In advertising, a lunch hour usually lasts more than 60 minutes.) Eating is one way. Socializing is another.

For years, the author made it a practice to share his lunch whenever possible with at least one associate, client, or vendor, ignoring the somewhat dubious medical maxim that mixing business with pleasure puts unwelcome pressure on the digestive system, leading to constipation. Shoptalk seems to flow easily across a dining table, especially if it is washed down with a drink or two. As often as not, that midday break represents a welcome change from jangling telephones, last-minute crises, and unannounced office visitors. (Interestingly enough, according to Henry Mintzberg, a management theorist, the average corporate executive, in the office and away from the lunch table, may have as many as fifty projects going at the same time, often disposing of items in 10 minutes or less. How about that for cultivating ulcers?)

If no lunch partners are available, a quick snack at the nearest coffee shop still leaves time for a *tour de force* in information gathering in such places as;

Department stores	Trade shows
Art galleries	Museums
Book stores	Auctions
Fashion shows	Seminars
Photography exhibits	Parks

Chapter Six
Getting Set to Create

To create, to produce an idea, you must first of all make up your mind that this is what you want to do.

Obvious? Maybe so, but it is easier said than done. Merely to put the mind in motion is not enough. In itself, that does not automatically bring forth a gushing of viable ideas. Only when the mind has been organized (remember all that talk about purposeful activity in Chapter 1?) will it begin to function productively, the way in which it is supposed to.

Concentration is the key.

Another thing: A sharp line must be drawn between the *real* problem and other problems that have nothing to do with the basic issue. This too, sounds simple. But it is not. For example, speculation about the client's reaction to the idea, method of paying for it, and thick headedness (there are clients who are thickheaded) may all be important ramifications of the assignment, but dwelling on them too long will only block your creativity. They have little bearing on the real problem and will not bring you one iota nearer to the solution.

Nine Ways to Put Yourself in the Mood

1. *First of all, get started.* Like everyone else, you will probably have dozens of perfectly good excuses for postponing the inevitable, that is, getting started. Pencils need sharpening, your friends are waiting for your phone call, you must have a cup of coffee to wake you up, and so on. All right, do what you have to do, but eventually face up to it: there is work to be done.

2. *Jot down whatever comes to your mind.* Moving your hand is an activity of sorts; at least, you are doing *something,* as opposed to doing *nothing.* The greater the number of ideas you put on paper, the better your chances of coming up with one you like. Any idea, no matter how trifling it may strike you at the moment, may signal the beginning of something bigger and better.

Do not make note taking a full-scale production. Scribbles will do. Forget about semantics or even rules of grammar. Leave your sentences dangling in midair, split your infinitives, or write diagonally across the page if you wish; no school marm is looking over your shoulder just now. *What* you say is infinitely more important than *how* you say it.

Make sure your note pad is large enough to accommodate your free-swinging penmanship. There is nothing more annoying than having your fist continually sliding off a page like an errant elbow at the bar after a few drinks.

Go ahead and doodle to your heart's content. Pictures inspire words, and words inspire pictures.

3. *Resist the temptation to drift into flights of fancy.* As we have said before, applied imagination is a form of discipline. Daydreaming is anything but that. Fantasies are fabri-

cated by restive minds to provide the dreamer with a means of escape from reality.

4. *Keep your eye on the target.* This stanza from *Blight,* by Ralph Waldo Emerson, is a classic:

> Give me truths;
> For I am weary of the surfaces,
> And die of inanition. If I knew
> Only the herbs and simples of the wood,
> Rue, cinquefoil, gill, vervain and agrimony,
> Blue-vetch and trillium hawkseed, sassafras,
> Milkweed and murky brakes, quaint pipes and sundew,
> And rare and virtuous roots, which in these woods
> Draw untold juices from the common earth. . . .

However, this type of stream-of-consciousness writing has no place in advertising copy. The technique stands in the way of the message.

5. *If you do not succeed at first, try again.* Keep reexamining your ideas. (This is another reason why it is good to have them listed on a piece of paper.) Go back to the beginning if necessary. Keep asking yourself these vital questions: Who is buying the product? Why? Who *could* be made to buy the product? What are the main selling features? Which selling feature lends itself most dramatically to verbal or pictorial interpretation? What type of contribution are you expected to make in the first place? (New creative approach? New technique in execution? A new product? A new application for the product?)

6. *Talk it over with a friend.* Your best sounding board is another professional: a writer, art director, photographer, television director. But you may find conversations with lay people—a salesman, shopper, secretary, or your favorite newsstand owner around the corner— just as stimulating. One of the best ways to collect your thoughts is to share them with someone else.

The author finds that *dictation* disencumbers the mind. Talking to another person is a form of communication, in this case between an

172. TV commercial — performer saying "hello" to his mother — waving at the camera

173. Computerized "Beauty Exercise" booklet — loose pages — "problem areas."

174. — protective shield for spray can — painting — attachable so it can be used repeatedly

175. "Manwatchers" — TV commercial?

176. Horoscope for dogs — astrology

177. Mousetrap — called "Better Mousetrap" — one that chemically destroys the mouse

178. Air-rights on top of brownstone houses — who owns them? Valuable piece of real estate.

179. Book idea: "Confessions of a male chauvenist pig."

180. Sell theatre tickets in bulk to corporations

181. "Beauty Cruise" — 10 days — only for women — complete make-up, exercise, fashion, etc. courses offered aboard.

182. Plastic garbage bags for campers — "keep America beautiful" printed on it.

183. Yogurt Icecream?

The author keeps a good-size notebook close by, even at night, to jot down his thoughts if and when they occur. Critical evaluation is withheld at this point.

author and a stenographer. Her smile, raised eyebrow, puckered lips tell the way she feels about what is being said. Much of this book was dictated from rough notes.

7. *Plan ahead.* Know what and how much you want to accomplish in the next several hours, days, or even weeks. Project your schedule as far ahead as possible.

An advertising executive in a well-known creative shop always has a month-at-a-glance calendar on his desk to help him apportion his time wisely. Continually on the move, he lines up his appointments several weeks in advance. This gives him a chance to prepare material for meetings, get to the point quickly, and save time. He is careful to set aside at least 2 hours a day for quiet contemplation behind closed doors so that he can have the privacy he needs to concentrate on purely creative problems.

Another executive, head of an art department in a large New York agency, has his secretary keep a magnetic-grid board above her desk. Colored tacks serve as a guide to account assignments. With this device, she is able to keep track not only of his time but also of that of eight other art directors working under his supervision.

If you are able to assign priorities to the next day's assignments, by all means do so as early as you can. Your subconscious mind will keep working on the problem even while you sleep, preparing you for a quick start in the morning.

8. *Stay with your schedule.* Once you have decided on your agenda, stick to it. Resist the temptation to get sidetracked, no matter how much fun there may be in the offing.

Always have a good-size, easy-to-see clock nearby. (Your wristwatch will not do; it takes too much effort to keep an eye on it.) Make sure the numerals are discernible from at least 15 feet so that everyone (including visitors) can see them. The louder the tick, the better. The sound will make people more conscious of the passing of time. All creative professionals in advertising are clock watchers. They have to

be. Every minute counts; there are always deadlines.

Know your limits of being able to stay with the same task, but be realistic. If you set impossible goals for yourself, you may be disappointed in your ability to deliver.

Much of one's staying power depends on the nature of the assignment. The writing of a free-flowing autobiography or the uninhibited slinging of gobs of paint on canvas to create an abstraction may call for more emotional than intellectual effort, making the hours go more quickly. Many creative professionals can become so thoroughly immersed in their work that they lose all sense of time. It is this ability to achieve intense concentration which enables some of them to complete their projects in record time. Handel composed *The Messiah* in 23 days; Johann Sebastian Bach often churned out church music (and even sonatas) on a weekly basis; Charles Hamilton, the prolific English novelist who created Billy Bunker, at the height of his career wrote 80,000 words a week; Belgian writer Georges Simenon has so far written

more than 500 novels; and British storyteller John Creasey once wrote two books in a week. Equally impressive are the speed records set by certain artists with a flair for a rapid, impressionistic art style. Picasso sometimes paid for his dinner by means of a quick sketch on a paper napkin. Van Gogh could turn out a painting a day. And one of the most popular illustrators in America, Ted De Grazia, has done some of his best work in less than 10 minutes. Several of his drawings used on greeting cards sold more than 1 million copies.

9. *Avoid interruptions.* Develop your powers of concentration. If your work calls for privacy, find yourself a place where you can get away from the crowd. And do not feel guilty about your desire to withdraw. The need for seclusion does not automatically turn one into a confirmed misanthrope; the famous philosopher Diogenes did all right by using a barrel for an office.

One of the most common interrupters, and perhaps the rudest, can be your telephone. Have your secretary, receptionist, or spouse take

---

These are exceptions, however. Most of us ordinary mortals cannot work that fast and wilt more rapidly.

After a while, attention wanes. Generally, these are the time limits for sustained creative activity:

	Average Attention Span	
Fiction writing	5 hours
Nonfiction writing	3 hours
Fine art painting	7 hours
Sculpting	7 hours
Representational painting	6 hours
Poetry writing	2 hours
Marketing-plan writing	3 hours
Advertising copy	2 hours
Advertising layout	3 hours
Brainstorming (active participation)	2 hours
Delivering a speech	1/2 hour

There are no rules, of course. At times, solutions come quickly; these are the lucky breaks. The author of this book, for example, working around the clock in an inspired fit of frenzy, was once able to turn out a 120-page best-selling book, *How to Live with a Neurotic Dog,* in 8 days, or about 60 hours. Its sequel, *Games Dogs Play,* took only a little longer. For another publishing venture, *How to Play Golf in the Low 120's* with collaborator Howard Zieff, more than 100 photographs were shot in a studio in 4 successive days, or about 48 hours. Progress has not always come that easily, however. It took almost 600 hours of hard work to complete this book, *Systematic Approach to Advertising Creativity.*

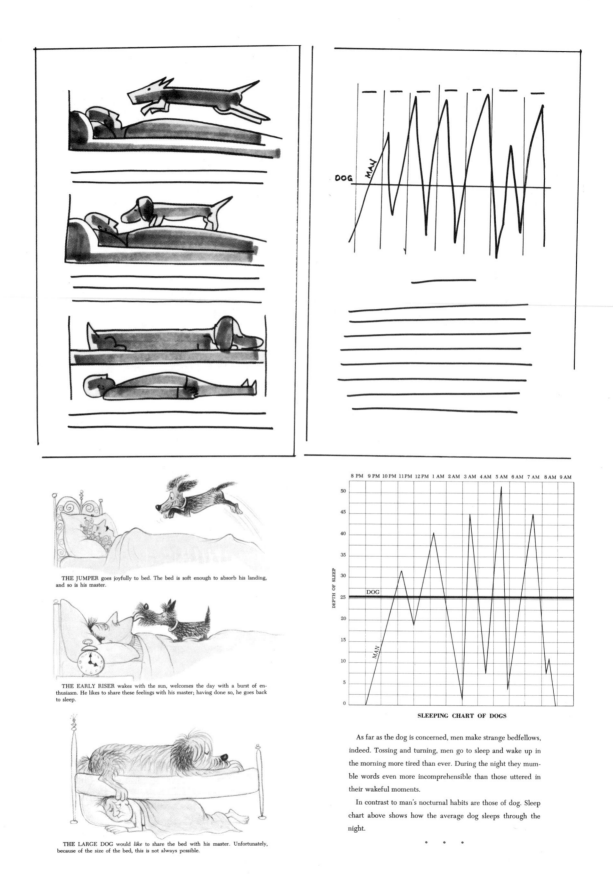

THE JUMPER goes joyfully to bed. The bed is soft enough to absorb his landing, and so is his master.

THE EARLY RISER wakes with the sun, welcomes the day with a burst of enthusiasm. He likes to share these feelings with his master; having done so, he goes back to sleep.

THE LARGE DOG would *like* to share the bed with his master. Unfortunately, because of the size of the bed, this is not always possible.

SLEEPING CHART OF DOGS

As far as the dog is concerned, men make strange bedfellows, indeed. Tossing and turning, men go to sleep and wake up in the morning more tired than ever. During the night they mumble words even more incomprehensible than those uttered in their wakeful moments.

In contrast to man's nocturnal habits are those of dog. Sleep chart above shows how the average dog sleeps through the night.

* * *

The author's captioned sketches provided the cartoonist Eric Gurney with information for finished art. Close collaboration made it possible to reduce hit-or-miss experimentation and finish the book quickly.

92

At-a-glance calendars come in many forms; all are conducive to develop time consciousness, an essential part of planning.

calls when you need privacy. Or take the receiver off the hook.

Ten Ways to Keep Going

1. *Work up a sweat: exert yourself physically.* Just stretching your limbs will make you feel better. Stand on your toes, take a deep breath, extend your arms. Jog in one place, bend at your waist, do push-ups on the floor or against the side of your desk. Take a walk if you have the time, spend a few hours at the local YMCA or YWCA (or whichever your favorite athletic hangout happens to be), swim, play a game of volleyball or tennis with friends.

2. *Turn on the music.* A good way to relax is to listen to your favorite sounds: classical, country, rock, or even a human voice brought to you by courtesy of your radio or record player. Close your eyes, lean back in your chair, and listen. There is solid evidence that music improves not only people's dispositions but their productivity as well. The chief proponent of piped-in office music, Muzak, is well aware of this; on the basis of computer-fed "stimulus quotients" between 0 and 7, this company changes to "progressively brighter and more stimulating music in mid-morning and again mid-afternoon," when, research shows, productivity tends to taper off.

3. *Reach for a snack.* Keep crackers or a few pieces of candy in your desk drawer. If you work at home, raid the kitchen periodically. The author has a compact 18-inch-high refrigerator installed in his office. It is filled with cheese, crackers, soft drinks, fruit, and, luckily with no weight problems to worry about in this case, candy bars.

4. *Take a coffee break.* Caffeine perks up the spirit. Only if consumed excessively (more than six cups of coffee a day) can it be considered medically harmful to people in good health.

Those concerned about their well-being may take comfort in the fact that Balzac downed 40 cups of coffee a day while working on a novel.

93

Caffeine Sources

SOURCE	APPROXIMATE AMOUNTS OF CAFFEINE PER UNIT
Beverages*	
Brewed coffee	100–150 mg/cup
Instant coffee	86–99 mg/cup
Tea	60–75 mg/cup
Decaffeinated coffee	2–4 mg/cup
Cola drinks	40–60 mg/cup
Prescription medications	
APCs (aspirin, phenacetin, caffeine)	32 mg/tablet
Cafergot	100 mg/tablet
Darvon compound	32 mg/tablet
Fiorinal	40 mg/tablet
Migral	50 mg/tablet
Over-the-counter analgesics	
Anacin, aspirin compound, Bromo Seltzer, Cope	32 mg/tablet
Easy-Mens, Empirin compound, Midol, Vanquish	32 mg/tablet
Excedrin	60 mg/tablet
Pre-Mens	66 mg/tablet
Many over-the-counter cold preparations	30 mg/tablet
Many over-the-counter stimulants	10 mg/tablet

SOURCE: *American Journal of Psychiatry.*
*Based on an average 6-ounce serving for coffee and tea and a 9- to 10-ounce serving for cola.

Voltaire did even better than that with his daily quota of 50 cups. Talleyrand liked his coffee "black as a devil, hot as hell, pure as an angel, and sweet as love." All these men lived full, productive lives.

5. *Turn on your television set.* One way to switch your mind off is to switch on the tube. Relax with a program that makes minimum demands on your intellect. There are plenty of these around, especially in the afternoon.

6. *Light up a cigarette, cigar, or pipe.* Used in moderation (fewer than six cigarettes a day), tobacco probably does not live up to its name as a killer. And there is another side of the coin: psychologists say that the act of puffing provides oral satisfaction. For that reason, tobacco acts as a sedative. Your powers of concentration will probably improve.

7. *Read or look at pictures.* Anything will do: newspaper, magazine, book. Your subconscious will keep running even while you are just looking. And you will be surprised: a word, sentence, or picture can spark a brand-new idea, a new direction.

8. *Phone a friend.* Listen to the voice of someone you like: your spouse, son, daughter, friends. Check out the weather. Or dial a joke.

9. *Take a catnap.* Many famous people, including Winston Churchill and Thomas Edison, used this method to keep going all day and into the night. Some business people do the same. Even 10 or 20 minutes of dozing off can work wonders. A half hour is ample; anything over an hour may be a waste of time.

Research indicates that thinking performance improves when the subject is lying down. Students at Colgate University were able to compute mathematical assignments about one-tenth quicker (and about 15 percent more accurately) in a prone position than when sitting upright. As a matter of fact, researchers suggested that perhaps employees with problem-solving jobs be supplied with work beds in their offices. And so it seems that putting one's feet on the desk is not such a bad idea after all; what the sitter loses in dignity, he more than makes up in a richer flow of thoughts.

Actually, it is not the intensity of sleep but the degree of relaxation that counts. It is not even necessary to be sound asleep to derive the full benefit from resting. As in meditation, it is the knack for shutting out outside distractions—freedom from exertion and strain—that is the key factor. As in other forms of relaxation techniques, it is the mind that has to be set at rest, more so than the body.

10. *Get away from your office if at all possible.* This is not to suggest that you should leave the office whenever the mood strikes you. Deadlines make this impossible. However, a break in the routine may just be what you need to replenish your energy.

GETTING HIGH DOES NOT MEAN GETTING MORE CREATIVE

The use of psychoactive drugs (such as hallucinogens) or the gulping down of a few drinks may open the door to a new fantasy world, but not necessarily the sort that provides the kind of input which is so sorely needed for solid advertising, campaigns.

It has yet to be demonstrated that inhaling, imbibing, or popping pills in the mouth enhances one's business judgment.

There are those who disagree. But they are confusing visual images with viable ideas. And in a field where every person is held accountable for his or her recommendations, confusing the two conceptions can give rise to dire consequences.

One of the problems with drugs and drinks is that under their influence the mind *appears* to function better. Nothing could be further from the truth.

The words or drawings put down on paper in a state of euphoric bliss look very different when examined ex post facto under more sober circumstances.

Another problem with both drugs and alcohol, and perhaps an even more serious one, is that they both are addictive. Dependence upon them does not have to be physical to create problems in users' professional careers; as long as they look to these agents as an emotional crutch to help them through the rough times, they are addicts. The chances are their dependence on such agents will influence their modus operandi.

Creative problem solving is never easy; almost always creators must encounter a number of failures before reaching success. It is important that during this trial-and-error period they keep their wits about them.

No doubt, turning to drugs or alcohol will lift their spirits. But that can wait until after office hours when they are no longer held accountable for the ideas they have been submitting to paying clients.

GETTING HIGH DOES NOT MEAN GETTING MORE CREATIVE: COMMON SENSATIONS

Sight

"I can see patterns, forms, figures, meaningful designs in visual material that do not have any particular form when I'm straight, that is, just a meaningless series of lines or shapes when I'm straight."

"When I look at pictures, they may acquire an element of visual depth, a third-dimensional aspect. . . ."

"I can see new colors or more subtle shades of color. . . ."

"Things in the periphery of my vision look different when I'm not looking directly at them. . . ."

Hearing

"I can hear more subtle changes in sounds; for example, the notes of music are purer and more distinct, the rhythm stands out more. . . ."

"I can understand the words of songs which are not clear when straight. . . ."

"When I listen to stereo music or live music, the spatial separation between the various instruments sounds greater, as if they were physically farther apart. . . ."

"If I try to have an auditory image . . . it is more vivid. . . ."

Touch

"My sense of touch is more exciting, more sensual. . . ."

"Touch sensations take on new qualities. . . ."

"Some surfaces feel much smoother, silkier. . . ."

"Some surfaces feel much rougher, irregular . . . and the roughness or graininess forms interesting patterns."

Interpersonnal Relations:

"I have feelings of deep insights into other people, how they tick, what their games are (regardless of whether they actually check out later)."

"I find it very hard to play ordinary social games."

"I talk a lot less."

"I am less noisy and boisterous at parties."

Taste

"Taste sensations take on new qualities. . . ."

"I enjoy eating very much and eat a lot. . . ."

"If I try to imagine what something tastes like, I can do so very vividly. . ."

"I crave sweet things to eat, like chocolate, more than other foods. . . ."

Smell

"Smell sensations take on new qualities. . . ."

"Smells become richer and more unique. . . ."

Space-Time Perception

"When I walk someplace my experience of the distance covered is quite changed. . . ."

"Time passes very slowly. . . ."

"Distances between me and things, or between me and other people seem to get greater. . . ."

"Events and thoughts flow more smoothly; the succession of events in time is smoother than usual. . . ."

"I get so lost in fantasy or similar trips in my head that I completely forget where I am, and it takes a while to reorient after I come back and open my eyes. . . ."

Thought Processes

"I appreciate very subtle humor in what my companions say, and say quite subtly funny things myself. . . ."

"Commonplace sayings or conversations seem to have new meanings, more significance. . . ."

"I give little or no thought to the future, I am completely in the here-and-now. . . ."

"Spontaneously, insights about myself, my personality, the games I play, come to mind when I am stoned and seem very meaningful. . . ."

Memory Functioning

"My memory span for conversations is somewhat shortened, so that I may forget what the conversation is about even before it has ended (though I may be able to recall it if I make a special effort). . . ."

"I can continue to carry on an intelligent conversation even when my memory span is so short that I forget the beginnings of what I started to say; for example, I may logically complete a sentence even as I realize I've forgotten how it started. . . ."

"I can't think clearly; thoughts keep slipping away before I can quite grasp them. . . ."

"My memory span for conversations is very shortened so that I may forget what the start of a sentence was about even before the sentence is finished. . . ."

"I spontaneously remember things I haven't thought of in years. . . ."

"If I read while stoned, I remember less of what I've read hours later."

"I think I've said something that actually I've only thought."

"My memory of what went on while I was stoned is poor afterwards. . . ."

Constructive revelations? Maybe, for a psychoanalyst to take notes, but not for a creative advertising practitioner to do his or her job well.

(Courtesy of Psychology Today)

Space does not permit a thorough examination of the complex relationships between meditation and creativity; that subject alone could fill another volume. However, with so many thousands of Americans (including many who work in the advertising field) using meditation as a shortcut to creativity, the issue deserves a brief discussion.

It should, of course, be apparent to the reader of *The Systematic Approach to Advertising Creativity* that the premise of this book collides head on with those murmured by the various gurus, all of whom would rise indignantly from their lotus position at the very mention of the words *intellectual discipline*. But to be fair to them and their considerable following, let us first give credit where credit is due.

There Is a Time and a Place for Doing Everything or Even for Doing Nothing

No doubt our hectic pace of living more than justifies the notion that we all need to take a breather once in a while. Few of us escape the physical and emotional consequences of living on this side of the globe. To be sure, some of us give it a try. But the value we place on *tangible* evidence of success makes total relaxation (as defined by Oriental philosophy) difficult, if not impossible. Competition reigns supreme in our civilization. We turn to hobbies to calm our nerves, only to find that our efforts are being compared with those of others also collecting coins or doing needlepoint. Our approach to sports, another form of "relaxation," follows a similar pattern. In

golf, all scores are posted in country-club locker rooms to figure out the latest handicaps; in jogging, we strive for speed and distance; and in fishing, we compare the size of the latest catch. We are a nation of checks and double checks on every possible type of human endeavor, from our intelligence, leadership potential, verbal reasoning, and mental maturity right down to our sexual performance.

No wonder that the peace-of-mind market has become a major growth industry. It appears to be just what the doctor ordered. At least, meditation offers us a legitimate excuse to get away from it all.

Is Everybody Happy?

Another peripheral benefit of various relaxation exercises is that they promise inner harmony, which has become an all-important preoccupation in today's hedonistic society, aptly labeled the "Me Decade" by Tom Wolfe. Relaxation, so goes the theory, brings on happiness; in fact, one invites the presence of the other. And with happiness come new and remarkable creative insights. How can you lose?

Let us repeat that it is not within the scope of this book to examine the various aspects of meditation; only the question regarding creativity concerns us here. It appears, however, that it is precisely at this point that spiritual leaders and advertising professionals part company.

With Creativity Goes Tension

The primary goal of all meditative techniques is to relieve tension and

thus increase productivity. Theory has it that the deeper the trance, the higher the success rate is bound to be.

Statements made by Peter McWilliams, offered in *The TM Program: A Basic Handbook* (Fawcett World Library, New York) typify his genre. In comparing transcendental meditation with another homemade emotional placebo, the relaxation technique (invented by Dr. Herbert Benson), the author uses the absence of tension as a major criterion. Since Dr. Benson's technique involves breathing exercises and the constant repetition of the word *one*, McWilliams is quick to point out that "some control of the mind is involved here, in contrast to TM which is *effortless*" (italics his). He continues with a straight face: "The difference between the effort involved in saying 'one' each time you exhale, and the effortlessness of the TM technique may not seem too great initially; but when you begin multiplying the effort involved by twenty minutes, by twice a day, by the rest of your life, the drudgery becomes obvious. And here we should also mention that the TM technique is not contemplation, which is thinking *about* something." The conclusion: "Effort, concentration, trying and mind control have no place in the TM program."

Another guru, Gopi Krishna, displays even more enthusiasm about his particular brand of intellectual woolgathering: "When I look within I am lifted beyond the confines of time and space, in tune with a majestic, all-conscious existence, which mocks at fear and laughs at death, compared to which seas and mountains, suns and planets, appear no more than flimsy rock riding across a blazing sky; an existence which is in all and yet absolutely removed from everything, an endless inexpressible wonder that can only be experienced and not described." All this is achieved by concentrating intently on a spot above the eyebrows for approximately 3 hours each morning after breakfast.

Unfortunately, the "state of least excitation" (also known as Tao, the kingdom of heaven, and by contemporary psychologists, the "vacuum state") is hardly conducive to producing a viable idea.

Adam Smith, in his perceptive book *Powers of Mind,* expresses the problem succinctly:

I get suspicious of the promises [of the spiritual leaders] to help creativity and intelligence, because they make it sound like a twist of the key makes you a genius. . . . It's like: ah, tap the right side, the old subconscious, and there is genius. Well, maybe, if you've been working at something eighteen hours a day. Why don't people remember that James Joyce learned Norwegian just so he could read Ibsen, and Edmund Wilson learned Hungarian just so he could read Molnar, and there were lots of translations in both cases, and for all his exquisite right-sideness, Einstein carefully figured out he could wear the same jacket all week and not have to spend thirty seconds thinking about clothes, so he could spend eighteen hours thinking about geometrodynamics, space and time. Not much time goofing off for those fellas.

There is a notable lack of scientific evidence that absence of tension sharpens creative acumen.

In fact, it seems that some degree of anxiety (a state of mind to be avoided at all costs, caution the gurus) actually improves performance under certain circumstances. Keyed-up athletes set new world records in the most demanding contest of all, the Olympic Games. Some of the most memorable speeches have been made during periods of intense national crisis. And war, perhaps one of the most stressful of all human-created situations, has turned people of ordinary backgrounds into overnight heroes. Closer to home are our creative colleagues who do their best work under the pressure of impending deadlines.

Drawn during a business conference, these doodles by agency principal Arnold Arlow show a vivid imagination and considerable artistic flair, but as advertising campaign ideas (as he would be the first to admit), they leave something to be desired. They merely suggest a rich but undirected flow of thoughts by an active mind.

Learn to Ignore Negativism in Other People

Later in this book, the various aspects of selling an idea will be discussed. At this point, suffice it to say that in advertising, as in most businesses, there will always be those in authority to accept or reject recommendations made by others. Their reactions may be based on a number of factors, their own disposition being one of them. Some people naturally take to ideas. Others try to find problems. For the sake of one's peace of mind, it sometimes pays to make an effort to find out why the idea meets with resistance. The reasons may be wholly subjective. Here are some points worth considering:

1. Is the idea clear to everyone?
2. Has somebody else (unbeknown to you) already produced the same idea?
3. Does the idea offer a solution to the specific problem?
4. Does it go against someone's likes or dislikes?
5. Are you bucking office politics?
6. Are you the right person to make the presentation?
7. Are you presenting your idea prematurely or too late?
8. Are you encroaching on someone else's prerogatives with your idea?
9. Is the audience too preoccupied to listen?

Let Your Working Environment Put You in the Right Frame of Mind

Many creative people prefer working in the midst of clutter. Others insist on clean desk tops. This is entirely up to the individual.

Before you decide to join the clutter-loving cult, however, stop and think of the time it takes to look for misplaced items. Having observed office procedures for many years, this writer found that 5 to 10 percent of the average employee's day is spent, sometimes frantically, in searching for pieces of paper. Executives with secretaries beat the odds, but not by much.

It is important, therefore, that whatever your personal predilection, you still have an assigned place for every item, large or small, important or unimportant, permanent or temporary. If tacking notes on a cork wallboard, lining up potted plants in the office corner, and piling stacks of books on the windowsill is your idea of being organized, so be it, as long as you know *where* everything is exactly *when* you want it.

A number of studies show that looking for things not only consumes time but also affects one's mental equilibrium. Psychologist Lawrence Baker of New York University has isolated a whole gaggle of psychological quirks associated with disorganized behavior. In his studies, he found that more often than not chronically depressed people live in messy environments. This is why in the last few years a whole new profession has sprung up to aid untidy executives. Called *systems analysts,* members of these clean-up squads charge $125 to $250 a day for creating a semblance of order. In the opinion of corporations that hire them, this is a small price to pay for increased efficiency and, usually, a boost in morale.

A quick way to organize and save money in the long run is to buy the kind of furniture that not only looks good but also lives up to its promise as a repository. Remember, you cannot put things away unless there is a place to put them. Take your time to shop around for exactly what you need.

Desk This may be among your most important pieces of furniture, not only in the office but also in your home. Find one with a top large enough to accommodate the things you use, such as an oversize sketch pad. There is a current trend among creative people to have dining tables (including some that they have discovered at antique shows) stand in for office desks. If that suits your fancy, well and good. But does a table have enough drawer space for all your papers?

Bookcases, Cabinets, and Wall Units Books have a way of proliferating; people tend to become attached to them. Every now and then, however, even the most ardent bibliophiles must clean house to make room for new editions. In that case, all musty volumes must go to a warehouse, a secondhand bookstore, or, better still, some worthwhile charity such as the Salvation Army or Goodwill, in the form of a donation and a tax deduction.

Modular units can be expanded or stacked to fit the user's particular needs. They are usually attractive enough to pass for furniture. Many are designed to harmonize with other storage units, such as filing cabinets or desks.

Wallboards Even though wallboards are put up vertically, they can be used as catchall space savers. Layouts, proofs, notes, forms, memos, and other material can be accommodated, opening up much-needed desk-top space.

Wastebasket One of the most practical pieces of furniture.

Filing Cabinets Two basic kinds of cabinets are available: standard and lateral. Both come in letter and legal size, the number of drawers being optional. If space permits, use the lateral type: it accommodates a larger number of folders in a single drawer and makes them more accessible. If you have a problem storing oversize flat sheets such as full-page newspaper ads, consider a blueprint cabinet with convenient roll-out drawer units.

A Few Words about Filing Systems

You may need several filing drawers, some that you can share with others in the office (mostly correspondence, records, job envelopes) and some that you wish to set aside for your private use. Basically, you can file according to:

1. *Client.* Correspondence, job descriptions, ideas (used and unused),

copy and layouts, proofs of finished ads, proofs of competitive ads.

2. *Date*. Chronological order makes it possible to track down material quickly, provided you have a good memory, a low turnover in secretaries, or both.

3. *Subject*. Take major categories and keep subdividing them:

Competitive Advertising Everything created by the competition, including proofs, news releases, and so on.

Correspondence Correspondence subdivided by client, projects, or both, and by vendors, legal matters, media, interoffice memos, job applicants, office supplies, and personal services.

Financial Data Cost of photography, art, and TV and print production.

Legal Matters Rules, regulations, articles in trade journals, and standard forms.

Media Mechanical requirements of media and quantitative and qualitative data.

Miscellany All other written material.

Miscellaneous A file of pictures of interest.

Photographs Keep transparencies in envelopes, boxes, vinyl nests, trays, or slide cabinets specially designed for such material. If photo-graphs are very large, reduce them photostatically for filing purposes.

Production Type specimen sheets, standard color swatches, samples of reproduction, samples of envelopes, paper stock, impositions, folding and binding methods, and new production techniques.

Suppliers Photographers, artists, art suppliers, equipment firms, copy services, printers, engravers, lithographers, model agencies, talent, stylists, propmen, set designers, paper suppliers, retouchers, photostat houses, messenger services, boardmen, audio-video services, television postproducers, directors, typographers, employment agencies, and organizations. Keep small photostatic copies of their work if needed.

Resist the temptation to branch out into too many new and sometimes much too esoteric classifications. The organization specialist Stephanie Winston advises: "It's better to have a small number of fat files than too many thin files. With fat files, you have to hunt 5 minutes for a paper, but at least you can find it."

Keep track of *every* print or broadcast ad (script) you have prepared for clients for a minimum of 2 years. Put proofs in large ring binders (one for every client) in the order of publication date. This legend, appearing under each proof, will help to identify it quickly.

Date	Medium	Size	Job Number	Miscellaneous

Binders

Binders for large-size material, such as charts, newspapers, clippings, art reproductions, and proofs, come in rigid covers with matching lining and an easy-to-snap multiring. Most can accommodate 125 pages or more of paper, plus two or three dozen acetate protectors. Some have built-in easels so that the work can be displayed at eye level. Typical insert sizes in inches are as follows:

$8^1/_2 \times 11$	14×17
$11 \times 8^1/_2$	17×14
11×14	18×24
14×11	24×18

The last-named size is large enough to accommodate newspaper-size material.

NOTE: To make proofs last a long time, have them mounted on laminated boards. These are handy, especially at new-business presentations.

[*Courtesy of Studio-Craft, Inc.*]

FURNITURE: ART FOR ART'S SAKE
Tabourets, consoles, and files are made for art directors, illustrators, production people, and just about everybody who is anybody in the field of graphic arts. Handsomely designed, they fit into any room, office, or home.

The above tabouret offers plenty of storage space. Only 30 inches long by 20 inches deep by 20 inches high, it has room for a full range of art supplies. Stacks of layout pads go on the lower shelf, while oversized type books, directories, and the like can be neatly stacked in the larger bin. Two other pieces of furniture for designers are shown on the right.

MINI OFFICE AT HOME This compact 48$\frac{1}{2}$-inch-wide handcrafted cabinet by Norsk has many unique features: pull-out lamp, file drawers, adjustable shelves holding large reference books and typewriter, and glide-out stationery shelves. The generous 46$\frac{1}{2}$- by 21-inch pull-down writing surface closes magnetically. Space units like these encourage organized working habits.

Creative Habitats

Creative people are hypersensitive to their surroundings. They often become their own interior decorators, putting their personalities and aesthetic-psychological theories into the office's ambience.

The author: "This is where *Systematic Approach to Advertising Creativity* was written. Picture window, facing the East River, provides natural daylight, cheerful sunshine, and inspiration. Located in midtown Manhattan, twenty-two stories above street level and street noise, the interior of this triplex studio is designed to make clients feel right at home. The color scheme is red, white, orange."

George Lois: "The office itself should be sparse but architecturally warm. Many people think my office is cold, but I think it's warm as hell. I think the people and the work serve as the 'decoration.' My office must be immaculate, with no distractions. Only in one area are there any ads hanging."

Ron Travisano: 'I wanted to do it a bit like a barber shop—not just the chairs, but poles and all. It makes it distinctive.''

Bill Gold: "If anything, I guess you'd call my tastes eclectic. The surroundings are my personality—almost a typical show business atmosphere.''

Herb Lubalin: "You spend more than half your life at your job, so your environment should be like your home. I don't like clean desks, cold environments, and contemporary surroundings. I like the warm, cluttered look. I want to make my clients comfortable so they'll come here rather than me going there.''

Rosa Cann: "The office is small, but low furniture (the cot and the crate) make it look and feel bigger, and I feel less confined in my thinking.''

[*Courtesy of* Art Direction, *the magazine of Visual Communication*]

Chapter Seven

Ideation: The Way It Works

You, the reader, are now about halfway through this book and more than half way up that symbolic pyramid which appears on the cover. The top of the climb is now within sight.

With information stored away in your mind, the climb is getting easier little by little, and faster. Closing in on the solution, you are, however, also growing increasingly impatient with yourself. What you want now is to see results, tangible evidence of your efforts: the big idea.

All right.

Let us move on and take the next giant step.

The More the Merrier

At this point, you probably feel that you have several pretty good ideas buzzing about in your head, like insects around a light. So be it. It is perfectly common, as any creative professional will tell you, to have quite a few ideas before hitting upon the one *definitive* solution. Many ideas fall by the wayside before you get the one you are looking for. Do not let that slow you down.

Keep the ideas coming. Examine not one, but *all* your ideas from *all* angles. Then, make your selection. Reject if you must, but also learn to accept. **Acceptance is as important as rejection.** Creativity is a positive, not a negative, undertaking.

Perhaps this is as good a place as any to remind the reader that its title notwithstanding, this book is not designed to inhibit the natural, free flow of ideas. The emphasis here is simply on building up to the ultimate solution, step by step, in some kind of logical sequence, using information gathering for a start. More information generates more ideas. The larger the selection, the better the chances for finding the right one.

There is conclusive evidence that quantity breeds quality. Brain Reserve, Inc., a group of four independent top creative advertising professionals working for blue-chip clients, often winds up with as many as 300 ideas at a single session and in less than a day. Such a performance is exceptional but not unusual. Says Alex Osborn, one of the foremost exponents of applied imagination, "The best ideas seldom come first." He reports that in his experience 70 to 80 percent more ideas are produced during the second half of brainstorming sessions (an invention of his) than during the first.

But Sooner or Later You Must Make a Choice

There comes a time, of course, when you must stop examining the alternatives and move in decisively on a *single* idea, the one that you think best answers the particular problem. This culling process is an interesting and rewarding intellectual exercise and is closely structured along the lines of problem definition, as discussed in Chapter 2. Remember that exercise? There information was put into three categories, labeled "nonessential", "essential", and "very essential" by order of preference.

The same modus operandi works at this end; only the labels have been changed. Ideas, too, can be separated into three categories. In this case, let's call them "no good", "so-so," and "good."

Obviously, the first category is of little or no consequence to us here. Thrown into this scrap pile are ideas that turn out to be impractical, costly, dull, or simply, and most important, off target.

The next category consisting of the so-called so-so ideas, deserves a slightly better treatment. Most of these ideas are practical; that is, they are affordable, logical, and more or less on target. So they should not be dismissed too quickly; perhaps in the future they will prove to be of use.

However, in advertising a good idea must be much more than just practical: it must be *inspired*. That is, it must be interesting enough to capture the attention of the millions of people caught more or less unawares. We are now looking at the tip of the pyramid: the good ideas. Not only do these ideas meet the criterion of being practical, but they are inspired as well, usually being spiced with an element of surprise. It is from this group that the winner emerges.

The Big Idea

As you keep screening out your ideas, you may (if luck will have it) encounter what is commonly and lovingly referred to in the trade as the "big idea." Then champagne will flow, with you cheerfully picking up the tab.

Not every idea can be construed as a big idea; nor is it necessary that every idea fit that description. The need for ideas is so intense in advertising that thousands of them must be improvised day after day as a matter of routine. It would be unrealistic to expect that every product turned out of this giant fantasy-making machine meet the stringent requirement of a big idea par excellence.

Curiously enough, top creative professionals all have the uncanny ability to recognize a big idea at once. They sense its presence, as if by osmosis. It is worth noting that such a large group of individualistic and sometimes highly opinionated people should be able to agree on what *is* and what *is not* a big idea. Yet, the subject invites few arguments, even though until now no one has been able to define the exact meaning of the term. Not even Webster. At the annual presentations of the regional conventions of the American Association of Advertising Agencies, where the unveiling of big ideas has long been part of the tribal ceremony, there are at least as many definitions as there are key speakers uttering them. Some say that all big ideas are based on a unique *marketing concept* (as in the exclusive selling of Tupperware through "housewife hostesses"). Others insist that a big idea is just another name for the *creative platform* (as in "You have a friend" for Chase Manhattan Bank), and it is this that acts as the launching pad of all that follows. Still others maintain that the secret of success lies in *execution* (as in the use of one Alan Rippy, a 5-year-old youngster demonstrating the size of a McDonald's Jumbo Jack Burger by stuffing it into his mouth). Who is to say which definition is right or wrong? They overlap. Most creative platforms are solidly grounded in marketing concepts, and vice versa. Along the same lines, *execution* often reflects the campaign theme.

It appears that about the only common denominator of big ideals is that they are basic. Like the proverbial paper-clip idea, a big idea is usually simple in concept, inviting an immediate "Why didn't I think of that?" reaction. It is never just a play on words, a superficial visual gimmick. Most big ideas, in fact, are so obvious that they are surprisingly easy to explain, and often without visual aids.

What Is a Big Idea? A Few Examples

Avis: We try harder.
Hathaway Shirt eye patch
Braniff: The end of the plain plane.
Chase Manhattan: The friendly bank.
Schaefer: The one beer to have when you're having more than one.
Clairol: Does she or doesn't she?
Join the people who've joined the Army.
(There is a story connected with this advertising theme.
It goes like this:
GENERAL: "And why do you like jumping out of airplanes, soldier?"
TROOPER: "I don't, sir."
GENERAL: "Then why are you here?"
TROOPER: "Because I like being around people who do, sir.")
Benson & Hedges: Cigarette break.
The nicest people ride Honda.
Volvo: The car for the people who think.
Perdue: It takes a tough man to make a tender chicken.
Hawaiian Punch
Gillette: The dry look.
Meow Mix: The cat food cats ask for by name.
Kodak film: For the time of your life.
Fighting cavities is the whole idea behind Crest.
The Olivetti girl
Charles Atlas: 97-pound weakling.
Maxwell House: Good to the last drop.
Greyhound: Leave the driving to us.
Marlboro country
Noxema shaving cream: Take it off, take it all off.
Lay's potato chips: Bet you can't eat just one.
Scope's medicine breath
AMF: We make weekends.
AT&T: Let your fingers do the walking.
Midas: We're shock specialists. We have to do a better job.
Container Corporation of America: Great ideas of Western man.
It's the Pepsi generation.
United Airlines' friendly skies
Kellogg: Best to you each morning.
There's a Ford in your future.
Smirnoff: It leaves you breathless.
I dreamed I was wearing a Maidenform bra.
Please don't squeeze the Charmin.
Nobody but nobody undersells Gimbel's.
New York Times: All the news that's fit to print.

Air travel: Fly now, pay later.

Geritol: For tired blood.

Virginia Slims: You've come a long way, Baby.

Ladies Home Journal: Never underestimate the power of a woman.

Florists Telegraph Delivery: Say it with flowers.

United School of Music: They laughed when I sat down at the piano, but when I began to play. . . .

Bell System: The next best thing to being there.

Fortunoff: The source.

Morton Salt: When it rains, it pours.

Mennen skin bracer: Thanks, I needed that.

Cutty Sark: Don't give up the ship!

Dr. Pepper: America's most misunderstood soft drink.

Volkswagen: The bug.

Alka-Seltzer: On the rocks.

What Every Creative Person Can Learn from the Binary System

The way of computers seems a far cry from what we commonly like to think of as the creative process. Certainly, none of these electronic prodigies ever conceived an idea as we understand it. Yet, to give credit where credit is due, they are superb problem solvers in their own right.

The key lies in their ability to answer any sufficiently crisp question by a single binary digit: 0 or 1, yes or no. In this respect, a creative person, who tends to look for several answers to several questions all at the same time, can learn a good deal from his or her "simpleminded" computerized peer.

Just think of it. The binary approach to problem solving prevents the computer from being sidetracked by irrelevancies such as "What will my boss think of the idea?" "Why am I doing this?" "I'm working too hard."

Nor does the computer go to the nearest bar to drown its sorrows if a particular question does not lend it-

self to an easy solution. It simply goes on and breaks down the problem into further components by the process of elimination until it finally finds one that can be answered positively **or** negatively. (One can be as useful a bit of information as the other in problem solving.)

In some ways, then, a computer follows the explorations of a finely honed creative mind. Human beings, too, in their quest for a solution, go on extended branching-out expeditions. But here the similarity ends. For the computer has no personal ax to grind to keep making discoveries for its own sake. It clearly wants to get the whole thing over with as quickly as possible.

Reluctance to stop examining the spectrum of possibilities and say "This is it," in the everlasting hope of finding something just a little better, is perhaps a commendable trait, but one that often tries the patience of clients looking for signs of progress. Perhaps computers are trying to tell us something about the art of problem solving, namely, that in the final analysis all the answers to any problem boil down to two simple words in the English language: yes and no.

CREATIVITY BY PROCESS OF ELIMINATION: HOW A NEW CADILLAC WAS NAMED

Naming a new car is a serious business. It took the management of the General Motors Cadillac Division almost a year of winnowing more than 400 suggestions before selecting the winner.

The new car was to be a compact Cadillac designed to carry its passengers in the highest attainable level of luxury and to compete with foreign luxury cars such as the Mercedes 450E and the Jaguar XJ12L. The car would be expensive, in the middle to upper range of the Cadillac lineup.

Recommendations came from advertising-agency employees, the marketing staff, and executives within the company. These were submitted to a group of ten to twelve people, mostly from marketing, sales departments, and the advertising agency, and were rated with one to five stars, much as in movie ratings.

By process of elimination, strong names were retained for further study. They were investigated for awareness, association with Cadillac, and shades of subtle meaning. Surviving names were then presented for reaction to owners of Cadillacs and other luxury cars and, finally, to top General Motors officers, including the president and the chairman of the board.

General Guidelines

1. Suitable for Cadillac in terms of up-scale, high-quality luxury implications.

2. Preferably easily associated with Cadillac so that the company would not have to spend a great deal of money on advertising to develop relevance.

3. Easily pronounced.

4. Having a reasonably apparent meaning so that it would not have to be defined through advertising (Chevrolet had a difficult time with Vega in this respect).

5. Lacking negative meanings, either generally distasteful or insulting to an ethnic or racial group.

6. Without braggadocio (for example, delegance, dellegante), as the car's essential definition is one of elegance.

7. Having a possible association with smaller size or economy of operation.

8. A French name would, of course, be appropriate for Cadillac.

9. Having a possible suggestion of worldwide appeal, as Cadillac does plan to be more aggressive in stopping the inroads of luxury imports and to branch out into export markets.

10. Possessing a possible tie-in with patriotism for the same reasons.

11. The name had to look proper on the car and in advertising.

12. Finally, the name had to be legally available and not be associated with a competitor's product.

List of Names Submitted

Amati	Cabriolet	Cadillac Leland	Carriole
Americus	Cadillac Allegro	Cadillac Mignon	Cartier
Arcadia	Cadillac Attache	Cadillac Normandy	Castellian
Aspen	Cadillac Biarritz	Cadillac Renaissance	Cavalier
Barcelona	Cadillac Charisma	Cadillac Road America	Charme
Beau Villeur	Cadillac Compagnon	Cadillac St. Moritz	Charmont
Beaupre	Cadillac Concept II	Cadillac Town Sedan	Chartres
Berkshire	Cadillac Concord	Cadillac Urbana	Chatelain
Bolero	Cadillac Crest	Cadillac Vignette	Classic/Classico
Bonaventure	Cadillac Dauphin	Caleche	Concept (III)
Bordeaux	Cadillac De Leon	Camelot	Concord
Brevette	Cadillac Elanceur	Canterbury	Conquester
Brougham Suburban	Cadillac Encore	Capitan	Conquistador
Caballero	Cadillac Envoy	Caravelle	Conserver
Cabretta	Cadillac L'Aiglon	Caroche	Constitution

Corona	Elantour	Legend	Revere
Counselor	Eldorado II	L'Elan	Rochelle
Couronne	Elevado	Leland	St. Nicholas Degrave
Courtier	Essex	Lexington	San Laurent
Cygnet	Exemplar	Liberte	Sedan De Cite
D'Alentour	Emplexl	Libre	SeVille
DaVinci	Garonne	Lido	Sheffield
De Integro	Gascony	Luxury	Sierra
Deauville	Grand Monde	Majestic	Somerville
Debonair	Hautton	Marseille	Sorrentian
DeEllegante	La Aygnette	Medici	Sovereign
DeLegance	La Espada	Merlette El	Tarnet
Delphine	La Estrada	Minuet	Torrero
Director	La Mancha	Noblesse	Tourismo
Du Monde	La Salle II	Park Avenue	Town Brougham
Du Reveil	La Scala	Patrice	Triomphe
Du Villageur	Laumet	Patrician	Verlaine
DuQuesne	Laurel	Pontchartrain	Versailles
DuVoisineur	Le Cygne	Prince	5.75 GL (Gran Lux)
Elancer	Le Nouviau	Provencal	60 Special
Elanceur	L'Eclipse	Regis	

Accepted and Tested by the Marketing Department

Allegro	Du Monde	L'Aiglon	Renaissance
Biarritz	Encore	Leland	St. Moritz
Concord	Envoy	Lexington	Seville
Constitution	La Salle	Mignon	
Corrone	La Scala	Normandy	

Preferred by the Design Center Product Clinic

Allegro	Encore	Envoy	La Salle

Researched among luxury-car owners

Allegro	Du Monde	La Salle	Seville
Couronne	Envoy	St. Moritz	

Most preferred names

La Salle	St. Moritz	Seville

Final choice made by management

Seville

Rationale for Final Choice During research, Seville did not produce any negative reactions. It did not have quite the positive thrust of La Salle or even St. Moritz, but it certainly lacked the controversy of La Salle (years ago a car named La Salle did not sell). Moreover, it had other things going for it:

1. The name was easily associated with Cadillac, being very close to DeVille (The division's biggest seller), and many people remembered the top of the line from 1956 to 1960, the Cadillac Eldorado Seville models.

2. The Spanish province and city of Seville are renowned for their history, art treasures, and architecture—an up-scale association.

3. There was the possibility that, in the future, the current Eldorado might be replaced by a smaller coupe, in which case Cadillac could retain the Eldorado name plate and perhaps call the smaller sedan Eldorado Seville, reuniting these two name plates, and the coupe Eldorado Biarritz (another valued Cadillac name from the past)—something with a slightly sportier flair. Thus "Seville" appeared to be the most practical choice.

CREATIVITY BY PROCESS OF ELIMINATION: HOW TELEVISION COMMERCIALS WERE CONCEIVED FOR A PUBLIC SERVICE CAMPAIGN

Research shows that while there was no lack of interest in organ donations (7 out of 10 people expressed willingness to make such a donation), most people simply did not know how to make a posthumous commitment. The purpose of this campaign was to overcome this information gap and, at the same time, to demonstrate to the medical community and to various government agencies (particularly Medicare) that the success of an organ procurement program very much depended upon a professionally executed mass-media advertising campaign.

[*Campaign created by the author*]

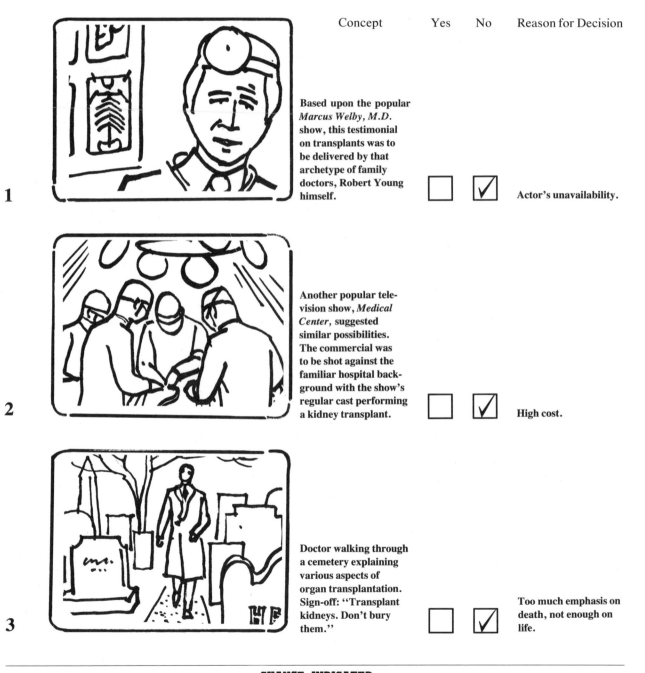

	Concept	Yes	No	Reason for Decision
1	Based upon the popular *Marcus Welby, M.D.* show, this testimonial on transplants was to be delivered by that archetype of family doctors, Robert Young himself.	☐	☑	Actor's unavailability.
2	Another popular television show, *Medical Center,* suggested similar possibilities. The commercial was to be shot against the familiar hospital background with the show's regular cast performing a kidney transplant.	☐	☑	High cost.
3	Doctor walking through a cemetery explaining various aspects of organ transplantation. Sign-off: "Transplant kidneys. Don't bury them."	☐	☑	Too much emphasis on death, not enough on life.

CHANGE INDICATED

A more upbeat approach needed. Avoid funereal connotations.

	Concept	Yes	No	Reason for Decision

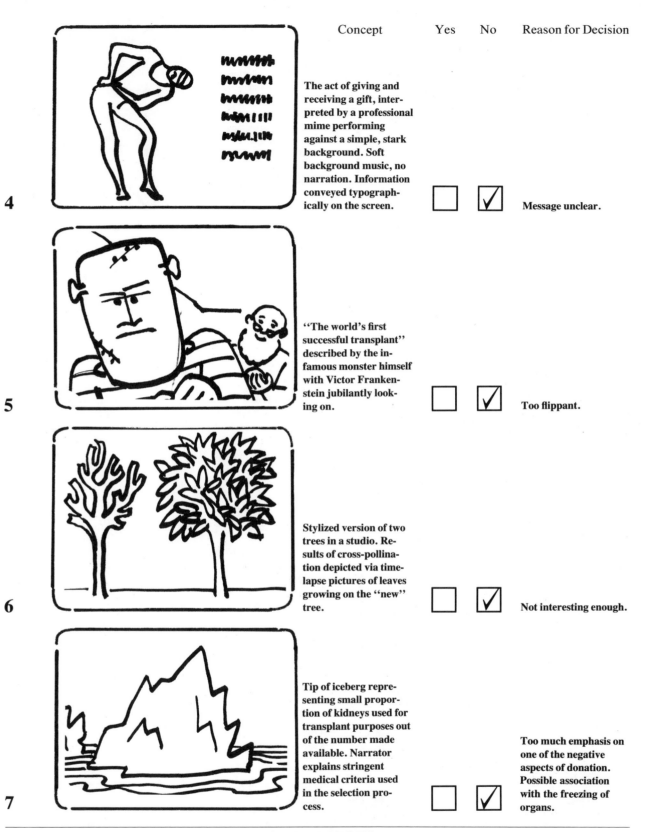

4 The act of giving and receiving a gift, interpreted by a professional mime performing against a simple, stark background. Soft background music, no narration. Information conveyed typographically on the screen. ☐ ☑ Message unclear.

5 "The world's first successful transplant" described by the infamous monster himself with Victor Frankenstein jubilantly looking on. ☐ ☑ Too flippant.

6 Stylized version of two trees in a studio. Results of cross-pollination depicted via time-lapse pictures of leaves growing on the "new" tree. ☐ ☑ Not interesting enough.

7 Tip of iceberg representing small proportion of kidneys used for transplant purposes out of the number made available. Narrator explains stringent medical criteria used in the selection process. ☐ ☑ Too much emphasis on one of the negative aspects of donation. Possible association with the freezing of organs.

CHANGE INDICATED

Impact of real-life situations, as opposed to imaginary ones, was becoming increasingly apparent. The decision was reached to use only actual transplant recipients or donors, or both, in the commercials.

	Concept	Yes	No	Reason for Decision

8

Two candles flickering against a dark background with the shorter one slowly dying out. Concurrently, the flame shoots higher from the taller candle as background music picks up. Life through organ donation is explained.

☐ ☑

Light going out is synonymous with dying; the message is too blunt.

9

CBS live newscast on an actual kidney transplant (a first on television) had the makings of a 60-second commercial, especially the scene showing the various procedures.

☐ ☑

Dialysis showed up as a poor second choice to transplant, still a somewhat controversial issue among members of the medical profession.

10

Slot machine ringing up the jackpot symbolizes a perfect match of kidneys (at least four compatible antigens), which minimizes the prospect of immunological rejection. Happy recipients surround the machine and wave at the camera.

☐ ☑

Slot machine connotes risk taking.

11

A young man named Sam Fleisher nearly lost his job in a camera store because of failing eyesight. A cornea transplant saved his vision, and presently he became manager. In this commercial, he looks over a camera and suggests that "it's easier to get parts for a camera than for people."

☑ ☐

This spot was produced, garnering four major awards. However, it emphasized cornea transplants. Commercials covering other organ transplants were needed.

Concept	Yes	No	Reason for Decision

12 Group recipients (of all ages, sexes, and races) riding bicycles through the park are identified by name. Voice-over explains how a transplant (eye, kidney, and so on) made it possible for these people to live happy, normal lives again. Donor card shown at the end of the commercial. ☑ ☐ All types of transplants were represented here. Shot by photographer Bert Stern, the commercial was praised for its artistic excellence. As a public service announcement, it was given more than $500,000 worth of free exposure on the air by networks and individual stations.

13 Howling Wolfe, an old-time blues singer and guitar player, has been waiting for his transplant for several years. Sitting next to an artificial-kidney machine, he sings about his fate, accompanied by his guitar. ☐ ☑ Patient died just before the commercial was to be shot.

14 George Butcher was a professional musician unable to find employment while undergoing dialysis three afternoons a week. In this commercial, he reenacts the scene of receiving an unexpected phone call from the hospital early one morning, announcing the availability of a kidney. ☑ ☐ This award-winning commercial was also well received by all transplant programs throughout the country. Mr. Butcher proved to be an accomplished actor, inspiring a 15-minute movie based on his true life story with him as the star.

15 Supreme authority on ecclesiastical matters, the Pope himself explains the position of the Catholic Church in in regard to organ donation. ☐ ☑ Only one religion, the Roman Catholic, is represented.

Use the same concept, but include other faiths.

	Concept	Yes	No	Reason for Decision

16

Three dignitaries, representing Catholic, Protestant, and Jewish faiths, discuss aspects of organ donation from a religious point of view.

☐ Yes ☑ No

Religion appeared as too controversial a subject.

17

Expressions of love (between individuals and God, men and women, parents and children, citizens and country) shown in colorful animation. Last scene shows the culmination of generosity, the donor leaving behind the gift of life, his body.

☐ Yes ☑ No

Too expensive.

18

Script was prepared to reflect Phyllis Diller's rambunctious, self-effacing personality, as she offers her "less than perfect body" to posterity to an unseen but enthusiastic audience until the very end of the commercial, when her last line, "My hair, anyone?" is met with stunned silence.

☑ Yes ☐ No

The popularity of Phyllis Diller made this commercial a favorite with television stations all over the country. Her tongue-in-cheek presentation did not detract at all from the essential integrity of the message.

19

Anny Krilovitch received her kidney shortly before this commercial was shot. Here, family and friends throw a mock birthday party to celebrate the beginning of her "second life." At the closing, Anny, now no longer on a strict diet, takes a bite of her birthday cake.

☑ Yes ☐ No

Movie director Len Steckler supervised this commercial; performers were neighborhood children and family members.

CAMERA STORE: 60 SECONDS

A true story about a man whose cornea transplant restored his sight 5 years ago and who now works as a manager of a camera store. He narrates: My name is Sam Fleisher. Five years ago I almost lost my job in this camera store. I was going blind. But now I can see again. Someone left me a cornea for transplant. You know you can make any part you need for a camera. But for people . . . spare parts just don't come easily. Sometimes they don't come at all. Which brings me up to what I wanted to say . . . More organs are needed for transplantation. Not only corneas but kidneys, livers, blood, and other parts. Transplants do work. I know.

PHYLLIS DILLER DONATES HER BODY: 60 SECONDS

Her face and body have long been the butt of this famous comedienne's self-effacing jokes. Here she donates it all to posterity, to the merriment of her audience. Ms. Diller carries a donor card.

Says she: You know, for years people made fun of my body . . . some even said it was less than perfect.

I meant to talk to you about that.

Because I want you to know that I'm donating it to posterity.

Oh, be quiet.

I'm talking about my kidneys, eyes, and all the good parts, silly.

You see this Donor Card? My name is on it. Phyllis Diller. Maybe someday this will save someone's life.

You know, there are thousands of people out there waiting for organs.

Yours and mine. And some die waiting. Now as far as I'm concerned, they can have whatever they need. After all, I'll be gone and they'll still be around. So why not?

Thank you.

My hair anyone?

THE EVOLUTION OF AN IDEA: DISCOVER BY DOING

Ideas feed upon themselves. Some errors in creative judgment become apparent only after they have been committed, suggesting other and more effective alternatives. Such is the nature of the creative process. In this instance, through trial and error the following facts emerged:

1. An *upbeat creative approach* was more effective in terms of both media acceptance and public reaction.

2. Use of *actual recipients or donors* not only was more economical (no residuals had to be paid) but also lent credibility to the presentation.

3. *Umbrella campaign* promoting the donation of several organs (kidneys, eyes, and so on) made it possible for five important local public service organizations* jointly to support a public education effort, for the first time in history.

4. Use of the *Uniform Donor Card* in the commercials brought immediate and measurable response. These statistics were useful in obtaining financial support from the United States government through Medicare.

Too grim

Too much humor, detracting from message

Too abstract, not people-oriented enough

Realistic, believable, hitting on the right tone for message

Too gruesome

Still too gruesome

Switch

Not serious enough

Switch

Too abstract

Switch

Modify

Get testimony

Modify

Offbeat but still believable

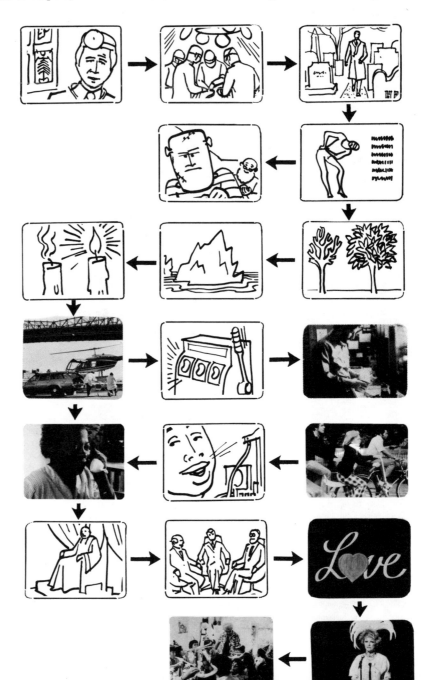

*Eye Bank for Sight Restoration, Inc.: Kidney Foundation of New York, Inc.: National Association of Patients on Hemodialysis and Transplantation, Inc.: New York–New Jersey Regional Transplant Program; Ruth Gottscho Kidney Foundation.

Chapter Eight

When Technique Is the Idea

Sometimes, technique—writing style, choice of illustration, typography, layout—is so distinctive that it becomes the single most memorable feature in an advertisement. In this case, the manner of execution, more than any other factor, is the big idea. We shall see numerous examples on the following pages. The contributions of experienced craftsmen, such as artists and writers in an advertising agency, are particularly important in this area.

Gimmickry or a Solid Idea?

At the hand of an advertising professional, *technique never overpowers the message*. Technique is not selected for its own sake. Like everything else in advertising, it is determined only after careful analysis of the basic purpose of the campaign.

Technique can never make up for lack of a solid advertising concept. Many brilliantly executed campaigns have failed for this very reason: there was no viable creative platform, marketing concept, or product features on which to build meaningful copy claims. Today's consumers are a sophisticated lot. Average persons are quite able to decipher the difference between style and substance. Impressed as they may be by the theatrical production values of a commercial,

they are unlikely to make a purchase just to show their appreciation for having been so royally entertained. One way to find out when and where a technique may be getting in the way is to study audience playbacks carefully. Whenever such comments as "It was a funny commercial", "Who was the model?" "I enjoyed the background music," and "Beautiful photography" are made by viewers with any consistency, take heed. This is a sure danger sign that the viewers' attention has been drawn away from the meaning of the message and to the fine points of execution of the commercial.

Big Picture or All Copy?

There is much ado in advertising about the relative merits of pictures as opposed to words. The fact is that there are probably no hard-and-fast rules regarding this issue. As in everything else, form follows function in advertising too.

Writers who doodle and designers who scribble (there are many of both kinds) are usually able to come up with the "perfect" balance between words and pictures. They are aided by their ability to form a mental picture of the final ad. Only a few of us have that inspired an imagination.

So, more often than not, we have art directors and writers both busily grinding their respective axes. Some

writers genuinely feel that the message must be spelled out in every detail, ignoring the subtle yet dynamic aspects of picture talk. At the other extreme are the art directors who so embrace the axiom "One picture is worth 1000 words" that they would just as soon do without the English language altogether.

Perhaps it should be noted here, in support of our visually minded colleagues, that the impact of pictures, especially on the television screen, may be such that the message can be delivered with few or no words and sometimes more effectively. In settling arguments, perhaps both art directors and writers should take note of the policy followed by most television stations in the country: when the picture is lost in a commercial because of some electronic fluke, 75 percent of the time cost is rebated to the advertiser. When the sound is lost, the figure is only 25 percent. Or, according to a survey conducted by Anny/SAM/MAC, more than twice as many magazine readers are captured by a picture in an ad than by a headline. And more of the same: In a 30-second announcement on the services of his own agency, Julian Koenig of Copywriters Hall of Fame played himself walking toward the camera, flashing on a business card. Not a word was spoken.

One thing is certain: it takes a close and understanding relationship between writer and art director to produce the proper blend of words and pictures.

The Lazy Man's Way to Riches

'Most People Are Too Busy Earning a Living to Make Any Money'

I used to work hard. The 18-hour days. The 7-day weeks.

But I didn't start making big money until I did less—a *lot* less.

For example, this ad took about 2 hours to write. With a little luck, it should earn me 50, maybe a hundred thousand dollars.

What's more, I'm going to ask you to send me 10 dollars for something that'll cost me no more than 50 cents. And I'll try to make it so irresistible that you'd be a darned fool not to do it.

After all, why should you care if I make $9.50 profit if I can show you how to make a *lot* more?

What if I'm so sure that you *will* make money my Lazy Man's Way that I'll make you the world's most unusual guarantee?

And here it is: I won't even cash your check or money order for 31 days *after* I've sent you my material.

That'll give you plenty of time to get it, look it over, try it out.

If you don't agree that it's worth *at least a hundred times* what it cost you, send it back. Your *uncashed* check or money order will be put in the return mail.

The only reason I won't send it to you and bill you or send it C.O.D. is because both these methods involve more time and money.

And I'm already going to give you the biggest bargain of your life.

Because I'm going to tell you what it took me 11 years to perfect: How to make money the Lazy Man's Way.

O.K.—now I have to brag a little. I don't mind it. And it's necessary—to prove that sending me the 10 dollars... which I'll keep "in escrow" until you're satisfied... is the smartest thing you ever did.

I live in a home that's worth $100,000. I know it is, because I turned down an offer for that much. My mortgage is less than half that, and the only reason I haven't paid it off is because my Tax Accountant says I'd be an idiot.

My "office," about a mile and a half from my home, is right on the beach. My view is so breathtaking that most people comment that they don't see how I get any work done. But I do enough. About 6 hours a day, 8 or 9 months a year.

The rest of the time we spend at our mountain "cabin." I paid $30,000 for it—cash.

I have 2 boats and a Cadillac. All paid for.

We have stocks, bonds, investments, cash in the bank. But the most important thing I have is priceless: time with my family.

And I'll show you just how I did it—the Lazy Man's Way—a secret that I've shared with just a few friends 'til now.

It doesn't require "education." I'm a high school graduate.

It doesn't require "capital." When I started out, I was so deep in debt that a lawyer friend advised bankruptcy as the only way out. He was wrong. We paid off our debts and, outside of the mortgage, don't owe a cent to any man.

It doesn't require "luck." I've had

more than my share, but I'm not promising you that you'll make as much money as I have. And you may do better; I personally know one man who used these principles, worked hard, and made 11 million dollars in 8 years. But money isn't everything.

It doesn't require "talent." Just enough brains to know what to look for. And I'll tell you that.

It doesn't require "youth." One woman I worked with is over 70. She's travelled the world over, making all the money she needs, doing only what I taught her.

It doesn't require "experience." A widow in Chicago has been averaging $25,000 a year for the past 5 years, using my methods.

What *does* it require? Belief. Enough to take a chance. Enough to absorb what I'll send you. Enough to put the principles into *action*. If you do just that—nothing more, nothing less—the results *will* be hard to believe. Remember—I guarantee it.

You don't have to give up your job. But you may soon be making so much money that you'll be able to. Once again—I guarantee it.

The wisest man I ever knew told me something I never forgot: "Most people are too busy earning a living to make any money."

Don't take as long as I did to find out he was right.

I'll prove it to you, if you'll send in the coupon now. I'm not asking you to "believe" me. Just try it. If I'm wrong, all you've lost is a couple of minutes and an 8-cent stamp. But what if I'm right?

Sworn Statement:

"I have examined this advertisement. On the basis of personal acquaintance with Mr. Joe Karbo for 18 years and my professional relationship as his accountant, I certify that every statement is true." [Accountant's name available upon request.]

Bank Reference:
American State Bank
675 South Main Street
Orange, California 92668

- - - - - - - - - - - - - - - -

Joe Karbo
17105 South Pacific, Dept. 432-B
Sunset Beach, California 90742

Joe, you may be full of beans, but what have I got to lose? Send me the Lazy Man's Way to Riches. *But don't deposit my check or money order for 31 days after it's in the mail.*

If I return your material—for *any* reason—within that time, return my *uncashed* check or money order to me. On that basis, here's my ten dollars.

☐ Please send Air Mail. I'm enclosing an extra dollar.

Name _____

Address _____

City _____

State _____ Zip _____

© 1973 Joe Karbo

This ad pulled several hundred responses each time it appeared in newspapers and magazines, paying for itself several times over. Long copy, set tight, gives readers the impression that they are being told the whole story with nothing important left out. Had the copy been greatly reduced to make the ad more pleasing to the eye, coupon returns probably would have suffered. Beautiful pictures, judicious use of white space, and other layout devices *in this case* would have been inconsistent with the deliberately unslick, almost amateurish ambience.

Contrary to a popular myth, the cheese of Holland is neither expensive, nor strong tasting.

The headline "It won't bite" tells the story. Anything more not only would have been superfluous but also would have weakened the impact of the ad.

Combining an institutional message with information on specific merchandise, the world's largest retailer of silver and jewelry (Fortunoff, the Source) gives the reader something to look at *and* think about.

Pictures and words work well together when there is a strong rapport between the two chief creative protagonists in advertising, the copywriter and the art director. Each appreciates the fact that their modes of expression are as interdependent as the nucleus and electrons in the atomic structure.

Sizing up the Taste Level of the Audience

In selecting the "right" technique for an advertising campaign, the psychology of the audience may be even more important from an advertising point of view than the intrinsic value of the illustration itself. Picasso might may had a problem in selling breakfast cereal.

The overwhelming majority of Americans (research consistently supports this statement) still gravitate toward realism in art. "It sure looks like him," said of a portrait, is one of the highest forms of compliment to be bestowed upon an artist in this country, connoting that the artist has mastered his or her craft. Despite museum curators' and painters' contentions to the contrary, the most popular paintings are still those with which the public can readily identify. It is no coincidence that the highest price ever paid to a living American artist was paid to Andrew Wyeth for one of his high-fidelity photographic renderings. And the Society of Illustrators, a group of artists who probably pay as close attention as anyone does to the commercial art scene in America, has always encouraged realism in its annual exhibits as if by force of habit. It bears noting that not a single recipient of the society's coveted Medal of Honor given for "distinguished achievement in the art of illustration" has ever called himself an abstract painter, despite the fact that all of them have a designer's unerring eye for composition. Among the Hall of Fame members are Norman Rockwell, Floyd Davis, Walter Briggs, Al Parker, Al Dorne, Robert Fawcett, Peter Helck, Austin Briggs, and Steven Dohanos—all pictorial storytellers of people and places. Thus, in communicating with a mass audience, consider your subject matter first and style second.

Greeting-card manufacturers, such as Hallmark, give subject matter (landscapes, flowers, dogs) priority over technique (loose, tight, or stylized). Theme-oriented shows consistently draw a larger audience than those based on the work of a single artist. Both the Metropolitan Museum of Art and the Whitney Museum of American Art come around to dealing with themes in their special exhibits. The Museum of American Folk Art never used any other approach. Its show with the cat as a central motif predictably drew the largest crowd in the history of the institution; it is clear that more people are interested in cats than in art.

Mass marketers of fine paintings, such as department and art stores, the largest of which sell more than 250,000 moderately priced paintings a year, with frames providing most of the income, also find that their patrons tend to take a rather pragmatic approach toward the buying of art.

Requests tend to run along the following lines:

Subject: "We'd like to have something patriotic."
Size: "We have some wall space over our fireplace."
Color: "Something to go with our sofa . . . here's a swatch to compare."
Medium: "An oil painting, maybe, or something washable."

And finally,

Style: "Oh, I don't know too much about art, but. . . ."

The preference for realism explains the preponderance of photography in advertising: approximately 80 percent of all pictures use that technique.

Readership studies demonstrate that, all other things being equal, photography wins easily over illustration.

This is not to suggest that art directors should ignore any of the graphic techniques available today, photographic or other. For one thing, the brush is still more facile than the lens. For another, many "in" people take pride in their familiarity with art styles, such as Art Déco, Pop, and psychedelic, and feel attracted to the advertiser who, like themselves, appears to be aware of trends.

[Courtesy of Brown & Bigelow Advertising]

Reproductions of the famous poker-playing dogs by C. M. Coolidge, first issued in 1906, are still in print. Popular demand for this kind of calendar art, though labeled "corny" by many critics, has always been great and will probably remain so. Today's best sellers: Sierra Club's Wilderness Calendar and the Tolkien Middle Earth Calendar.

[Courtesy of Norcross]

This birthday card is typical of its kind, one that is much in demand. The subject matter is as important here as the art technique.

Few artists received as wide acclaim for their work as Norman Rockwell. To his credit are more than 300 covers for _The Saturday Evening Post_ in its heyday, in addition to some 2000 illustrations for various advertisers. A shrewd observer of the American scene, he created characters familiar to all of us.

118

Most art directors prefer photography when showing the "real thing": it helps to sell the product. The quiet beauty of an uncrowded beach is brought home by a simple, unretouched photograph taken for the Golden Rock resort. Similarly, it is the veracity of the camera that lends extra credibility to Aziza's mascara ad.

WHEN ILLUSTRATION WINS OVER PHOTOGRAPHY: EXCEPTIONS TO THE RULE

Marlboro cigarettes switched from photography to water-color paintings to accentuate the difference between Marlboro lights and regulars . . . while preserving its well-established masculine campaign theme. Department stores (shown here is a newspaper ad by Saks Fifth Avenue) are always searching for unusual art techniques to make their advertising look different from their competitors'.

It *creates a mood* for the product.

It helps *attract* the right type of audience.

It *sets apart* the advertiser's message.

It builds campaign *consistency*.

There are thousands of art techniques from which the advertising art director can choose. It helps to be familiar with as many as possible so that he or she can have the largest possible pool in seeking just the right talent.

This book cover, designed by superrealist Don Smith for a Ballantine science fiction series, is typical of its genre, one that beats photography at its own game. Turning a dream into reality, it is especially effective in this context. The same approach finds many applications in the advertising field. [Illustration by Boris Vallejo]

These sketches by Mary Jo Quay are realistic too, but her feel for fashion comes through unmistakably. They are quite different from the meticulously executed rendering on the left.

Pen-and-ink product illustrations (this one is for Hoffritz cutlery) show up the merchandise well and lend themselves to newspaper reproduction. Scrupulous attention to details makes drawings as convincing as their photographic counterparts.

GERRY GERSTEN

Represented by
Cullen Rapp
251 East 51 Street
New York, N.Y.
212 PLaza 1-4656

Most commercial illustrators are capable of changing their technique with their assignment. This one-page minicollection of illustrations by Gerry Gersten demonstrates his sure control of the pen, the pencil, and the brush.

SOME OF THE ART TECHNIQUES USED IN ADVERTISING

Abstract	Optical
Acrylic	Oriental
Airbrush	Ornamental
Antique	Paper sculpture
Aquatint	Paste-up
Art Nouveau	Pastel
Artist's market	Pencil
Benday	Photography
Calligraphy	aerial
Caricature	candid
Cartoon	miniature
Charcoal drawing	portrait
Children's drawings	stroboscopic
Collage	wide-angle
Conventional	Photoart combination
Crayon	Pointillism
Crosshatch	Pop
Decorative	Primitive
Drybrush	Psychedelic
Drypoint	Relief
Duotone	Romantic
Etching	Sampler stitching
Fine art	Sand painting
Finger painting	Sculpture
Flow pen	Silhouetting
Foil	Stippling
Futuristic	Stencil
Gouache	Stick figures
Hatch	Surrealism
Impressionistic	Symbolism
Initials	Tapestry
Lettering	Tempera
Line drawing	Typography
Loose sketch	Vignette
Modernism	Wash drawing
Montage	Watercoloring
Nonrepresentational	Weaving
Oil painting	Wood carving

This list is far from complete. It does not include new techniques, such as animation and stop motion, generated by makers of TV commercials.

A NOTE ABOUT AMERICAN TASTE: IT IS FICKLE

Art techniques fall in and out of favor with amazing rapidity in the United States, occasionally even within a few months.

The reach of mass media, changing lifestyles, and a never-satisfied gluttony for the new are among the reasons for the nation's short attention span.

Volatility makes it important for the advertising art director to keep a close watch on all forms of the arts, not only the graphic arts but also trends that "happen" in painting, literature, theater, music, dance, fashion, and architecture. There is much reciprocity between one type of art and another; a change in one inevitably makes itself felt in the other.

Fashion illustrators have the widest of all creative latitudes. Their art styles are often so individual that their work itself may serve as a theme on which to build an entire campaign, as in the case of Larry Laslo with his graphic interpretations for Hattie.

Somewhere between cartoon and real life are the drawings by Little Moon. Inspired by illustrations used some 50 years ago, she came up with her own contemporary version of them.

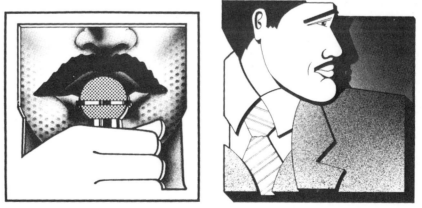

A totally new technique is being explored in these black, white, and shades-of-gray illustrations by Jack Messling. Although they are not fashion drawings in the traditional sense, their simplicity connotes sophistication, and they blend right in with the look of the *Gentlemen's Quarterly*.

Just what is meant by a cartoon? That is a matter of individual interpretation. All the illustrations on this page could be called cartoons, even though they look very different. This is one of a series of posters for Del Monte executed in the manner of a child's drawing.

Charles Saxon is one of several name cartoonists active in the advertising field. His approach lends itself to wide commercial applications; although his drawings are not realistic in the strict sense, his characters are instantly identifiable.

One of the least inhibited and fastest on the draw of all cartoonists is Bill Charmatz. Spontaneity lends a peculiar charm to his drawings. Wally Neibart's characters are more tightly drawn but are exaggerated enough to pass as cartoons.

Working under the aegis of the same studio may be a number of different illustrators, representing a wide gamut of graphic styles.

Where does illustration stop and design begin? The question may be only a matter of semantics. An instinct for composition enables most illustrators to pass as designers. Bary Zaid's silhouettes show his fine understanding of space relationships. Below, the typographical design for a Pioneer Moss advertisement is more the work of a designer than that of a typographer.

An innate sense of design often shows up on the television screen as well. Bob Abel photographed forty-two separate camera passes over the same footage as he superimposed his artwork on live photography in this unique commercial for Seven-Up, "the UNcola."

125

Many artists develop their own distinctive styles early in their careers. Some of the best artwork is produced by young talent and can be had at affordable prices. Celebrating the bicentennial year are six graphic interpretations of America out of fifty-six submitted by students at the School of Visual Arts in New York.

More and more photographers are able to put a strong personal stamp on their work. It is really this which separates one photographer from another, more so than the variety of cameras they own, the size of their skylights, or the number of laboratory assistants they have working in their darkrooms. Not surprisingly, photographers carry their individual styles into television when and if they decide to become film directors, as many do.

(top) Editorial photography, whether used for editorial or for advertising purposes, is recognizable by its straightforward, no-nonsense approach. Master of the art form, Leon Kuzmanoff lets his camera record nothing but the truth in this strong, unretouched portrayal of a farming couple, with their life story etched deeply on their faces.

(right) A very different kind of approach to his subject is taken by fashion-beauty photographer Stan Shaffer of Bloomingdale fame. Actions and facial expressions are all planned carefully. To stylize the setting, the background is kept stark. Top models—Denise Hopkins, Tony Spinelli, Janice Dickenson—having developed the ability to "see themselves through the photographer's eyes," can offer their own considerable creative contributions.

The photographer as cartoonist came into his or her own in the last couple of decades, and not without the pioneering work of Howard Zieff, whose talent in this area brought him fortune and fame. A master of his craft, Zieff has an uncanny knack of bringing out the best in his models, even novices, such as a photography salesman and a laboratory assistant posing here for the book *How to Play Golf in the Low 120's*. To the right is a color picture shot in the studio by Stephen Steigman for Pfizer, spoofing Emanuel Leutze's famous painting of Washington crossing the Delaware River.

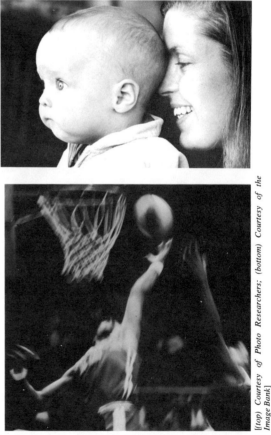

Many photographers have the instincts of a designer, just as illustrators do. Hugh Bell manipulates his graphic elements, lights and shadow, in this fine composition.

Some photographers specialize in certain types of photography. On top is one of thousands of baby pictures taken by Suzanne Szasz, a past mistress in the handling of unruly tots. Unfazed by the problems of indoor lighting is sports enthusiast-action photographer Mel DiGiacomo.

Technical know-how can be an important factor in the creation of unusual photographic effects. Raised high above the ground by a boom-type lift, John Paul Endress took this remarkable color photograph of Eastern Airlines' president and crew from an aerial work platform.

Panoramic 360° photography by Douglas Mesney, using a camera that revolves around a tripod, offers an unusual view of Fifth Avenue.

The wide-angle lens of a camera is a powerful tool in the hands of a knowledgeable photographer, making near objects appear very large and distant objects very small. This gives the impression that things are nearer to or farther from the camera than they really are. In these photographs, Phil Mazzurco demonstrates how to ignore the rules of perspective. Automobile manufacturers, always looking for ways to make their cars appear longer and sleeker, are understandably fond of this photographic technique.

Imaginative photographers know how to inspire their models. Shown here are a few of the 288 frames which Barry Evans took in about 3 hours. Neither subject had modeled professionally before.

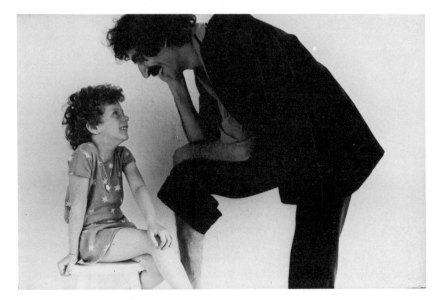

Still-life objects, like people, can be photographed in many different ways. With modern lighting and camera techniques, the photographer has a wide range of options from which to choose. This photograph by Arthur Beck makes a cherry pie look appetizing under the watchful eyes of a home economist in the studio.

In this still life Michael O'Neil is using his instinct for composition. Casual as the table setting may seem, nothing whatever has been left to chance.

A different mood is created in this *trompe-l'oeil* photograph by Ben Somoroff. The tones, mostly browns and reds, are muted. This is a low-key photograph—an interesting change of pace on the pages of today's magazines, dominated almost entirely by high-key photography. NOTE: It is important to bear in mind that all good professional photographers can switch styles to accommodate an advertiser's needs. Here, Ben Somoroff decided to use a low-key technique as best to convey the quality of silverware.

Stock photographs can be beautiful, too. Color transparencies like these, reproduced here in black and white, were culled from the thousands available at Four by Five, Inc., in New York, one of the several stock-photograph houses distributing high-quality pictures.

For a realistic approach, stock drawings are made available for subscribers of the Metro Newspaper Service, one of the firms which provides easy-to-reproduce black-and-white and color mats to local retail stores. Middle of the road in art style, these illustrations have a grass-roots appeal all their own.

Love is a basic human emotion, enjoying universal appeal. It can be interpreted in many ways, limited only by the imagination of the copywriter and the art director and their understanding of the psychology of their audience.

MANIPULATING THE PERSONALITY OF AN OBJECT PHOTOGRAPHICALLY

A single object, in this case a chair, adopts human qualities as the photographer manipulates camera angles, lights and shadows, composition, and background.

Elegant

Unassuming

Loving

Uncordial and cordial

Cheerful and cheerless

And Now Back to the Illustrator A sensitive artist like his colleague behind the camera, the illustrator also has the power to have his object assume a variety of roles. Here Jerry McDaniel, with the aid of a pen, a brush, and a dexterous hand, shows how it is done.

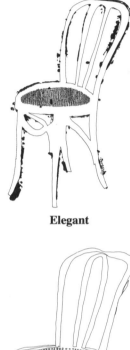

Elegant

Feminine

Masculine and feminine

Masculine

[*Photographs were taken by Alfred Gescheidt for another book by the author,* Visual Persuasion: The Effect of Pictures on the Subconscious, *published by the McGraw-Hill Book Company*]

OLD MASTERS: SOURCE OF INSPIRATION

Since the day primeval man reached for a piece of singed wood to record his impressions on cave walls, artists have been busily developing their own personal styles, many of which have found wide commercial application. Examples are shown here. They are Francis Bacon Gerard's romanticized oils, the frankly erotic pen-and-ink drawings of Aubrey Beardsley, the uninhibited brush strokes of Picasso, René Prinet's famous painting *The Violinist,* which came to symbolize Dana perfume for more than 35 years (no copy was ever needed to tell the story, just the name of the provocation, Tabu; it was assumed that was what stopped the music). A few of the fine artists of more recent vintage whose styles have been adapted commercially are Charles Dana Gibson, N. C. Wyeth, John Held (creator of flapper Margie), May Wilson Preston (tots and babies for Gerber & Johnson in the 1920s), Gluyas Williams, Rube Goldberg, J. C. Leyendecker (creator of the Arrow Collar man), and Russel Patterson (known for his miniskirted, patent-leather–haired flappers).

Says Thomas W. Laughlin, director of creative services of Clinton Frank Advertising, about his agency's colorful two-page magazine illustration: ''This particular ad received more response from readers than any other we have created in recent years. The Dean Food Company has received scores of letters and phone calls requesting reprints. To quote one of the writers: 'Maxfield Parrish must be turning over in his grave . . . with envy.' ''

O C T O B E R

Old movie stills are made available by some public libraries and museums, pictorial archives, stock-photograph houses, and motion picture studios. They can be used effectively in advertising, sales presentations, house organs and the like to highlight various copy points.

As might have been expected, Art Déco of the late 1920s and the 1930s again became a favorite with designers after a 40-year hiatus. Its economy of line and judicious use of white space fit the mood of contemporary advertising. A strange but compatible bedfellow with almost any art style, even photography, it turns up at the most unexpected places. And its black-and-white linear treatment (still one of the most striking color combinations) lends itself to reproduction on the grainiest paper.

Above is a full-page newspaper ad for a Baskin Robbins ice cream store. The graphics are typically Art Déco—an artistic subtlety that perhaps went over the heads of a few Midwestern housewives but nonetheless was efficacious.

Below are a few of the many typefaces based on the rich legacy of the Art Déco period.

Old pictures like this project a different meaning when used in a new context. Contemporary dilemmas, such as human contamination of the environment, urbanization, and overpopulation have been chronicled by many bygone artists, as shown in this print, one in the Bettman Archive's 3-million-plus collection of graphic memorabilia.

BENTLEY light

EXPRESS express

FLAPPER LINED

[Courtesy of M. J. Baumwell Typography]

137

GEOMETRY: A PERENNIAL SOURCE OF GOOD DESIGN

Almost everything around us, be it a building, fashion, furniture, typography, or, for that matter, nature's creations, is in some sense geometrical in construction. That is because the principles of good design are compatible with strict mathematical formulas. The architects of ancient Greece realized this, as do most of today's commercial artists. They know that symmetry, logic, and tidiness can produce greater visual lucidity. Going from the past to the present are a few examples shown on these pages.

The textbook definition of *advertising layout* is "the arranging of various elements within a given space," with the art director in charge. Geometrical gambits can have considerable visual impact, as in this double truck for Jamaica or the trademark designs shown below.

flowers

[*From Yasaburo Kuwayama:* Trade Marks and Symbols]

138

DANSKINS ARE NOT JUST FOR DANCING

THEY'RE FOR DOWNHILL RACERS, CROSS-COUNTRY TREKKERS, HIKERS, CYCLISTS, AND EVERYONE WHO'S ABSOLUTELY ADDICTED TO OUTDOOR SPORTS. TURTLENECK RACING STRIPE BODYSUIT AND TRICOLOR BICYCLE STRIPE BODYSUIT 17.50. MATCHING LONG JOHNS 8.75. ALL MADE OF DANSKIN'S HEAVYWEIGHT COTTON AND LYCRA® SPANDEX BLEND IN SIZES S, M, L. AVAILABLE AT LORD & TAYLOR AND OTHER FINE STORES. WRITE FOR BROCHURE NY11. DANSKIN, INC., 1114 AVENUE OF THE AMERICAS, N.Y. N.Y. 10036.

DANSKIN

The layout for Danskin is based upon subtle geometric space relationships, as are the label designs for Wilson's New Zealand whisky and Giumarra sherry, both created by Gould & Associates. The shape of the bottle was designed to complement the label.

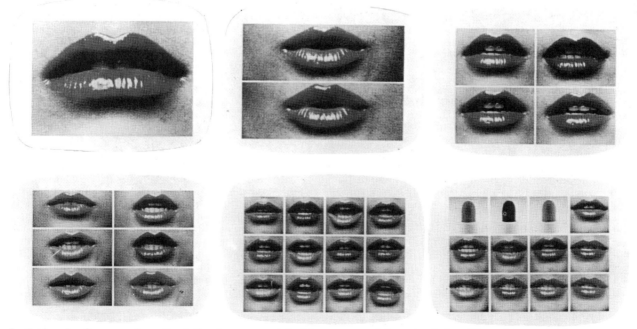

In the hands of an experienced art director, even a television commercial can be designed by using geometric principles. Movement becomes as much a part of the design as the composition of individual frames. In this dramatic 30-second spot created for Max Factor, the lips, painted in shades of lipstick, are moving in unison.

139

THE ART OF BORROWING, CONTINUED: THE VISUAL TWIST

It is not only a particular art style (steel engravings made in 1851) that can lend itself to adaptation, but also a basic layout format, such as this one, based on the "strip" continuity technique. Using that technique is artist Stanley Metzoff with thirty-two guests of honor (from Benjamin Franklin to a newborn baby) making their appearance on his bicentennial telephone-directory cover.

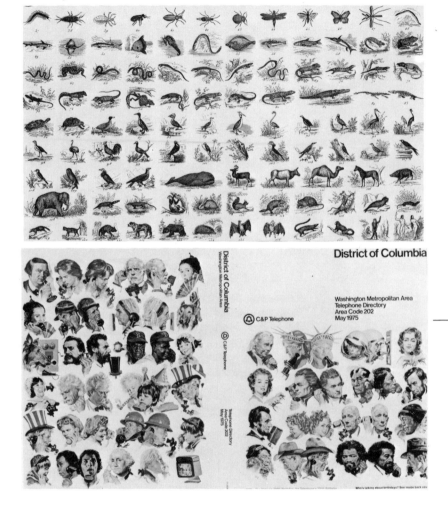

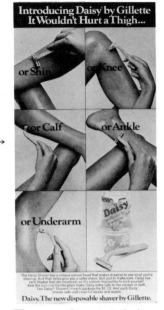

The same layout technique is used in these ads, too.

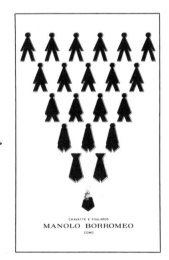

A drinking glass on top of a person's head first appears in an eighteenth-century silhouette print and then

many years later, in a completely different context in a modern magazine advertisement.

140

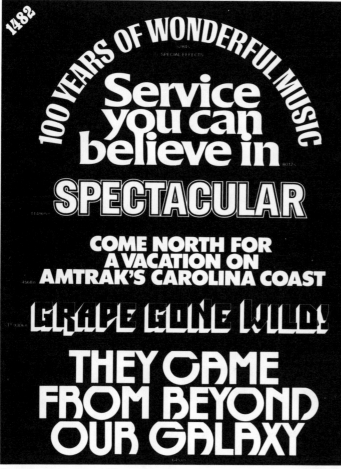

Sample page from Photo-Lettering, Inc., shows the flexibility of photocomposition, an increasingly popular process based on reproducing type on film. The size and spacing of words can be manipulated and fit into almost any given area.

The choice of typefaces, the weight of body text, and the relationship between type and illustration ultimately rest with the designer. They are his or her instruments; the designer must orchestrate them to achieve the desired effect.

We need two sharp
secretaries, a
classxey reception-
est, and kxwixtwo
xxxxyxxx
accxuratxe clexrk
typists.
Call Mr.Ivey foxr
an appointment at
xxMetzdorf Adv.,
526-5361.

When type is the illustration itself.

extra-light 8755n
abcdefghi
jklmnopqr
stuvwxyz
1234567890¢$.,?!e'∞⚭

book 8756n
abcdefghi
jklmnopqr
stuvwxyz
1234567890¢$.,?!e'∞⚭

medium 8757n
abcdefghi
jklmnopqr
stuvwxyz
1234567890¢$.,?!e'∞⚭

Bloomingdale's has proprietary rights to a typeface designed for exclusive use. The same type style appears in most of the store's graphic material to establish graphic continuity.

The choice of typeface, elongated here by the artist to fit the space, plays an important part in design-centered projects, such as letterheads, packaging, and displays.

[Courtesy of John N. Schaefer, Inc., New York]

Conversion of halftones to line does away with many problems inherent in printing on newspaper stock. Over fifty different textures are available.

A wide variety of design motifs, in addition to more than 2000 typefaces and sizes and texture sheets, are now printed on a matte-finish film which can be transposed in one piece onto the mechanical, ready for reproduction. Template sheets, like this one prepared by Chart-Pak, can be made to the client's specifications.

STILL ANOTHER SOURCE OF INSPIRATION: PRODUCTION TECHNIQUES FOR PRINT AND TELEVISION

Some of the most exciting creative opportunities in design come through innovations in production technology. To mention a few: phototypesetting, which spawned more than 1000 new typeface designs in less than a decade; giant offset printing presses able to combine from five to ten different high-speed operations in a single run; computerized typesetting; high-speed newsprint color-printing tape; mechanical binding tape; improved film and tape editing and transfer techniques; and the use of multiple-track sound-recording facilities.

Computer-generated animation on tape offers new and colorful design opportunities. Monitoring the commercial in the control room permits the director to keep refining the commercial electronically up to the last minute, making changes on the spot and adding optical effects.

Illustrations in various sizes of people, flora, cars, and other subjects on transfer sheets make it possible to create entire landscapes in minutes and very inexpensively. This architectural rendering was pieced together from various design elements furnished by Cello-Tak.

142

ANIFORMS
212-688-5255

Manipulating his animated alter-ego cartoon character on a full-size screen from a cubicle, the puppeteer-commentator keeps an eye on his audience through a peephole in the wall. From here he can engage in a spontaneous conversation with any person through a speaker system. This unusual form of animation was developed by Aniform.

[*Courtesy of Young & Rubicam, Inc.*]

Live-action photography of a revolving 4-foot (1.2-meter) model of a Remington shaver and five separate air-brush backgrounds fused into 800 different mattes proves once again that as far as quality of film production goes, television commercials can be on a par with the best that Hollywood has to offer.

Synthavision, another type of computer-generated animation, makes objects disappear and reappear, dance, explode, warp, flop, break, change colors, or flatten out on the screen, all at the whim of the production director.

[*Courtesy of Mathematical Applications Group, Inc., Elmsford, New York*]

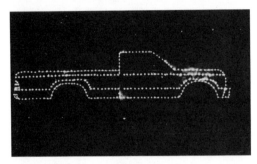

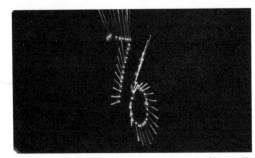

A fireworks display simulated in a studio spells out the campaign theme and then forms an outline of a Dodge truck on the screen.

Concealed behind one-way mirrors set up next door, cameras recorded the reactions of customers leaving an ice cream parlor where a number of the flavors had been replaced with Sealtest ice cream, bought straight from the freezer in a supermarket. As anticipated, users were unable to tell the difference in taste and were pleasantly surprised to find that they had been eating what they thought was "supermarket ice cream."

On-air interviews like this are popular with advertisers, and rightly so. A script, even when recited by an accomplished performer, rarely can match the credibility of consumers expressing their reaction in *cinéma vérité* style.

The same distinctive graphic technique (enlarged blue dots) is used in both print and television advertising for Sylvania Blue Dot light bulbs. The product is called simply (though tongue in cheek), Dots. "Dot's our flash cube. Dot's our light bulb. Dot's it, folks," says the announcer.

Chester Gould's comic strip drawing style inspired this Gillette commercial, introducing the Dry Look.

Old-style cartoon drawings gave this TV commercial a welcome change of pace.

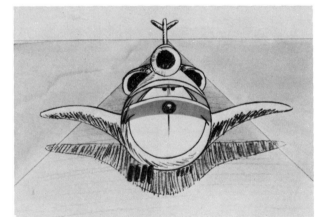

The use of a grainy, rough-line drawing style sets this American Airlines commercial apart from other airlines' advertising.

A colorful Sesame Street approach was used in this Dial dry deodorant television spot, with light coming through a rotoscopic device.

Commercial for Eastern Airlines makes ingenious use of the familiar.

Childlike drawing lends unique charm for this spot for Holiday Inn.

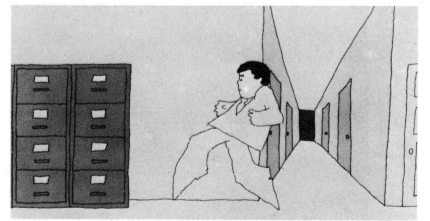

Some of the most successful animated television commercials are the result of close collaboration between name artists, with their own art style, and animation technicians. The loose, "improvised" sketching style of Bob Blechman sparked these frames for the 3M Company.

145

In demand are models who resemble real people. Most modeling agencies and TV directors maintain an extensive list on file of just such performers. On the left is Henry Ferrentino of Funnyface, a model who looks like anything but a professional model. Above are performers of a different type: their claim to fame is that they bear an uncanny resemblance to well-known personalities. Both are from John Hoffman's Look-a-Like modeling agency.

1. Bill Russell: Well, I have this friend, Ron. He's a very dear friend of mine. We met when I was playing with the Celtics, and he was pretending he was a basketball player. And, I used to play and he would watch. And, we became friends because I admired the way he watched.

2. Ron Watts: Bill Russell. Oh yeah, short guy, built like a fireplug. I know the guy.

3. Bill Russell: No. Actually he was not that bad a basketball player. He wasn't good, but he wasn't bad.

4. Ron Watts: He masqueraded as a player-coach then. I was the coach of the team, it can now be revealed for the first time.

5. Bill Russell: [Chuckle] He is the type of guy you don't introduce to anybody in polite society.

6. Ron Watts: Actually, I taught Bill Russell everything he knows about coaching. I made him what he is today. Nothing!

7. Bill Russell: He's always the same, crazy!

Spontaneous locker-room banter between two celebrated athletes and good friends, Bill Russell and Ron Watts, prompted several AT&T Long Lines television commercials. The men were allowed to improvise, letting their true personalities come through.

146

USE OF TECHNIQUE FOR SURPRISE EFFECT

Pictures pique readers' or viewers' curiosity. They induce them to read the message. This, basically, is one of the most important functions of an advertising illustration (showing the product is another). It is not necessary that the picture tell the whole story or even persuade readers to buy without the aid of copy. The two elements are totally integrated.

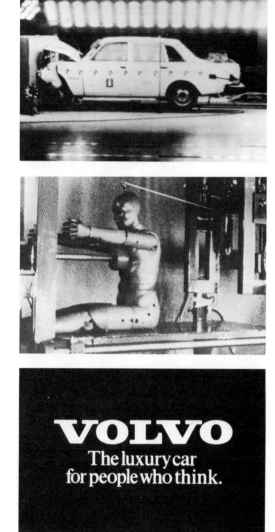

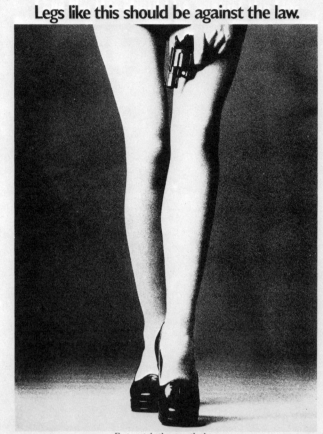

Legs like this should be against the law.

Fortunately they are the law.
Angie Dickinson is Sgt. Pepper Anderson in "Police Woman" a new series starting on Channel Seven at 9 o'clock tonight.

The picture intrigues readers, but they must read the caption to learn its full meaning.

VOLVO
The luxury car for people who think.

Demonstrating Volvo's crash-worthiness, this slow-motion-picture sequence shows the car meeting a stone wall head on, all to the soft accompaniment of Vivaldi-inspired music by Warner/Levinson. The juxtaposition of the two contrasting moods adds impact to the message.

BILL STETTNER
37 EAST 29TH ST., NEW YORK, N.Y. (212) MU 4-4058

Leaning figures in this Klopman logo cause the reader to do a double take.

Graffiti inspired a new form of art in this ad.

A burning match about to set the whole stack ablaze builds up to suspense in this photo by Bill Stettner.

147

Join the vast array of art directors and writers who use shock treatment to gain attention—words and pictures that startle. Avoid overkill, however. Remember that it is not enough to stop readers. They must also be persuaded to buy.

This homely Hi-Sci humanoid is hardly what the reader would expect to see in an advertisement. Relevance justifies his presence.

SFX: Natural sounds.

ANNOUNCER: Where does your candidate stand on the killing of baby seals?

SUPER: Where does your candidate stand on the killing of baby seals? Demand an answer.

Realism makes this commercial for the International Fund for Animal Welfare completely believable and shocking.

Anyone who has sex once, just once, can get syphilis or gonorrhea.

VD is spreading like the plague through our neighborhoods. Hitting people you'd least expect to get it.

In the suburbs, VD is more prevalent than chickenpox. Finding that hard to believe is one of the reasons it's spreading so fast.

So don't think it's not your problem.

Antibiotics cure VD and prevent its spreading. So it's ironic there's so much VD around when it's so easy to prevent or cure.

If you're curious or confused, get information or a pamphlet at a pharmacy or health clinic.

If you need help, see a doctor.

VD is for everybody.

A Public Service of This Magazine & The Advertising Council. Americas Social Health Association.

**We're worried about the cost of living.
She's worried about the cost of staying alive.**

In the face of such overwhelming need, the Lutheran Church in America is reaching out in Christ's name through the Love Compels Action/World Hunger Appeal for immediate help for starving people. We can make a difference, but only if we make an effort.

For further information write
Love Compels Action/World Hunger Appeal, Lutheran Church in America, 231 Madison Avenue, New York, NY 10016

Very straightforward talk about a very delicate subject.

A reportorial, no-nonsense photograph proved to be a wise choice for this ad.

Tasteful execution makes this advertisement an aesthetic delight despite its controversial content.

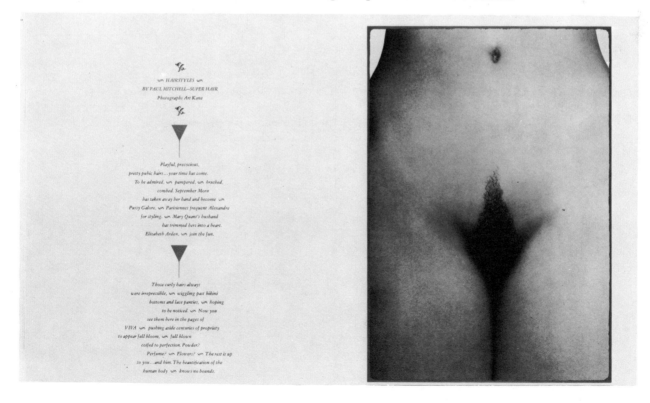

Publishers have always been among the most thoughtful observers of the graphic scene, quick to seek out top talent in photography, illustration, typography, and design. Paradoxically, the fees paid for editorial work often fall below those in advertising, owing to budget restrictions and the apparent willingness of contributors to have a credit line make up for lower fees. One of the mysteries of the business is why the editorial presentation should be as good as, and often superior to, that of advertising when, in fact, both appear in the same publication and appeal to the very same audience. A possible explanation is that while advertisers tend to underestimate the sophistication of the reading public, publishers do not.

Spread in *Mademoiselle*. A free, uninhibited use of space, yet in keeping with sound design principles.

Vogue **magazine has long set the pace in photography and illustration. Meticulous attention is paid to fashion, accessories, makeup, and choice of models. These pictures were taken by Irving Penn.**

Some of the best examples of typography can be found in newspapers. *The New York Times* is a consistent winner of awards in this area. More ebullient in spirit but also tastefully designed are the pages of *The Village Voice*.

Graphic imagination is particularly prevalent in the record and book field. As in the case of publishers, illustrators are willing to accept lower payments in return for greater creative freedom.

[Courtesy of designer: Henrietta Condak; artist: Richard Ness]

Chapter Nine

When Media Selection Is the Idea

Selection of media is basically a creative problem. No two publications or TV and radio stations are exactly the same or reach exactly the same type of audience. Each media vehicle stands on its own. And, since media decisions must always blend in with the total marketing strategy, it requires a searching, imaginative mind to take advantage of the subtle relationships between the elements.

With this in mind, there is usually a close interaction between creative and media departments in an advertising agency. People in the creative department are always seeking new applications for existing media or, at times, even go as far as inventing totally new media vehicles to carry the message. To illustrate, using the sides of Volkswagens ("beetle boards") for advertising was chanced upon by an observant young art director.

It was an advertising copywriter who first turned to the United States Post Office for help in selling products to special-interest audiences; he called his method *direct mail,* and the name stuck. A magazine-space salesman, responding to a group of restive minds in a large, big-clout advertising agency that wanted a triple-page space inside the cover to accommodate an actual-size photograph of a portable Smith Corona typewriter, developed the gatefold inside-cover concept with the aid of his colleagues back at the printing plant.

By the same token, in true two-way street fashion, artists and writers can absorb a great deal of information from their media friends. Marketing strategies are often brought into clearer focus via rapping sessions between the two groups, each representing its point of view and coming up with just the right solution.

Creative Media Strategists

Here is how to recognize members of the species:

They Have a Working Knowledge of Not One Medium but All Available Media They have no preconceived notions about any medium and play no favorites. Most of all, they do not automatically chalk up television as the "most potent medium" for each and every occasion.

They Are Willing and Eager to Explore New Avenues of Communication They are just as curious about new types of media as are their counterparts in the creative department, whether the new media are T-shirts, solicitation over the telephone, blimps, or the handing out of handbills on a street corner. They keep a close watch on the ever-shifting media scene and anticipate new developments.

They Know That Human Beings Are Superior to Computers They put both in their right perspective. They are aware of the fact that computers can be only as creative as their programmers are; it is the chef who makes the meal, not vice versa.

They Know That Basically Advertising Still Deals with Individuals, Not Economic Entities Such as Households or Zip Codes Their media decisions are qualitative as well as quantitative. There is more to the definition of a target than a heap of statistics.

They Select Their Media According to the Needs of the Advertiser They put the advertiser first, not the other way around.

They Know That All Good Media Buyers Must Be Outstanding Negotiators They are acutely aware of the fact that media costs depend on many variables: economic developments, seasonal changes, supply and demand, and, last but not least, the advertiser's ability to drive a hard bargain.

They Listen They always listen carefully.

When Media Selection Is the Big Idea

As mentioned above, creative media buyers do not live by the rules: they make their own. And so they often make advertising history as the first to adopt a new course. Below are a few examples of bold media decisions.

- Doubleday Advertising Company carried geographic market segmentation to its ultimate refinement when it advertised *My Son the Jock,* a book written by Fairfield County resident Gerald Green, in the October issues of Magazine Networks' Fairfield County editions.
- Introducing its feminine napkin, Kimberly-Clark used bound-in samples of the product in *Family Circle, Woman's Day,* and *Seventeen.*
- Shell Oil put all its advertising dollars into a single medium, newspapers, for more than a year. Then it purchased only full-page advertisements.
- Celanese took 100 pages of advertising in a single issue of *Harper's Bazaar.*
- Setting a new record, the Ford Motor Company placed a 10-minute commercial on the network movie *The Robe.* Not to be outdone was General Motors, which bought all available time on three major networks to introduce its new models.
- L'Oreal Preference hair coloring filmed its 30-second TV commercial not in color but in black and white to bring home the point that "the condition of your hair is just as important as the color." The closing product-identification tagline "Because you're worth it." turns to color, with copy adding "in color or black and white."
- A manufacturer of a drain cleaner bought in the plumbing section of the Yellow Pages a display ad which recommended his product as an alternative to calling in a plumber.
- Armstrong Cork put Dutch-door inserts in magazines to show how ceilings and floor textures can change the feel of a room. Alternating the half pages, top and bottom, readers could experiment with their own decorating ideas.
- *Apartment Life* bound its complete 142-page magazine in *Anny,* a publication reaching the advertising community, swelling that particular issue to 7 times its normal size.

- Canada Life printed its financial report for the whole year on the back of a poster which it mailed to stockholders.
- A manufacturer of a stay-awake pill ran an intensive cartoon advertising campaign in college newspapers a few days before midterm cramming.
- A low-cost late-night schedule on radio was purchased by the same advertiser, this campaign being aimed at drivers trying gamely to stay awake in those late hours.
- A media director persuaded a large manufacturer of silverware to open a street-level store in New York City, thus meeting the requirement of an important metropolitan newspaper to qualify as a local retailer to purchase space at 40 percent below the national advertising rate.
- Using posters on the sides of an ice-resurfacing machine at hockey games, *The New Yorker* alternated its message between the first and second periods, each time rooting for a different team and thus keeping all the fans happy.
- Popcil Brothers, a manufacturer of housewares, personal items, and sporting goods, promoted its products via a $4 million television campaign running only 3 times a year: a month before Christmas and on Mother's Day, and Father's Day.
- Promoting X-rated movies, Tandar Four placed a number of commercials on late-night cable television for Paramount Picture's *Emanuelle* and *The Joys of a Woman.*
- Turning to mass media to promote his paintings, artist Chris Burden bought 30-second commercials on WNBC-TV and WOR-TV. "Paid for by Chris Burden—Artist" appeared at the closing.
- Since scratch-and-sniff was introduced in 1967, the use of odors in advertising and promotion has surged onward. The 3M Company's Pine Top Lakes used pine fragrance in its direct-mail advertising to sell land subliminally. Another company, United Airlines, scented its advertising message with the sweet smell of oranges to lure travelers to California.
- It is believed the biggest full-color newspaper ad was created by American Honda Motor Company. A two-page insert measuring 30 by 22 inches (76.2 by 55.9 centimeters) ran in *The National Observer.* A large printing overrun (at minimal cost) on 70-pound (31.8 kilogram) coated stock provided an effective window-display piece for the more than 600 Honda dealers from coast to coast.

An excellent example of an imaginative use of media. The emblem appears against a black background on the right-hand page in *The Creative Black Book,* then against white on the opposite side of the same page, now on the left side.

MEDIA SELECTION: AS THE CREATIVE PERSON SEES IT

	Creative Disadvantages	Creative Advantages
Newspapers	Loss of fidelity, especially in reproduction of halftone illustration. More than ad-format variations among newspapers. Variance in column widths. Difficulty in controlling ad position on page.	Almost any ad size available. Impact of black against white (still one of the most powerful color combinations). Sense of immediacy. Quick response; easy accountability. Local emphasis. Changes possible at short notice.
Magazines	Size not as large as those of newspapers or posters. Long closing dates, limiting flexibility. Lack of immediacy. Tendency to cluster ads. Possible difficulties in securing favorable spot in an issue.	High-quality reproduction. Prestige factor. Accurate demographic information available. Graphic opportunities (use of white space, benday screen, reverse type). Color.
Television	No time to convey a lot of information. Air clutter (almost 25 percent of broadcasting is nonprogramming material). Intrusiveness (TV tops list of consumers' complaints in this respect). Capricious station censorship.	Combination of sight and sound. Movement. A single message at a time. Viewer's empathy. Opportunity to demonstrate the product. Believability: "What you see is what you get."
Radio	Lack of visual excitement. Wavering attention span (many listeners tune out commercials). Inadequate data on listening habits (when is the "listener" really listening?). Fleeting nature of message.	Opportunity to explore sound. Favorable to humor. Intimacy. Loyal following (the average person listens regularly to only about two stations). Ability to change message quickly.
Direct Mail	Damper of state, federal, and postal regulations on creative experimentations. Censorship often unpredictable. Formula thinking encouraged by "proven" direct-mail track records.	Graphic and production flexibility, such as use of three-dimensional effect (folding, die-cuts, pop-ups). Measurable. As scientific as any other form of advertising. Highly personal.
Posters	Essentially a one-line medium with only a limited opportunity to expand on the advertising message. Inadequate audience research, especially in transit advertising.	Graphic opportunities. Color. Large size. High-fidelity reproduction. Simple, direct approach. Possibility of an entirely visual message.
Point of Sale	Difficulty in pinpointing audience. Failure of retailers to make proper use of material submitted to them.	Opportunities for three-dimensional effects, movement, sound, and new production techniques.

All these factors play or should play a part in making media decisions. This is why, with apologies to Marshall McLuhan, the medium is *not* always the message. There are times when it is the nature of the message that dictates the medium.

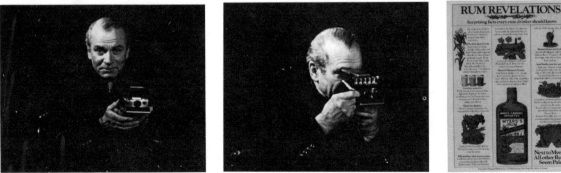

This is a demonstration for the Polaroid SX-70 Land Camera. Sight, sound, and movement were called for—in short, television. In any other medium, the format would have been entirely different.

Copy here is complex. Wisely, Meyer's chose print for its message.

Buying Cost Efficiencies Imaginatively: Television

Theoretically, TV-commercial time rates are based upon such conditions as the size and type of audience delivered, the length of the commercial, and the time of day in which it is used (day-part designation). So much for theory. In reality, costs depend more on esoteric considerations, such as the degree of demand, seasonal factors, the clout of the advertiser, and, last but not least, the negotiating skill of the buyer. (The cost of the same media package can vary as much as 50 percent depending upon who is buying. Stations have been known to offer seven or eight different rates for the same spot.)

These factors will *always* affect the price tag:

1. *Buying in bulk*. This practice lowers costs. For example, a contract for 500 commercials annually may bring a discount of 6 percent. The heavier the scheduling, the larger the discount. *Frequency discounts,* a variation of bulk discounts, are available when spots are used continually for a given period, such as 26 weeks. Spots can also be purchased at a saving on the basis of a *package plan* which included participation in several programs (high- and low-rated).

Savings opportunities motivate many sophisticated advertisers to commit themselves to schedules as much as 4 or 5 months ahead of time. Large corporations working through major agencies or buying-time services sometimes lock up 80 percent of station time long before air time, especially when prices appear to be on the rise, as they do during presidential elections, Olympic Games, or sudden spurts of economic activity.

2. *Seasonal buying*. Some months are lighter than others. Normally, the size of the audience decreases as much as 20 to 30 percent during the summer, with a commensurate drop in prices. In one year, the spot-sales division of a major network in New York, for example, offered 1 minute for $1200 in May and June; the same spot sold for $3000 in October, November, and December.

3. *Special availabilities*. Astute time buyers develop a sixth sense about time "avails" and move in at the peak of the buyers' market. One network, for example, faced a last-minute cancellation on its 1-hour spectacular 3 days prior to broadcast. A large Midwestern bakery picked up the time at a 30 percent discount. In another situation, a 60-second spot in the New York metropolitan area became available during an Orange Bowl football game. A large men's clothing store grabbed it at a 35 percent discount less than a day before air time. On another occasion a major airline, American, purchased evening commercial time at rock-bottom rates the same day on which it was used. Savings vary between 5 and 40 percent or even more for such "clearance sales."

4. *Time flexibility*. Certain discounts offered by stations are fairly standardized:

a. Run-of-station plans (ROS). These are comparable with newspaper run-of-paper (ROP) programs. Reduced rates are provided by the station, which then has the option to run the spot at its selected time. In most cases, advertisers do not know in advance when their commercials are going to be aired, since stations lock up their logs only a day or less in advance. However, it is possible to have stations guarantee that not all the commercials will be run in batches and that a given percentage will be aired at different times during the day.

b. Preemptible pricing. This practice saves money for advertisers willing to have their spots bumped by other advertisers offering a better deal to the station. As a matter of courtesy, most stations warn advertisers several days in advance that their commercials will be preempted so that they have time to make adjustments in their schedules. Since stations keep close track of their commercial inventories, most can advise advertisers of other availabilities well in advance.

5. *Program flexibility*. In most cases, the quickest way to reach the largest number of people is to buy into or next to, say, one or several of the twenty-five top-rated shows. Obviously, this is easier said than done.

Once a prime-time program has achieved a Nielsen rating of 20 or better, the price of a commercial minute may hover in the $100,000-per-minute area (cost per 1000 in that case would be around four homes per penny). Only large advertisers appealing to a mass market can justify that kind of one-time investment. More often than not, advertisers may have to consider other options, such as *daytime programs* (which may give them up to twice the number of commercials for the same cost and a more accurately profiled audience target), *late shows, reruns* (some reruns enjoy high ratings and can be bought economically on groups of stations), *spot coverage* (buying different day parts, different stations), *piggybacking* (buying two spots back to back for different products by the same advertiser), *multisponsorship arrangements* (with up to six unrelated advertisers sharing the same program period), *cooperative buys* (dividing the expense of the commercial with another advertiser selling the product, such as a local retail store, usually on a 50-50 basis), or *barter arrangements* (trading time or merchandise for the advertiser's goods or services).

The Rating Game: Who's on First?

One way to win or lose is to be able to make a commitment prior to the exposure of a program and before the ratings are in. With forty to fifty new entries each season vying to fill some 3000 hours of prime time, there is a plethora of programs from which to pick.

The three major networks, NBC, CBS, and ABC, and, occasionally, independent packagers, preempting prime time with nationwide series of their own), usually run a close race for rating supremacy. About 1 in 3 of new network prime-time entertainment series launched each year survives the first full season. The results are based upon winning more than one-third of the total prime-time audience (about 60 percent of the 70 million-plus television households, representing more than 150 million viewers), which manages to remain on an amazingly constant level during most of the week, with Friday being slightly under and Sunday slightly above average.

Contrary to popular belief, it is not primarily the intrinsic quality of the program that determines its pulling power; as in a horse race, the rest of the field has much to do with the outcome. (One media service forecasts ratings of new TV fare in terms of schedule position alone, without even bothering to view the show.) If a particular program is superior to others appearing exactly at the same time, it will emerge a winner. View-

ers, watching the television screen during certain times of day by force of habit, will stay with the show that is least objectionable to them.

Profit-conscious network executives are aware of this phenomenon. They jockey for position on a day-to-day, hour-to-hour basis. With the focus on prime time—the peak viewing hours between 8 and 11 p.m. which bring in about half of the profits—all three networks have the same amount of air time to sell during prime time: six minutes an hour, except for movies, where the allotment is stretched out to seven minutes. The price for a commercial varies, depending on the size and demographic composition of the audience. It is estimated that every prime time rating point equals about 2 million viewers, which, in turn, can easily mean a difference of $2 million in advertising revenue, or over $25 million in revenues over the course of a full year. Since rating points mean money, it is difficult for a network to resist the temptation of "hyping" its figures, particularly

during the crucial 4-week "sweep" periods (each quarter of the year) when the shows are being rated by the various services. *Bunching* shows is one way to preempt viewing time; the average TV watcher would just as soon not make an effort to get up and switch the dial. *Counterprogramming* is another ploy used by the networks; as mentioned above, ratings rise predictably in the face of feeble opposition. If the show fails to live up to expectations, it is often yanked off the air with maximum dispatch—sometimes within a few weeks time.

Pity the advertiser asked to make an up-front investment on the basis of a pilot film or the outline of a special program or, as often as not, several of them. It is not unusual for large advertisers to buy into as many as 100 to 150 different programs, sometimes playing the market through "scatter" buys. Like everyone else, they must make their own predictions, hoping that their handicapping system is as good as their competitors'.

TYPES OF PROGRAMS

Comedy
Drama
Western
Variety
Situation/comedy
Adventure/travel
Medical
Law enforcement
Science fiction
Game shows
Newscast
Miniseries
Documentary
On-spot reportage
Investigative reportage
Interview
Religious/inspirational
Talk show
Movies
Sports
Specials
Musical variety
Dance
Educational
Children
Amateur

[Courtesy of Viacom]

[Copyright Paramount Pictures Corporation]

Network or off-network reruns can offer excellent buying opportunities to advertisers looking for the right time period in which to reach their prospects. In ratings, about 1 out of 10 of these programs finds its way right back to where it came from: the coveted top twenty programs in Nielsen's ratings. In smaller markets, where budgets have a good deal to do with program content, nearly all local shows during prime-access time are syndicated reruns, talk shows and local newscasts being the notable exceptions. Shown here are two perennial rerun programs. Generally speaking, it takes about 150 markets to reach about 90 percent of the nation's households.

How to Pick the Right Program: A Quick Review

1. *Audiences welcome familiar faces.* Established stars do not guarantee success (nothing does), but they certainly help. Several top shows are merely spin-offs from other series featuring the same performers. For those looking for viewers' opinions, Performer Popularity Poll of Marketing Evaluations provides annual likability reports; scores are broken down into demographic categories. One of the favorite maxims of the industry is that it is easier to attract a faithful following with a regular pattern of characters, situations, or even catch phrases.

2. *Programs people say they like to watch and those they do watch are not necessarily the same.* Typically, results become skewed by the human tendency of wanting to say the right thing. In a survey of 10,000 viewers by the Screen Actors Guild, for example, only 2.1 percent of them admitted that they liked sports, 1.9 percent expressed an interest in game shows, and 28 percent voted for documentaries. Ratings tell a different story. Some football and baseball games attract more than 50 million viewers. Almost half of local access time is filled with some form of audience-participation shows. Documentaries, on the other hand, rarely get top ratings.

3. *Violence always was, and unfortunately still is, a favorite American spectator sport.* According to a number of studies, about two-thirds of TV viewers claim that they oppose violent shows. However, more than half of those who expressed their dislike of violence continued to tune in such shows. Networks give their viewers what they want; approximately seven brutalities, many of them fatal, occur on television every hour. It also bears mentioning that almost 50 percent of American households today own at least one gun (and every third owner is a woman).

4. *Subjectivity should never interfere with program evaluation.* For example, nearly 35 million people watch soap operas on a regular basis, while nonwatchers, including many media buyers, look down their noses at this form of entertainment as designed for the shallow-minded. And so the industry keeps perpetuating its own particular brand of old wives' tales about the "typical" soap-opera viewer. The fact is that about 1 out of every 4 such viewers enjoys an income of more than $15,000, more than 50 percent of them finished high school, and many went to college. Such audience demographics are just right for some of the less pseudointellectual advertisers, including by far the largest TV advertiser, Procter & Gamble. This company sponsors nearly half of the daytime dramas. Says one of their executives: "Soap-opera characters are realistic and believable and do things that a lot of the viewing public does."

DAY	DATE	TIME	RATING	SHARE	HOMES	WOMEN
Monday.	7/14	8–9 P.M.	7	17	447	113
Tuesday	7/15	8–10 A.M.	2	14	122	93
Tuesday	7/15	3–4:30 P.M.	5	18	273	211
Thursday	7/17	12 noon–2 P.M.	8	35	477	291
Thursday	7/17	3–4 P.M.	5	21	303	255
Friday	7/18	4–5 P.M.	4	15	244	166
Monday	7/21	5–7 A.M.			DNA	
Thursday	7/24	5–7 P.M.	3	11	224	167

Apollo-Soyuz Space Mission Time-Period Data, July 1974, WNBC-TV, New York)

NOTE: All daily numbers reflect Monday–Friday averages.
See ARB (American Research Bureau) sheet for estimate.

Show audiences are often projected in advance by the network offering spot avails to advertisers. Here is an estimate, prepared by WNBC-TV, New York, on live coverage of the 9-day United States–Soviet space mission.

Designation	Hours
Daytime (Monday-Friday)	7:30 A.M.–4:30 P.M.
Early evening	4:30–7:30 P.M.
Nighttime	7:30–11 P.M.
Late evening	11 P.M.–1 A.M.*
Weekend day	12 noon–6:30 P.M.
Early-late news	5:30–7, 11–11:30 P.M.*
Children's programming	7–8:30 A.M., 4–6 P.M. (Monday–Friday) 7 A.M.–2 P.M. (Saturday) 7 A.M.–12 noon (Sunday)

*In Eastern and Pacific zones; 1 hour earlier in Central and Mountain zones.

CPM: The Way It Works A measure commonly used to determine basic broadcast costs is cost per thousand (CPM) per commercial minute. For example, a nighttime network advertiser may estimate the costs as follows:

Total television homes: 50 million.
Network lineup of 150 stations reaching 90 percent of television homes: 45 million.
Program rating of 25 percent of these homes: 11,250,000.
Time cost for a half-hour program: $65,000.
Program cost: $45,000.
Total of time and program costs: $115,000.
Cost of reaching 1000 homes (total cost divided by homes reached): $10.
Cost per commercial minute ($10 divided by the 3 minutes of commercial time allowed): $3.33.

The cost per commercial minute in 1962 for all programs on network television was $3.71 for nighttime and $1.70 for daytime.

When agencies and clients convene to talk over their broadcasting plans, the discussion often turns to GRPs (gross rating points). One GRP is 1 percent of all potential adult television viewers (listeners in radio). It is a handy figure since it reflects both *frequency* and *reach*, for example, to get to 50 percent of the adult viewers in a market requires 200 GRPs a week for 4 weeks. A heavy schedule would be 800 rating points, or enough to have a meaningful impact on any given market.

ALL FOR ONE, ONE FOR ALL: REACH, FREQUENCY, LENGTH OF MESSAGE, TYPE OF AUDIENCE, AND CREATIVE CONTENT

The temptation to buy time and space on the basis of well worn media shibboleths, such as "Frequency makes up for reach" or "Reach makes up for frequency" is understandable. Unfortunately, as any experienced planner will agree, buying media is not that simple. For one thing, the *content* of a commercial may have as much to do with its effectiveness as its *placement*.

Messages that come on strong tend, like an often-told joke, to wear out their welcome quickly. Such commercials should be scheduled far enough apart so that the viewers' patience will not be tried by overexposure. This is a lesser problem with reminder commercials, such as those used by many large soft-drink advertisers. The emphasis here is on entertainment.

Reactions even to the same commercial will, of course, vary with the audience. Young viewers tend to react favorably to the sound of their favorite rock singer, but he is less of a hero to an older and more sedate audience. A liberated spokeswoman exuding self-assurance may find greater rapport with her career-minded listeners than with some housewives who would rather raise children than cain in the office. Nor should the optimum length (10, 30, or 60 seconds) of a commercial be judged on the basis of true-and-tried formulas without careful examination of its creative content. Short rapid-fire commercials that try to get too much into a limited time period can actually prove to be more intrusive to viewers than their longer, more comfortably paced counterparts.

Moreover, the program surrounding a commercial can have an important effect on the viewers' reaction, just as does the editorial environment in print.

Shows that grab viewers, such as dramas or suspense stories, create a whole new set of unique problems; viewers may resent the interruption. Says Arthur Eikoff, an expert on direct-response advertising: "We favor passive viewing programs, such as game shows, talk shows, movies, and syndicated series where people don't mind being interrupted. The worse the program, the better the response."

Television advertisers such as Coca-Cola, make no overt attempt to generate immediate sales by proselytizing viewers. They can afford to rely on pleasant-sounding lyrics in place of a hard-sell pitch; their product no longer needs introduction. The commercial featuring the song "I'd like to teach the world to sing in perfect harmony, I'd like to buy the world a Coke and keep it company" brought an average of 5000 letters a day each time it appeared. Such commercials can be shown at relatively frequent intervals. As a rule, music "softens" the commercial. It can—and often does—provide background mood for the spoken word.

DEVIL: Diet Conscious?

Let me tempt you with a rich, fattening hot chocolate. Go on, you need a little extra fat to keep out the cold.

ANGEL: You devil—I've got a heavenly surprise for you. That's Alba '66 with all the devilishly rich taste of regular hot chocolate, but only half the calories. It's everything hot chocolate should be but without the devil to pay.

DEVIL: ALBA'66. The taste you don't have to resist when you're on a diet. Well, I'll be . . .

Alba's hot cocoa mix, a new product, was announced for the first time in this commercial. Here, a strong, no-nonsense presentation proved to be the right thing; an overly subtle approach might have gone unnoticed. Commercials of this type tend to wear out their welcome more quickly if shown in too rapid a sequence; they need breathing space between exposures.

Buying Cost Efficiencies Imaginatively: Print

Historically, the rate cards of publications tend to reflect more accurately actual media costs than do those used by television stations. This is true because a publication is flexible enough to adjust its number of pages to advertising volume. Base circulation figures, one of the most important criteria for setting rates, change less throughout the year than they do on television, particularly when subscriptions dominate newsstand sales (more than half the sales of national magazines) and distribution is committed ahead of time. Characteristically, the term *guaranteed circulation* was coined by publishers, not by television-network executives.

1. *How to pay less for what you get.* As in all buying, the ability to buy in quantity is the prime factor. Almost all the newspapers and magazines have their *bulk discounts* (cumulative space), *frequency discounts* (based on the number of insertions for a specified period of time), or, in some cases, *combination discounts* (space bought by the same advertiser in several magazines published by one company).

Other money-saving opportunities worth mentioning are the purchase of *remnant space* (advertising appears whenever space is available), *positioning* (less desirable positions in some publications may cost less), *geographic* and *demographic editions* (an advertiser buys less than full circulation to reach a selected group of readers), and *marriage splits* (several advertisers buy the total circulation of a magazine, each using only a portion of that circulation).

2. *How to get more for what you pay.* Less obvious a factor, but equally meaningful, is the increased profitability of the kind of advertising which takes optimum advantage of the character of the medium in which it appears. The medium often dictates content. Here are just a few of these qualitative considerations, a little esoteric perhaps but nevertheless important:

Dominance Larger ads are more effective in terms of "noted" and "read most," but not necessarily in relation to cost. Doubling space does not automatically attract twice as many readers. In some cases, it may be more prudent to build readership gradually through repeated insertions.

Color As a rule, the use of color in an ad increases attention value as well as readership by as much as 50 percent, but the cost can be high. The advertiser must decide if, in terms of sales, color is worth the premium. Some products need to be presented exactly the way they appear to the eye: a black-and-white picture simply does not tell the whole story. In this case, the additional expense may be justified.

Repetition The same ad can be repeated a number of times with no appreciable loss in attention value. In most cases, with intervals less than a month readership stays about the same even after six or seven exposures. In fact, in a number of instances repetition of the *same* message has actually raised "noted" and "read most" scores.

Frequency in the Same Publication Generally, the cumulative impact of a campaign (a series of ads that carry the same basic message though implementing it in a different way) increases substantially with insertions. On the average, a professionally executed campaign is good for at least 2 years.

Editorial Environment This factor is important from two points of view. First, the editorial content of a publication has much to do with the quality of its readership; women's service magazines are read primarily by housewives, daily newspapers by people living in the area they cover, hobby magazines by those pursuing a particular hobby, and so on. In this way, the publication preselects the audience. Second, the environment puts the reader in a receptive frame of mind to read the advertising message.

SIZE VERSUS DOMINANCE

Editorial copy adjacent to this ad boosted readership and saved the retail store $500 on space which it would have paid for an additional column. Eye-movement studies show that scanners (people going through a newspaper fortuitously) are more inclined to notice an advertisement of less than a full page.

▼

This two-page spread in the prestigious *New York Times* heralded the beginning of a year's monthly full-page–ad campaign for a relatively little-known commercial bank, the J. Henry Schroder Company. Up to that time, the advertiser had only used small, 200-line newspaper insertions, concentrating on high frequency. The move to large-space advertising was made in order to develop a corporate image—that of an important institution.

▶

Schroder is not th

, MAY 21, 1963. THE NEW YORK TIMES, TUESDAY, MAY 21, 1963.

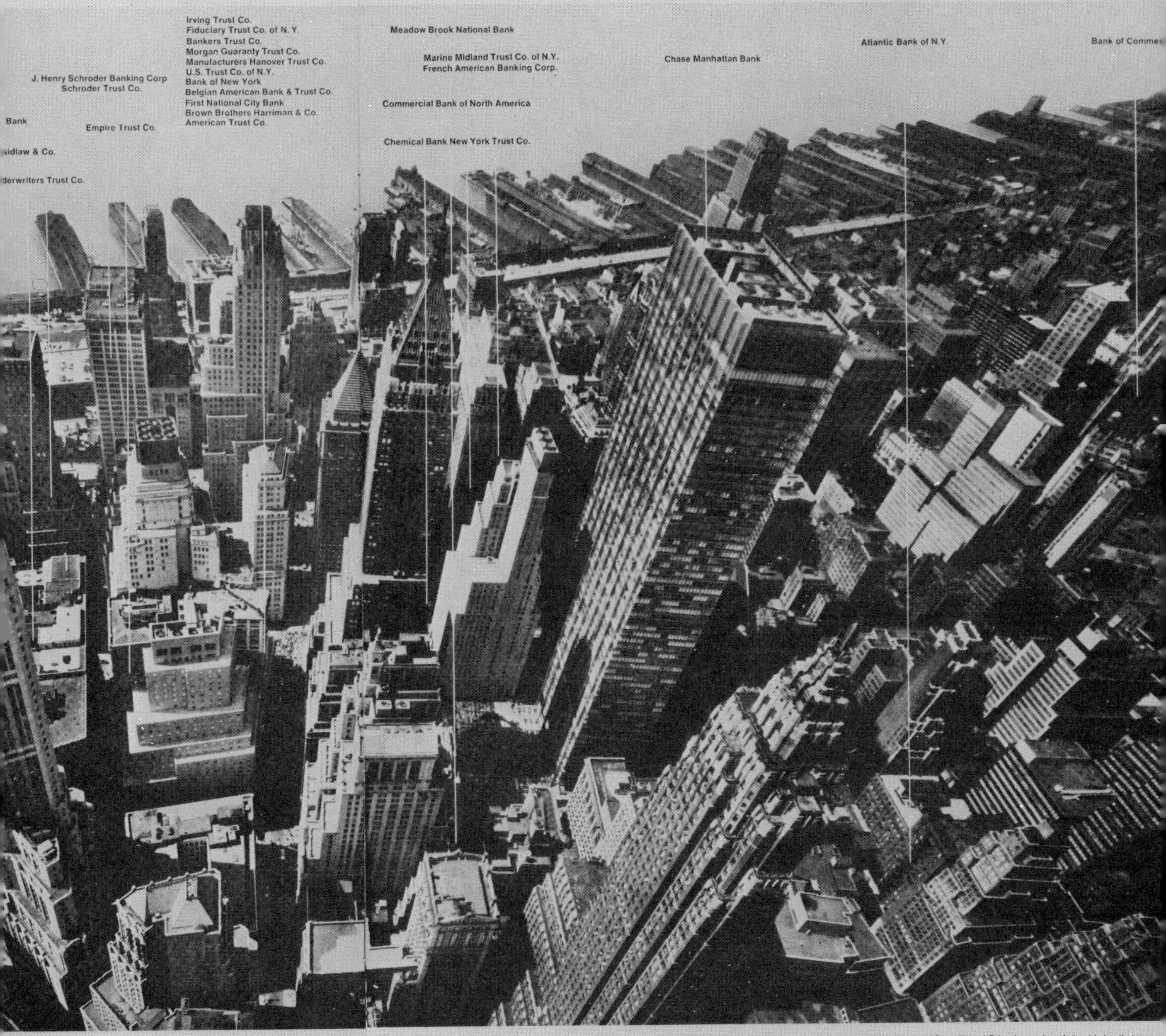

Irving Trust Co.
Fiduciary Trust Co. of N.Y.
Bankers Trust Co.
Morgan Guaranty Trust Co.
Manufacturers Hanover Trust Co.
U.S. Trust Co. of N.Y.
Bank of New York
Belgian American Bank & Trust Co.
First National City Bank
Brown Brothers Harriman & Co.
American Trust Co.
J. Henry Schroder Banking Corp
Schroder Trust Co.
Bank
Empire Trust Co.
aidlaw & Co.
derwriters Trust Co.
Meadow Brook National Bank
Marine Midland Trust Co. of N.Y.
French American Banking Corp.
Commercial Bank of North America
Chemical Bank New York Trust Co.
Chase Manhattan Bank
Atlantic Bank of N.Y.
Bank of Comme

bank in New York City

Nor are we right for every business man.

For example, if you need ten million dollars in a hurry, Schroder is not your bank. It may take us several days to get you that much money. And anyway, we prefer to keep our loans in the neighborhood of two million or less.

That is because we are not the largest bank in the United States (Chase Manhattan is larger). We are a medium-sized bank (forgetting about the London office for the moment).

We like our size and act the part.

Sure, we have reasons to be proud. Our assets are over $241,000,000 in the United States alone. Behind us are 159 years of world-wide financial leadership. Among our clientele you will find some of the most respected names in industry and finance. But have we allowed success to spoil our straight-from-the-shoulder banking philosophy? Never!

Our senior officers answer the phone as often as any of the 449 employees, except Margaret, the switchboard operator. Pride? Yes. Pretensions? No.

Executives at Schroder are knowledgeable in all phases of banking, whether corporate funds, short term investments, pensions, estate handling, loans, trusts, global financing, and even the administration of personal wills. No customers need go desk-hopping at Schroder to find out the "right" officer for the right answer.

If you like the way we do business, please make yourself at home in our offices at 57 Broadway.

If you don't like the way we do business, there are 56 other commercial banks in New York.

J. Henry Schroder Banking Corporation **Schroder Trust Company**

A digest-size ad dominates the full-size page. The editorial copy surrounding this colorful free-form layout for Catalina makes the ad stand out from its environment.

This 5- by 7-inch ad for the Air Force, covering a full page in *Reader's Digest,* is hard to miss. An ad of the same size would fare less well on a large newspaper page. The size of an ad is relative to the space that surrounds it.

Ads for Brut aftershave and antiperspirant spray on facing pages reinforce one another.

Four quarter-page ads overwhelm these two magazine pages.

Two facing single-column ads "own" this page in *Time*.

This is actually a full-page space unit, masquerading here as two horizontal half-page ads.

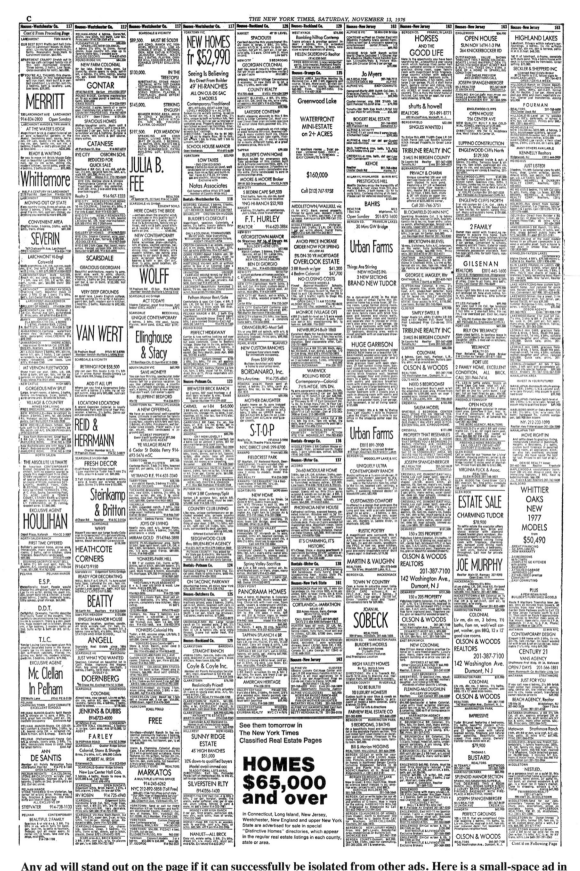

Any ad will stand out on the page if it can successfully be isolated from other ads. Here is a small-space ad in *The New York Times*, representing a change of pace in a full-page cluster of classified ads.

A refreshing change of pace was Volkswagen's use of black-and-white photography, employed as much to convey unpretentiousness as for reasons of parsimony. The campaign represented this company's answer to Detroit's color-happy display of its favorite chariots.

Tell him your media story over lunch at Brennan's, $39. Then remind him in Ad Age, 3¢.

A lot of the media talk that goes on in Dallas goes on at Brennan's. And small wonder.

It's an excellent place to sit comfortably with your client. And tell your media story over a terrific dish such as Filet of Redfish Gelpi.

Too bad that you can't take all of your clients to Brennan's every week. They'd never forget you and you'd enjoy a lot of delicious lunches.

But all dreaming aside, how do you keep your story in the minds of clients you can't afford to take to lunch all the time? Especially in today's financial climate.

With Ad Age, that's how.

A full page ad in Ad Age reaches 68,000 people at a cost of just 3.2¢ each.

And those people are not just in media, but in marketing, client services, management and creative. All kinds of marketing and advertising people who should hear what you have to say.

And Ad Age is the best way to reach them.

So, if you want to spread your message and keep it alive, think of Ad Age.

You can't afford to feed all of our readers Filet of Redfish Gelpi. But you certainly can afford to feed them your message.

Put your 3¢ worth in Ad Age.

Crab Louis; redfish sauteed in lemon butter with capers, pimientos, green peppers and almonds; Crepes Fitzgerald; coffee and a bottle of Chateau Olivier '70. Lunch for two, about $39, including the usual gratuity.

Color used on the right-hand page creates an impression of not one but two continuous full-color pages.

Some kid may get away with murder tonight

Children fifteen and younger are killing, raping and robbing every night in New York City.

One out of every five arrests for major crimes last year involved someone under sixteen. The maximum sentence — for murder: a year and a half in training school.

Next week. NewsCenter 4 begins a series of reports on this new breed of delinquents.

Killer Kids. 6:45 pm

NewsCenter 4
We get it *all* on.
Chuck Scarborough at 5pm. Tom Synder at 6pm — Channel 4

Billion Dollar Makeover

Americans spend a pretty penny having nose bobs, chin jobs, face lifts — buying wigs, moustaches, chest pieces — shaping up at fancy gyms and spas.

We spend $1 billion a year on cosmetics alone.

Join us next week for a look into the business of being beautiful — what can be done, who's doing it, and what it costs.

Vanity. Thy Name Is Money. 5:55pm

NewsCenter 4
We get it *all* on.
Chuck Scarborough at 5pm. Tom Snyder at 6pm — Channel 4

Conveying a newsy impression are these ads by the National Broadcasting Company. Readers associate stark black-and-white photographs with wire-service pictures, which appear regularly in metropolitan newspapers. The use of color in this case would probably have weakened the impact of the campaign, not increased it.

166

For male readers only:

Cox's knows how difficult it is for men to pick just the right Valentine gift for someone. We keep that in mind when you come in to Cox's. We know that you also feel sort of embarrassed when you're poking around in the lingerie department, for example. Well, relax. We'll help. Let's say you had in mind giving someone a bright red hot water bottle with a pink rose on it and filled with perfume. Right off the bat we would very politely and adroitly question the appropriateness of the gift. We would suggest a few other items. If you insisted on the hot water bottle, we would tell you that we didn't have one that matched your description. If that would disappoint you terribly, and you still insisted on such a gift because your romance depended on it, do you know what we would do? *We would make one for you.* No fooling, that's what we would do. You see, at Cox's it's very important to us that every customer gets the kind of service and satisfaction that he can't get at any other store. That's the way we are.

No other scotch makes you wonder what you did to deserve it.

Color commands attention and helps readership, but is it worth the additional cost? That depends on many factors. Change of pace is one, as in this full-page ROP Cox's department store ad amid black-and-white newspaper articles: the giant water bottle is vivid red. Eye appeal is especially important in food, cosmetics, fashion, furniture, and travel advertising.

A lot of blonde without a lot of bleach.

The use of a second color requires graphic restraint on the part of the art director. A second color serves a definite function (other than decorative), as in this Schwan-Stabilo ad for felt-tipped markers, highlighting words in the body text. In the Yellow Pages ad, yellow is used to emphasize the signature; everything else on the page is black and white. Cutty Sark puts second color to good effect, using it as a solid background for quick identification in its full-page magazine campaign.

Three posters in a row vied for the attention of one of the most blasé customers in the world, the New York subway rider. They appeared in more than 300 stations. (A small but meaningful consolation prize goes to the J. Walter Thompson agency, which had to grapple with the logistics of arranging some 1000 sheets in their correct order.)

(below) Two identical coupon ads juxtaposed in *The New Yorker* have invited multiple subscription orders.

This ad pulled a 15 percent greater response in its second time around in the same publication, with only 2 days between insertion dates.

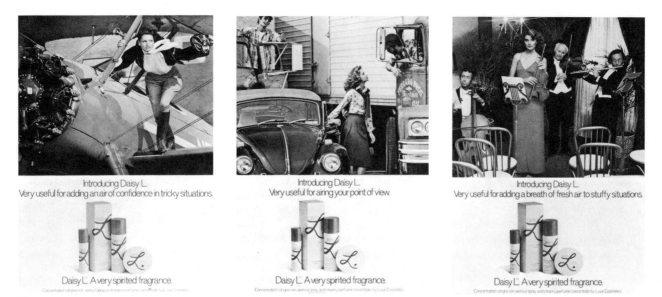

Three full-color ads for Daisy L. of Love Cosmetics ran on three consecutive pages in the same magazine, building up to higher readership.

This series of full-page two-color ads appeared for several months preceding the New Year. Repetition increased coupon responses.

This highly successful introductory ad for instant Maxwell House, a classic in its genre, ran continually for 2 years without any substantial change in graphics or copy. No one got tired of the same message—not even the advertiser.

Retention Several studies show or try to show that advertising makes no lasting impression; that its impact has the endurance of a rain cloud passing through the summer sky. Typical are the reports in *Media/Scope* by Eugene Pomerance and Hubert Zielske, who found that half of the readers forget an ad 4 weeks after it has appeared; the figure goes up to 75 percent in 11 weeks.

The author takes a more optimistic view on the subject of memorability. Given a strong creative base (a circumstance sometimes ignored by statisticians), a campaign can become firmly fixed in the mind of the reader (viewer or listener) for a very long time, perhaps even for several decades. To illustrate, here is a simple test. Which of the following advertising slogans are still current today?

Avoid five o'clock shadow.
Better things for better living.
Breakfast of champions.
Pause that refreshes.
Does she—or doesn't she?
Double your pleasure, double your fun.
Everything's better with Blue Bonnet on it.
Fifty-seven varieties.
Fly now—pay later.
Getting there is half the fun.
Good to the last drop.
If it's Westinghouse, you can be *sure*.
If it's Borden's, it's got to be good.
For those who think young.
Progress is our most important product.
Quality goes in before the name goes on.
Say it with flowers.
Select, don't settle.
Snap, crackle, and pop!
The closer you get, the better she looks.
There's always room for Jello.
Never underestimate the power of a woman.
When it rains, it pours.
Where there's life, there's Bud.
Winston tastes good like a cigarette should.
You have a friend at Chase Manhattan.
You're in good hands with Allstate.

Actually, only one ("Good to the last drop") has survived! If you scored poorly, do not despair. Join the club. Most people overestimate the number of slogans which they think are still being used in the best *déja-vu* tradition. This once again

goes to show the *effective* slogans do not die or even fade away; only ineffective ones do.

A note of interest: optimum effectiveness may be achieved by alternating thrusts of concentrated advertising with periods of inactivity. Breathing time of 2 to 6 weeks between flights can stretch out a campaign and may actually increase its cumulative impact.

Content More important than any other single factor in the success of an advertisement is its creative content. Not even the most astute media buyer can make up for the indiscernibleness of a poorly conceived ad. Research supports this statement. Having studied such factors as size, color, position of ads in the publication, seasonal changes, effect of the thickness of magazines,

and the influence of editorial matter perhaps more thoroughly than anyone else, the veteran Daniel Starch still concedes in an unpublished manuscript: "Years of readership studies have shown consistently that whether a large or small number of people read an advertisement is determined by three sets of factors: *(a)* the natural, inherent product, *(b)* subject interest of people, and *(c)* the characteristic of the advertisement itself." He concludes: "The powerful, controllable factors are within the advertisement itself, what it says and how it says it."

This highlights the point, made repeatedly in this chapter, that responsibility for the success of an advertising campaign depends upon *both* the media planner and the creative department.

This unusual ad, featuring a Budweiser T-shirt emblem, appeared in the *Chicago Sun-Times* and the *Chicago Daily News* in red and blue. A hot iron transfers standard newsprint (plastic textile dye mixed with solvent-based rotogravure printing ink) to cloth. Thousands of readers responded to the offer.

A series of nameless teaser ads in *The New York Times*, describing the kind of people who read *Psychology Today*, brought an avalanche of inquiries the following day from both potential subscribers and advertisers. Curiosity grew steadily during the week. On Friday the sponsor's name was revealed.

In an unusual move, the Institute of Outdoor Advertising displayed a picture of the reigning Miss America, Shirley Cothran, on 10,000 of its panels to demonstrate the impact of the medium. Ten times as many people were able to identify her after 2 months.

This chapter is as good a place as any to put the so-called mechanical requirements of media in perspective. Never should these requirements be allowed to become creative encumbrances. On the contrary. Media is or should be a creative person's freest of all playgrounds. Space and time are his or her domain. The creative person can do with them whatever he or she wants. Yes, posters under certain conditions (as in railway, bus, or subway stations) can be copy-heavy. Magazine and newspaper ads can be all type and no pictures. Radio spots can convey vivid visual messages through the use of "picture words" (this is why many agencies insist that their art directors participate in "writing" radio commercials).Vinyl sound sheets make publications "talk," and scratch-and-sniff pages can make the printed page smell sweet. Folding techniques can add a third dimension to a flat sheet. In-store displays can be made to sing to customers.

Wordless ad for Bank AmeriCard uses a poster technique in *Time*. It achieved one of the highest "seen-associated" scores in the history of that publication.

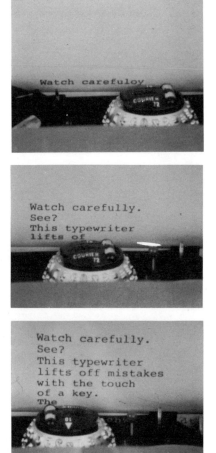

The message is spelled out by IBM's erasing typewriter on the TV screen (silence can be golden in television, too) in this 30-second demonstration commercial. Research indicated that the message came across loud and clear nonetheless.

This campaign, for the Metropolitan New York Ford Dealers Association, using ads that looked like but did not sound like the classified ads they actually were, successfully kicked off Ford's youth-oriented compact car. The informal tone used in the accompany copy offers a startling change of pace from others on the page.

G. M. What's good for the country, also best for the city and suburbs? Stallions, Engine Charley says, call your local Ford dealer.

Fu Man Chu—Yan is fun? Make 1976 your Year of the Stallion.

New York magazine's all-copy 4- by 5-foot "Help You Get Around" station poster appeared at bus stops throughout Manhattan, offering a nearly 2000-word message to decipher while waiting for a bus. Who says a poster has to be all picture?

It is possible for an advertiser to gain broad exposure in many different media while always carrying the same basic message, albeit differing in execution. Many advertisers, particularly in consumer-oriented companies (General Foods, Colgate, General Motors, among others), use ten to twenty different media vehicles to carry their advertising campaigns.

Experienced art directors and writers should have no difficulty whatsoever in adapting a single creative theme to any medium.

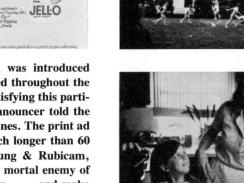

Same campaign but different execution: new Jell-O gelatin was introduced through both print and television. The identical recipe was used throughout the campaign. On television, real housewives demonstrated how satisfying this particular dessert could be. At the end of each commercial, the announcer told the audience that the recipe would be found in that month's magazines. The print ad carried the recipe, which the housewife could examine for much longer than 60 seconds. Says Alex Kroll, creative managing director of Young & Rubicam, responsible for this campaign: "Television was not born as the mortal enemy of print. We did not try to duplicate or merely reinforce television . . . and make print fall flat by trying to compete with television."

Switching from the printed page to outdoor posters, Coppertone changed its layout to suit the format. A picture of only one model appeared on the billboard as opposed to the three who were shown in the magazine ad. Large, simple display took the place of body text. Fewer products were shown. Directed toward motorists, not magazine readers, this poster conveyed the message in seconds.

174

Choosing Media: The Fine Art of Making Comparisons

Cost per thousand (CPM) is often presented as the last and irrefutable argument for choosing one medium vehicle over the other. This is still the media buyer's Holy Grail.

Unfortunately, like most rigid formulas, this, too, has loopholes if indiscriminately applied to every situation. That is particularly true today. Times have changed. With increased emphasis on market segmentation, more and more advertisers are interested not only in quantitative but in qualitative evaluation of media. And so it should be.

The exact composition, geographical, demographic, and psychological, could be just as important a media consideration as the sheer number of readers, listeners, or viewers. That is why it behooves today's media planners to study in depth any medium they are about to recommend to their clients. If possible, they should spend time with the newspaper or magazine in which an ad is slated to appear and go through it. They must read the articles, look at the pictures and put themselves in the readers' place. They must settle down in front of a television set and watch the program they have just been introduced to through brochures left by a television time salesperson. They must get into their cars and pay personal visits to poster locations (postings) that they are about to include in their media plans. They must have conversations not only with computers but with consumers as well. In short, they must try to gain firsthand knowledge of the medium they are about to buy and feel its impact as though they themselves were buying the product. No CPM figure offers that experience.

SELECTIVITY: THE TOTAL LOOK AT MEDIA[a]

MEDIA	GEOGRAPHIC	DEMOGRAPHIC	SPECIAL INTEREST	PSYCHOLOGICAL	AVERAGE CPM (AUDITS)
Posters					
Highway	*****	***			$0.10–0.35
Street	*****	****			
Station	*****	***	*		
In-car	*****	**			
Point of sale	*****		**		
Newspaper	*****	**	*		$2.25–3.20[b]
Television					
Spot:					
Daytime	****	***	*	*	
Fringe	****	***	**	**	
Prime	****	***	*	*	
Network					$2.25–3.00[c]
Daytime	**	**	*	*	
Fringe	**	**	**	**	
Prime	**	**	*	*	
Cable TV	****	**	*****	*****	
Radio[d]					
Spot	*****	****	*****	****	
Network	*****	***	***	***	$0.60–1.50[e]
Magazine					
General	***	****	****	***	
Trade	*	***	*****	**	$1.50–3.50[f]
Special interest	*	**	*****	****	
Direct mail	*****	*****	*****	*****	$1.50–20.00[g]

Source: Doyle Dane Bernbach, Chicago and New York
[a]Graded by star system; maximum; five stars.
[b]Based on 1000 lines.
[c]Based on a 30-second commercial.
[d]FM tends to be better targeted than AM.
[e]Based on a 60-second commercial.
[f]Based on a black-and-white page.
[g]Production costs included.

Off the Beaten Track: Special Media

Creative media buyers have numerous opportunities to add to their usual television-radio-newspaper-magazine fare. Specialized media represent excellent opportunities not only in terms of savings, but also in ability to reach a highly segmented audience group.

Rampant entrepreneurship in the field makes it difficult to keep abreast of all the specialized media services at a given time. New projects enter the marketplace at a rapid rate, while others are rejected for lack of success. Therefore, it is wise to investigate before making a firm commitment.

Advertising via Telephone Several companies offer this service. It is estimated that approximately 7 million consumers are reached daily through this medium; of these, estimated 2.8 million are "willing to listen." It is possible to purchase 30- to 35-second messages in which the advertiser supplies the company with relevant sales points. They can be taped, introduced by a live-pitch person or both. Recorded announcements lasting from 1 to 4 minutes can be purchased as part of weather, time, news, or stock exchange messages. "Where to buy" telephone services identify retailers of specific products upon consumers' inquiries.

Aerial Banners and Lights Banners, usually more than 30 feet (9 meters) long, are pulled by low-flying planes. After dark, traveling aerial lights can display messages of up to 90 characters. The cost is less than $100 per hour for banners and slightly more for aerial light flights.

Airborne Neon Signs These signs are advertising messages about 200 feet (61 meters) long which are suspended under the plane's body. The traveling speed and the route must be specified by the advertiser. Rates are negotiable.

176

Balloons and Kytoons Ad balloons range from 2½ to 7½ feet (from 0.8 to 2.3 meters) in diameter. Kytoons are nearly twice as long. The advertiser's message is imprinted on the balloons or on side panels attached to kytoons. Airborne heights vary from 200 to 800 feet (from 61 to 244 meters). The balloons and kytoons may be made individually on request. Costs vary, starting at $2 for small balloons.

Beetle Boards Advertising messages are placed directly on the bodies of student-owned automobiles (Volkswagens) with preprinted, precut decals. Owners are handpicked on the basis of grades, driving records, affiliations, appearance, and personality. This method has been conceived primarily as an on-campus medium, although programs are available in many metropolitan markets throughout the country. The service is available on approximately 100 campuses; once an advertiser has been accepted, product exclusivity applies. The basic marketing rule of thumb for prime saturation is about one beetle board per 5000 students.

Belt Buckles Custom-made for the advertisers, buckles can be used as self-liquidating premiums. The cost depends upon the amount of metal alloy in the buckle, the type of finish, the mold complication, and the quality of the belt. It ranges from $5 to more than $15.

Blimps Since the blimps are owned and leased by Goodyear, availability to advertisers is limited. The cost varies.

Bowling Scorepads and Displays Advertising is printed along the margins of bowling pads. One-quarter of league bowlers' cards are available for this purpose. The cost is $2500 for about 100,000 scorepads and $5000 for 1 million personal scoring cards.

Bus Posters and Cards Illuminated posters are available at bus-stop shelters which provide protection for as many as twenty-four persons. Transit outdoor posters are available in king size (side of the bus), tail-light size (rear of the bus), and bus-o-rama size (along the roof line and sometimes back-lit fluorescently). "Total bus" service features the same poster inside and outside the bus. The average passenger rides the bus for 23 minutes. More than 40 million Americans, or nearly one-quarter of the total population, travel to and throughout their cities by bus. Almost every major artery in every major city is covered by a bus route. Rates depend on the *showing* (the type of route covered per month).

Bus-Stop Shelters Advertising in shelters is available in most cities with a population of 500,000 or more. Two panels per shelter offer an excellent opportunity for ad-message visibility at all times. They are often protected by vinyl plates and are kept clean and free of stickers or graffiti by local businessmen, who construct them on a partnership basis with Busstop Shelters, Inc. Panel sizes and rates vary, but the

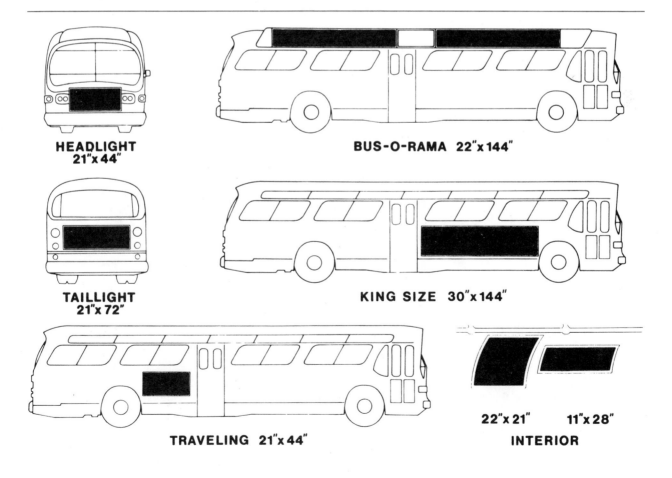

HEADLIGHT 21"x 44"

BUS-O-RAMA 22"x 144"

TAILLIGHT 21"x 72"

KING SIZE 30"x 144"

TRAVELING 21"x 44"

22"x 21"   11"x 28"
INTERIOR

cost can reach $400 per panel. This medium is popular with national and local advertisers.

Calendars Calendars offer a year-round opportunity to advertise and are especially suitable for local advertisers. The method of distribution provides a prime-prospect audience.

Campground and Trailer Guides Approximately 70 percent of all vacationers and travelers who are recreational-vehicle campers purchase these books. Travel guides are usually updated annually, and they enjoy a fairly up-scale ($15,000-plus) readership. The cost varies from $500 to $15,000 per four-color page.

Cable Television Signals are transmitted through coaxial cables rather than through the air for reasons of improved reception, adequate coverage to homes outside the primary-signal range, or special programming. Cable television is noted for its ability to provide a multitude of channels: about twenty today but eventually forty or even sixty. Programming may be produced in the stations' studios. Basic cable systems charge different rates for airing programs on their leased channels, ranging from as much as $250 an hour for prime time in a major market such as New York to more than 10 times as much if the telecast is national. A few public-access channels offer commercial time for more than $100 a minute. Operating in most of the United States, they achieve an average penetration of TV homes of more than 10 percent; in some major markets, this figure more than doubles. At this time, no accurate audience data are available. Nielsen does not rate public-access channels at present, and except for making an educated guess as to coverage (for example, 250,000 in the southern half of Manhattan), the sponsor is hard put to learn the exact return on investment.

About 12 million subscribers are connected to the nation's 3500 cable systems. Operators predict, somewhat optimistically, that this figure will grow to 75 million by 1980. Through satellites, programs may be distributed nationally. The new pot of gold at the end of the rainbow, is *pay cable,* involving an additional monthly charge to subscribers of such services as Home Box Office, in New York City, for events without commercial interruptions.

Campus Advertising More than 2000 college papers accept advertising; they are read by more than 80 percent of the students. Video-tape programming, operating through heavy traffic hours (10 A.M. to 6 P.M.), is found on many campuses. It is rented to the colleges and is shown on an average of 30 times a week. Commercial time is available to the sponsor.

Clocks The name of the product or the advertiser may appear on the face. These are distributed by a sales force to local accounts.

Closed-Circuit Racetrack Advertising Commercials of various lengths are available on closed-circuit monitors at racetracks. The cost is approximately $50 per 60-second commercial, depending upon attendance.

Computer Clock Spectaculars Fully illuminated display units suspended at a high level are vandal-proof. Still transparencies can be animated. The cost of 150 clocks is about $14,000. Advertising space is also available on computer-station timetables.

Cooperative Newspaper Inserts Assembled on a full page-ad, usually in color, are ad coupons for many brands, from many manufacturers, distributed by one company, such as the Marketing Corporation of America. The cost is $1 per 1000 coupons circulated, compared with $5 for a newspaper or magazine insert paid for by a single advertiser and $14 for direct mail.

Coptermedia This method uses thousands of light bulbs mounted on a 40- by 8-foot (2.2- by 2.4-meter) billboard frame on a slow-flying helicopter. The effect is that of a brilliant flying electric sign floating about 500 feet (152 meters) above the ground. Rates are approximately $200 per hour, depending on the total length of the flight.

Criterion Boards These consist of three-sheet posters and junior posters (six to eight sheets). The boards are usually placed near shopping centers and local stores, sometimes as freestanding structures at eye level. They are available in almost all major cities and towns. A three-sheet poster costs approximately $25 to $35 a panel.

Demonstrators Demonstrators are hired sales help at retail outlets, trade shows, fairs, and so on. They can generally perform any kind of function, from that of receptionist to that of hostess. Costs start at approximately $30 a day.

Flash sign "Rheingold Beer" appears on the news flash of the Allied Chemical Building in Times Square, New York. A photograph of this message appeared in a TV commercial.

Direct Mail Whether this type of vehicle comes under "special media" is a moot point; it is included here only because it is still considered as such by many large advertisers accustomed to thinking of "mass media" in terms of television, magazines, newspapers, radio, and possibly posters. To many people direct mail—by far the largest portion of a $50 billion plus annual direct selling industry—is a "major" medium.

Formats of direct mail vary so much that it is impossible to generalize about costs. Depending upon the size and type of the audience—the more selective the mailing list, the higher the cost of the mailing—the advertiser may spend anywhere from 20¢ (including postage) to $20 or even $50 per piece. His payoff depends on the number of "returns," or more precisely, *paid-up* orders. To be able to evaluate the true costs, they always must be compared with the cost of selling through other and more traditional sales channels, such as retail outlets.

Based on past experience, a surprising variety of products lend themselves to this selling method. It has yet to be proven that less expensive product lines are more profitable when sold directly. Cars, homes, and real estate have all been sold with the help of the U.S. Post Office. The greatest users of direct mail are magazines, newspapers, credit card companies, insurance companies, fund raisers, and stores.

A classic mailing package consists of a mailing envelope, letter, circular, or brochures (folder, booklet, broadsize) and some type of response mechanism, usually an order or reply form. Within and outside this format, the direct mail advertiser can enjoy complete creative freedom.

The basic costs of any direct mail selling must include:
Mailing lists
Creative cost of the mailing piece (layout, copy, finished art, typography)
Production cost (stock, engraving and printing, folding and inserting)
Postage (carrier costs)
Fulfillment (order processing)

General overhead (research, testing, staff, rent)

Film Distribution Services are available to assure bookings in theaters, cable networks, local television stations, business and community club meetings, and resorts. Programs can be less than 10 minutes (for movie showings), longer than 30 minutes (for schools), or 27 minutes (for television). Prints are shipped out and monitored. The advertiser pays only for certified showings. Costs are $20 for each of the first ten certified telecasts, discounts being applied to quantity until the straight rate of $10 is achieved. The cost of film production is absorbed by the advertiser. The average cost is about $20,000 for a 12 to 15 minute film. Often, the sponsor is mentioned only during the credits.

Flash Sign Message in the form of moving lights that flashes on and off or circles in a continuous band around buildings.

Giveaway Prizes For merchandise in the low-price range (less than $450) offered in game shows, the manufacturer must pay a fee (usually slightly more than half of the price of merchandise) and donate the prize. For more expensive merchandise (such as cars), networks pay the dealer's cost and, for every 10-second minicommercial, deducting $1000 to $1500. Hotel accommodations can be exchanged for 10 seconds of promotional time. Criteria for acceptance vary among the more than twenty network shows, reaching 5 million to 7 million viewers during the daytime and about 3 times as many at night. Acting as brokers between producers of giveaway shows and manufacturers are merchandise consultants, who operate on a percentage basis. Networks have their own merchandise departments specializing in this area.

Handbills Handbills are distributed by agents. TDI and firms supplying demonstrators are major sources for distributors.

Hotel-Lobby Displays These are wall-hung or freestanding displays of an advertiser's products.

Hotel Television Prerecorded cassettes and films provide closed-circuit programs geared to hotel guests. They are available nationwide. Costs vary, depending upon the type of closed-circuit TV used.

Independent Television Networks Supplementing the three major networks (which can be dialed on nearly 90 percent of sets in the United States) are several broadcast systems which, through well-established bases, specialize in producing shows, placing them on network affiliates (NBC, CBS, and ABC) and other local stations and selling spots to national sponsors. Three of the largest are the Hughes Television Network, TVS Television Network, and Mizlou Television Network (MTN). Another is the Spanish Television Network. Free of the pressure of having to produce 18-hour programming day after day, these independent agents can operate with a great deal of flexibility in selecting types of programs that have not yet been accepted by major networks for lack of firm evidence of a trend. Hence, the advertiser can use an independent network to try out new concepts or to telecast live events and can also program overflows. Most of the networks can deliver a CPM of less than $2 for a 30-second spot with a guaranteed reach of 85 percent of all television homes, with Nielsen ratings to support exposure.

Kiosks Some major cities offer space on concrete litter receptacles located at major commercial intersections. Rates are based upon the length of exposure and the number of display sides.

Magazine Television This system provides televised discussions and views of top business and government officials offered on videotape to subscribers, primarily of the business community. Currently, no commercial advertising is accepted, but because of the quality of the audience the concept has possibilities.

Maps Advertising space is available on maps, atlases, and globes on an exclusive or multisponsorship basis. Most maps are given away, but they can be used as premiums or can be sold for a specific purpose.

Midnight Postings Various sign and display companies undertake postings on buildings, fences, subways, and the like. This form of defacement is unwelcome to authorities, and thus the need for a late hour.

Multiple Outdoor Displays The copy face can be changed mechanically. The service is available at airports and bus terminals and costs approximately $25 per unit.

Newspaper Supplements and Free-standing Inserts Supplements are usually 11- by 13-inch (28- by 33-centimeter) publications printed in color, black and white, or combinations of the two. The number of pages varies from eight to any multiple thereof. Inserts can be produced by the advertiser or by the newspaper. More than 1500 newspapers accept supplements, and many offer split runs upon request, with carrying charges based upon circulation.

Freestanding inserts are frequently used by direct-response advertisers. These, too, are folded into the publication, with considerable latitude in size, weight of paper, and other mechanical requirements.

On-Pack Advertising A full-side panel of a quart (0.9-liter) or a half-gallon (1.9-liter) milk container is available for imprint. It is estimated that messages of this type reach nearly 60 percent of the United States population. The cost ranges from $1.50 to $2 per 1000.

Paper-book Advertising Bound-in inserts are available in gatefolds, four-page spread, and single pages. Hand-inserted cards serve as bookmarks. Costs range from $7 to $9 per 1000; hand-inserted cards are more expensive. Approximately 350 million pocket books are sold annually. The audience can be pinpointed by book title.

Paper Towels Dispensers containing 200 sheets of towels carry an advertiser's message in up to three colors. The cost is approximately $25 per year per dispenser.

Park Benches The back rests of benches provide advertising space about 2 feet (0.6 meter) high by 6 feet (1.8 meters) long. The ads can be placed at strategic locations such as bus stops and the vicinity of shopping centers. Costs range between $15 and $25 a month.

Phone Covers Advertising on plastic telephone book covers can be purchased from several companies. The medium is used primarily by local retailers.

Plugs Networks are equipped to incorporate visual mentions in their shows, using cars, fashions, appliances, jewelry, hotels, airlines, and so on. Because the plugs are a part of the show, their effect can be wholly subliminal and therefore highly effective. Costs vary, but they can frequently exceed $25,000 for repeated exposure.

Prefiled Catalog File Industrial catalogs serve the buyer more than they do the seller; readers order directly from listings which include a sales representative, agent, and distributor (if further information is required). Because descriptions are fairly comprehensive, these catalogs enable the buyer to make comparisons and selections. There are organizations that collect manufacturers' catalogs and inserts and bind them in prefiled catalog files, which are indexed, classified, brought up to date, and distributed.

Premiums Approximately half of the items used by nonretailers are self-liquidating (they pay for themselves). Combination offers, straight giveaways, and coupon plans comprise most of the others. Major

premiums consist of housewares, toys, novelties, cutlery, utensils, sports equipment, and even trading stamps, often offering the customer a wide selection.

Protective Binders Opaque or clear plastic covers used to protect magazines in waiting rooms, beauty parlors, and barbershops can be imprinted. Rates are negotiable with the producer of the binder. Some airline magazines offer similar services.

Public-Channel TV Programs Corporate underwriting is made available by several stations; it costs from $25,000 to more than $2.5 million. A series can be picked up by other stations and even by a network, although this cannot be guaranteed. Ratings are hard to determine, but they can be quite high—more than one-third of tuned-in sets in some cases.

These shows are also welcome additions to audio-video presentations in schools.

Scales Scales can be placed in high-traffic areas. A full-color, illuminated, 11- by 14-inch (28- by 36-centimeter) transparency flips a small mirror in which the passerby sees himself as he steps on the scale. A yearly contract allows a new message every 3 months.

Shirt Boards and Wrappers The message is printed on the shirt board and shirt bands. Advertisers specify their market areas. A million shirt boards printed in full color on both sides would cost approximately $30,000.

Shopper Information Systems These may be fixtures with pockets containing "take-one" literature, located in high-traffic areas in stores. About 80 percent of the material has some type of direct-response device.

Shopping Bags Bags are offered to grocery chains on a regionally exclusive basis. A shopper's checklist is printed on both sides, and advertisers can have their names printed on the list next to or in place of the category designation. Advertising imprinted on plastic, vinyl, or paper shopping bags which are distributed at trade shows, department stores, or other locations also belongs in this category.

Shopping-Cart Miniboards Attached to supermarket carts, this form of advertising is being revived. Displays can also be inserted on each side in a faced frame on the first panel of the cart. The average supermarket has a traffic flow of some 35,000 shoppers a month. Costs vary from $1 to $3 per sign per month.

Shopping-Mall Television Systems Large color television screens (usually a couple of dozen) are placed at strategic points in shopping malls.

Sidewalk Paint Many sign-painting and display companies offer this service, even though most cities have ordinances prohibiting the defacing of sidewalks. The message is airbrushed on the sidewalk by means of precut stencils.

Skywriting and Skytyping Skywriting consists of a single plane able to spell out a twenty-five letter message per flight. Using five planes, skytyping is 15 times as fast, providing a letter every 90 seconds. In perfect weather, the message is visible in a 15-mile (24-kilometer) area. The cost is approximately $400 per twenty-letter message.

Slide Charts These charts can be tailor-made to aid customers in their calculations of, for example, shipping rates, calorie intake, metric conversion, gasoline mileage, or other figures directly or indirectly related to an advertiser's products or services.

Sound Sheets These are vinyl sheets, transparent or in seven colors, containing 12 to 15 minutes of sound on each side. Lightweight and thin, they are easy to mail, can be bound into publications, used as free inserts, or employed as direct-mail pieces. Prices depend on the size of the sheets (length of sound), quantity, and center imprint ($25 for the first 1000 and $5 to $9 for each additional 1000).

Spanish-Language Television Network Sometimes called the fourth TV network, this chain of fourteen stations serves 13 million Hispanic consumers in their mother tongue throughout the United States, in-

181

cluding New York, Chicago, Los Angeles, and four locations in Texas. Research indicates that minimizing the language barrier improves commercial retail sales as much as 2½ times.

Special Reproduction Matchbooks There are two types, those made for cigarette companies and those made for special promotions. The matchbooks are distributed through vending-machine operators, tobacco and drug wholesalers, chain stores, and supermarkets and by direct mail. Approximately 15 billion books are used annually. Message retention is high. The cost ranges from $40 per 1000 upward for smaller orders; it is less in the case of large volume.

Spectaculars Outdoor signs are especially effective in high-traffic areas. Long-term contracts are desirable since initial production costs can be high, often exceeding $100,000.

Spin-o-Rama Three posters, mounted together on shopping-center parking lampposts, are activated by the wind. One or all panels can be purchased.

Sponsorship Generally, sponsorship means the financial backing of a major event or personality, capitalizing on publicity derived from this support. Funding (scholarship, buildings, and so on) and prize money (going toward winners' purses) are types of commercial sponsorship. The cost is governed by the degree of participation and by the person, event (which may assume the sponsor's name), or subject. For example, $250,000 has purchased exclusive sponsorship of ten automobile races.

Stadium Posters Parks, sport arenas, and Little League stadiums are often ringed with boards for advertising messages. In some parks, electric scoreboards are equipped for the same purpose. Costs vary, ranging from $10,000 to $75,000 per year, depending on attendance figures.

Station and Terminal Displays Island showcases, direct-phone centers, floor exhibits, and commuter clocks are available at nationwide public transportation centers. One-,

two-, or three-sheet posters (in some locations, six-sheet posters) enclosed by frames can also be shown at such locations.

Prices depend on the strength of the showing.

Store Casts Many large stores have in-store speaker systems which are used for the store's purpose, but they make time available for commercial messages.

Subway Posters and Cards More than half of the city population regularly rides the subway. Posters can be displayed at stations (one-, two-, and three-sheet) or in cars at various locations (side positions or above doors). The height of side cards is 11 inches (28 centimeters; 16 inches, or 41 centimeters for above the door), and widths are 11, 14, 21, 28, and 56 inches (28, 36, 53, 71, and 142 centimeters). Same-size posters fit inside the coaches. Rates are based upon runs (number of cars per month).

Sugar-Packet Advertising It is estimated that approximately 30 million adults handle these packets daily; almost two-thirds of them are used during office hours when few other advertising messages compete for the consumer's attention. Space is sold in 1 million units for 4-week time segments at approximately $1.70 per 1000 packets, ranging from a small section of a city (one that is selected for limited coverage) to the top twenty-five markets in the country.

T-Shirts This plain white garment has been transformed into a kind of personal fashion statement for people of all ages, but about 80 percent of the wearers are 25 or younger. Advertising emblems intrigue Pop Art–conscious wearers.

T-shirt premium offers typically pull 2 percent or more in responses.

A "smell" T-shirt uses the microencapsulation process to simulate a smorgasbord of smells from bananas to root beer. Bright, sparkling rhinestones complementing the colorful design by Sherry Manufacturing Company for Bright Side shampoo, makes the T-shirt shown a favorite with young people. Two ads depicted are typical of the many self-liquidating T-shirt promotions conducted by corporations.

"Talking" Mannequins A blank face is constructed to simulate the spokesman's features. Film footage of the spokesman is then projected onto the mannequin, bringing it to life. The mannequins can be rented.

Taxicab Advertising The back panel of front seats, the outside rear, and displays built on the roof (14- by 48-foot, or 43- by 14.6-meter, space on the 5000 fleet-owned vehicles in New York City) provide day and night exposure (cabs travel between 100 and 250 miles daily in a large city). Trips last an average of 15 minutes. Rates depend on the number of taxis used and the contract period.

Rear-screen slide projectors facing riders are also available in some major markets.

Theater-Screen Advertising Commercials ranging from 30 seconds to 2½ minutes are screened at performances in most indoor and drive-in theaters at approximately $6 per 1000.

The average national movie audience consists of approximately 500 million people per week, with women and younger people dominant.

Toll-Free Numbers Large retail chains relying on mail orders have been placing more than half of their orders by telephone for many years. The 800 operator can be requested to suggest additional products to customers, trade up to higher prices, quote prices, offer product information, suggest gift giving, give the name of the nearest dealer, accept a membership application, offer credit options, and suggest alternative methods to facilitate delivery of merchandise.

Truck Posters These are designs mounted on a monthly basis on the sides of interstate trucks. The American Trucking Association es- timates that there are an average of 500 million exposures per month. The cost is approximately $35,000 and is slightly higher for 4- by 10- foot (1.2- by 3-meter) posters on Railway Express trucks. Illumination is available on some vehicles.

Vending-Machine Advertising The display, which is placed on the sides of the vending machine, measures about 6 by 8 inches (15 by 20 centimeters). Machines can be isolated or grouped. The minimum schedule covers a 4-week period. The cost depends on volume and period of exposure, starting at less than $1 per machine.

Word-of-Mouth Advertising This is accomplished through club luncheons primarily for women, which are hosted by skilled buying counselors. Products are explained, displayed, taste-sampled, and couponed. The potential audience is half a million persons during the 39-week season, and they influence the decisions of an additional 1,500,000 households. The cost is approximately 10 cents per customer.

Yellow Pages More than 5000 directories are used by some 65,000 households in the United States. Space units range upward from two one-half columns or on-line trade listings. Layout and typography are regulated by the publisher. The yearly cost of one-sixteenth of a page in the top 100 markets ranges from $34,000 to more than $100,000. A nationwide single-contract plan is available.

Chapter Ten

When the Product Is the Idea

A product may be so different from its competitors' wares that the advertisement practically writes itself. Such is a creative person's dream ad; it is effortless. A piece of straightforward copy may be all that is necessary, perhaps with a head-on photograph of the product thrown in for good measure.

However, such choice assignments are few and far between. The simple fact is that in today's marketplace many different products perform the same *basic* function. Most of them have to do with the everyday needs of the average American male or female: the cleaning of clothes, the economy of driving, the elimination of odors, the killing of bugs, the feeding of pets, and so on. So to highlight the differences between products is still left largely to the professional advertising practitioner.

Products, Products, Products

Needless to say, the tidal wave of "new" products has left many an artist and writer in advertising in a greater quandary than ever. More products were introduced in the last decade than in the preceding 50 years. Dancer Fitzgerald Sample, an advertising agency whose estimates are usually on the conservative side, put the figure at 100 or so a month.

Most modern corporations are very much new-product–oriented; new products are their hope for still better times, the carrot to be dangled before stockholders. And the end is not in sight. Campbell Soup not so long ago managed to introduce more than ninety new products in a single year. The Eastman Kodak Company unveiled seventeen consumer photographic products designed to strengthen its line all at one time at a press conference.

Thus, it is hardly surprising that a large supermarket today is likely to have more than 8000 different brands and products fighting for their place in the sun, or more accurately, under the fluorescent ceiling lamps. And in a typical drugstore there are some 40,000 items on the shelves, with many more at the door waiting to join the fray. Some of the items are about as closely related to drugs as a toilet seat is to an oval picture frame.

Some observers cannot help but wonder what effect such an influx has on the marketplace. One of them is Edward Buxton, editor of *Ad Daily*. He relates that during his trip to a supermarket he found 45 brands of breakfast cereals, 150 different kinds of snacks, 35 varieties of bread, and more than 30 flavors of ice cream, despite the fact that nearly 50 percent of ice cream eaters routinely choose vanilla (chocolate follows, with 10 percent). In his book *Promise Them Anything,* he

wonders: "It would seem incredible that a manufacturer would make a product that he knew beforehand would appeal to less than one percent of the population. Yet they do it every day. More than 25 brands of cigarettes hold less than one percent of the market. Popular Virginia Slims is considered by Philip Morris to be a very successful brand. Only 1.2 percent of the smokers buy it" (Stein and Day, New York, 1972).

A Little Goes a Long Way

But in the $15 billion-plus cigarette industry 1.2 percent goes a long way. The same is true of many other product categories (for example, 1 percent of the market share would place a pantyhose manufacturer among the top ten in the field). The size of the pie encourages more and more entries, no matter what the product category. Of course, not all "new" products are new. Quite a few are nothing more than a modified version of their predecessors; some are downright incestuous.

Lists of new-product introductions by major corporations published monthly by *Advertising Age* provide a few insights. In one typical list only one of the twenty-four items could be considered a major breakthrough (a cigar developed by American Brands with a charcoal-impregnated inner wrapper claimed to reduce cigar odor significantly). The rest were merely refinements of an existing product: Hi-C fruit, another liquid concentrate; Datril acetominophen in liquid form; a low-calorie beer under the Schlitz name; a low-tar version of Salem menthol cigarettes; Murine eye drops; Purex liquid laundry detergent; and, from Campbell Soup, another single-serving entry.

Whatever Happened to Product Difference?

None of the above is intended to suggest that product difference has lost its traditional *sine qua non* status. In fact, the proliferation of products makes preeminence all the more essential. The sounding off of one housewife at a panel discussion conducted by the Bloom Advertising Agency in Dallas, Texas, underscores that point: "Who needs to walk into the supermarket and find an entire long row of beans? I mean how many kinds of beans can you eat? I don't need 16 different kinds of pinto beans. I don't need 25 different kinds of pinto beans. Who needs all of this? I think it's foolishness. Housewives are not so foolish. Housewives are more interested in quality, and they don't need 99 new products every year. They are not dissatisfied with some of the good stable ones." Her outburst was followed by applause. It is safe to say that advertisers would have greeted her statement with considerably less enthusiasm.

As mentioned above, the products that emerge victorious are those that are perceived to be unique by consumers. Note the word *perceived*. A product difference, no matter how important it seems to the advertiser, means nothing to consumers unless they (and not only the advertiser) perceive it as such. What consumers care about most is the way in which product difference will affect them: change their life-style, increase their earnings, make them look better,

improve their performance with the opposite sex. Consumers can afford to be selfish creatures; being on the paying end, they can dictate their wants. Advertisers have no choice but to play up to these creatures. They can do so by making sure that product differences are clearly understood by consumers and perceived as *genuine selling features*.

Perception occurs on several levels. Some filters through on a subconscious level, but feelings are as important in making a sale as any mental process. Here are some of the factors that affect ultimate purchasing decisions:

1. Consumers' perception of the *company*. Who are the manufacturers? What is their reputation?
2. Consumers' perception of the *product features*. What does it do?
3. Consumers' perception of the *product benefits*. What does it do for me?
4. Consumers' perception of the *package*. Does it protect the product? Does it make the product easier to use? Is it attractive? What does the label say?
5. Consumers' perception of the *advertising* itself. Is it accurate? Informative? Honest?

Obviously all these things (physical attributes, promise, package, price, and advertising of the product) are perceived by consumers in totality as a *single communication package*.

KISS the USP

KISS stands for (in the words of a marketing director of a nationally known food chain) "Keep it simple, stupid." Blunt as it may sound, the formula has worked for him, as it has for many other business executives.

USP, on the other hand, is short for "unique selling proposition," invented many years ago by Rosser Reeves of Ted Bates & Co., Inc. Following in the wake of this basic and important advertising concept were "product difference," "new-product model," "single concept," and other semantic coinages mean-

ing much the same thing, namely, *the consumer's impression of the product reduced to its essence*.

It is vital that the selling proposition of a product be simple. There are limits to the amount of information that the human brain is able or willing to absorb. The average person has a reading vocabulary of 25,000 to 50,000 words, the latter suggesting exceptional verbal fluency and the probable presence of a superior mind. Most people have difficulty in dealing with more than seven units at a time. Therefore, most consumers quickly lose interest in, or soon forget, an advertising message which unduly taxes their level of comprehension.

Says Ed McCabe, founder of his own agency and a member of the Copywriters Hall of Fame: "Monosyllables work best. Say it simply. Don't beat around the bush."

The Art of Positioning: Some Good Examples

Astute planning, a simple selling proposition, and consistency in advertising have entrenched these products firmly in today's marketplace. They are well positioned in the mind of the buying public.

Cadillac: quality car
Chevrolet: American car
Volvo: rugged car
Datsun: economy car
The New York Times: thorough and authoritative newspaper
Daily News: people's newspaper
Howard Johnson: family eating place
Marlboro: cigarette for men
Virginia Slim: cigarette for women
Chivas Regal: expensive Scotch
American Tourister: sturdy luggage
AT&T: the telephone company
IBM: the computer company
Xerox: the copying company
Steinway: the piano company
Midas: the muffler-installing company
Polaroid: instant photography
Club Méditerranée: inexpensive vacations
Crest: the cavity-fighting toothpaste

Like products, retail stores also suggest very definite images (with positive and negative values) in the minds of consumers. People patronize stores for a number of reasons. These may be tangible benefits, such as quality of merchandise and service, location, parking facilities, special promotions, pricing, and store policies. Or the reasons may be more subtle. Store ambience, the method of displaying the merchandise, advertising graphics, and, most of all, self-identification with the store (the sense of comfort derived from shopping there) also play an important part in attracting customers. Research (based on the currency of stores' own mailing lists) shows that average shoppers feel at least as much loyalty to the store as they do to the products they find there. Less than one-third of consumers purchase the same product for more than 6 months, while most of them stay with the same store in established communities for 5 to 10 years and sometimes for a lifetime.

Good retail advertising reflects consumers' concept of the store. Execution has much to do with that. Choice of art style (fashionable, realistic, deliberately crude, and so on) or photography (high-key, low-key and so on), typography (heavy or light, free or tight), handling of display copy and layout techniques (for example, use of white space, number of items displayed on the page) all work toward that end, albeit often in a subliminal fashion.

In some cases, nuances of execution are given short shrift by overly item-oriented retailers who tend to judge the effectiveness of their advertising solely on a short-term rather than a long-term basis. Perhaps these die-hard pragmatists should remember that the so-called hard-sell approach need not run counter to image-building advertising. The two approaches, in fact, often complement each other. Certainly, the image of the store is as important a factor in making a sale as any other. Examples of how merchandise and image advertising can be made to work together are shown below and on the next few pages.

Before

After

King's Super Markets boldly dispensed with the usual supermarket look in its advertising campaign. On the basis of findings by an independent researcher, Oxtoby-Smith, it was brought to light that this grocery chain had already firmly entrenched itself in the minds of shoppers as a source of high-quality food and other household merchandise at a somewhat higher price.

So Warren Pfaff Advertising set out to prepare a series of ads that helped to reinforce the store's image. The agency presented an organized shopping list (right) instead of the old, untidy carnival of hopped-up numbers (left). The good looks of these ads in no way interferes with their practicality as a shopping guide. Each ad provides the shopper with an easy-to-read list of items and prices.

Another example of an image-building advertising campaign (and yet with elements of hard sell) is Barney's, the world's largest men's apparel store. Barney's, like so many other clothing stores, started out in limited circumstances. Only a generation ago, it was just another modest-size discount store on Manhattan's lower West Side. The story goes that Barney Pressman, the immigrant founder and the only salesman in the store in those days, would stand in front of his establishment with a long cane in his hand so that he could pull prospects in through the door. Be that as it may, his fame spread rapidly. More and more uptown customers took the trouble to come downtown to visit the store. And that was how a former hole in the wall grew into an imposing three-story building taking up an entire city block.

Still, Barney's out-of-the-way location at Seventh Avenue and Seventeenth Street had certain connotations; among other things, it suggested bargain prices to the general public. For quite a while, management saw no reason to dispel this notion. In fact, along with the promise that it could fit men of any shape and size, Barney's talked about the value of its merchandise as often as it could. For many years, the slogan "Calling All Men to Barney's" had as familiar a ring to the average New Yorker as Ohrbach's "Business in Millions, Profit in Pennies", or the low-overhead theme used by Robert Hall Clothes, then in direct competition.

Men's tastes changed with the times, however, and so did the store's selling approach. The fashion revolution of the 1960s did not escape the attention of founder Barney Pressman and his astute son and heir apparent, Fred. Both agreed to phase out price merchandising in print and on radio advertising. Instead, the copy centered on fashion. The word *selection* ("Select, don't settle") had come to mean more than just size, tailoring, and perfect fit; it connoted a choice of name brands and some of the world's best-known designers. To dramatize its fashion orientation, Barney's divided its 100,000-square-foot (9290-square-meter) interior into a number of individual "rooms," each with its own fashion point of view. It branched out into selling other fashion items. Social amenities were introduced. They gave the store a special ambience. The tone of advertising kept pace with the changes; for example, the store's coffee shop was described in a newspaper ad as a place where "you can retire for a bit of wine and imported cheese and fruit."

In its fifty-third year, Barney's added women's tailored clothing to its line of merchandise as a crowning touch. Today, the store is a fashion center, a place out-of-town tourists are told to visit, a venerable New York institution.

Through the years, Barney's award-winning newspaper, magazine, radio, and television ads have become as talked about as the store itself. As in most retail success stories, they have helped to make what today is the store's image.

Typical two-page ad in *The New York Times*. Barney's uses major metropolitan newspapers and prime-time television to carry its advertising messages.

187

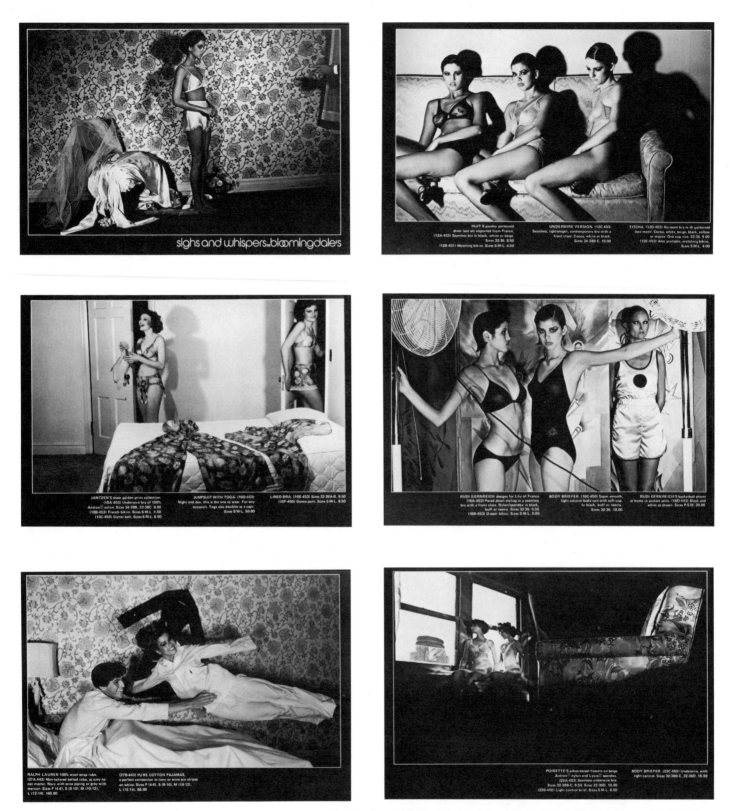

sighs and whispers...bloomingdale's

HUIT 8 paisley patterned sheer lace set imported from France. (12A-453) Seamless bra in black, white or beige. Sizes 32-36. 8.50 (12B-451) Matching bikini. Sizes S-M-L. 4.50

UNDERWIRE VERSION. (12C-453) Seamless, lightweight, contemporary bra with a front close. Cocoa, white or black. Sizes 34-38B-C. 10.00

TITCHA. (12D-453) No-seam bra with patterned lace motif. Cocoa, white, beige, black, yellow or mauve. One cup size, 32-36. 9.00 (12E-453) Also available, matching bikini. Sizes S-M-L. 4.00

JANTZEN'S sheer garden print collection. (10A-453) Underwire bra of 100% Antron® nylon. Sizes 34-38B, 32-38C. 9.50 (10B-453) French bikini. Sizes S-M-L. 4.50 (10C-450) Garter belt. Sizes S-M-L. 6.50

JUMPSUIT WITH TOGA. (10D-453) Night and day, this is the one to wear. For any occasion. Toga also doubles as a cape. Sizes S-M-L. 50.00

LINED BRA. (10E-453) Sizes 32-36A-B. 9.50 (10F-450) Dance pant. Sizes S-M-L. 8.50

RUDI GERNREICH designs for Lily of France. (16A-453) Pared down styling in a seamless bra with a front close. Nylon/spandex in black, buff or tawny. Sizes 32-36. 9.50 (16B-453) Diaper bikini. Sizes S-M-L. 5.00

BODY BRIEFER. (16C-450) Super smooth, light control body suit with soft cup. In black, buff or tawny. Sizes 32-36. 18.00

RUDI GERNREICH'S basketball player at home in acetate satin. (16D-443) Black and white as shown. Sizes P-S-M. 20.00

RALPH LAUREN 100% wool wrap robe. (27A-443) Man-tailored belted robe, as only he can master. Navy with wine piping or grey with maroon. Sizes P (4-6), S (8-10), M (10-12), L (12-14). 165.00

(27B-443) PURE COTTON PAJAMAS, a perfect companion in navy or wine pin stripes on white. Sizes P (4-6), S (8-10), M (10-12), L (12-14). 56.00

POIRETTE'S silkscreened flowers on beige Antron® nylon and Lycra® spandex. (22A-453) Seamless underwire bra. Sizes 32-38B-C, 9.50. Sizes 32-36D. 10.00 (22B-450) Light control brief. Sizes S-M-L. 6.50

BODY BRIEFER. (22C-450) Underwire, with light control. Sizes 32-38B-C, 32-36D. 16.50

In keeping with its image, Bloomingdale's delighted its sophisticated clientele with a beautiful twenty-four-page bedroom-wear theme brochure from which these pages are culled. Sensuous, world-weary models pose languidly in front of Guy Bourdin's camera. The result is a fashion catalog with only the slightest hint of commercial overtones.

188

How to Build a Better Mousetrap or Invent a New One

Roughly, only about 2 out of every 10 new products survive for more than 3 years. In some industries, as in the 170-brand cigarette market, the success rate is less than 20 percent. A changing economy, unforeseen competition, poor marketing and advertising, lack of distribution, legal obstacles, and lethargic retail acceptance are some of the reasons for the high mortality.

The most important, however, is the most obvious one: lack of genuine demand.

It appears that this simple fact is quite frequently overlooked by even the most experienced marketers, people who should know better. That is true because many manufacturers, surrounded by members of their own organizations, are so close to production problems as to lose sight of a sound marketing plan. It is this total immersion in the *making* of a product as opposed to *selling* it that plays havoc with so many new-product introductions. Pity the artist, writer, and account executive who get saddled with a product concocted in this fashion. Whether or not they like the product for which they create advertising, it is unlikely that there is much they can do in the way of basic product changes at this point.

Fortunately, more and more manufacturers are taking advantage of the innate marketing instincts of the creative advertising people while there is still time. They consult writers and art directors at the early planning stages. Some of the best ideas for new products have been generated through such joint efforts. With that in mind, it may be in order here to cite some of the basic elements that go into successful new-product introductions.

1. *Ask consumers*. Every new product or service has its own *raison d'etre*, usually determined through careful consumer research. Give prospective users an opportunity to express their needs. Whether these are real or imagined should make little difference at the cash register. Consumers may not be able to come up with an exact blueprint for the product they want, but they will offer a clue or two as to the attributes that they would most like to have.

2. *Continue your dialogue with consumers*. Keep touching bases. More than one factor leads to purchase decisions; the product is only one. Packaging, product nomenclature, pricing, and advertising are some of the others. Remember that it is the totality of the presentation that counts, not the parts.

3. *Watch consumers react in the marketplace*. That means the supermarket, drugstore, or wherever the purchase is being made. If costs of getting the product on the shelf are prohibitive, try simulating the circumstances.

4. *Learn from failures*. The fact that others did not get off the ground with a similar or the same product should not stop you from trying again. There could have been a variety of problems which had nothing to do with the product itself. First, find out what these problems were. (Poor advertising could have been one.) Then try skirting around them.

5. *Look for the flaws in existing products*. Frequently, negatives lead to the discovery of basic problems, only to inspire new solutions. For example, detergents left fabrics stiff: enter fabric softeners. Synthetic fabrics picked up static electricity, causing unpleasant side effects: enter static preventers.

6. *Keep an eye on the changing marketplace*. Watch the latest reports, not only those issued by the slow-paced Census Bureau but also the ones published by various marketing research organizations, syndicates, media, trade associations, and advertising agencies. Shifts in population—geographical, demographic, psychological—set the stage for new life-styles and new buying trends. In Chapter 3 we touched upon this important source of stimulation for new-product discoveries.

7. *Keep an eye on the changing economy*. In times of prosperity, new demands for products and services arise. But, as we have pointed out before, recession, too, offers a gamut of marketing opportunities.

8. *Find new uses for old products*. Many products have been restored to life by finding new applications for them. Baking soda enjoyed a sudden resurgence in sales when some 150 new uses were "discovered" for it in a series of ads. Demand for margarine more than doubled in a year when it was reintroduced as cooking butter. The new positioning of Pledge furniture polish as a dusting aid started it off on a new career as a household item.

9. *Extend that line*. This is considered one of the simplest ways of inventing a new product and one that has often proved successful. With distribution channels already established, the manufacturer may be one up on competitors. This is why so many large companies keep adding brands to their product line even if diversification means encouraging competition among their own divisions. Procter & Gamble, one of the most sophisticated marketers in the United States, assigns its products to as many as ten different agencies, each using a different campaign theme: Tide (makes clothes "white"), Cheer (makes clothes "whiter than white"), and Bold (makes clothes "bright"). The three household detergents fight among themselves for an increased market share.

10. *Maximize mileage*. One form of line extension is to add *servicing* to a product. Selling automotive parts (at almost 3 times the original factory price) can yield a substantial profit to automobile manufacturers, not to mention the source of livelihood they provide for several thousands of automobile repair services. Following the same principle, the RCA Factory Service Plan offers up to five service coupons and 24-month coverage to owners of its television sets.

11. *Change the product*. Even the slightest modification can make a big

difference in sales. Almost always, consumers will view the change as an improvement or even conceive of the end result as a new product. Changes can be made in;

Package (bigger, easier application, new label, better design)
Product attributes (consistency, color, flavor, weight)
Price (lower, higher, two for one)
Name (new, modified)

12. *Respect your insights.* Inspiration for a new product can occur at any time and in any place. For example, a better way may suggest itself as you go about performing a routine chore at home or while you are at work or at play. Whatever your inspiration, do not ignore it because it came on the spur of the moment. Examine it from every angle. Check it out with your friends.

13. *Have patience.* It usually takes 4 to 6 months for a new product to make any kind of penetration. Figure on spending about $1\frac{1}{2}$ times as much on the introduction of a new product as you would on one already established.

A Few Words about Test Marketing: Minimizing the Risk

Most new products requiring sizeable up-front investments go through some form of finding-out process. This can be done on a small or an extensive scale, requiring expenditures that run into the millions. The more popular methods are *blind-use testing* (unmarked products tested by users, usually in their homes), *sampling* (product tested by up to 10,000 people), *panel discussions* (group of selected people examining and reacting to the product in the presence of an experienced research person), *central-location testing* (street interviews), *direct mail* (questionnaires and product samples sent to prospects), *coupon ads* (ads with a built-in response mechanism), and

computer-aided techniques (actual buying situations simulated). The most accurate measurement of course, is that of testing a product in an actual, geographically confined, controlled marketplace, usually backed by advertising. This procedure is known as *test marketing*.

The philosophy of test marketing is simple. The problem lies mostly in execution. Here are some of the do's and don'ts:

1. *Make sure that you are testing your entire selling program, not the product alone.* Sampling the product will give the manufacturer some ideas about applicability and consumers' reaction to various features. But use of the product is not the same as selling it. That may be contingent upon a variety of factors, including the way the product is advertised.

2. *Select the right-size test market.* The market should be large enough to provide the advertiser with projectable information, yet not so small as to be a lone, atypical island in the vast United States marketplace. The key is projectability. At present, Milwaukee, Minneapolis, Denver, Phoenix, and Peoria (the most typical of all) rank high on the list with the three largest cities, New York, Chicago, and Los Angeles, also gaining in favor. The most reliable way to test a new product is via multimarketing (up to twenty cities). Generally, there should be at least two, and preferably more, geographically dispersed test markets plus a control area, representing between 2 and 3 percent of the national population. The optimum investment per market is a $250,000 expenditure for the minimum of 6 months that is required to measure results.

3. *Watch media activity.* A test market must be reasonably self-contained from the point of view of media coverage, with as little overlap as possible from nearby areas. This shifts the focus primarily to newspapers, regional magazines, radio, and spot television. The cost of advertising, of course, is reduced through the purchase of national media. A medium can be considered national when it achieves more than

30 percent household penetration.

According to Ira Weinblatt and Martin Friedman of Dancer Fitzgerald Sample, minimum criteria for selection should include three to five TV stations, four radio stations, a daily and a Sunday newspaper, a supplement, and a selection of regional issues of national magazines.

4. *Define your audience.* Prime prospects should be represented in all test markets, not only demographically (income, family size, education) but also psychographically (purchasing habits, attitudes, life-style).

5. *Check retail reception.* This may be a propitious time to find out about the feelings of those who ultimately must sell the product on a one-to-one basis to the consumer. Find out about retailers' preferences, the type of support they would like to have in addition to advertising.

6. *Keep an open mind.* Look for weak spots as you test.

Keep refining your target to avoid more expensive errors in a national expansion.

What Creative Professionals Can Learn from Test Marketing

It behooves creative professionals to follow test-marketing developments closely. From their point of view, the results will be a fair indication of what will take place if and when the product is distributed on a more extensive basis.

Analyzing consumer reactions, creative practitioners will gain insight not only into the product and its package but into the effectiveness of their advertising campaigns as well. For another thing, they will see perhaps for the first time, their advertising in print and broadcast in the context of the total editorial environment, exactly as it appears to the ultimate consumers.

New Product Development: The Y & R Method

Aware of the difficulties inherent in new-product introductions, Young & Rubicam has its own team of creative research and marketing experts to assist advertisers in this area. Consumers' needs are carefully analyzed and emphasized at every step of the way.

INTRODUCING GAINES SUPER EGG-BURGER

Because just like you, your dog needs a little variety.

Gaines is now offering a new deluxe burger, twice the size of the regular Gaines-burger, with plenty of protein-rich egg mixed in.

GAINES SUPER EGG-BURGERS are a full feeding, balanced formulation of protein, fats and carbohydrates, containing beef by-products, vegetables, vitamins and eggs added . . . all the wholesome nutrients your dog needs.

Each burger is individually wrapped and pre-measured for completely accurate feeding. No fuss with can openers or mess with leftovers. Each of these burgers equals a one pound can of dog food.

CONCEPT AD COPY
PRIOR TO G.F. LEGAL CLEARANCE

A lot of people feed eggs to their dogs for a lot of different reasons.

Some because their dogs love the taste.
Some because eggs make their dog's coat look shinier and healthier.

And some because they think eggs are just plain good for dogs. Period.

At Gaines . burger, we agree with a number of these reasons. Which is why we're introducing new Gaines . burgers with egg.

The first dog food ever made with real, fluff dried eggs. (We don't think there's a dog around who won't like the taste.)

Gaines . burgers with egg contains all the nourishing vitamins, minerals and bone meal every dog needs. And one thing every dog loves. 30% beef and beef by-products.

What's more, as you'd expect from Gaines . burger, never any cans or leftovers to worry about.

New Gaines . burgers with egg.

For people who know what's good for a dog.

Introducing Gaines-burgers With Egg.
A well-balanced diet for good looking dogs.

Today's dog looks better. Dresses better. And leads a healthier life. Because, unlike the dogs of yesteryear who were fed whatever was handy (table scraps, etc.), today's dogs are fed a well-balanced diet.
The kind of diet your dog will get when you feed him new Gaines-burgers with Egg. They're made with real protein-rich egg. (Three whole dried eggs in every package of twelve burgers.)
And, just like regular Gaines-burgers, they're made with beef, beef by-products, vegetables, vitamins, and minerals—everything your dog needs to keep him healthy, happy, and looking his best.
Gaines-burgers with Egg come individually wrapped. Two burgers have as much nourishment as a one-pound can of dog food.
One more thing: there are no messy cans or leftovers to bother with. No odor either.
New Gaines-burgers with Egg. For today's dog.

ANNCR: Eggs.
The best natural source of complete protein.
Everybody loves them. People love them. Dogs love them.
Up until now it wasn't easy for a dog to get an egg for himself.
But now there's new Gaines • burgers with egg.
The moist meaty taste dogs love . . .
plus a quarter of a real egg in a burger.
So why not give your dog a taste he'll love . . . and all the goodness of real egg. Give him new Gaines • burgers with egg.

191

Consumer Research As a Form of Test Marketing

Many advertisers feel that new-product testing often can be made *prior* to moving into the marketplace —and thus can save the cost of distribution and advertising. It is true that consumers are quite able to verbalize their needs. There are many marketing and research organizations as well as advertising agencies that have developed interview techniques just for that purpose.

Here, for example, is how Michael Amoroso Inc., a marketing group, goes about assessing new product ideas—and determining the chances for success:

Step 1: Disciplined Ideation. The process starts with ideas, which we usually phrase in terms of known or hypothesized consumer needs.

Step 2: Opportunity Identification. Once we have generated a number of ideas (within a pre-determined market or product category), the task is to select the ones *with the most potential.*

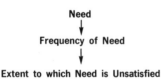

Need
↓
Frequency of Need
↓
Extent to which Need is Unsatisfied

Step 3: Creative Implementaion. Our actual creative effort, then, focuses on the identified high-potential opportunities. The opportunity description becomes, in effect, the *creative platform* we use to design a viable product concept.

Michael Amoroso calls the method "focused creativity." His sounding board constitutes about 1000 people. The approach represents a prototype of new-product testing—sans the expense of a roll-out test market. A word of caution: his type of testing shows only what *not* to do —a product idea whose time has not yet come.

As pointed out before, the ultimate test of any new product lies in its ability to survive under actual marketing conditions. There is no substitute for front-line experience.

An economic slowdown should not stop new-product activity. There is *always* a need for something new. When the unemployment rate climbed above 7 percent during a period of recession, this writer offered a fifty-page "confidential report," *How to Get a Better-paying Job—without Asking for It.* Advertised in *The Wall Street Journal*, it prompted many thousands of readers to send $10 in the hope of getting some good advice.

192

GETTING TO KNOW THE PRODUCT: WHERE SOME OF THE BEST ADVERTISING IDEAS HAVE THEIR START

Always looking for subtle distinctions, writers and art directors are particularly well qualified to translate product *features* into product *benefits*. This is where creativity often begins. There are a number of ways to find out about a product from the consumers' point of view. One is to use it or to talk to someone who is using it. Another is to ask a company sales representative (or even the president, who may be the most articulate salesperson of all) to go through the motions of selling the product to you. Others in the corporation, such as engineers, R&D staff, and factory workers, may also provide fresh insights, as may retailers who deal with products all the time. And, of course, there are the standard sources of information, such as trade magazines, books, and competitive advertising campaigns. Whatever you do, spend as much time as you need in examining the product or service which you are going to write about. The lists below offer a few clues as to what to look for.

PRODUCT PROFILE

Physical Properties		Performance	Aesthetic and Social Considerations	Subjective Evaluations
Size	Variegation	Engineering	Design	Fashionableness
Weight	Pulpiness	Durability	Distinctiveness	Conventionality
Texture	Moisture	Structure	Tone quality	Newness
Shape	Dryness	Storability	Ornamentation	Opportuneness
Density	Vapor	Preciseness	Elegance	Economy
Rigidity	Fragrance	Efficiency	Attractiveness	Noticeability
Pliancy	Tone quality	Velocity	Daintiness	Audibility
Elasticity	Mellifluousness	Salubrity	Decorousness	Familiarity
Roughness	Strength	Permanence	Naturalness	Restorativeness
Brittleness	Consistency	Automatism	Unpretentiousness	Exclusiveness
Powderiness	Temperature	Versatility	Simplicity	Masculinity
	Transportability	Practicability	Colorfulness	Femininity
		Feasibility	Flashiness	
		Comfort	Fragrance	
			Odor	
			Savor	
			Tactility	

SERVICE PROFILE

Purpose		Performance	Subjective Evaluation
Repair	Exchange	Speed	Dependability
Delivery	Buying	Economy	Efficiency
Cleaning	Selling	Comfort	Productiveness
Improvement	Production	Convenience	Authority
Protection	Reproduction	Completeness	Attentiveness
Education	Rent	Specialization	Courtesy
Health	Lease	Frequency	Inventiveness
Beauty	Information	Regularity	Responsiveness
Finance	Art	Durability	Thoroughness
Entertainment	Emergency	Flawlessness	Fashionableness
Law	Travel	Accessibility	Usefulness
Transportation	Public service	Need	Importance
Religion	Government	Safety	Salubrity
Communication	Social Service	Conformity	Informality
Environment	Storage	Skill	
Pleasure	Funeral	Experience	
Nourishment	Military		

As we said earlier, consumers want more than anything else to know about the product itself and how *they* can benefit from using it. This to them, is one of the main purposes of advertising.

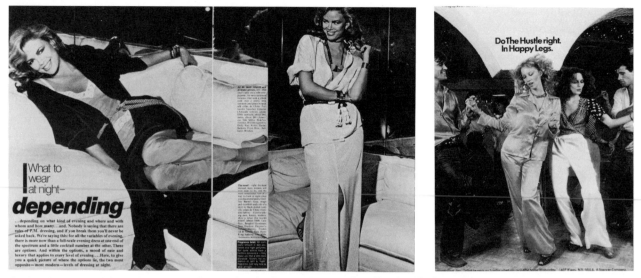

In fashion advertising, the center of attention is always the merchandise itself. Consumers, especially women, want to know as much about it as they can. Generally, women surpass male purchasers in detail consciousness, perhaps because of their experience in shopping. Showing off the garment in its best light, creating an illusion of wrinkle-free perfect fit, has long been acknowledged to be a formidable artistic challenge by those who would rather see clothes drape naturally in their photographs. Editorial art directors and photographers often succeed in getting around the stilted, mannequinesque look, showing the way to their colleagues in the advertising field. Bob Richardson, a student of movement of the human body, took these photographs, which appeared in *Vogue*. The advertisement is for Happy Legs.

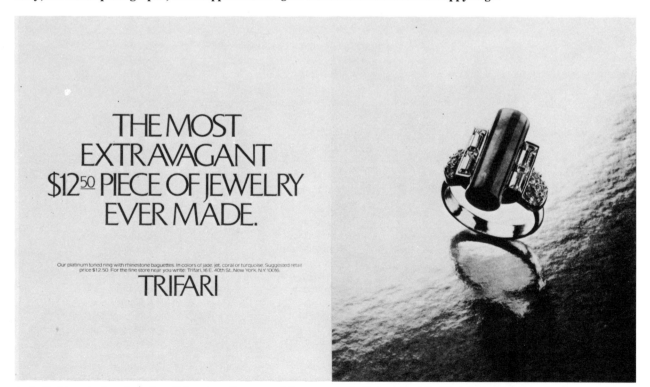

As in fashion, in jewelry advertising, too, the crux of the message is the product itself. Admirable restraint is much in evidence in this Trifari advertisement: Interplay between pictures and headline, "The Most Extravagant $12.50 piece of Jewelry Ever Made," emphasizes the low bargain price but without sacrificing the quality image.

Most retail ads are designed primarily to convey information about the merchandise. Readers, most of whom are women, want to know the particulars. (After the strike of a major newspaper, research uncovered the fact that women readers missed regular retail ads more than any other feature in the publication.) This is why the straightforward, no-nonsense copy and realistic product illustrations of Hoffritz, Aynsley, and the Howard Miller Clock Co. work hard for these advertisers. Though simple in layout, both ads display graphic flair and excellent taste.

"Sell the sizzle, not the steak" is an old, well-worn adage. It works in advertising, too. Here, the Sovereign luxury apartment is putting the adage to good use, presenting a panorama of Manhattan as a status symbol.

"Show me" is still presented as a challenge by people from Missouri—and all the other states. Mark Eden proves its case with photos taken before and after. Less libidinous, perhaps, but just as convincing is the ad designed for Hartmann.

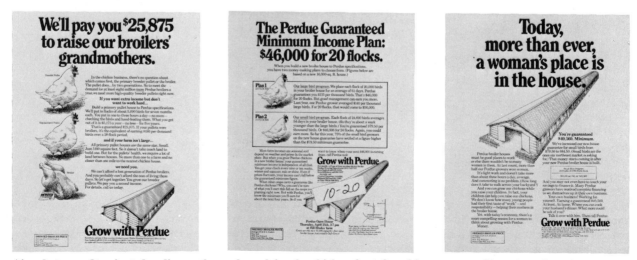

Aimed at a profit-oriented audience, these ads explain why chicken-farm franchises are a good long-term investment.

196

Beautymist Panty Hose.
Everything looks better through Beautymist.
Especially your legs.

SFX: NATURAL SOUND

GIRL: May I help you, Sir?
MAN: Yes, stick 'em up . . .

GIRL: Oh! I see you're wearing Beauty-mist Panty Hose.

MAN: Yeah? How did you know?

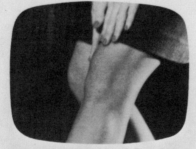

GIRL: I wear them myself. They fit just perfectly.

They're so soft and smooth and com-fortable.

And so sheer! I mean, they really im-prove your appearance.

MAN: Oh, they do?

GIRL: Yes, would you smile for the camera, please?

DRAMATIC MUSIC

DRAMATIC MUSIC

ANNCR: Somehow, everything looks bet-ter through Beautymist.
GIRL: Especially your legs.

Television offers an excellent opportunity for demonstrating product use, presenting many successful examples of hard- and soft-sell combinations. Copy points (perfect fit, softness, comfort, and sheerness) are ingeniously covered in this commercial for Beauty Mist pantyhose.

ANNOUNCER: Watch these sunglasses carefully. They'll change . . . by themselves from light to dark, as the strength . . . of the sun changes. Here's 5 minutes of exactly what happens . . . compressed into 5 seconds. (Silence) They're called Photosun sunglasses. Developed by Corning. Ask about them . . . where you get your professional eye care.

ANNOUNCER: Taking pictures of the family gets easier all the time. Now with the new Keystone Pocket Everflash you can forget all that monkeying around with flash cubes. Just drop in the film and shoot. Because the Keystone has its own electronic flash built right in. It's so simple, even a person can use it. The Keystone Pocket Everflash, the newest member of the Keystone Everflash family.

(Music throughout)

ANNOUNCER (Swayze): This is John Cameron Swayze for Timex. Over the years you've seen the Timex take a licking and keep on ticking. But how will Timex Martin stand up to the full weight of an elephant?

(VOICE-OVER) This ponderous pachyderm packs four crushing tons! (SFX) Ouch!

(DAVE): Ouch!

(VOICE-OVER) Dave, can you get that watch?
What time is it?

DAVE: Time to get a new Timex.

ANNOUNCER: Well, you know, it worked in rehearsal.

Chapter Eleven

A Limbering-up Exercise: 201 Ways to Get an Idea

There is time for strict mental discipline. But there is also time for uninhibited mind stretching. The two approaches to problem solving are not inconsistent, any more than following a fixed training schedule is with boxing. So, go ahead and loosen up once in a while. Improvise. Free-associate. Try a variety of approaches:

1. Turn it[1] upside down.
2. Stretch it.
3. Shrink it.
4. Change its color.
5. Make it bigger.
6. Make it smaller.
7. Make it round.
8. Make it square.
9. Make it longer.
10. Make it shorter.
11. Make it visual.
12. Make the most out of a circumstance.
13. Put it into words.
14. Put it into music.
15. Combine words and music.
16. Combine words, music, and picture.

[1]Whatever *it* happens to represent, as layout, words, picture, package, product, advertising campaign, marketing strategy.

17. Combine picture and music.
18. Eliminate the words.
19. Eliminate the picture.
20. Silence it.
21. Use repetition.
22. Make it three-dimensional.
23. Make it two-dimensional.
24. Change the shape.
25. Change a part.
26. Make it into a set.
27. Make it a collector's item.
28. Sell it by subscription.
29. Sell it by subscription only.
30. Animate it.
31. Mechanize it.
32. Electrify it.
33. Make it move.
34. Reverse it.
35. Make it look like something else.
36. Give it texture.
37. Make it romantic.
38. Add nostalgic appeal.
39. Make it look old-fashioned.
40. Make it look futuristic.
41. Make it a part of something else.
42. Make it stronger.
43. Make it more durable.
44. Use symbolism.
45. Be realistic.

46. Use a new art style.
47. Change to photography.
48. Change to illustration.
49. Change the typeface.
50. Tell your story by picture caption.
51. Make the ad look editorial.
52. Make the editorial look like an ad.
53. Use a new advertising medium.
54. Invent a new advertising medium.
55. Make it hotter.
56. Make it cooler.
57. Add scent.
58. Change the scent.
59. Deodorize it.
60. Make it appeal to children.
61. Make it appeal to women.
62. Make it appeal to men.
63. Lower the price.
64. Raise the price.
65. Change the ingredients.
66. Add new ingredients.
67. Twist it.
68. Make it transparent.
69. Make it opaque.
70. Use a different background.
71. Use a different environment.
72. Glamorize it.
73. Use optical effects.

74. Use another material.
75. Add human interest.
76. Change consistency.
77. Put in a different container.
78. Change the package.
79. Make it compact.
80. Miniaturize.
81. Maximize.
82. Eliminate.
83. Make it portable.
84. Make it collapsible.
85. Go to the extremes.
86. Summerize it.
87. Winterize it.
88. Personalize it.
89. Make it darker.
90. Illuminate it.
91. Make it glow.
92. Make it flicker.
93. Make it sparkle.
94. Make it light up.
95. Make it fluorescent.
96. Make it heavier.
97. Make it lighter.
98. Tie in with a promotion.
99. Run a contest.
100. Run a sweepstake.
101. Make it "junior" size.
102. Make it grow.
103. Split it.
104. Understate.
105. Exaggerate.
106. Sell it as a substitute.
107. Find a new use.
108. Subtract.
109. Divide.
110. Combine.
111. Use the obvious.
112. Rearrange the elements.
113. Lower it.
114. Raise it.
115. Divide it.
116. Mix it.
117. Translate it.
118. Speed it up.
119. Slow it down.
120. Make it fly.
121. Make it float.
122. Make it roll.
123. Pulverize it.
124. Cut it into pieces.
125. Put sex appeal into it.
126. Condense it.
127. Bend it.
128. Match it.
129. Tilt it.
130. Suspend it.
131. Make it stand upright.

132. Turn it inside out.
133. Turn it sideways.
134. Weave it.
135. Mask it.
136. Make it symmetrical.
137. Make it asymmetrical.
138. Partition it.
139. Pit one against another.
140. Sharpen it.
141. Change the contour.
142. Encircle it.
143. Frame it.
144. Coil it.
145. Fill it up.
146. Empty it.
147. Open it.
148. Misspell it.
149. Nickname it.
150. Seal it.
151. Transfer it.
152. Pack it.
153. Concentrate it.
154. Spread it out.
155. Alternate it.
156. Solidify it.
157. Liquefy it.
158. Jellify it.
159. Soften it.
160. Harden it.
161. Vaporize it.
162. Intonate.
163. Make it narrower.
164. Make it wider.
165. Make it funny.
166. Make it satirical.
167. Use short copy.
168. Use long copy.
169. Attach an instruction sheet.
170. Find a second use.
171. Prefabricate it.
172. Sell it as a kit.
173. Purify it.
174. Sanitize it.
175. Make it more nourishing.
176. Put in in a bottle.
177. Put it in a can.
178. Put it in a box.
179. Put it in a jar.
180. Put it in a pot.
181. Wrap it.
182. Fold it.
183. Unfold it.
184. Extend credit.
185. Offer it free.
186. Offer it at cost.
187. Make a special offer.
188. Add comfort.
189. Offer protection.

190. Use a different texture.
191. Sweeten it.
192. Sour it.
193. Moisten it.
194. Dry it.
195. Dehydrate it.
196. Freeze it.
197. Project it.
198. Make it blander.
199. Make it more pungent.
200. Simplify it.
201. Combine any of the above.

Take Coffee, for Example

Here is how to apply the foregoing what-if approach by way of free association. The subject in this case is coffee.

Color Should coffee always be coffee brown or perhaps another color? Black? Green? Light brown? Are there any copy claims that could be based on specific and palate-tempting color-taste associations?

Taste Does pungent coffee taste sell coffee? Or should the brew be mild? Sweet? Perhaps a sweet taste would have a particular appeal to weight-conscious coffee drinkers who would like to cut their sugar consumption. The same is true of cream. Could powdered cream be premixed with instant coffee and advertised as the "instant cup of coffee"? How about mixing *both* powdered cream and sugar with instant coffee and promoting the mixture as a spoonful of coffee ready to serve?

Caffeine Content Perhaps there is room for a new brand, half caffeine (for stimulation) and half caffeine-free (for better health). Or an artificial stimulation for a tonic effect could be added to compensate for the absence of caffeine. Additives? Caffeine citrate (costing little more than 1 cent per tablet) sold with the jar or independently at the supermarket? How about flavored coffee, for example, mint, vanilla, or chocolate? Powdered vitamin or mineral supplements added? Mild amphetamine content? How about more information on the label, specifying recommended intake, depending upon the size, age, and working habits of the user?

Package Does it have to be round? (Square containers are easier to ship and to stack on supermarket and kitchen shelves and in refrigerators.) Would a wider jar with a larger opening better accommodate a coffee spoon? What about measuring aids? Spouts for pouring? Scores on sides of jars? A can divided in the middle with airtight wax paper to keep the bottom half fresh? A jar that could serve as a drinking glass after use? Small plastic packets filled with instant coffee similar to tea bags? Coffee in tablet form to mix with hot water? Decanters? Could these be made into collector's items, offering a series of designs or colors? Junior coffee jars? Family coffee jars? Plastic jar tops that could be used as cups? Other material used for packaging such as wood, broadcloth, cotton, wax paper, vinyl, silver, silver foil, or tinfoil? Add coffee fragrance to the package? Coffee packaged in plastic cups with handles on them?

New Uses Recipes for different seasons, celebrations? Coffee beans for cooking purposes as in coffee cake or ice cream? New kinds of mixed drinks such as cordials, cocktails, punches, and hot drinks laced with coffee? Coffee for hospital patients (cornflakes were first developed for this purpose) and, once established as a restorative, advertised as such to the general public? Coffee for watchdogs? Coffee-flavored cigarettes, pipe tobacco, lozenges, toothpaste? Brands of coffee served in fine restaurants, then sold to coffee aficionados? Mix coffee with other ingredients (bran,

molasses, herbs, caramel)? Other new brews and brands? "Keep alert" coffee, brewed specially for police and fire departments, doctors, and nurses, served perhaps in a booster-dose pill form? "Keep going" coffee, brewed for the Red Cross to distribute and the Salvation Army and bars to serve free to any patron who has had a few too many drinks? "Good night" coffee mixed with barbiturates that encourages a good night's sleep? "Good morning" coffee, braced with heavy caffeine, brewed to wake people up? Coffee machines set off by an alarm-clock mechanism which starts brewing coffee automatically in the morning? Coffee to sooth hangovers? Electric percolators built in desks, yachts, cars, and campers? Use as an aphrodisiac? As an appetizer? Coffee dispensers for the home, classroom, and waiting rooms? Espresso makers manufactured in the United States, and sold to a mass market? Coin-operated espresso makers to grind the coffee beans and brew a steaming "fresh" cup of coffee in less than half a minute to use at service stations and airports? Vats of heated coffee grounds for people to bathe in to "relax sore muscles, knock off pounds, and alleviate high blood pressure and circulatory disorders," offered as in the Koso-Sauna bathhouses in Tokyo, Japan?

New Channels of Distribution Company-owned gasoline stations having their own private brands. For example, Texacoffee? Have takeout cups of coffee at popular truck stops and restaurants? Coffee-vending machines at highway rest stops? In libraries? A spoonful of powdered instant coffee ("Just add water") in paper cups to be distributed in

offices, schools, and homes? Small battery-operated coffee makers made for outdoor camping and sold as part of camping gear? "Change your coffee maker, not your brand" advertising campaign? Take-it-with-you vacuum bottles filled with hot coffee promoted? (Coffee brewed at home costs about 6 cents a cup versus 30 cents a cup for the vending-machine product.) Selling exotic coffee beans through mail-order advertising, in special gourmet publications, radio, late-late movies on television? Selling attractively packed coffee beans in supermarkets in the gourmet section? In restaurants? In theaters? Distributing samples at "Coffee is for everybody" exhibits in roving vans?

Special Promotions Free spoon hidden in every tenth instant coffee jar? Gift certificate for a year's supply of coffee? Decanters filled with coffee sold as gifts? National "Have a cup of coffee" day when a cup of coffee is yours for the asking, free? Coffee thermos bottles distributed at supermarkets near coffee shelves? Name brands sold via vending machines? Popularizing coffee brown as an "in" fashion shade? Huge Pop Art coffee cans with logo imprints to be sold in stores? Brochures written by medical (including psychiatric) authorities, on the effect of coffee? Reprints of these articles on labels? Coffee cups as premiums? Segmenting coffee drinkers by profession (for example, doctors, students, secretaries, business executives, truck drivers, teachers), demographic data (men, women, young, old, blue-collar, white-collar), and life-style (warm and cold climate, night owls, heavy readers, late-late–show watchers) for advertising campaigns directed at them?

Chapter Twelve

Getting the Most Out of Creative People

The behavior patterns of the creative species, like those of the Pygmies of Africa or the penguins of Antarctica, have for some time been a subject of scientific scrutiny. Unfortunately, most of the investigations have been conducted by such people as physiologists, biochemists, neuroanatomists, sociologists, and psychologists—observers all, not participants.

The fact is that the functions of a creative brain can best be understood by an "insider." One has to have one to know one. For the creative brain operates in mysterious ways. Logic and lunacy share quarters under the same pate, thriving on paradoxes. Even the founding father of psychoanalysis, Sigmund Freud, admitted his confusion when it came to the creative process. So in this chapter we shall take the simple route to understanding the creative mind, that is, from the point of view of a "doer"—based on dealings with hundreds of creative professionals, and often changing sides of the desk.

Are Creative People as Different as They Say?

Probably. It stands to reason that, sooner or later, constant preoccupation with problem solving, sometimes several steps removed from so-called reality, will leave its mark on the personality of an individual. And why not?

Intellect and emotion are not that far apart.

Frequently, the same traits that enable creative people to excel in their professions are the very ones that make it difficult for them to cope with the mundane and, to them, boring chores of everyday living. They have little or no patience with many of the standards set by the establishment. Needless to say, this attitude causes a few problems, especially in the structured environment of a large corporation.

The Profile of Creative People: What It Takes to Understand Them

Most, if not all, creative people have a surprisingly clear understanding of their mission in life. Part of their self-image is a keen awareness that, yes, they are *different* from the "others"; they are creative.

A number of studies confirms this. Raymond B. Cattell's Early School Personality Questionnaires, for example, indicate plainly that students, even at first-grade levels, already pigeonhole themselves as *either* creative *or* noncreative. The creative

202

see themselves as a unique species not only from an intellectual point of view (more original, efficient, productive) but from an emotional one as well (more sensitive, receptive). The concept of self then becomes a legacy of childhood and a permanent feature of character. By way of example, the psychologist Bruce C. Bergum of Texas Agricultural and Mechanical University found that creative faculty members (those who published books and articles regularly) claimed to be "more compulsive, living closer with their emotions and were less inclined to join such team sports as baseball, football, basketball or hockey." Those who never had anything published saw themselves as "relaxed, pleasant individuals, who were more comfortable agreeing to group decisions."

It goes without saying that such a self-image produces strong and often opinionated personalities. Those who have worked with creative practitioners are only too familiar with the symptoms.

At the risk of being accused of dealing in generalities, the following are hints of the more typical characteristics:

1. *Creative chauvinism.* Creative professionals (and that term, by broad definition, includes anyone who makes a living on the strength of creative ability) tend to take considerable pride in their powers, which enable them to make something out of nothing—a feat outside the reach of lesser human beings. It goes without saying that this feeling of omniscience works against winning popularity contests in the office or anywhere else, for that matter. Many creative people, however, do not mind at all being set apart from the general population, if only to reinforce their self-image, soothe their egos, and, probably, fatten their paychecks.

Typically, creative people will do all they can do to defend their exalted position. Rallying around the same flag they often look for and find comfort in solidarity. There are more than 5000 professional creative clubs in the United States, or more than 5 times the number organized for marketing or even for advertising people. Several of these groups are incorporated and have memberships larger than those of most country clubs. Awards bestowed every year for outstanding performance (art and copy) far surpass, if not in quality then in quantity, all others in the advertising field put together. Moreover, there are more than 100 avant-garde graphic magazines that circulate exclusively among members of the creative inner circle. They are printed on glossy stock and usually are written in a lingo especially created for their readers. Perhaps "secret code" would be a better name for it.

Nor does the cultivation of separateness stop here. Creative people like to *look* creative. To emphasize their anomalousness, they prefer to wear casual attire, even to boardroom meetings if possible. It almost seems that to become a member of the fraternity, the first step is to look the part. In fact, absence of the look can be more conspicuous than its presence. Here is the way adman Tom Little of McDonald & Little described the phenomenon in *Madison Avenue:* "Jonis Gold has a theory about creativity and personal appearance. Jonis believes that people tend to be creative in the reverse proportion to how creative they look. I noticed that myself when I attended a creative conference recently.

"There were a lot of creative hacks and grunts who looked like riders and sorcerers. The creative chap they came to hear looked like an accountant."

2. *Volatility.* Creative people's fierce commitment to ideas, mostly their own, perplexes those who either on purpose or by accident must deal with them in business. The question usually boils down to this: what is an idea worth? Average business executives tend to view an idea as just another form or proposal, the kind that routinely passes over their desks every day. It is just the beginning of a project in need of analysis from a corporate and financial point of view. The brunt of the responsibility for the success of an idea thus rests more heavily with the receiver than the giver. Needless to say, creative people do not always share this view. They perceive ideas not as suggestions but as the final, and possibly the only, solution to a given problem: hence the high premium they put on it.

The all-too-familiar swings in temperament in creative people are almost always due to the importance they attach to ideas—to the effort they feel they have made to get them.

When they feel that the solution to a problem is within reach, their spirits soar.

Conversely, when they feel that they cannot close in on a solution, they experience a sense of profound despondency.

3. *Naïveté combined with sophistication.* Equally puzzling to business executives is the ambiguity of creative people. "Sometimes he is so brilliant he amazes me," said the president of a large advertising firm, describing one of his top art directors to a client. "And sometimes he has a block for a head."

That pretty much sums up the sentiments of many executives. But here, too, there are two sides to the coin. As pointed out earlier, creativity is not a matter of sheer intelligence, as defined in the usual sense. Rather it is something that encompasses a wide spectrum of intellectual qualities, on occasion contradictory. Among them are curiosity, enterprise, impatience with established tradition, outspokenness, subjectivity, a search for unusual relationships, a flair for drama, and the wish to be ahead of the times. Sometimes, these traits have a tendency to make creative people look very smart; at other times, not smart at all.

4. *Hero worshiping.* With the emphasis on creative performance goes idolization of those responsible for it all.

This approach also may be a source of confusion for business executives more interested in the commercial aspects of an idea than the thinking behind it.

The intrinsic value of the lighting technique used by a photographer, the sound effects used in a radio commercial, a new kind of typographical treatment designed by an art director, or the paint texture favored by an illustrator as a creative contribution may seem much too trivial to executives to warrant all the fuss.

Business executives must remember, however, that the world of creative professionals consists of just such accomplishments. The fine points in execution are very important to those who make a living at it; it is their reason for being. And should money be a yardstick, business executives may be interested to learn that such "insignificant" innovations often bring many thousands of dollars to their inventors.

5. *Need for approval.* Not many artists and writers like to admit or even to be aware of the fact that they care particularly about other people's reactions to their work. Such an I-couldn't-care-less posture is especially prevalent among poets, painters, sculptors, and others who wear artistic independence like a gold chain around the neck.

It is true, of course, that many creative people become so deeply engrossed in their projects that for all practical purposes they cut themselves off from most of the outside world. But this may be only a superficial phenomenon. Like everyone else, creative people, too, have a need to communicate with fellow beings and to maintain a sense of belonging. Approval of their work by others serves as an affirmation not only of their professional competence but of their personal worth.

6. *Competitiveness.* Another well-concealed facet of the creative personality is aggressiveness, but again appearances can be deceiving. Behind that easygoing, up-with-the-organization countenance may be the spirit of a warrior. This is not altogether surprising when we consider the importance creative people place on creative talent. With their egos so greatly involved with professional success, they are easily drawn into combat.

Interestingly enough, most creative people (particularly before they reach the higher executive plateaus) prefer to wage their battles on the merit of their work rather than on personal charm. By and large, they find office politics bewildering and gladly delegate that end of the business to those with a knack for it, such as account executives.

How to Accept an Idea or Kill the Goose That Lays the Golden Egg

The most propitious time to assure creative persons of their worth is when they submit their ideas— a brief, and from their point of view not particularly welcome, whistle-stop on their extended ego trips. Many artists and writers view such meetings as head-on confrontations between two opposing camps, with winners or losers emerging from the scrimmage. That is why the reactions of others to their ideas can be so meaningful to them. As a rule, it is politic to be *personal* when an idea is acceptable and *impersonal* when it is not.

Saying Yes This is an opportunity to praise creative people, not only for their professional competence but for personal qualifications as well: hard work, imagination, intelligence, sense of responsibility. Top executives in many advertising agencies make it their business to congratulate all staffers on the success of a campaign and in *writing*. Credit is given where credit is due, specific names being mentioned. Notes like this can prove to be excellent morale boosters, especially if they are circulated freely among people in the organization.

Particularly appreciated are compliments which are made in front of clients. However, some agencies feel that, because of the business risk, this is carrying generosity a bit too far. Creative people singly or in pairs, have been known to walk away with accounts as bait to attract offers for higher-paying jobs or even to use the business to found shops of their own. That, however, should not cause an agency to keep its writers and artists in the closet. Sooner or later clients will find out who originated the campaign anyway.

One way to handle this sensitive matter and to encourage a close and uninhibited exchange between the client and the creative staff is to have a clear understanding of the legal obligations of everyone involved. A noncompetitive clause in written employment contracts goes a long way in setting the record straight. Such clauses make it impossible, or at least very difficult, for art directors or writers to cultivate hip-pocket accounts for their own selfish interests.

It should be kept in mind, however, that for courts to uphold restrictive covenants the loss of a job ought not interfere with a person's fundamental right to earn a livelihood in his or her chosen profession. For this reason, the terms of such an agreement must be specific. The agreement must define the nature of the business which it is supposed to cover (advertising), geographical limitations on other employment (if the ex-employee goes to another town and provides advertising services for a local business, this may not be construed as a competitive account), duration (usually 2 years after leaving the job), and names of clients included in the agreement (those with the agency while the employee was working there).

Since courts are becoming increasingly wary of restrictive covenants in employment contracts, it is best to look for forms of agreement that have stood the test of time (see *Warren's Forms of Agreement,* published by Matthew Bender & Co., Inc., New York) and to have an attorney go over the stipulations with a fine-tooth comb.

Saying No This, of course, is a much more difficult task than saying yes. Here is how to soften the blow:

Rule 1. Give the presenter an opportunity to state his or her case.

Rule 2. Hint at possible alternatives by way of questions rather than answers.

Rule 3. Be precise in your comments; analyze the weaknesses of an idea, not those of its originator.

Maintain a positive attitude. What exactly is wrong with the idea? Has it failed to solve a specific marketing problem? Is it inconsistent with the creative platform? Does execution (art, copy, production) veer away from the basic concept? Or does the fault lie with the basic concept itself? If the technique blocks the message, perhaps it is only the technique that needs tinkering with. Conversely if the technique is acceptable but not the concept, this can be the beginning of a totally new concept. (Such a beginning often suggests itself.)

Rule 4. Show the presenter examples of work (proofs of ads, campaigns, photographs, artwork, and so on) created by others to solve similar problems. Remember, one idea can lead to another. Moreover, you are staying outside the presenter's creative prerogatives by supplying him or her only with information, as opposed to specific solutions.

Rule 5. Resist the temptation to psychoanalyze the client and give reasons why the client will *not* buy the idea. The chances are that your listener will think it is up to you to cope with this situation. As far as the listener is concerned, one never knows until one tries. (And he or she may be right on that.)

Creative people like to feel that it is the function of an account executive to act as a shock absorber between them and the client, representing the viewpoint of the agency. A show of no confidence is bound to undermine your authority with them.

Rule 6. Avoid the mention of irrelevancies in your explanation for turning down an idea; these will only add fuel to the fire. In this respect, there is much that account executives can learn from members of the legal profession. Much of the background normally presented at business meetings would summarily be thrown out in a courtroom by the judge as *nihil ad rem,* or "not to the point."

Rule 7. Do not let your personal taste, good as it may be, get in the way of sound business judgment. Consumers' reactions to an idea may not be the same as yours, even

if they do happen to be your demographic kin.

Should Creative People Attend Clients' Meetings?

More and more clients want to be in direct contact with the creative people responsible for the work turned out. This may irk certain account executives who feel that things would go more smoothly with them in total charge. Be that as it may, the trend toward maintaining client-creative contacts is growing. Many creative people are well qualified to expound their views; their natural, have-I-got-something-for-you enthusiasm makes them persuasive salesmen indeed. And, of course, they are knowledgeable about the various production details connected with their own ideas as they go into execution, and they have the ability to answer questions expertly.

There are many creative people, however, who feel put upon in having to explain their ideas to a critical audience. Some unconsciously resent having to explain their ideas at all. Under these circumstances, the presenter may not live up to his promise. If that is the case, it is up to the account executive (or whoever heads the meeting) to help the creative person refine his or her presentation technique.

Here is how an account executive can help creative presentation run smoothly.

1. *Introduce the creative people to the client at the beginning of the meeting, briefly describing their responsibilities and backgrounds.* If a creative person is an art director, writer, musician, or one of the members of a special creative team (art director–writer, art director–producer, art director–writer–producer, or the like), describe his or her (and their) functions so that the client understands the type of people he or she is dealing with.

2. *At some point, give the creative*

people the floor. One way to stop a business meeting from turning into a shouting match is to let all participants know in advance that they will have a chance to speak their minds. This will effectively prevent everyone from throwing ideas on the table and avoid confusing the client as to just what the agency is recommending.

3. *Rehearse if at all possible.* Time-consuming as rehearsals seem to some creative people ("What do you want from me? The client isn't even there to listen."), they can be very helpful. Invite as many people as possible to these preliminary practice bouts. This is the time to refine the schedule and work out the details. Nothing gives people as much confidence as having been through it all once before.

4. *Keep individual presentations short and to the point.* Let each creative person know how much time he or she has to speak. A written agenda helps. Have it ready for the meeting so that everyone can see it and stick to it.

5. *Avoid controversy in front of the client.* As far as the client is concerned, he or she is dealing with an organization, not with individuals. The client will not welcome the role of settling feuds between creative people or between members of the creative department and the account executive.

6. *Have the teams make a joint presentation.* Members of a team will complement each other, especially if they happen to represent art and copy. Sometimes they will even throw bouquets (not bricks) at one another.

7. *Cultivate unanimity between members of the agency.* A meeting of minds will come as a welcome relief to the client. (The client knows full well from experience how difficult it is to achieve such a consensus.) Be generous with credits; build up not only individuals but departments. Your supportive attitude makes sound business sense. For one thing, the client will have good feelings about the agency. For another, everyone will leave the meeting feeling better about himself or herself. That pays dividends; dis-

gruntled employees can be expensive. As likely as not, they may keep asking for raises to salve their bruised egos and repeatedly prove their worth to themselves. This is why so many shops that treat their employees callously often have higher-than-average overhead—up to one-third more. Incidentally, this circumstance works both ways: art directors and writers are willing to make financial sacrifices for the privilege of working in a creative agency which cultivates originality.

Passing on Ideas: How to Get the Most Out of Your Suppliers

In Chapter 2 we discussed the type of basic information creative people employed by an advertising agency must have to get started on a project. This section deals with another aspect of information flow, that between the creative people and outside services. Since the prime responsibility of an advertising agency is to conceptualize advertising (not necessarily execute it), outside services are often called in to lend an expert helping hand in implementation.

Most advertising people and clients as well find themselves working with suppliers at one time or another, particularly during the initial stages of a campaign when plans are being formulated. Cases in point are TV preproduction meetings with five to ten people participating, discussions between copywriter and typographer to choose a typeface, and a casting session.

It is important at such meetings that all participants have a clear understanding of the area of their responsibilities and the limits of their authority. Certainly, the final selection of suppliers should be left to those who are most conversant with the specific requirements of the job. If a musically inclined copywriter is in charge of writing the lyrics, he should have a chance to talk with the composer. Art directors, *not*

marketing or production people, should have prime contacts with photographers or illustrators, television production executives and art directors are best suited to work with camera crews, and so on.

It is also well to remember that not every supplier is concerned with all phases of advertising. Many are interested only in their job areas, not in overall advertising problems. If they do not want to touch all bases, they should not be asked to do so unless the information materially helps them to understand the nature of their particular assignment. A typographer, for example, may find audience demographics of little or no value. A photographer will be hard put to find a meaningful relationship between the latest Arbitron figures and lighting technique. A designer would just as soon not get involved in the nuances of corporate financing.

Tell a supplier only what he or she needs to know.

Who Deals with Whom

These are the primary lines of communication between the advertising agency and its outside suppliers:

Art Director
- TV music and sound
- TV editors
- Audio-video services
- Free-lance writers
- TV producers and directors
- TV performers

Copywriter
- Illustrators
- Photograhers
- Retouchers
- Engravers
- Typographers
- Art-mechanical studios
- TV performers
- TV music and sound
- TV editors and optical houses
- TV producers and directors
- Designers
- Audio-video services
- Sketch people
- Printers
- Lettering people
- Animators
- TV laboratories
- Tape houses
- Casting directors

Print Production
- Engravers
- Paper suppliers
- Printers
- Typographers
- Binders
- Mechanical department
- Shipping

TV Producer, or Art Director, or Both
- Commercial TV producers and directors
- Casting directors
- Makeup people
- Fashion coordinators
- Set designers
- Camera operators
- Performers
- Recording studios
- Mixing studios
- Home economists
- Audio-visual services
- Animators
- Art studios
- Composers
- Musicians
- Tape houses
- Artists
- Props
- Editors
- Film libraries
- Optical houses
- TV laboratories
- Hair stylists
- Choreographers
- Legal services
- Shipping

What Outside Suppliers Really Want to Know

In passing on information the keynote again is *relevance*. Mentioned before was the tendency to pass on too many specifics about a job, in an earnest attempt to give the supplier a complete background. Mentioned here should be the understandable human tendency to engage in gossip. What is commonly referred to as the grapevine in the advertising community is nothing more than the exchange of notes between friends. Names of people about to be hired or fired, accounts "up for grabs," the latest about office power politics, and campaigns about to break are just some of the revelations that are freely bruited about in the guise of providing information. Needless to say, these juicy morsels, fascinating conversation pieces as they may be, accomplish little in getting a specific assignment on its way.

Here is the type of information that suppliers need to know:

ILLUSTRATOR WORKING FROM A ROUGH-COPY CONCEPT OR LAYOUT

Nonessential Statistical marketing and sales data, quantititative media information (circulation, reach, frequency, and so on).

Essential Corporate history, competitive advertising.

Very Essential Creative platform, mechanical requirements (size, color, possible reduction or enlargement, stock, method of reproduction, printing process), headline, amount of text, choice of typography, type of readership, budget, date of delivery, approval stages (rough, comprehensive, finish), flexibility of layout (freedom to make changes and to what extent), use (which media and how often), seasonal requirements (summer, winter, all year, and so on), information on the product (size, material, important selling points, qualities), general purpose (image building, introductory, and so on), ownership, copyright, credits, legal requirements. A layout is helpful, but it is not necessary.

DESIGNER

Nonessential Statistical marketing and sales data, quantitative media information.

Essential Corporate history, competitive advertising, method of distribution (if the assignment is package or point-of-sale design), projected life-span of the design.

Very Essential Creative platform, mechanical requirements (size, possible reduction, stock, reproduction method, printing process, binding and folding techniques), shipping problems, type of audience, budget, date of delivery, approval stages (rough, comprehensive, finish), testing method (prototypes, pilot), use (in advertising corporate letterhead, trucks and so on), information on the

product (size, qualities, material, important selling points), purpose (corporate look, booklet, single ad, campaign format, logotype), ownership, copyright, allocation of credit. A rough layout is helpful, but some designers prefer to work without it, interpreting the basic concept.

PHOTOGRAPHER

Nonessential Statistical marketing and sales data, quantitative media information.

Essential Corporate history, competitive advertising.

Very Essential Creative platform, mechanical requirements (size, color, possible reduction or blowup, reproduction method, printing process, binding and folding techniques, stock, contrast required, number and size of prints, size of the original negative, reproduction), type of audience, choice of model, headline, amount of text (as part of the layout), date of delivery, minimum number of pictures from which to make a selection, shooting schedule, flexibility of layout (possibility of changes), use (choice of media), seasonal requirements, information on the product, props, fashion, general purpose, ownership of the negative, copyright, credit given, legal requirements. A layout is helpful, but it is not necessary.

RETOUCHER

Nonessential Statistical marketing and sales data, quantitative information, corporate history, competitive advertising, creative platform, media information.

Essential Flexibility of layout, general purpose, headline, type of audience.

Very Essential Mechanical requirements (size, color, possible reduction or enlargement), contrast required, flaws to be corrected, mood of picture, reproduction method, printing process, binding and folding techniques, name of photographers (for additional prints), budget, date of delivery, information on product, legal requirements. A photograph, preferably several prints or a negative, or both should be submitted.

ENGRAVER AND LITHOGRAPHER

Nonessential Statistical marketing and sales data, statistical information, corporate history, competitive advertising, general purpose, audience composition, creative platform.

Essential Information on product, legal requirements.

Very Essential Mechanical requirements (size, color, type of plate), maximum reduction and enlargement, binding and folding techniques, halftone screen, line conversions, type of halftone (square, silhouette, combination, and so on), stock, contrast, printing process, approval stages (rough proofs, color-correctible separations), number and types of reproduction proofs required, budget, delivery date, use, shipping (name and address of recipient other than the agency), number and size of duplicate plates needed. Oversize artwork and mechanical ("copy" in engraver's parlance) should be submitted.

PRINTER

Nonessential Marketing and sales data, statistical information, corporate history, competitive advertising, audience demographics, general purpose, creative platform.

Essential Information on product.

Very Essential Mechanical requirements (size, color, stock, color specifications, contrast, type of printing machine, binding and folding techniques, ink to be used), approval stages (on-spot checking, first run, final run), budget, delivery data, maximum overtime, number and type of reproduction proofs required, use (which media), shipping, duplicate plates needed, legal requirements. Plates and a layout dummy should be submitted.

TYPOGRAPHER

Nonessential Marketing and sales data, statistical information, corporate history, competitive advertising, audience demographics, information on product, creative platform.

207

Essential General purpose.

Very Essential Typesetting method to be used, mechanical requirements (type point size, type specimen, kerning, line spacing, arrangement of lines, paragraphing, maximum reduction and enlargement, mixing of type styles, use of initials, use of hyphens, stock, binding and folding techniques, color, ink), budget, date of delivery, editing and correcting process, method of approval (master proof, corrected proof, number of reproduction proofs required), use (which media), arrangement of elements on the page (layout), possibility of using type on reverse, reproduction from type (offset, letterpress, intaglio). Typewritten text and type layout or a mark-up copy should be submitted.

ART STUDIO AND MECHANICAL DEPARTMENTS

Nonessential Marketing and sales data, statistical information, corporate history, creative platform, quantitative media information.

Essential Type of audience, competitive advertising, information on product.

Very Essential Mechanical requirements (size, color, stock, reproduction method, binding and folding techniques, color correction, color separation, use of transfer type, use of photostats, use of original or existing art, material needed for reproduction, tone indication, hand lettering, scaling, retouching, cropping, overlays), approval stages, budget, date of delivery, maximum overtime, arrangement of elements on the page, shipping, legal requirements. If possible, all the elements should be submitted simultaneously.

TELEVISION PRODUCERS AND DIRECTORS

Nonessential Marketing and sales data, quantitative media information.

Essential Audience composition, corporate history, projected cycles.

Very Essential Creative platform, day part scheduled (indicating type of audience), seasonal schedule,

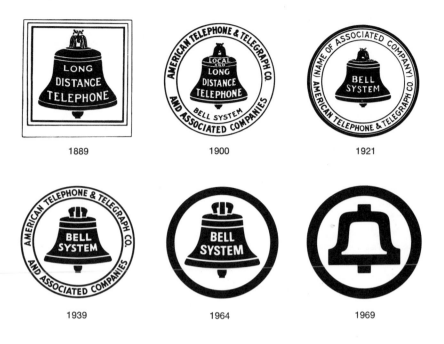

1889   1900   1921

1939   1964   1969

Modernizing the trademark of a leading public utility fell within the province of a designer. Little information had to pass; this was primarily a graphic assignment.

FROM ART DIRECTOR TO PHOTOGRAPHER: PASSING ON AN IDEA

Instructions given to the photographer, Howard Zieff, were minimal in this case. The picture concept (the story) was decided through an art director's thumbnail sketch, which was discussed with the client for approval. All other aspects of the actual shooting—lighting, composition, fashion, and even casting—were left to the photographer, who is known for his warm, humorous approach to human-interest pictures.

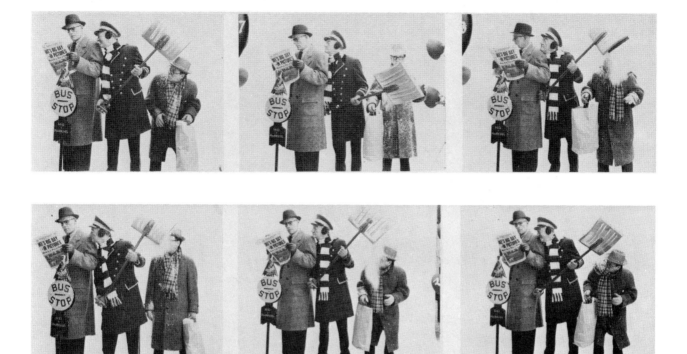

Photographs to choose from.

Finished poster.

general purpose, competitive advertising, length of commercial, cut versions (10, 20, or 30 seconds and so on), information on product, mechanical requirements (soft or hard focus, lighting, use of titles, opticals, typography, artwork), pacing (slow, fast), music and sound, script, budget, delivery data, method of approval (who is to approve what and when), shooting schedule, degree of agency participation in preproduction, postproduction, or both, possible use of stock shots, type of location required, props, fashion, makeup, casting requirements, names of people responsible for postproduction, number of prints required, legal and censorship problems (buy-outs and residuals), payments, budget (detailed breakdown), union contracts, shipping (type of stock needed, station requirements, names of people at stations responsible for airing commercials, names and addresses of stations). A storyboard is helpful, but it is not necessary.

TELEVISION SOUND AND MUSIC

Nonessential Quantitative media information, marketing and sales data, corporate history.

Essential Type of audience, general purpose, use, location, video technique, print advertising, supporting broadcast.

Very Essential Information on the product, lyrics (if any), creative platform, length of commercial or radio spot, musical art form (ballad, march, rock, blues, folk, country, bluegrass, classical, jazz, soul, combinations, and so on), tempo (slow, fast), method of mixing (wild sound, direct recording, syntonization, presync, postsync, dubbing), number of sound tracks available, sources of music to be explored (original, stock), special sound effects (original, stock, background, sound bridges), manner of speech (stressed, unstressed, regional, accented, pretentious, conversational, unaffected, laconic, curt, pompous, tongue in cheek, drawling, nasal, hoarse, brash, raspy, sententious, and so on), canned or stock music

(tape, film, recording), video (for television or multimedia-presentation use), budget, date of delivery, prints, credit lines, legal requirements, second use (as a record). A storyboard of the finished cut is necessary.

TALENT: MODELS AND PERFORMERS

Nonessential Marketing and sales data, statistical information, corporate history, audience demographics.

Essential Information about media, type of competitive advertising, general purpose, seasonal schedule.

Very Essential Words and illustrations in the advertisement, creative platform, length of commercial, type of photography, background music and sound, video technique (film, tape, live, color or black and white), shooting schedule (days, hours), wardrobe, accessories, makeup (time allowed for makeup on location), other performers, rehearsal time, sound mix, contractual agreements (noncompetitive clause, single or multiple scale, payments for casting sessions, payments and repayments, projected coverage, guarantees, seasonal commercial, buy-out, session fees, holding fees), use of service (principal, extras, on camera, off camera, musician, name talent), postproduction participation (mixing, dubbing), tie-ins (print or broadcast, special promotions), names and addresses of producer, photographer, and fashion coordinator, transportation. A script or storyboard (or both) is helpful.

Helping Outside Services to Make Effective Contributions

As the advertisement (print or television) is carried into its final form and more and more people participate in its execution, suggestions will pour forth from all corners. It is up to the ever-vigilant art director,

producer, or other person in charge of the project to screen them. If he or she finds that the ideas of others are inconsistent with the creative platform or that they are unsound from a marketing point of view, they should, of course, be held in abeyance. This is not to suggest, however, the person in charge should close his or her mind to possible improvements. It makes good business sense to encourage creativity at all times, regardless of the source, though always with an eye on the estimated budget.

This last point is particularly important. There is always a temptation to refine an idea, to make it better. But this luxury often calls for expenses not projected in the original budget. So if the illustrator has a few ideas about interpreting the headline, or the typographer feels able to improve upon the art director's original type specification, or the television director, while shooting a commercial, discovers that the script could be made to sound more natural with a little doctoring, then, of course, all should be invited to suggest improvements, but not before costs (including possible overtime) have been determined.

If the changes must first be approved, authorization should come from the right source. All too often, under pressure of time approvals are given much too casually (''let's try it''), only to discover later to everyone's chagrin that someone else in the corporate hierarchy should have been consulted about the change in the first place.

Since there is always room for some improvement, experienced producers anticipate a few (or not so few) changes during the various stages of implementation. These need not be financially embarrassing *provided* these simple rules are followed:

1. *Present layouts and storyboard only as a form of recommendation.* That is what they are, not a finished piece of work. Be certain that the client or other person who approves them understands the difference between a sketch and the final illustra-

From this layout, prepared by J. Walter Thompson, the typographer gets an accurate idea of the kind of type to use.

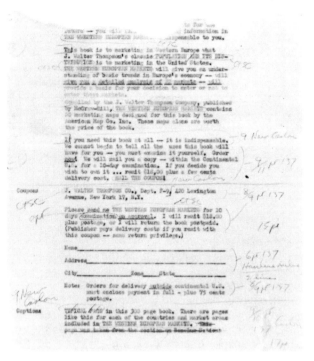

Shown here is part of the copy.

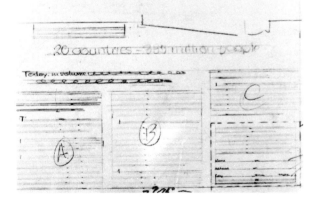

This tissue was prepared along with the marked-up manuscript.

Final proof of the advertisement.

tion. Gain this person's confidence so that you will be given sufficient creative elbowroom.

2. *Include a contingency fee in your budget for changes.* Carefully laid-out guidelines on the stretchability of the budget will prevent postmortem surprises.

3. *Do not invite suppliers to make a creative contribution unless you feel a need for it or they happen to offer one.* It is best to assume a wait-and-see attitude in this respect. If your suppliers think they are expected to make suggestions, they are likely to throw in a few, good or bad, to make a favorable impression.

4. *The purpose of the ad should be clearly understood by everyone involved.* The more explicit the platform, the less chance for a costly creative faux pas.

5. *Remember that not all suppliers approach creative assignments in the same manner.* Different people handle problems differently even if they have the same job titles. There are television directors who think their function is limited to shooting the storyboard exactly as it is indicated on paper. (In some agencies, or with some art directors, this is all they are expected to do.) Others feel that they have been hired not only for their specialized skill but also for their creative insights, and they will improvise freely during shooting. One photographer, today a leading movie director in Hollywood, responded to every storyboard brought to his studio with his own version (to delight of art directors who worked with him). Similarly, illustrators, photographers, typographers, and musicians may also have strong opinions about the nature of their assignments. And designers, who are least dependent upon the art director's sketches, always do.

6. *Take time to get your ideas across.* It bears repeating that few outside creative suppliers have exactly the same realm of experience —or levels of comprehension. It is well to remember that spoken words are open to different—and very personal—interpretations. The meaning of such words as "lively" or "static" or "sensuous" or even "dark red" are always in the ear of the listener. Since most assignments are given verbally, this is an important point to keep in mind. Terminology can play havoc with the best of intentions. Anyone giving out assignments knows from experience that the results can often be nothing like what was originally envisioned.

One of the best ways to avoid confusion is to rely less on words and more on tangibles, such as pictures and sound, in conveying the nature of an assignment. If it is a particular mood that is required, the wisest course yet may be to show a piece of art resembling the final product. There are plenty of picture sources from which to pick (Art Directors Yearbook, Illustrators and Photographers' Annuals, to mention only a few). Similarly, as any house painter will testify, color swatches go a long way in helping to define the exact nature of the color wanted—hue, tint, and so on. (Even white has over thirty varieties; all in all, there are in excess of 3000 color pigments in commercial use today.)

When discussing a sound, the parties may again be speaking in riddles to one another. Words such as "romantic" or "upbeat," for example, mean different things to different people. That is why it is often helpful to actually listen to a few sample melodies and then discuss them.

Take maximum advantage of suggestions made by your suppliers. Accept their expertise in the following areas:

PHOTOGRAPHER

Yes	Maybe
Design	Copy
Color	Production
Choice of model	techniques
Fashion	Applications
Accessories	Sales effective-
Props	ness
Design	

TYPOGRAPHER

Yes	Maybe
Design	Copy
Applications	
Production	
techniques	

ACTORS AND MODELS

Yes	Maybe
Makeup	Choreography
Fashion	Script
Accessories	Camera
Acting style	movements
Speech delivery	Types of shots
Vocal arrange-	Method of
ments	payment
Mixing	Legal require-
	ments

ILLUSTRATOR

Yes	Maybe
Design	Sales effective-
Typography	ness
Color	Copy
Symbols	
Applications	
Production	
techniques	

DESIGNER

Yes	Maybe
Design	Copy
Typography	Sales effective-
Color	ness
Applications	
Production	
techniques	

JINGLE WRITERS, COMPOSERS, MUSICIANS

Yes	Maybe
Musical score	Sales effective-
Jingle	ness
Voice part	Legal require-
Arrangement	ments
Instrumentation	Applications
Beat	
Mixing	

TV DIRECTORS AND PRODUCERS

Yes	Maybe
Script	Music
Sound effects	Sales effective-
Opticals	ness
Casting	Legal require-
Fashion	ments
Makeup	
Accessories	
Location	
Scenery	
Camera	
movements	
Types of	
shots	
Graphics	
Background	
Type of	
film	
Processing	
Editing	
Mixing	

The Creative Point of View

Creative people often appear to live in a world of their own. Their approach to things, their value system, and often their language are unlike most people's. This only indicates their total immersion in their work, however, and not much more. A few examples follow:

Here is how Lawrence Lotner describes the use of type in annual reports of the previous year in an article in *Art Direction* magazine:

> This year showed several radical departures in type design. James Cross set the text for Carter Hawley Hale Stores, Inc. in large italics printed in grey to avoid conflict with the photography. Frank Schulwolf used neon typefaces through The Orange Bowl's report and mixed it with handwriting, script and even some printed matter for the disclosures. . . .
>
> Hot metal is still preferred by many designers. It's easier and cheaper on corrections. Tscherny uses hot metal exclusively. He says that mixing it with a photo face changes the texture of the report.

Here are opinions expressed by the film maker Steve Horn in an interview with Eastman Kodak:

> I've never even shot a commercial on tape. [Film] is an important accessory to me, just like a Polaroid print is when I'm shooting a print ad. It is especially helpful because I direct through the camera. And it lets me re-check things like lighting and timing.
>
> But the texture of film itself cannot be replaced by tape. It's the subtleties you get by playing with the light. By overexposing or underexposing.
>
> To me 99% of a picture is light, and what the light looks like when you take the picture. And that's why I take that picture on film.[1]

And his talking about a shooting experience for Volvo:

> We couldn't allow the rain to come down too soon because it would soften the shot of the car while it was under sunshine. But when the light under the rain changed, it could only change so much before it got too dark for the picture.

[1]*Courtesy of Eastman Kodak Company.*

The basic concept, a man studying a book, gave artist Bob Weaver a chance to contribute a few ideas of his own. Instead of a single sketch, he offered six interpretations, leaving the art director with a wide range of options.

GIVE ARTISTS THEIR HEAD AND WATCH WHAT THEY DO WITH IT

Once creative, always creative. When Saks Fifth Avenue, a leader in the field of high fashion, approached top art directors and graphic and industrial designers to collaborate with the store's own fashion designers, the results were dramatic, somewhat to the surprise of those who believed that creative people were able to move only within the confines of their particular specialties.

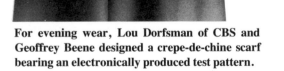

For evening wear, Lou Dorfsman of CBS and Geoffrey Beene designed a crepe-de-chine scarf bearing an electronically produced test pattern.

Stephen Burrows, inspired by Niels Diffrient's industrial designs, created this streamlined, all-purpose jump suit.

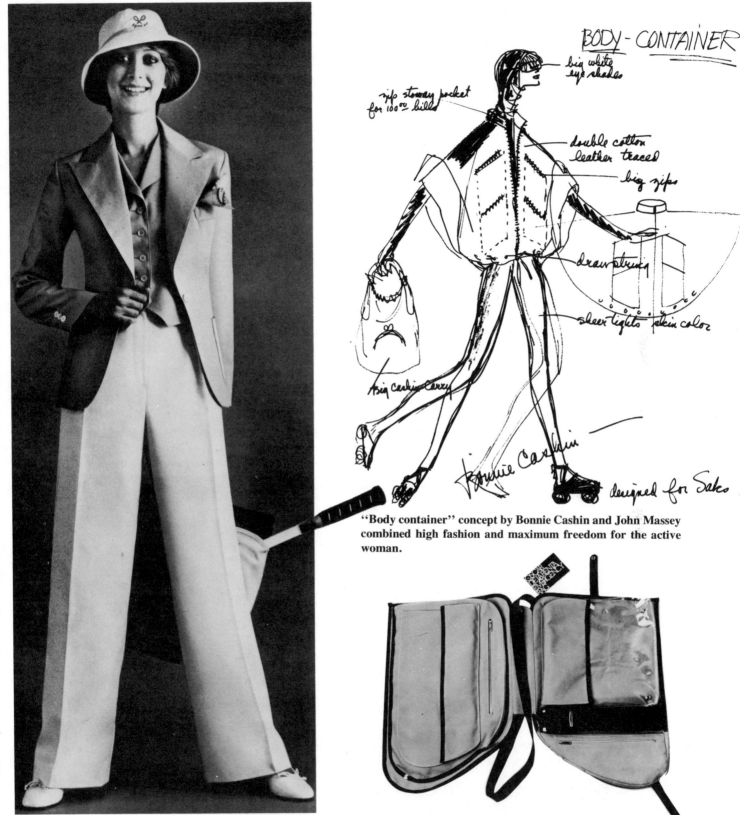

BODY-CONTAINER

big white
eye shades

zip stoway pocket
for 100°° bills

double cotton
leather traced

big zips

drawstring

sheer tights skin color

big cashin carry

Bonnie Cashin

designed for Saks

"Body container" concept by Bonnie Cashin and John Massey
combined high fashion and maximum freedom for the active
woman.

This smartly tailored, coordinated tennis ensemble
was put together by Frank Smith of Evan-Picone
and the designer Jack Roberts.

There is a place for everything in this fashionable and
compact emergency getaway kit conceived by Henry
Wolf and Oscar de la Renta.

215

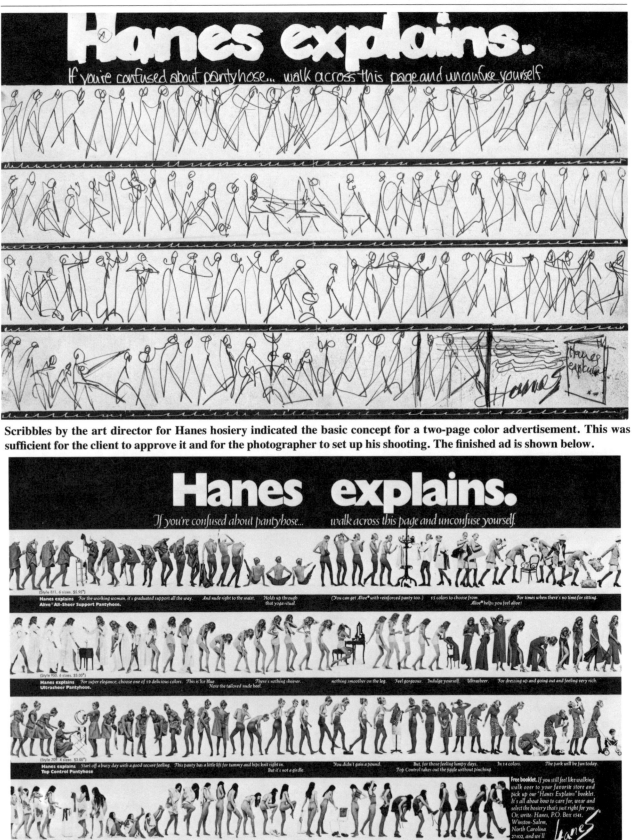

Scribbles by the art director for Hanes hosiery indicated the basic concept for a two-page color advertisement. This was sufficient for the client to approve it and for the photographer to set up his shooting. The finished ad is shown below.

216

MECHANIC AND PARKING LOT

MECHANIC:	Let's have a heart-to-heart talk. One honk for yes, two for no, O.K.?
CARS:	Honk.
MECHANIC:	You think you're getting the right kind of treatment?
CARS:	Honk. Honk.
MECHANIC:	Tired of worrying about your valves and plugs?
CARS:	Honk.
MECHANIC:	Does your idle leave you cold in the morning?
CARS:	Honk.
MECHANIC:	And when you get onto a highway, does some of that old pep and bounce seem to be gone?
CARS:	Honk.
MECHANIC:	That's called hesitation. Do you like hesitation?
CARS:	Honk. Honk.
MECHANIC:	Isn't it about time you improved your standard of living? Work up with a start instead of a sputter?
CARS:	Honk. (Longer honk.)
MECHANIC:	O.K., O.K., don't blow a gasket. I got something for you. Something that will make you feel a lot better. It's Exxon with HTA. HTA is an additive that may help prevent hesitation. Interested?
CARS:	Honk.
MECHANIC:	O.K. If you're tired of hesitation and you want a better life, you gotta get some Exxon. And you gotta get some soon. Are you with me?
CARS:	One long, loud, continuous honk.

A single storyboard, scrawled on a sketch pad with a felt-tipped pen, and a typewritten script were all the elements that Exxon needed to approve the idea for this 60-second commercial. Production estimates were submitted from these two pieces of paper.

Last-minute changes in prices made long-range planning for Pathmark's television campaign difficult and often impractical. Many decisions had to be made in quick reaction to news flashes on pricing, hard-to-get items, and new menu ideas arriving at the studio at the last minute. Spokesman Jimmy Karen and home economist Ruth Cowlell were on a 24-hour alert, always ready for action. Wisely, the client gave wide creative authority to his advertising agency, Venet. At times, he saw his commercials for the first time on his home television set.

217

I GO THROUGH THE MOTIONS OF PLAYING HARD-TO-GET...BUT I KNOW THAT HE KNOWS THAT I THINK HE'S SOMETHING SPECIAL.

BUT THAT DOESN'T MEAN I'M GOING TO CHANGE MYSELF JUST TO IMPRESS HIM.

I JUST WANT TO BECOME THE BEST POSSIBLE ME. MY HAIR COLOR, FOR INSTANCE, HAS TO LOOK ABSOLUTELY NATURAL. THAT'S WHY I LIKE NICE 'N EASY. IT LETS ME ... BE ME.

IF YOU SAY IT SELLS THE MOST, I GUESS THAT'S WHY.

(MUSIC UNDER) GIRL (VOICE-OVER): I go through the motions of playing hard to get. But I know he knows that I think he's something special. But that doesn't mean I'm going to change myself just to impress him. I just want to become the best possible me. My hair color, for instance, has to look absolutely natural. That's why I like Nice 'n Easy. It lets me be me. If you say it sells the most, I guess that's why.

One-minute commercials for Nice 'n Easy were shot with few preconceived notions. Fresh-faced models, most of whom were appearing on television for the first time, were encouraged to be themselves and "project their natural spunkiness." The first batch of six commercials was shot in a day, each in a single continuous take and without the benefit of a sketch or a final script. Later, as the theme became better established, rough storyboards like this were used by the agency, Doyle Dane Bernbach, for discussion and approval purposes.

218

Sizing Up People Who Do the Creative: The Three T's

The reception area of an advertising agency often looks more like the waiting room of a theatrical agent in search of talent for an upcoming Broadway play than a corporate facility. Men, women, children, and sometimes even pets are gathered here, many people with their "books" (sample portfolios) in their laps.

Finding the right person for an assignment is of particular concern to advertising agencies, especially for members of television and art departments, whose professional competence may be measured by their knowledge of available talent. This is why agency television producers or directors are always on the lookout for promising new film technicians, directors, actors, and musicians; art directors, for photographers, TV directors, animators, illustrators, typographers, and designers; and production managers for typographers, engravers, and printers. In metropolitan areas, the number of such specialists may run into the thousands. With the influx of fresh talent, the list must be updated constantly.

Those who interview applicants for permanent staff positions may also find themselves as busy as traffic cops during rush hours. Despite its critics, the advertising field always attracts more job applicants than it can absorb. According to a government source, more than 2500 advertising college graduates enter the scene every year. It is not unusual to find between 100 and 200 applicants vying for jobs in the $7000-to-$30,000 salary range.

One four-line classified ad in the Sunday New York Times for an assistant art director's job generated more than 200 inquiries on Monday morning, keeping two secretaries on the phone all day. And this happened at the height of prosperous times.

Perhaps this is why interviewers so often approach the task of seeing people rather wearily. Looking for shortcuts, they learn after a while to read between the lines of typewritten résumés and to respond to portfolios, sample reels, and demonstrations quickly.

By and large, experienced interviewers use three T's as criteria to size up their applicants' creative qualifications: traits, talent, and track record. For the benefit of those sitting on either side of the desk, it may pay to examine each of these T's more closely.

TRAITS TO LOOK FOR

Motivation Creative persons *must* enjoy their work, both emotionally and intellectually. Money alone is not enough; ego fulfillment (doing good work) is just as important, and sometimes more important to them.

Reliability This is an important requisite in any job, but particularly in a service business, where the human factor plays such an important part.

Fiscal Discipline Entrusted with other people's money, creative persons must feel a sense of responsibility for every dollar they spend. They must be able to work within a budget and to feel comfortable in doing so.

Administrative Ability Sometimes it is impractical to pass on a myriad of administrative details to creative persons; their time can be put to better use. However, they know better than anyone else how they want their ideas executed, and so they must also be familiar with and interested in preproduction and postproduction details.

Curiosity This trait was highlighted in Chapters 4 and 5, and there is no need to dwell on it here. Suffice it to say that lazy minds produce lazy ideas.

Temper Much of this trait is as indigenous to the creative process as heat is to cooking.

Ambition Life in advertising is never easy, and only the hardiest survive. Those with a strong ego are better equipped to absorb the shocks.

Salesmanship In advertising, creative talent must go hand in hand with a desire to sell. It should be pointed out, however, that selling in advertising need not always involve personal contacts; the preparation of a successful commercial appealing to a mass audience does not call for the temperament of, say, a door-to-door salesman. Some of the best-known creative stars in advertising are about as sociable as a mole making its way underground.

Composure Some people thrive under pressure, and with their adrenal glands working double-time they actually perform better. Others lose their composure. In the advertising business, where every job has a deadline, the former plainly have an easier time of it. However, stress tolerance is an acquired trait. Unseasoned graduates may just need a little time to grow accustomed to the pace.

TALENT TO LOOK FOR

Writing Skill It is difficult to say whether writing ability is a natural or a learned skill. There are convincing arguments on both sides. One thing is certain: professional writers write a lot and upon the slightest provocation. Their craft is a compulsion with them, bordering on the neurotic. As a creative director at a major agency, this author has interviewed hundreds of aspiring copywriters and found that all good writers are earnest about their trade. They often feel the urge to compose poems, plays, or short stories in addition to writing advertising copy. Lack of drive throws serious doubts upon the legitimacy of an applicant's literary aspirations.

Not all poets, novelists, or playwrights make good copywriters, of course. Writing advertising copy is an art unto itself. The hallmark of good copywriters is their ability to produce one-liners, innate salesmanship, genuine interest in the product, marketing sense, and, most of all, a stubborn insistence that they communicate with their audience, even at the sacrifice of textbook grammar. They do not particularly relish using all the 900,000-odd words which make up the English-American language (by far the richest in the world). And, unlike most others in the literary field, they do not use their writing for the purpose of unburdening their souls, airing their political views, or reminiscing about their early-childhood experiences. Nor do they subscribe to the somewhat shaky premise (a recurring theme with counterculturists) that getting paid for their efforts inevitably leads to corruption of the mind.

Visual Imagination Some people (not only artists) are able to think in terms of picture images as well as in words. In advertising, this is an important and well-paid asset. Ours is a visually oriented society. At least two generations have been raised on television; our educational system has come to accept visual aids as a routine teaching device; magazines and books (particularly the so-called mass-market paperbacks) are becoming increasingly graphic. And advertisers are going along with the trend.

But even art directors differ in their ability to visualize. Some of the best designers cannot draw a realistic figure to save their souls. Others, keeping up with developments in art, photography, typography, production techniques, and the like, excel in ferreting out the talent to execute a basic concept but have no particular interest in designing. Still others are accomplished renderers (they can put it on paper) but fall short in basic selling concepts. Finally, there are those who confine their creative contributions to specific media, such as television, print, or package design, and develop expertise mostly in these areas.

A good indication of talent is sample books and reels. Art directors strong in basic ideas usually show a number of graphic interpretations of a headline, sometimes by crude but meaningful thumbnail sketches. Designers try to display a little more polish in their portfolios; they know that type, colors, and other graphic nuances are as much an integral part of a basic design concept as is the advertising message. Renderers, on the other hand, are aware that their chief value lies in their drawing ability, and they usually include in their presentations samples of tight comprehensives, some that are only a small step removed from the finished version.

The wide variety of creative expressions makes it all the more necessary for the interviewer to know exactly the *type* of contribution he or she is after. A large selection of talent is available even within a single job category. Moreover, people differ greatly in the *degree* of their talent. People with top talent, while no doubt the most desirable, demand high fees for their services. Thus, it may well be economic folly to look for their contribution if the job does not really call for it.

Nor is it particularly wise to hand an assignment to a person whose area of expertise lies elsewhere. For example, some assignments (for example, corporate logotypes) require an acute sense of design. Obviously, this belongs in the bailiwick of a designer. On the other hand, pictorial composition plays a relatively minor role in shooting a television commercial *cinéma-vérité* style; there is no need to look for a sense of design in choosing the director who will supervise that kind of scene. And so it goes. A senior art director's interpretive visual sense may be more important than his or her rendering ability. (Some advertisers demand tight comprehensives, but many are able to approve an entire campaign on the basis of rough sketches.) The nature of television art directors' creative contributions are, by virtue of the medium, totally different from those offered by their colleagues in print; their feel for movement, sound, and timing may be much more important than their knowledge of typography.

Advertising Know-How Polished craftsmanship should not be confused with advertising savvy. The two complement each other, and together they represent a *coup,* but it is possible to have one without the other and still do well. A television director may, for example, excel in his or her ability to direct performers yet have merely cursory interest in the art of selling. Similarly, some of the best name designers are only fair-to-middling advertising professionals. Still others, such as photographers, directors, illustrators, designers, fashion coordinators, actors, typographers, and other people working at the periphery of advertising, may be eminently successful in their respective fields without ever having been called upon to solve marketing problems.

Good Taste This is one of the most elusive qualities of all. Obviously, to be able to judge taste in others, anyone who sits in judgment must possess good taste. Good taste is not necessarily synonymous with creative ability, of course. There are many photographers of excellent taste whose beautiful pictures lack true originality, perhaps because their high artistic standards inhibit them from trying. At the other extreme are those who take special (some say, perverse) pleasure in discarding the traditional dicta of good taste in the hope of making new graphic discoveries; some of the Pop Art illustrators belong in this category.

TRACK RECORD TO LOOK FOR

Past Clients People with top talent usually have a long list of clients and ex-clients. It is a good idea to take more than a cursory glance at applicants' past accomplishments.

It is not unusual for an established photographer or television director to have worked for as many as 50 or even 100 different clients. Many major production houses (some represent and provide facilities for up to a dozen directors) have more than 1000 television commercials to their credit and probably several movie shorts for theatrical or other forms of distribution.

Repeat business is a vote of confidence. On the other hand, the fact that a supplier has executed only a single assignment for a client does not necessarily imply a lack of talent. Some clients, always looking for a miracle which will make their sales go sky-high, are notoriously fickle. They might have had quite a number of esoteric reasons for bounding from one supplier to another, but none that has much to do with the work itself.

Neither do the résumés of those looking for staff positions always tell the whole story about applicants' backgrounds. There is usually more there than meets the eye. People switch jobs for a wide variety of reasons. Account shifts are one; they often compel management to let some of the best creative talent go. Moreover, personality clashes may leave a strong-willed art director or writer with no alternative but to seek solace elsewhere.

As a rule, fleeting stints of employment (less than 2 years), like a series of short-lived marriages, portend more of the same. (Generally, the higher the salary range, the longer the job tenure.) Job hopping can become habit-forming. The answer to such a nomadic existence may lie with a psychoanalyst, not with a boss.

This is not to suggest that periods of long employment always indicate an abiding sense of loyalty. People stay with the same company for many reasons, including some that are more personal than professional in nature. Typically, some of today's most respected advertising professionals have taken a zigzag road to riches, having held many positions in their careers. More often than not, low creative standards have forced them to make the moves.

Circumstances All this brings us to the importance of the working environment. By that, more is meant than piped-in music or a cushiony sofa at the wall; what we are talking about is the *total psychological climate*. This is all-encompassing: coworkers, caliber of work, office morale, or even the boss, who may stand in the way, all play a part.

Credit Hogging The birth of an advertising campaign can be a mys-terious process. With several people participating in the event, it is hard and sometimes impossible to pinpoint authorship.

Harry W. McMahan has shrewdly alluded to this circumstance in *Advertising Age* (December 1975), in which he describes the creator of a television commercial in this manner: "The man most responsible for the Marlboro cigarette creative concept now takes off with his own agency." Note the word *most*. The implication is clear that more than one person was responsible for the campaign.

Who is to say where ideas originate? They may begin with an actor improvising at a television studio, an art director jotting down a headline to go with a picture concept, a copywriter showing doodles to an art director; and even a client presenting his or her point of view to an agency. No wonder there is never a shortage of idea claimants in advertising. After all, the main staple of the industry is ideas; paychecks and entire careers are built on them. Perhaps this is why creative credits for celebrated advertising campaigns, such as those done for Volkswagen, Avis, and Alka Seltzer, are shared by enough people to fill a telephone book.

The author had firsthand exposure to the credit-hogging phenomenon by way of his "Let Your Fingers Do the Walking" theme for AT&T. At the writing of this book, no fewer than five advertising agencies (including some major ones) claim responsibility for this campaign, not to mention several dozen copywriters in whose portfolios or sample reels the theme appears in one form or another. This is in spite of the fact that the original series of ads was conceived by the author several years ago in the closed-door privacy of his office at Cunningham & Walsh. But such is life. Some campaigns call for continuous implementation, and the line between concept and development can become so vague as to be genuinely confusing.

Specific Account Experience It may be helpful for the account executive to know the distribution patterns of a product, for a copywriter to be thoroughly familiar with its selling features, and for an art director to understand its physical properties so he or she can best illustrate it. However, mere familiarity with a product is not to be confused with creative talent. One is no substitute for the other. It is the sign of competent professionals that they can tackle *any* assignment on *any* product.

Combination of Backgrounds A mixed bag is often the best kind there is. Some of the most successful photographers served their internship as agency art directors. Probably the majority of television directors in New York have flirted with print photography at one time or another. Others, working in advertising agencies, have written books, articles, and plays, supervised movie shorts, painted pictures, and invented (and taken out patents on) new products.

Recommendations and Résumés Friends and business associates—with emphasis on the latter—are probably still the best source of information about an applicant's qualifications. To gain insight, nothing can replace the experiencing of day-to-day personal relationships. The old adage "The work speaks for itself" has a ring of truth but suggests woefully little about working habits.

Letters can tell a lot—or very little. Skilled interviewers learn to tell the difference between a carefully crafted, and always polite, document and one that bubbles with genuine enthusiasm.

Résumés are an excellent source of information. The lack of one may show a cavalier attitude about job hunting, in itself a telling comment about seriousness of purpose. (There are exceptions to this, of course. Not every applicant is expected to have a résumé.) Curiously enough, the manner of presentation often reveals as much about its author's organizational ability, writing skills, perspective, salesmanship, ambition, and creative talent as a verbal interview.

It is advisable to keep on file all records on any job applicant—whether he or she is "it" or not. Needs change. Even if the applicant has found another job, the résumé may motivate an employer to make contact at some later date.

Discovering New Talent Lack of a proven track record does not necessarily indicate a dearth of talent. There may be a number of valid reasons why the work of an artist or a writer has not yet been published. Youth, lack of clients, budget limitations, a slow economy, and just plain tough luck are some of them.

Budget-conscious buyers always keep their eyes on up-and-coming, unrecognized, and, it is hoped, still-hungry talent. Some of these young men and women may be recent college graduates (see Chapter 8) waiting for their first break. Others, among them some of the most imaginative designers of all, have been concentrating on graphics for album covers, magazines, or books but have not yet moved into advertising.

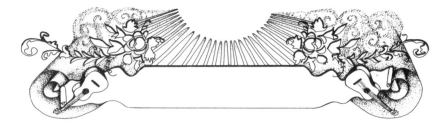

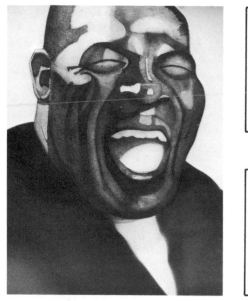

Where the Talent Is

Advertising people, using outside services, often face the problem of tracking down talent. Schools are only one place to go. Here are some others: amateur and professional clubs, associations, and guilds; manufacturers (for example, Eastman Kodak); columnists; trade exhibits; art studios; consulting and editorial services; agents; conferences; museums; ad agencies; advertisers; television stations; TV production studios; printers, artists, and photographers; and magazine, newspaper, and book publishers.

The artists are ordinarily given credit lines on the work that is reproduced.

Many excellent talent lists also are available (see Chapter 5). The most comprehensive ones are in *The Creative Black Book, Literary Market Place, Writer's Market, Artist's Market, Independent Advertising Services, The One Show, The Annual of American Illustration*, and, of course, the *Yellow Pages*.

Talent shows up early, even in the classroom. Shown here is work done by recent graduates of Pratt Institute, Brooklyn, New York, part of more than 300 illustrations, designs, and photographs reproduced every year in the RSVP catalog of the institute.

From top to bottom, left to right: Nancy Ohanian, Fred Marshall, Sharon B. Reiter, and Marc Weinstein.

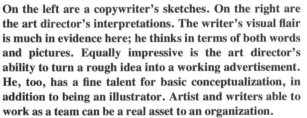

On the left are a copywriter's sketches. On the right are the art director's interpretations. The writer's visual flair is much in evidence here; he thinks in terms of both words and pictures. Equally impressive is the art director's ability to turn a rough idea into a working advertisement. He, too, has a fine talent for basic conceptualization, in addition to being an illustrator. Artist and writers able to work as a team can be a real asset to an organization.

Unfortunately, case histories such as the one shown here rarely find their way into sample books. Once the job has been completed, there is a tendency to throw out scraps of paper which would allow a step-by-step reconstruction of the campaign's evolution.

So there is no way for interviewers to find out who has contributed what; what they are shown is the end product. Only on-the-job performance will give them the information they need to evaluate the creative ability of applicants.

Guided by a fine, innate sense of design, top art director Helmut Krone of Doyle Dane Bernbach produced these award-winning ads, as he has for years for many other products. Note his sensitive handling of display copy and body text, his use of white space, his way of making all elements work together harmoniously on the printed page. This art director not only works with concepts but keeps a close watch on production. He does many of his own mechanicals, making subtle but important graphic contributions up to the last minute.

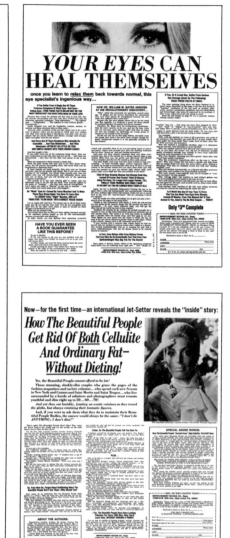

Here is the work of art director Sidney Koblenz of Megaman, Inc., an expert in laying out mail-order campaigns. Graphic nuances such as letter spacing and the use of white space play a less important role here; curiously enough, they may even prove to be counterproductive in Koblenz's type of advertising. According to the number of coupon returns, overly slick, letter-perfect execution of advertising actually works against getting responses. It takes a special breed of talent to know what appeals to a mail-order audience.

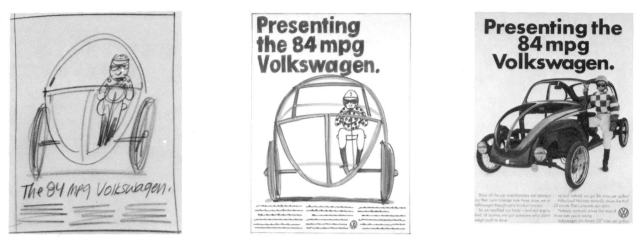

This art director developed the ad from the very inception. First came a small (4- by 5-inch) but professional thumbnail sketch to dramatize the headline "The 84 mpg Volkswagen." Another rough layout followed, this in full-page newspaper size (15 by 22 inches) to be shown to the client. Once approved, the layout became the blueprint for the photographer, typesetter, and paste-up person.

The comprehensive layout (bottom) for this two-page magazine ad was prepared by a team consisting of a professional renderer and a paste-up person. Staffers like these are often employed by an advertising agency to carry out their art directors' rough layouts (top).

Few art directors have creative director Ron Howell's knack for indicating human figures. Detailed sketches like these set the tone for the Norman Rockwell nostalgia photographs taken by Marty Evans in his campaign for Kawasaki motorcycles.

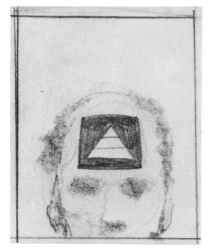

Quick sketches like these indicate vivid visual imagination. The ability to conceptualize ranks among the most sought-after skills in the graphic field and is one that commands the highest salaries.

Designer-visualizer Gene Frederico uses a collage of magazine photographs in his layout to simulate the appearance of the final ad. The best way to indicate photography still is to use actual photographs. Art directors whose budgets restrict them from taking experimental pictures for layout purposes often turn to using already published material.

Chapter Thirteen

Executing an Idea: Who Does What

In an agency, the scheduling of advertising campaigns is part of doing business. Some organizations turn out as many as 100 ads, both print and broadcast, every week. Usually, they adopt the following procedure in the preparation of an ad:

1. *Client.* He or she defines the problem.

2. *Account executive.* He or she delivers the assignment from the client to the agency. The account executive may act on his or her own or be accompanied by members of the marketing, research media, or creative departments. He or she initiates the campaign and is held responsible by the client for its successful execution.

3. *Copywriter and art director.* They work in the creative department of the agency, providing concepts for ads. While responsible for the quality of the final product, copywriters and art directors in advertising agencies do not actually execute layouts but use outside specialists. The cost of execution is passed on to the client, usually plus a commission.

4. *Production manager.* He or she may be responsible for the technical execution of print or broadcast advertising or, in some cases, of both. Major involvement begins after the layouts or storyboards have been submitted to the client for approval.

5. *Research.* This may include pretesting or posttesting.

6. *Media.* Space (in print) or time (on radio or television) schedules may be purchased before, during, or after the concept has been ap-

proved, depending on the circumstances.

In view of the many details surrounding every job and the large sums of money riding on it, advertising agencies are careful to assure a smooth follow-through.

Their success depends on it.

It should be emphasized that the implementation of an idea does not rest with the idea person alone. The responsibility is spread among others throughout the various departments in the agency.

However, it behooves the idea person to stay with his or her idea long after it has left the typewriter or the drawing table.

IT IS UP TO YOU!

Better than anyone, the idea person knows what he or she wants. Others in the agency not only will welcome the idea person's participation but may insist on it.

This is why in the traffic system of most agencies accommodation is made for creative persons to have their say at various completion stages of their ideas, practically up to the last minute. Checks and double checks are built into the system to assure the best quality and, of course, to make certain that deadlines and budget requirements are met.

The following pages demonstrate how one organization, Cunningham & Walsh, a large and highly successful advertising agency, assigns areas of responsibilities among its various departments.

Section I: Administration

RESPONSIBILITIES OF THE TRAFFIC EXECUTIVE

The traffic executive is responsible to the account executive for the efficient movement of projects through the agency and for obtaining the necessary approvals at each stage.

The traffic executive:

1. Issues the job order and any revision orders to all involved personnel as indicated by the account executive and confirmed by the creative director.

2. Will schedule meetings with the account executive and the business manager and issue a weekly status report showing due dates and the action to be taken on each print and television job.

3. Will secure approvals for all creative concepts (copy, layouts, and storyboards).

He or she will then verify that all jobs are in correct sizes, per schedule, correctly numbered, and properly identified; and keep copies of all creative work.

4. Will secure, before client presentation, a rough preliminary estimate from the art and print production departments for discussion with the client.

5. Will schedule *print* preproduction meetings including (when necessary) the creative director, art director, copywriter, account exec-

utive, director of legal services, and print production supervisor to discuss preproduction and legal problems and specifications for estimating the job.

6. Is responsible for securing approval for all phases (type, art and mechanical, proof) of print production to the completion of the job. The traffic executive will secure approval for TV storyboards and send scripts and storyboards and the commercial approval form to the business manager after client approval.

In the event of revisions, either in the creative stage or in the production stage, the traffic executive will make absolutely sure that all signatures are up to date.

7. Will release, after final approval, all material and insertion instructions to scheduled publications and then retire the job for billing to the client.

RESPONSIBILITIES OF THE ACCOUNT SUPERVISOR

The account supervisor is responsible for the coordination and maximum utilization of all agency departments to provide complete and effective solutions to client needs.

The account supervisor:

1. Will develop creative strategies with the group creative director.

2. Will agree with the group creative director on all material to be presented to the client. Any disagreement will be arbitrated by the creative director.

3. Will approve all print and broadcast material before it is delivered to publications or networks.

4. Will be responsible for obtaining any materials requested by legal services and for coordinating and obtaining all requisite legal reports or approvals.

NOTE: Prior to the development of the annual marketing plan for each client and management or group, the account supervisor should assess the importance of utilizing specialized agency departments such as research, sales promotion, and public relations. Securing early input from each of these departments will

help to channel ideas into the overall strategy before advertising has been completely developed. This makes a more orderly work flow as the advertising is prepared.

RESPONSIBILITIES OF THE ACCOUNT EXECUTIVE

The account executive is responsible with the creative group for the efficient movement of creative work through the agency. The account executive:

1. Initiates all work with a job order, which provides complete information on each job.

2. Involves all necessary agency departments.

3. Ensures sufficient time for the completion of job in coordination with the traffic executive or business manager and the group creative director.

4. Arranges to obtain all necessary approvals, including legal and network reports and approvals for management.

5. Obtains all necessary material for legal and network approvals. The account executive should make sure that the client is appraised of the content of the legal services reports or approvals, so that appropriate responses may be prepared or data gathered. Client legal and R&D departments (where appropriate) must approve all material *before* giving the agency final approval. All replies and data requested by legal services will be forwarded to both legal services and scientific services for appropriate comment or approval, or both.

6. Issues the commercial approval form for the traffic executive to transmit to the business manager and the director of legal services after formal client approval of estimates.

7. Obtains client approval of print layouts, finished art and mechanical and engraver's proofs; and TV storyboards, interlocks, optical check prints or answer prints, and video tape master and duplicate.

8. Ensures that proper media arrangements have been made prior to completion of production.

9. Obtains final legal and continuity clearance.

RESPONSIBILITIES OF THE GROUP CREATIVE DIRECTOR

The group creative director is responsible for the quality of the creative product and for its efficient movement through the agency. The group creative director:

1. Develops creative strategies with the account supervisor.

2. Agrees with the account executive on due dates for each job.

3. Must check with legal services at the earliest possible time and *in advance* of client presentation.

4. Consults the manager of scientific services if, in the opinion of legal services, the advertising contains a test, demonstration, or experiment or if the advertising is comparative in nature, to make sure that adequate data are available to support claims, to obtain assistance in the preparation of demonstration or production procedures, or to receive advice on the nature and extent of the data needed.

5. Has responsibility for the quality of all stages of commercial production and shares budget responsibility with the commercial producer.

6. Must approve *all* material produced by his or her group *prior to* client presentation and at each stage of print and TV production.

7. Is responsible for the allocation of his or her group's time to his or her accounts and for properly recording that time on time sheets.

RESPONSIBILITIES OF THE COPYWRITER OR COPY SUPERVISOR

The copywriter or copy supervisor is responsible to the group creative director for the quality of the creative product. He or she:

1. Must not begin any job unless he or she has received a job order with complete information including strategy and due dates.

2. Will consult with both legal services and scientific services, where appropriate, pursuant to the direction of the group creative director.

3. Will proofread and otherwise check all type proofs, engraver's proofs, commercial storyboards, and scripts.

4. Will, following client approval

of creative work, supervise and approve each step of television and print production until final release.

RESPONSIBILITIES OF THE ART DIRECTOR

The art director is responsible to the group creative director for the quality of the creative product. The art director:

1. Must not begin any job unless he or she has received a job order with complete information, including strategy and due dates.

2. Must consult with the print production supervisor prior to the preparation of any finished artwork.

3. Will prepare preliminary cost estimates and final estimates for print and art estimates for TV. If these estimates are exceeded, he or she must inform the traffic executive in print matters and the business manager in TV matters. They will then notify the account executive.

4. Will consult with both legal services and scientific services, where appropriate, pursuant to the direction of the group creative director.

5. Will, following client approval of creative work, supervise and approve each step of television and print production until release of materials.

RESPONSIBILITIES OF THE ADMINISTRATOR OF COMMERCIAL PRODUCTION

The administrator of commercial production is responsible for the overall administrative management of the commercial production department. The administrator:

1. Serves, in the absence of the director of commercial production, as the acting head of the commercial production department and assumes all responsibility for the department.

2. Assigns commercial producers and assistant producers to production projects.

3. Assists the commercial producer and the business manager in the preparation of commercial production schedules.

4. Facilitates the commercial completion and answer-print procedure.

5. Obtains final answer-print approval from the client (account executive) and prepares and distributes the completed answer-print approval form.

RESPONSIBILITIES OF THE COMMERCIAL PRODUCER

The commercial producer is responsible to the director of commercial production for the quality of each commercial and for its efficient budget control. The commercial producer:

1. Is responsible for involving himself or herself in the creative development of each commercial as soon as he or she has been assigned to it.

2. Is responsible, with the copywriter, for the proper timing of each commercial.

3. Is responsible for conducting prebid and preproduction meetings to achieve agreement on production details and to issue complete reports on each meeting. NOTE: The producer *must* have preliminary legal and continuity approval before setting up a prebid or preproduction meeting.

4. Is responsible, with the business manager, for preparing the final production estimate.

5. Is responsible for a production schedule, which he or she prepares with the business manager and the administrator of commercial production. Any additional time required must be cleared with the appropriate personnel through the business manager.

6. Is responsible, with the group creative director, for controlling the cost of the actual production and must notify the business manager, account executive, and administrator of commercial production of any expenditure above the estimate.

7. Is responsible for the correct signing of all scale talent contracts and for submitting them with the studio report form to the business manager.

8. Is responsible for the transfer of TV commercial printing or master material to the print procurement and distribution company and radio commercial master radio tapes to

the radio tape distribution company and for advising the administrator of commercial production, the business manager, and the broadcast operations coordinator.

9. Must arrange screenings for approval, with appropriate agency personnel concerned, at each stage of production.

10. Is responsible following client approval of the 35- and 16-millimeter answer prints, for advising the business manager to arrange for the transfer of the commercial production material to the storage company and for the preparation and distribution of the production completion report.

Assistant Producer As the title implies, the assistant producer will assist the commercial producer in all stages of a commercial production project.

He or she will also:

1. Prepare as-produced scripts and photoscripts.

2. Function as a commercial producer on specific assigned production projects.

RESPONSIBILITIES OF THE MANAGER OF BROADCAST BUSINESS AFFAIRS

The manager of broadcast business affairs is the supervisor for the business, talent payment, and broadcast operations departments. In addition, the manager is the agency's overscale talent negotiator and union code interpreter.

RESPONSIBILITIES OF THE BUSINESS MANAGER

The broadcast business manager reports to the manager, broadcast business affairs, and is responsible for estimating, coordination, budget control, and assisting the producer in liaison with account executives, traffic executives, production companies, talent, talent unions, and all other vendors. The business manager:

1. Is responsible, upon receipt of the commercial production approval form, for assisting the producer in setting up the prebid and preproduction meetings.

2. Assists the producer in the preparation of specifications sheets.

3. Is responsible, with the producer, for the preparation of the final production estimate.

4. Is responsible, with the producer, for the preparation of the production schedule.

5. Is responsible for issuing the formal production contract after receipt of a client-approved estimate.

6. Is responsible for the maintenance of thorough cost records of each commercial production.

7. Is responsible for approving and forwarding all commercial production bills *in duplicate* to the accounting department with date, client name, job number, and signature.

8. Must, in conjunction with accounting, see that all charges are promptly billed and the job closed when all costs are in.

THE DIRECTOR OF LEGAL SERVICES

The director of legal services is responsible for the legal review and approval of all creative material to ensure compliance with legal, network, and industry requirements. The internal traffic responsibilities of the director of legal services include:

1. The review of all creative material to determine whether each print ad or commercial complies with legal, network, and industry requirements.

2. The preparation and internal distribution of legal and continuity reports to be used initially as a guide by the account executive in presenting creative material to a client.

3. The submission of commercial storyboards, scripts, and finished commercials to the networks for continuity clearance.

4. The issuance of the preliminary legal and continuity approval. The director of legal services, after consultation with the director of commercial production and (where appropriate) outside legal counsel, may postpone or cancel the scheduled production of any broadcast or print ad if the information or material, or both, required by legal services has

not been obtained or if, prior to production, anything should occur which would negate the basis of the approval.

5. The issuance of the final legal and continuity approval once the commercial or print ad has been produced in accordance with legal or network guidelines, or both.

Section II: Creative Development

1. *Strategy statement.* Each account and each product within that account must have a current strategy statement. This strategy must be agreed upon by the client, account supervisor, group creative director, and research supervisor.

When dealing with a new client, a new campaign, or a major project, the proper management supervisor and the creative director and director of research must also approve strategy. No work will be initiated until a strategy statement has been devised.

2. *Job order*
   a. To start a project the account executive must fill out a job order form.
   b. No work will begin until this form has been *fully completed* and distributed.
      The form should include *strategy* (creative and marketing), all mechanical requirements, audience information, market information as applicable, legal considerations, due dates (no job will be begun without a due date acceptable to both the account supervisor and the group creative director), and any other applicable information.

3. *Internal creative review*
   a. Tissues or roughs should be prepared by the writer and the art director for review with the group creative director.
   b. When creative agreement has been reached in rough form, the director of legal

services should be consulted.
   c. The group creative director must check with legal services at the earliest possible time to ensure that all legal concerns have been recognized and fully discussed *in advance* of client presentation.
   d. If, in the opinion of legal services, the advertising contains a test, demonstration, or experiment or if the advertising is comparative in nature, the manager of scientific services will be consulted to make sure that adequate data are available to support claims and assist in the preparation of demonstration or production procedures or to advise on the nature and extent of the data needed.
   e. The creative department should then review the work with the account department. When agreement has been arrived at, comprehensives should be prepared for presentation to the client.
      NOTE: In the event that the group creative director and the account supervisor fail to agree, the creative director will make the final decision.

4. *Client presentation.* After internal agreement has been reached and *prior to client presentation,* the following procedures *must* be observed:
   a. All proposed creative material must be reviewed by legal services, which will then issue internal legal-continuity report or preliminary approval including, where appropriate, anticipated network or other considerations.
   b. All storyboards must be reviewed by the director of television production, and a producer assigned to each job. The producer will make sure that all boards are properly timed and will make whatever creative contribution is possible at this early stage.

c. All print should be reviewed with supervisor of print production to review and discuss production techniques.

d. The TV producer or print production supervisor will provide the traffic executive or business manager with a *rough* estimate for discussion with the client.

e. Before client presentation the following approvals must be obtained by the traffic executive: those of the art director, copywriter, copy supervisor, group creative director, and producer or print production supervisor; the legal services report or approval (where appropriate the account supervisor is responsible for ensuring the issuance of the appropriate report or approval); and the approvals of the account executive, account supervisor, and management supervisor.

5. *Revisions.* The account executive must notify the traffic executive in writing of *all* revisions, the reasons for the revisions, the new due dates, and all other pertinent information. The traffic executive will then issue a revision requisition. When the revisions have been made, the traffic executive will obtain all required signatures in a new signature block with current dates.

Section III: Print Production Procedures

1. *Preliminary estimate.* Before rough layouts are presented to the client, an estimate is given to traffic and marked ''Budget only.'' This estimate, which is based on verbal or rough specifications, is subject to change.

2. *Preproduction meeting.* After client approval, the traffic executive schedules a preproduction meeting including the creative director, art director, copywriter, account executive, and legal and production supervisor to discuss reproduction and

specifications for final estimating.

3. *Final estimate.* This estimate is given to traffic. Type, engravings, or printing cannot be ordered unless the production supervisor is advised in writing that a signed estimate has been received by the agency. *If an approved estimate has not been received by the agency, production must obtain written approval from the account supervisor to order any work.*

4. *Cost changes.* If the cost of production exceeds the estimate, a revised print production estimate is given to traffic explaining with an explanation.

5. *Type proofs.* When type proofs are received, they are given to the traffic executive for proofreading and approvals. (The production supervisor and the copywriter are responsible for proofreading.)

6. *Approval of art and mechanical.* When the mechanical is finished, traffic will check for accuracy and obtain approvals from the copywriter, art director, copy supervisor, group creative director, production supervisor, and director of legal services prior to submission to the account executive. The account executive is responsible for obtaining approvals from the account supervisor and the management supervisor.

7. *Approval of engraver's proofs.* When engraver's proofs are received, traffic is informed and will advise the art director and the account executive. All corrections from both the client and the agency are recorded on the proofs. When final corrections have been made, all approvals, including legal, are indicated on the proofs and filed in the traffic job jacket.

8. *Forwarding.* The traffic executive retires the job jacket and releases instructions and printing material to publications. He or she also coordinates the control of closing dates and necessary extensions to assure that all materials are released at the proper time.

9. *Completion of job.* Upon completion of the job, all invoices are requested from suppliers, approved by the production supervisor, and forwarded to the accounting department for final billing.

Section IV: Broadcast Production Procedures

1. *Approval for production*
   a. No job will be accepted for production without a production approval form signed by the account executive.
   b. The traffic executive must give this form to the business manager, the director of legal services, and the administrator of commercial production with copies of the commercial storyboard and photoscripts or scripts.
   c. The business manager and the producer are responsible for keeping the traffic executive informed of the status of all stages of production.

2. *Legal continuity.* The director of legal services determines the legal and continuity status of commercials. If a preliminary legal-continuity approval has not been issued, the director will discuss the status with the account supervisor and notify the business manager and the administrator of commercial production.

3. *Communication of approvals*
   a. The administrator of commercial production should confirm the commercial producer on each job.
   b. The business manager should notify the account executive if the estimate will be available on the date requested on the commercial approval form. If not, they will agree on an acceptable date.

4. *Prebid meeting and report*
   a. The commercial producer and the business manager will schedule a prebid meeting with the group creative director, copywriter, art director, account executive, and assistant producer to discuss bidding, casting, graphics, and the like.
   NOTE: When a commercial includes tests, demonstrations, or experiments which

illustrate product effectiveness, comparative efficacy, superiority, or the like (as defined by legal services), the manager of scientific services must attend the prebid meeting. The commercial producer is responsible for recording the decisions and agreements reached at this meeting and reporting these in a prebid meeting report prepared by the director and the administrator of commercial production.

b. The commercial producer and the business manager will then prepare the prebid meeting report.

5. *Bidding*
   a. On the basis of the prebid meeting report the producer and the business manager prepare copies of commercial production specifications and the bid form.
   b. The producer, business manager, and creative group will then meet with and obtain bids from production companies.
   c. The commercial producer and the group creative director will then meet with the director or administrator of commercial production to select a production company.

6. *Production estimates*
   a. The business manager will get costs for color correction or other necessary graphics, or both, from the art director.
   b. The business manager will prepare a complete commercial production estimate.
   c. The business manager will present the estimate to the commercial producer and administrator for approval before forwarding it to the account executive.
   d. The account executive will obtain client approval and deliver signed estimates to the business manager for distribution to the producer, group creative director, assistant producer, casting department, administrator of

the production department, and accounting department.

7. *Preliminary legal approval.* When all the information and material requested by legal services has been received from the account supervisor and found to be sufficient and when all preliminary network clearances have been received or are anticipated by the director of legal services, a preliminary legal-continuity approval form will be issued by legal services. Any legal or network production cautions will be indicated for discussion at the preproduction meeting. When a commercial includes tests, demonstrations, or experiments (as described in paragraph 4), the director of legal services will request the manager of scientific services to prepare a procedure to be followed during production.

No contractual commitments may be made and no preproduction meeting or commercial production may be scheduled until the client-signed or account supervisor–signed estimate has been received and preliminary legal-continuity approval has been issued.

8. *Production schedule.* On the basis of an air date obtained from the account executive, the business manager, producer, and administrator of commercial production will prepare a preliminary production schedule for discussion at the preproduction meeting.

9. *Preproduction meeting.* The commercial producer will schedule a preproduction meeting including all those listed in paragraph 4 plus production company and client representatives, to complete production details, including scheduling, casting, and any legal or continuity requirements.

10. *Talent booking and contracts*
    a. The commercial producer will instruct the casting department to book talent or prepare contracts, or both (in accordance with the client-approved estimate and any special instructions from the business manager).
    b. The commercial producer is responsible for obtaining signed contracts and com-

pleting the studio report form and returning it to the business manager.

11. *Production budget control*
    a. The commercial producer and the group creative director have full control over all operations on location, on a set, or in a studio and are responsible for maintaining costs within the client-approved estimate.
    b. Any increase over the estimated costs will be reported by the producer as soon as possible to the account executive, the business manager, and the administrator of commercial production on a production-screening report form.
    c. The account executive will indicate the proper disposition of these costs and will return the report to the business manager.

12. *Approval of film interlock or video tape master*
    a. The commercial producer and the group creative director will schedule a screening of the film interlock or video tape master (video cassette) for review by the director of commercial production and the director of legal services and subsequently for account group approval.
    b. The account executive and the commercial producer will schedule a screening for client approval after agency approval.
    c. Corrections indicated by the commercial producers are reported to the account executive, the business manager, and the administrator of commercial production on a production-screening report.
    NOTE: Whenever commercials include a test, demonstration, or experiment (as described in paragraph 4), the director of legal services will review the film interlock or video tape master (video cassette).

13. *Approval of optical-check print (film).* If approval of any interlock of

the optical-check print and track is necessary, the procedure outlined in paragraph 12 will be followed.

14. *Completion report and as-produced scripts*
   a. The commercial producer or assistant producer prepares a production completion report and an as-produced script.
   b. Copies of the completion report are sent to the business manager and the talent payment supervisor.
   c. Copies of the as-produced script are sent to the broadcast operations coordinator and the traffic executive.

15. *Approval of answer prints and tape masters*
   a. After client approval of the optical-check print, the commercial producer notifies the production company to transfer printing elements to the print-tape procurement and distribution company.
   b. The producer advises the administrator of commercial production, the business manager, and the broadcast operations coordinator.
   c. Answer prints and sample tape duplicates must be approved by the administrator of commercial production, the commercial producer, group creative director, and the client (account executive).

16. *Final legal-continuity approval*
   a. The first available composite prints or tape duplicates will be sent to the networks by legal services for final continuity clearance.
   b. When all clearances have been received and all previous legal services' requests have been answered, the director of legal services will issue final legal-continuity approval to release commercials for broadcast to the account supervisor, business manager, broadcast operations coordinator, and administrator of commercial production.

   c. *No commercial material may be released for broadcast scheduling until both the final legal-continuity approval and the commercial approval form have been issued.*

17. *Forwarding of commercial material.* After receipt of necessary approval forms the broadcast operations coordinator reviews the scheduling instructions with the account executive and the media supervisor and orders the necessary quantities of prints or tapes.

18. *Completion and closing out*
   a. The administrator of commercial production receives commercial reference prints or tapes, and schedules a screening for the business manager, the talent payment supervisor, and the broadcast operations coordinator.
   b. Prints and tapes are distributed to the commercial producer, the group creative director, and other offices of the agency.
   c. Broadcast operations sends copies of as-produced scripts to the assistant commercial producer along with a 35-millimeter film print.
   d. The assistant commercial producer selects key frames from each commercial, marking the as-produced script next to the appropriate copy, and forwards this material to the traffic executive for the production of quantity photoscripts.
   e. Broadcast operations also sends copies of the as-produced script to the creative director, group creative director, account executive, and director of legal services.
   f. The first air date for the commercial is to be shown on the script sent to the director of legal services.
   g. The business manager advises the production company to release and transfer the commercial production

material for cataloging and storage.
   h. The business manager sees that all charges have been received and forwarded to the accounting department and closes out the production job by written notification to the accounting department and the traffic executive.
   i. The original client-approved storyboard is returned to the traffic executive for permanent filing.

Section V: Sales Promotion Procedures

The complexities of the merchandising–sales promotion department require additional consideration in the development of creative material. The department's work encompasses all forms of media advertising as well as planning outlines, multimedia, sweepstakes, premiums, promotions, and so on.

Procedures outlined in the creative development section and print production procedures also apply to the merchandising–sales promotion department.

In addition, the department has the responsibility of formally estimating and recording time.

1. *Estimating*
   a. All preliminary or final estimates will be coordinated by the business and administrative manager or, in his or her absence, by the administrative assistant, working with all the people involved in each particular project.
   b. All estimates will be reviewed by the director of the merchandising–sales promotion department.
   c. If the preparation of an estimate is either impossible or impractical, or proceed-without-estimate form is to be used.
   d. This form will require the signature of the account executive or, when available, the client and will state the

reason for the lack of an estimate.

e. This form will be completed before the job is started. It will establish cost limits for creative time and out-of-pocket expenditures until a formal estimate has been prepared. It will also be used for nonbillable jobs.

f. If after the project has been started a change of direction is requested by both the account executive and the client, a revised estimate is to be prepared.

2. *Recording of time*

a. The time spent on each job is to be recorded on a day-by-day basis on the weekly time sheet form. This time sheet *must* be completed and given to the administrative assistant every Friday without fail.

b. The administrative assistant will record the time spent by each individual every day in the cost control ledger.

c. It will be the responsibility of the persons involved to keep track of the number of hours available, hours spent, and hours remaining on each project. If more time is justifiably needed, the business and administrative manager must be informed so that a revised estimate can be prepared.

d. Likewise, each individual will be responsible for reporting to the business and administrative manager the need for work when hours are available.

e. The traffic executive will advise the account executive of the cost and will receive approval from the account executive. He or she will add this information to the job requisition.

Section VI: Media Procedures

The media department is responsible for the development of the annual media plan for each client within the agency. The media supervisor works in conjunction with the account executive to obtain approval of the plan by the client organization.

Media plans will not be made final without consultation with the creative director regarding creative needs for space and time. Once approvals have been given, the following steps take place within the traffic system:

1. *Broadcast*

a. The account executive alerts the business manager, broadcast operations, and legal services that the first air date has been scheduled.

b. The media supervisor then sends memoranda to the business manager, broadcast operations, and the account executive, giving details of the upcoming schedule.

c. Once a firm media buy has been made, the media supervisor confirms air dates and markets to the business manager, broadcast operations, via the radio-TV forwarding instructions form.

d. The media supervisor will notify the business manager, broadcast operations, and the account executive via phone and follow-up memo regarding changes in or cancellation of a schedule.

2. *Print*

a. The account executive alerts the traffic executive and legal services that the first insertion date has been scheduled.

b. The media supervisor confirms in detail with the account executive and the traffic executive all the details of the print schedule.

c. The media supervisor confirms, with the account executive and the traffic executive, purchased insertion dates and publications via form or memo.

d. The estimator provides the traffic executive with a copy of the contract covering newspaper, magazine, or outdoor advertising.

e. The media supervisor notifies the account executive and the traffic executive via phone and follow-up memo of changes in or cancellation of a schedule.

6. The research department notifies the account group and the media department of market availabilities for alternative dates.

7. The account group and the media department jointly decide on the network vehicle on the basis of the rating of the show, the markets available, the brand's marketing considerations, the cost of any cut-ins, the cost of spot buys (if spots must be bought), network clearances for the markets (to avoid preemptions), competitive adjacencies, and the best possible geographic spread of the markets available.

8. The research department requests the structure of the test, indicating the date of airing, the vehicle (network, cut-ins, or spot buys), the markets wanted, and the name and length of the commercial.

9. A day or two later, the research department notifies the research firm of the approximate time or position of the commercial in the show on the basis of information received from the media department.

10. The research department notifies all concerned (client, account, media, broadcast operations) of the final test arrangements.

11. The research department secures a copy of the test commercial script from the producer of the broadcast operations department. It notifies the research firm as to the product and brand category and supplies a brief description of the commercial for use in the questionnaire. It also sends a copy of the script and, in some cases, a copy of the film to the firm for inclusion in the final report.

12. The research department approves the final questionnaire.

13. The media department orders the cut-ins or the spot buys and sends out reminder notices the day before the test. It also cancels any spot activity for the brand in prime time for 24 hours *before* and 23 hours *after* the test.

14. The broadcast operations department ships out the commercials.

Chapter Fourteen
Selling Your Idea to Others

Unless an idea is sold, it will remain merely an idea in somebody's head, an interesting conversation piece at a cocktail party, another page in a portfolio of layouts, a dream that never came true. And, from a more practical point of view, such an idea is unlikely to generate an income. Since it will be seen or heard by only a few, it will never catch the general public's attention or that of a client who happens to be searching for an agency to service his or her account.

It is little wonder therefore, that people in advertising are often judged and paid on the basis of their ability not only to create but also to sell what they (or others) have created. Nearly all top executives in the business are reputed to be what the trade press sometimes describes as people persuaders, able to think on their feet. At times, that is their major claim to fame.

Probably more than 25 percent of total person-hours in advertising (some estimates go as high as 50 percent) are spent in selling ideas, one person to another in offices, conference rooms, restaurants, parties, bar cars, and golf courses. At first glance, this may seem a colossal waste of time and a very expensive practice at that. But is it, really? The various approval stages met by ideas could be thought of as a giant multilayered sieve, grains of sand going through it. Presumably, only the finest ideas are allowed to pass by. Without this shake-out process, there would be many more ineffective and, therefore, more costly advertisements getting into print or on radio and television, with the consumer picking up the tab.

Selling, Selling Everywhere . . .

If you think total person-hours spent on the selling of ideas have just been overestimated, consider the following:

Copywriters must sell their ideas to *art directors, account executives,* and *clients.*

Art directors must sell their ideas to *writers, account executives, clients, print and television producers,* and often *vendors* such as *photographers, illustrators,* and *television directors.*

Media planners must sell their ideas to *account executives, clients, media representatives, researchers, marketing experts,* and sometimes *writers* and *art directors.*

Account executives must sell their ideas to *writers, art directors, media planners, marketing experts,* and *clients* (who are usually represented by several people). Moreover, the task of persuading *lawyers* that an idea will stand up under legal scrutiny may also be assigned to an account executive.

Vendors, offering a broad range of services in the creative fields (media, production, research, marketing, and public relations) must sell their ideas to *art directors, writers, account executives, print and television producers, researchers, marketing experts,* and, on occasion, the *advertiser* as well.

Advertising agencies must sell their ideas to *clients.*

And the buck still does not come to rest. As often as not, advertising functions are decentralized at the client's headquarters. Ideas are bounced from one department to another. *Advertising managers* must sell theirs to *brand managers* (or the other way around), *members of the staff* to *top management, top management* to intermediaries *(sales force, retail organizations, brokers, wholesalers),* and so on. It is only after all the approvals have been garnered (one survey points out that major decisions in large corporations can involve as many as forty people) that the idea is allowed to go into production so that eventually it will be in good enough shape to be presented to the ultimate jury, the *consumer.* Then he or she must be sold.

The Inherent Difficulties in Selling an Advertising Idea, No Matter How Good It Is

1. *Unlike an automobile, toothpaste, or a cake of soap, an advertising idea is only an abstraction.* It must be expressed in words and pictures to be put across.

2. *Advertising expenditure may be a sizable sum, sometimes running into several millions of dollars.* Its spending calls for corporate policy decisions.

3. *Advertising is an investment.* Commitments required by media make it imperative that the money be put up front; that is, a financial investment must be made prior to the implementation of the campaign. Approval of an advertising theme, even if it is presented only by way of layouts, storyboards, or scribbles on a piece of paper, thus is tantamount to spending money.

4. *Advertising budgets suffer from elasticity.* In times of economic stress, this corporate expense item is usually the first to be tinkered with. It is simpler to cut advertising budgets than to fire employees (and then in good times to try to rehire them), sell machinery, or juggle inventories. Rejection of an idea (or holding it in abeyance) is thus tantamount to saving money.

5. *The exact role of advertising in making sales and producing profits is difficult to determine.* Marketing is much too complex an undertaking to lend itself to quick analysis. Any increase in demand may be traced to a change in the product, an improvement in the sales force, new distribution channels, greater retail support, an economic upturn, or the like, with advertising remaining only a piece in the corporate jigsaw puzzle. Despite advertisers' wishes, advertising is far from being an exact science, and it is doubtful whether it ever will be.

Understanding Corporate Attitudes about Advertising in General

Each corporation, representing a group of people stepping to the music of the same drummer, has its own characteristic approach to advertising. Corporate policies vary with the industry, product experience, financial resources, and, of course, personal predilections of key executives.

It is important for the person who makes the presentation to recognize the corporation's basic and sometimes obdurate attitude toward advertising and not to take failure personally. Appearances notwithstanding, it may not be his or her particular presentation which meets resistance, but the more fundamental issue of *whether or not the corporation should advertise at all*.

Actually, not all corporations have the same need to advertise. As a rule, low-ticket items (under $5), which invite frequent repeat purchasing, require relatively large advertising budgets. On the other hand, high-ticket items and products not sold directly to consumers may survive with the aid of more carefully targeted and less costly advertising support.

The compilation of figures in the accompanying table shows average advertising sales ratios of various industries. However, none of these figures should be carved in stone. Every corporation, regardless of its product category, has its own set of problems. Its advertising budget will vary accordingly. Manufacturers of drugs, gum, cleaning and toilet preparations, candies, and sometimes tobacco and beer often plow between 5 and 20 percent of their sales back into spreading the good word through mass media. Here competition calls for aggressive advertising. The launching of a new product demands especially strong promotional backing, as the spending patterns of such large marketers as

General Foods, Colgate Palmolive, and Procter & Gamble show.

As a rule, there is no need to promulgate the value of advertising to top management. Corporate officers are usually astute enough to understand that advertising is one of the most potent selling tools available to them. Many, in fact, have become slightly inured to platitudes. Writes M. E. Ziegenhagen from the the executive side of his desk as director of advertising and public relations at the Babcock & Wilcox Company: "In companies that are marketing leaders, the chief executive is weary of being told he needs advertising; he knows it. He is wary of those who continually tell him, with a commissionable glint in his eye, that he needs more of it."[1]

This is not to say that an agency should not make a case for more advertising if it *honestly* feels that the client is missing out on important new business opportunities by unwisely skimping on the budget. In that case, supportive data (documented, if possible) on the value of more advertising will go far in overcoming skepticism. These areas may be explored:

1. *Industry averages.* This information is made available by the federal government in the *Statistical Abstract of the United States,* by trade publications such as the listing in *Advertising Age,* and by various other trade and media associations.

2. *Competitive spending.* Research, clipping, and monitoring services offer data on cost, advertising time, and space purchases made by competition. Reliable sources are the Advertising Checking Bureau, Inc., New York, which checks all daily newspapers in the country and also weekly newspapers and general consumer magazines; the National Research Bureau, Inc., Burlington, Iowa; the National System, St. Louis; magazines such as the *Harvard Business Review;* leading national advertising reports, such as those published by Media Records, Inc., listing expenditures by large

---

[1]Roger Barton (ed.), *Handbook of Advertising Management,* McGraw-Hill Book Company, New York,

national advertisers in newspapers; *The Standard Directory of Advertisers,* published by the National Register Publishing Co., Inc., Skokie, Illinois, showing billing breakdowns of some 17,000 corporations; Leading National Advertisers, Inc., providing reports of advertising in six media; Broadcast Advertisers' Reports, Inc., which covers network and spot TV and network radio expenditures), the Publishers' Information Bureau giving expenditures in consumer magazines for large national advertisers on a monthly basis; and Daniel Starch & Staff, Inc. Local and national media, trade associations, and, if perhaps indirectly, the federal government are additional sources for this type of information.

3. *Data on advertising effectiveness.* Case histories of advertising's sales effectiveness are available from several companies including the advertisers themselves, such as Campbell Soup, Mighty Dog, Kraft, British Airways, Lysol, Hallmark, and Alka-Seltzer (which increased sales by 52 percent in 6 years just by changing its creative approach). McGraw-Hill published a comprehensive study on the subject. It found that companies that were heavily involved in advertising had up to one-fifth lower sales costs than those that were not. Historical records are also made available by Daniel Starch & Staff, the Government Printing Office, and Media/Scope magazine. Several economists, among them Jules Backman, research professor of economics at New York University, offer cogent evidence that sales reflect increased advertising spending. Certain items, it was found, sold 3 times as fast with advertising as without it.

4. *Alternative budgeting methods.* Most companies base advertising appropriations upon sale volume (*A/S* ratio), but that is only one approach. Advertising based upon a percentage of the selling price received for each unit is another; comparative data are available. Moreover, experiments can be conducted in isolated markets. The campaign can be refined along the

Advertising/Sales Ratio of Various Industries Based upon Corporate Tax Returns (from "Advertising Age")

INDUSTRY	PERCENT	INDUSTRY	PERCENT
Manufacturing	1.25	Leather and leather	
Food and kindred products	2.27	products	1.60
Meat products	0.36	Footwear, except rubber	1.47
Dairy products	1.38	Leather and leather	
Canned and frozen foods	2.51	products not elsewhere	
Grain mill products	3.73	classified	1.85
Bakery products	2.16	Stone, clay, and glass products	0.59
Sugar	0.45	Glass products	0.69
Malt liquors and malt	4.06	Primary metal industries	0.28
Alcholic beverages, except		Fabricated metal products,	0.74
malt liquors and malt	3.62	except machinery and	
Bottled soft drinks and		transportation equipment	
flavorings	4.87	Metal cans	0.91
Tobacco manufactures	4.37	Cutlery, hand tools, and	3.30
Textile mill products	0.61	hardware	
Weaving mills and textile		Plumbing and heating	0.86
finishing	0.55	apparatus, except electric	
Knitting mills	0.96	Fabricated structural metal	0.35
Apparel and other fabricated		products	
textile products	0.76	Screw machine products,	0.33
Men's and boys' clothing	1.01	bolts, and similar products	
Women's, children's,		Metal stampings	0.38
and infants' clothing	0.62	Other fabricated metal	0.51
Miscellaneous apparel		products	
and accessories	0.61	Machinery, except electrical	0.83
Miscellaneous fabricated		Farm machinery	1.01
textile products	0.61	Construction, mining, and	0.62
Lumber and wood products,		materials-handling	
except furniture	0.36	machinery and equipment	
Furniture and fixtures	1.11	Metalworking machinery	0.85
Household furniture	1.22	Special industrial machinery	0.99
Furniture and fixtures,		General industrial machinery	0.77
except household		Office and computing	0.79
furniture	0.84	machines	
Paper and allied products	0.84	Service industry machines	1.12
Pulp, paper, and board	0.92	Other machinery, except	0.82
Other paper and allied		electrical	
products	0.78	Electrical equipment and	1.30
Printing and publishing	0.91	supplies	
Newspapers	0.18	Household appliances	2.27
Periodicals	0.95	Radio, television, and	1.44
Books, greeting cards,		communication equipment	
and miscellaneous		Electronic components and	0.90
publishing	3.15	accessories	
Other printing and		Other electrical equipment	1.14
publishing	0.40	and supplies	
Chemicals and allied		Motor vehicles and equipment	0.66
products	3.63	Transportation equipment,	0.37
Basic chemicals,		except motor vehicles	
plastics, and synthetics	1.19	Aircraft, guided missiles, and	0.30
Drugs	7.78	parts	
Soap, cleaners, and		Scientific instruments,	2.41
toilet goods	8.79	photographic equipment,	
Paints and allied		watches, and clocks	
products	1.32	Scientific and mechanical	0.98
Chemical products not		measuring instruments	
elsewhere classified	0.40	Optical, medical, and	3.67
Petroleum refining	0.40	ophthalmic goods	
Miscellaneous petroleum		Photographic equipment and	2.36
and coal products	1.44	supplies	
Rubber and miscellaneous		Watches and clocks	5.10
plastics products	1.30	Retail	
Rubber products	1.50	The average retailer spends	
Miscellaneous plastics		2 to 3 percent of gross	
products	0.73	income on advertising.	

NOTE: To those concerned about the high cost of sales in the United States, this point may be of interest: average per capita advertising in the United States comes to about $126.32 per year, or less than 1 percent average income per capita—a small token to pay for the most effective and least costly marketing system in the world.

way, each thrust offering new insights.

Some companies have no rule-of-thumb approach to their advertising appropriation. On the basis of much research, they adjust their expenditures to fit the problem at hand. This method is gaining favor and is used by a growing number of sophisticated marketers. Results dictate advertising budgeting in this case, not vice versa.

One sure way to demonstrate advertising effectiveness is through the use of a direct-response mechanism built into the advertisement, such as a coupon or a premium offer. The number of responses will reflect the impact of the campaign.

5. *Awareness data.* Lack of public awareness of a company or a product dramatically illustrates the need for more advertising. Suggest progressive bench-mark studies for the purpose of analysis, starting with low awareness.

6. *Most of all, whet clients' appetites by showing them better ways to advertise.* They are business executives. They will welcome ideas that hold promise and a fair return on their advertising investment.

Understanding Corporate Attitudes about Advertising Agencies

Advertisers differ not only in their approach to advertising but also in whether or not an advertising agency should be employed to do the advertising for them, as opposed to using their own in-house facilities or working on a project-to-project basis with outside modular creative service or consultants or with independent media-buying organizations. More than 80 percent of advertisers are in favor of having a single full-service organization at their beck and call. (Why else would there be more than 7000 advertising

agencies in the United States, many employing hundreds of people?) Be that as it may, considerable confusion exists among advertisers as to the functions of an advertising agency. Perhaps this is why some advertisers are skeptical about using them.

Here are the most common misgivings *some* clients have about *all* agencies, including their own, if they have any:

1. *Advertising agencies tend to overrate the value of their contributions.* True, some agencies are quick to take credit for success. On the other hand, there are clients who give none. They find it temperamentally difficult to accept that advertising can (as indeed it often does) send the sales curve spiraling upward on its own strength to a even larger extent than, say, modifications made in distribution patterns, sales personnel, management, the product, or packaging or any other changes instituted by the corporation.

2. *Advertising agencies do not get to the core of the problem; their sole concern is the preparation of ad campaigns.* Lack of information about the advertiser's more immediate problems (snags in production, inventory surplus, lack of distribution, financial matters) is often misinterpreted as a sign of indifference on the part of the agency. It is true, of course, that the more insights people have about a client's problems, the more effective their contributions will be. At the same time, it should also be pointed out that direct involvement in the client's problems does not guarantee high-quality service. The main function of an advertising agency is to produce advertising, present a fresh *outside* point of view to its client (preferably that of the consumer), and be fully conversant with the latest communication techniques.

3. *Advertising agencies should assume greater responsibility for sales results.* As a rule, advertising agencies, like lawyers and doctors (and plumbers, too) are paid for services on the basis of their efforts, not results. This practice irks many advertisers. They feel that good ideas are

worth more than bad ones and that compensation should reflect that fact.

4. *Agencies are unable to measure advertising effectiveness.* In some ways, this is true. However, considerable progress has been made in this area. Surveillance of advertising/sales relationships is growing increasingly sophisticated.

5. *Agency people are overpaid.* The salaries of creative stars often receive considerable publicity, partially owing to a knack for self-dramatization. By average standards, their salaries are on the high side, often exceeding $40,000 annually. Some make 2 or 3 times that. Such income levels may well be responsible for unconscious resentment between, say, a less affluent advertising manager and the person he or she considers to be a creative star in an advertising agency.

6. *Left to their own devices, agencies will recommend the services of highpriced suppliers to increase their commissions.* While many art directors or television producers, if given a free reign, do gravitate toward the most successful and probably the most expensive talent to execute their ideas, their motivation is not necessarily mercenary. The caliber of work is the usual attraction, not the relatively small increment on production expenses which agencies receive as a handling charge, usually 17.5 percent of costs.

7. *The traditional 15 percent commission on media costs encourages the agency to advocate the use of more expensive mass media.* For example, a buy into a single prime-time spectacular is suggested when in fact a well-planned but administratively more complex local daytime schedule might give the client better delivery at less cost. Or advertising in a mass publication is recommended when direct-mail or point-of-purchase material would actually be more productive from the client's point of view. Compensation methods, such as a fixed monthly payment, fixed payment charges against commission, a cost-plus arrangement, or project-to-

project fees, may offer a sound alternative to the traditional straight 15 percent commission system and may dispel some of the suspicions the client has in this area.

Understanding Individual Corporate Executives' Attitudes about Advertising

Anyone who has ever watched the expressions of people listening to an advertising presentation knows that no two persons' reactions to the same idea are ever exactly the same even if the people work for the same corporation. Chief executives probably have their own opinions about presentations (4 out of 5 chief executives participate in approving budgets), although their business judgment may compel them to allow their associates to speak up first. It pays to find out how he really feels about a presentation. If the chief executive has reservations, the presenter must address that problem. It is unlikely that many others in a corporation would risk contradicting a person who has the power to fire them.

Generally, if top management has an interest in mass marketing, it needs little convincing about the power of advertising. In some industries, such as tobacco and packaged goods, it is not unusual for the chief executive to have had that kind of background. A study by *Fortune* magazine shows that approximately 1 out of 10 top executives has reached the last rung of the corporate ladder through sales and marketing. This is nearly twice the number who have taken the legal or the financial route to the front office. With increased emphasis on marketing (nearly one-third of aggregate aftertax corporate expenses are chalked up to that activity in the United States), the trend is definitely toward putting more and more

marketing-oriented business leaders in charge of corporations.

Of all executives, presidents are most apt to delegate authority to others. Generally presidents tend to work through people and consider it part of their job to assign jobs to others. This is an important point to remember. While account executives are trying to explain ideas to them, doing their best to make a sale, chief executives' minds may be wandering off in other directions. They may be thinking about the caliber of the people responsible for the campaign in the first place. Probably more than anyone else present, they are aware that one way to improve the quality of performance is through a change of personnel or of the entire advertising agency.

Decisions made by a president, however, are not always as final as they may appear to be. In larger corporations especially, top executives learn to depend on the advice of their associates, many of whom are experts in their specialties. The chances are that the president's is a broad-stroke approach to problem solving, leaving the details of implementation to others. And so, back at the home office the same presentation may be studied by others in a company, this time without benefit of the agency. Thus, chief executives may be persuaded to change their minds several times before giving a campaign the nod.

The *advertising manager* may or may not hold the title of a corporate officer. According to one study, conducted by Robert M. Gray, former advertising and sales promotion manager of the Humble Oil & Refining Company, and Joseph B. Wilkinson, former vice president of McCann-Erickson, the odds are no better than 1 out of 3 that this executive will reach that lofty plateau. His or her functions cover a wide range of activities. According to a report by Bernard P. Gallagher, 1 out of 4 advertising managers is given the responsibility of preparing advertising budgets, but only about 1 in 20 is actually given the authority to approve them. In some companies, the advertising manager is instrumental in setting advertising policies. In

others, the manager is concerned mostly with the execution of a campaign. (In most corporations, however, the word *implementation* has a wider meaning than it does in an advertising agency.) Among the advertising manager's responsibilities may be the approval of ads and the media budget and, not infrequently, the weeding out process of advertising-agency selection.

In some companies, such as steel and oil corporations and public utilities, the advertising department is often part of an overall corporate communications or public relations group, with direct access to top management. It is not necessarily the size or the scope of the advertising budget that is responsible for this situation, but the needs and traditions of the industry.

Of all the people in the company, the advertising manager is most likely to be familiar with the mechanics of implementing an advertising campaign. He or she is the advertising expert in residence, so to speak. The manager may have held positions in copy, media, or marketing and thus be a fugitive from the publishing, public relations, or advertising fields.

The *marketing manager* usually works closely with the advertising manager (most corporations, to an even greater degree than their agencies, cultivate close integration between advertising and marketing functions. He or she is rarely as conversant with the day-to-day problems of executing an advertising campaign as is his or her counterpart in the advertising department; the manager's prime concerns are sales and distribution. However, 1 out of 3 corporate marketing managers is regularly consulted on matters involving budgeting. The marketing manager, too, is likely to have the president's attention in the selection of a new advertising agency.

The *brand manager* (product manager, division manager) is becoming increasingly important as the trend toward decentralization produces greater numbers of autonomous units within corporations. It is the brand manager's responsibility to submit advertising and marketing programs to the corporate headquarters for approval and then to use them as a basic guideline for most of the year.

The *corporate lawyer* has only recently become a regular guest at advertising meetings. Increased interference by governmental and consumer groups makes the lawyer's presence welcome and often imperative. The position of corporate lawyers is unique: they do not pretend to be creators of campaigns. Their direct involvement with the mechanics of execution is minimal. Their responsibility is that of being devil's advocates, guiding ads through the maze of various regulations, notably those issued by the Federal Trade Commission (FTC) and the Federal Communications Commission (FCC) in addition to about a dozen other groups that act as watchdogs of advertising practices.

And so corporate lawyers often find themselves in awkward predicaments. For hard as they may try to maintain positive attitudes, standing aloof from creative controversies, they are not always as successful as they would like to be. That is why many artists and writers feel that lawyers in advertising are spoilsports. But they often overlook the lawyers' main function, which is to avoid costly litigation and the bad press that usually accompanies it.

There is no reason, of course, why lawyers and creators of advertising should not be able to work together harmoniously. Both have the same goal: to create an advertising message that is both meaningful and lawful. Wise are the creative professionals who hone their skills by keeping up with the ever-changing advertising legal scene. New laws are constantly being formulated and interpreted by the courts as well as tested in the marketplace. Moreover, governmental agencies are paying greater attention than ever to recommendations of the industry's own self-regulatory bodies, notably the National Advertising Division of the Council of Better Business Bureaus, which issues its own newsletter, the American Association of Advertising Agencies (AAAA), the National Association of Broadcasters (NAB), the National Advertising Review Board (NARB), and local advertising review boards. And finally, there are the Postal Service and media censorship, both of which yield just enough power to stop advertising material from being published.

Most corporate lawyers will encourage suggestions from members of creative departments. They know that on occasion an outside point of view, subjective or not, can shed new light on problems. Furthermore, a few minor changes here and there in the campaign recommended by the creative department may be all that is required to make the ad pass official muster.

The *merchandising manager* is responsible for in-house promotions, dealers' aids, administration of promotions, and the like. He or she may also be called the *promotion manager*. In a creative presentation, the merchandising manager's department is most apt to look for tie-ins between advertising and merchandising.

Research and development (R&D) executives include the *new-product manager,* some or all of the people mentioned earlier, *laboratory engineers, production supervisor, medical staff,* and members of the *sales force.* Because of their background, people working in R&D will be concerned primarily with the product itself, perhaps more so than with its marketing aspects. A close rapport between consumer-oriented advertising executives and more product-oriented corporate technicians assures optimum success of a new product.

There may also be others present at advertising meetings to follow through on the various aspects of implementation. Among them are *assistant advertising managers, detail men* (brokers), representatives from in-house departments *(writers, artists, photographers), sales personnel,* and *trainees.* Generally, the larger the corporation, the greater the number of people involved in the marketing and advertising of the product.

HOW THE POLICY OF ONE COMPANY UNIFIES ADVERTISING: THE PROCTER & GAMBLE CREATIVE CODE

1. Housewives must be able to identify themselves with situations depicted in advertising, including those in slice-of-life commercials.

2. The housewife is a wife and mother, average in intelligence, below, or above.

3. She takes her job at home *seriously.*

4. Humor should be used carefully, and it should never offend the propriety of the average housewife.

5. Too much subtlety diffuses the message. Selling points should be made directly.

6. Positioning of the product is essential in overall marketing. Each of the competing brands of the company has its own copy platform. Tide makes clothes *white.* Cheer makes them *whiter than white.* And Bold makes them *bright.* Although advertising execution may vary from one product to another, it never departs from its preassigned role in the master plan. Variations are encouraged, executed, tested, and then evaluated.

7. For this company, television is the most effective medium. Approximately 90 percent of the advertising budget is spent here. Soap operas are favored slightly over game shows; housewives are depicted more favorably in the soap operas.

Corporate directives like this are often looked at askance by artists and writers in advertising agencies, who feel their creativity is being infringed upon. This need not be the case. The requirements laid down merely suggest a general direction. Within the guidelines, there is ample room left for creative experimentation. Few companies try out as many commercials in the actual marketplace as Procter & Gamble. Its management is always looking for new advertising ideas.

The Strategy of Selling an Idea:
The Pyramid Principle at Work Again

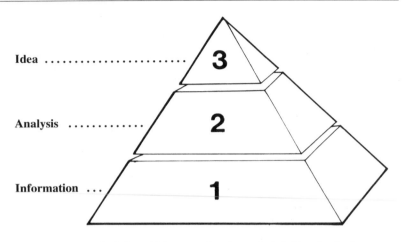

The pyramid principle, which proved to be so helpful in *developing* an idea, is also a useful tool in *selling* it. Letting the client gain an insight into the creator's thinking process shows how he or she has logically reached a conclusion. This lends an air of authority to the presentation, making it more acceptable to a business executive.

The Best Opener: What Is in It for the Advertiser?

Often it is advisable to outline from the client's point of view, in quick capsule form, the specific advantages of an idea before beginning a more detailed and lengthier description. Naturally, what the advertiser wants to know, first and foremost, is how the idea applies to his or her specific problem. To the practical-minded business executive, *the application of an idea is more important than the intrinsic value of the idea itself.*

Selling an Idea on the Telephone

Asking a busy executive of a corporation for an appointment over the telephone seems like an onerous task. Yet it may be the fastest, and perhaps the only, way to introduce an idea to the executive. For the most part, experienced business executives are more responsive to cold calls than it is usually thought. If executives have no time to see a visitor with something to contribute, they or their offices will probably make an effort to bring the idea to the attention of someone else. That is part of executives' job responsibility.

The question is often asked: Is a telephone call a more effective door opener than a business letter? Obviously, there are advantages and disadvantages to both. It is easier to establish a one-to-one relationship through a conversation than through a piece sent by mail. On the other hand, callers expose themselves to a possible turndown. This makes further overtures awkward if not impossible.

It is best to anticipate the general drift of the conversation even before reaching for the telephone receiver, possibly by putting some of the highlights on paper. Remember, however, that every idea has virtues as well as problems. Both aspects should be taken into consideration so that the caller will not be caught unawares.

As a rule, the fewer specifics revealed over the phone, the better the caller's bargaining position in later negotiations. The reason for the call is to whet the client's appetite, not to close a sale. It is best to omit the subject of remuneration at this point.

Remember that advertisers must *want* an idea before they decide how much it is worth to them. The more they want it, the more they will pay for it.

However, it is perfectly acceptable to inquire about the type of legal protection one can expect from a company, provided the idea can be protected (most ideas can be protected).

The following would be the structure of a typical get-acquainted phone call:

1. *Quick introduction.* Name, type of business, quick list of credentials to establish the credibility of the caller.

2. *Reason for the call.* Description of the idea, viability, type of problem it solves.

3. *Financial rewards.* Client's profit potential. However, bottom-line figures must be handled with care.

A knowledgeable business executive will view overly optimistic projections with skepticism.

4. *Icing on the cake.* Peripheral benefits.

5. *Asking for an appointment.* A brief outline of what you would like to discuss at a personal meeting (presentation of a sketch, outline, prototype, financial program, advertising support).

The client may suggest that you follow up the telephone conversation with something in writing. This is a reasonable request. You have nothing at all to lose and everything to gain.

A written document will reinforce your authorship and thus strengthen your legal position in the event proprietorship becomes an issue. And the client will have something to pass around to others in his or her organization.

Selling an Idea through the Mail

More can be conveyed in a letter than in a quick, perfunctory phone conversation. Here are a few comments about mail salesmanship.

That short documents are read and long ones are not is much too simplistic a statement to be taken at face value. If a message is interesting, it will be read. This is not to say that a writer should ignore all rules. Short paragraphs, succinctness, and underlining salient points encourage reading, but never at the expense of completeness. Enclosures on personal and corporate background, sketches, newspaper and magazine clips, comments by others, photographs, and a proposed advertising campaign lend credence to an introduction.

As in other forms of presentation, the letter writer should try to put the reader in a receptive frame of mind by arousing his interest in the first few paragraphs—preferably the opening statement. He should, if possible, strongly imply that he has a profitable solution to a problem which falls into the purview of the client. If the writer feels that the recipient is particularly suited to implement the idea, he should bring this to his attention quickly, listing reasons for his contention.

Some writers have a penchant for underscoring or CAPITALIZING the high points in their letters to invite scanning. This device works well in letters used in direct mail, as does the use of a second color, or even spot drawings. In some cases, such visual gimmickry helps to reinforce the message. However, a word of caution: Key corporate executives are quick to distinguish between "promotional material" and "personal correspondence."

Some writers prefer to send not one but several letters, mailed a day or two apart. The first letter may be the opener to stimulate interest. The next one goes into a more detailed description of the idea, the demand for it, urgency, costs, and so on.

How an Idea for a Television Commercial Was Sold over the Telephone
Even though the client had already approved another storyboard, he was told about a new and different idea for a commercial later in the day (the client accepted business phone calls at his home after office hours). First, he wanted to know why the agency felt this "new" version was better than the one he had already approved. He was told that this concept represented an improvement over the previous suggestion because it shifted emphasis to the interior of his store, particularly the ten shops, each with its own fashion point of view.

Could the plot of this commercial be explained to him on the phone, he asked. Yes. A cleaning woman notices a store sign at the entrance advertising 60,000 fashions. She shakes her head in disbelief; she needs to be convinced. So she proceeds to walk and ride the escalator through the store from floor to floor, room to room, counting aloud the number of suits. Her tally comes to 59,999. She stops, ponders, and finally says: "I must have missed one."

The client approved the concept on the basis of this 5-minute verbal description and without a storyboard. The commercial ran for 3 years during prime-time television in New York City and won several major awards.

Mr. _____

Department of Housing and Urban Development
451 Seventh Street, S. W., Room 9242
Washington, D.C. 20410

Dear Mr. _____:

We have studied your Federal Crime Insurance Program and feel strongly that it has great merit for a large segment of population subject to the problem for which it was designed. However, we found that viable as the concept may be, it has yet to receive the attention it deserves. Many people simply are not aware of its existence.

Through our contact with some of your servicing companies in this area, we gather that efforts have been made to market this product aggressively. Results, we are told, have been less than successful. As one insurance executive put it, "The program has not clearly demonstrated to the service companies that there is a large unmet demand for this product."

We think this is a premature conclusion. There is considerable, yet untapped demand for this type of insurance, particularly in high crime areas. For example, anyone living in New York City will testify that buying theft insurance today is prohibitive to thousands—and perhaps millions—of residents.

We believe that a more carefully targeted marketing thrust would better serve the interest of Federal Crime Insurance and at the same time rekindle the enthusiasm of the insurance companies assigned to implement the program. Apparently, most of your prospects are apartment and multifamily dwellers. It is this segment of the population on which advertising must concentrate. Those living in their own homes in low and medium crime rate areas already carry homeowners' policies. As a rule, they have little, if any, interest in purchasing additional coverage. Moreover, Federal Crime Insurance in these cases is in direct conflict with policies written by the very insurance companies with which you have contracts.

Therefore, we would like to suggest that you redirect your efforts on given target areas with a minimum of spillage through the use of tested direct-mail techniques and commence with a market-to-market roll-out program which expands on the basis of success.

For some time now, the writers of this letter have been active in the direct-response field, selling millions of dollars worth of insurance and information all over the United States. Our confidence in your program is such that we wish to make the following proposal.

244

We shall create, without charge, a direct-mail piece (consisting of an application form, letter, outer envelope, and enclosed response envelope) describing your program to prospects. The letter will be approved by you (and the insurance companies, if you wish) before we launch our initial test.

Once the mailing is approved, we shall select a test group of 10,000 to 20,000 prospects in the metropolitan New York and New Jersey regions, print the mailing piece, and mail it. This will be done at our cost and completely at our risk.

Recipients of the mailing piece will be asked to fill out the form and return it to us with the first 6-month premium. Upon receiving the applications, we shall turn them over to the servicing companies in the area. The insurance companies will then conduct the inspection of premises and issue policies to those prospects who pass the inspection. For each qualified prospect we shall receive a commission from you or from the insurance company equal to presently paid agents. We shall derive money from this program only through completed sales by our direct-mail campaign.

If the original test mailing shows that we can profitably enroll prospects, we are willing immediately to extend our direct-mail campaign to hundreds of thousands or millions of prospects, spending our own money and receiving compensation either from you or from the servicing companies only on the basis of actual policies issued.

We are doing this not only to make a profit but also because we feel that Federal Crime Insurance is of vital interest to homeowners and corporations throughout the United States who do not know where to look for adequate crime protection. Also, we feel that better-protected homes act as crime deterrents.

If you have any questions or if you desire more details, we would be delighted to meet with you at your earliest convenience to discuss our proposal at length.

Sincerely,

Stephen Baker
President
Stephen Baker Associates, Inc.

This twenty-eight page, two-color business-envelope-size booklet was designed to provide professional background information and fits comfortably the inside pocket of a jacket.

Cover

Stephen Baker

"Let Your Fingers Do The Walking"

Created for AT&T in 1962, this campaign is still being used extensively by all member companies of the Bell System. Today, the slogan ranks second in recognition.

Inside cover

Accounts, campaigns worked on (a partial list):

Chase Manhattan: "The Friendly Bank."
Smith Corona
Texaco
Folgers Coffee
Braniff International
L&M Cigarettes
Salada Tea
Johns Manville
21 Brands
Daily News
Sunshine Biscuits
Italian Line
French National Railroads
Jergens: Hand Comparison
American Home Products
AT&T: Yellow Pages
AT&T: Seminars, audio-video
Chock Full O'Nuts: Coffee, Nuts
Public Health: Air Pollution, TV
Chantilly Perfume
Gullistan Carpet
Barney: "Select, Don't Settle."
Avis Car & Truck Leasing
Monroe: "The Calculator Company."
Wohl Shoes
Fortunoff: "More For Less."
Ronzoni

Career, a brief glimpse: Vice President & Associate Creative Director of Cunningham & Walsh (12 years), Executive Vice President of Griswold-Eschleman (3 years), Founder and President of advertising agency. Nominated twice as "The Art Director Of The Year." Ad Age columnist. Author of 10 books. Over 60 awards in copy and art.

Liberty Life Insurance
Regional Transplant Program
Jaguar Car: "The Cat."
Western Electric
General Cigars
Southern Railway
Northwest Orient Airlines
Cook's Travel
McCall's Magazine
Childcraft

Page 1

Be the first on your block to plant a tree.

Let Barney's show you how to get rid of last year's fas

Two-page image-building ads, prime time TV commercials such as these—and the keen merchandising instincts of a client—helped Barney to become the world's largest men's clothing store. Cleaning

Page 2

...hions for fun & profit.

60,000 fashions—I can't believe it!

New Yorker Shop

1...2...3

59,998...59,999.

I must have missed one.

lady going through the store, counting suits, won the coveted "Best Television Commercial Of The Year" award in its category. It ran for 3 years, proving that retail commercials can have a long life.

Page 3

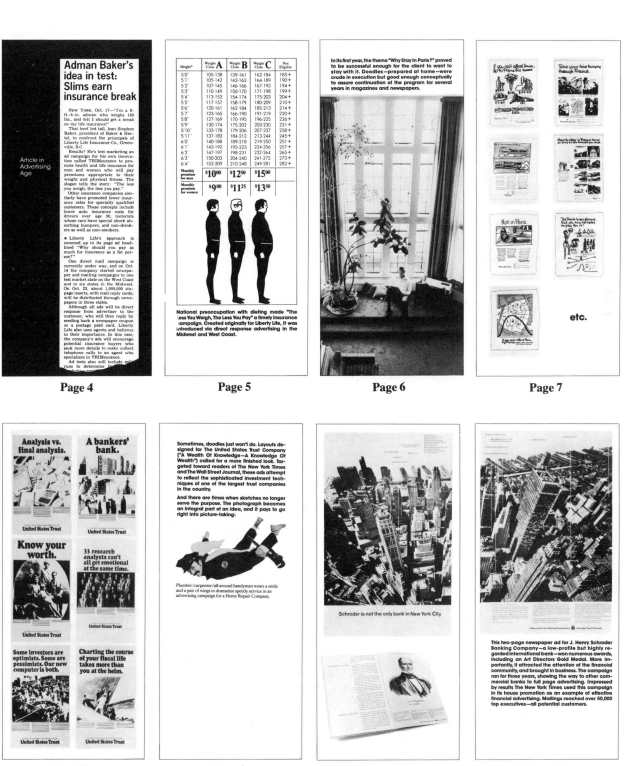

Page 4

Adman Baker's idea in test: Slims earn insurance break

New York, Oct. 17—"I'm a 6-ft.-4-in. adman who weighs 180 lbs., and felt I should get a break on my life insurance!"

That beef led tall, lean Stephen Baker, president of Baker & Hartel, to confront the principals of Liberty Life Insurance Co., Greenville, S.C.

Results? He's test marketing an ad campaign for his own innovation called TRIMsurance to promote health and life insurance for men and women who will pay premiums appropriate to their weight and physical fitness. The slogan tells the story: "The less you weigh, the less you pay."

Other insurance companies similarly have promoted lower insurance rates for specially qualified customers. These concepts include lower auto insurance costs for drivers over age 30, motorists whose cars have special shock absorbing bumpers, and non-drinkers as well as non-smokers.

■ Liberty Life's approach is summed up in its page ad headlined "Why should you pay as much for insurance as a fat person?"

One direct mail campaign is currently under way, and on Oct. 14 the company started newspaper and mailing campaigns in one test market state on the West Coast and in six states in the Midwest. On Oct. 23, about 1,000,000 six-page inserts, with mail reply cards, will be distributed through newspapers in three states.

Although all ads will be direct response from advertiser to the customer, who will then reply by sending back a newspaper coupon or a postage paid card, Liberty Life also uses agents and believes in their importance. In this case, the company's ads will encourage potential insurance buyers who seek more details to make collect telephone calls to an agent who specializes in TRIMsurance.

Ad tests also will include split runs to determine the

Page 5

Height*	Weight Class A	Weight Class B	Weight Class C	Not Eligible
5'0"	105-138	139-161	162-184	185+
5'1"	105-142	143-163	164-189	190+
5'2"	107-145	146-166	167-193	194+
5'3"	110-149	150-170	171-198	199+
5'4"	113-153	154-174	175-203	204+
5'5"	117-157	158-179	180-209	210+
5'6"	120-161	162-184	185-213	214+
5'7"	123-165	166-190	191-219	220+
5'8"	127-169	170-195	196-225	226+
5'9"	130-174	175-202	203-230	231+
5'10"	133-178	179-206	207-237	238+
5'11"	137-183	184-212	213-244	245+
6'0"	140-188	189-218	219-250	251+
6'1"	143-192	193-223	224-256	257+
6'2"	147-197	198-231	232-264	265+
6'3"	150-203	204-240	241-272	273+
6'4"	153-209	210-248	249-281	282+
Monthly premium for men	$10.00	$12.50	$15.00	
Monthly premium for women	$9.00	$11.25	$13.50	

National preoccupation with dieting made "The Less You Weigh, The Less You Pay" a timely insurance campaign. Created originally for Liberty Life, it was introduced via direct response advertising in the Midwest and West Coast.

Page 6

In its first year, the theme "Why Stay In Paris?" proved to be successful enough for the client to want to stay with it. Doodles—prepared at home—were crude in execution but good enough conceptually to assure continuation of the program for several years in magazines and newspapers.

Page 7

etc.

Page 8

Analysis vs. final analysis.
United States Trust

A bankers' bank.
United States Trust

Know your worth.
United States Trust

33 research analysts can't all get emotional at the same time.
United States Trust

Some investors are optimists. Some are pessimists. Our new computer is both.
United States Trust

Charting the course of your fiscal life takes more than you at the helm.
United States Trust

Page 9

Sometimes, doodles just won't do. Layouts designed for The United States Trust Company ("A Wealth Of Knowledge—A Knowledge Of Wealth") called for a more finished look. Targeted toward readers of The New York Times and The Wall Street Journal, these ads attempt to reflect the sophisticated investment techniques of one of the largest trust companies in the country.

And there are times when sketches no longer serve the purpose. The photograph becomes an integral part of an idea, and it pays to go right into picture-taking:

Plumber/carpenter/all-around handyman wears a smile and a pair of wings to dramatize speedy service in an advertising campaign for a Home Repair Company.

Page 10

Schroder is not the only bank in New York City

Page 11

This two-page newspaper ad for J. Henry Schroder Banking Company—a low-profile but highly regarded international bank—won numerous awards, including an Art Directors Gold Medal. More importantly, it attracted the attention of the financial community, and brought in business. The campaign ran for three years, showing the way to other commercial banks to full page advertising. Impressed by results The New York Times used this campaign in its house promotion as an example of effective financial advertising. Mailings reached over 50,000 top executives—all potential customers.

Page 12

In typical Phyllis Diller fashion, she struts back and forth the stage.

FOR YEARS PEOPLE MADE FUN OF MY BODY…SOME EVEN SAID IT WAS LESS THAN PERFECT.

Sound of laughter. She stops, addressing the audience.

I MEANT TO TALK TO YOU ABOUT THAT. BECAUSE I WANT YOU TO KNOW THAT I'M DONATING IT TO POSTERITY.

Whistling, someone boos. She turns, glares at someone.

OH, BE QUIET. I'M TALKING ABOUT MY KIDNEYS, EYES, AND ALL THE *GOOD* PARTS, SILLY. YOU SEE THIS DONOR CARD? MY NAME IS ON IT.

Close-up of Donor Card.

MAYBE THIS WILL SAVE SOMEONE'S LIFE. THERE ARE THOUSANDS OUT THERE WAITING FOR ORGANS…AND SOME DIE WAITING.

Back to Phyllis Diller.

AS FAR AS I'M CONCERNED, THEY CAN HAVE WHATEVER THEY NEED. AFTER ALL, I'LL BE GONE AND THEY'LL STILL BE HERE. SO WHY NOT?

Enthusiastic whistling, voices. "We want Phyllis Diller." applause. She musses her hair.

MY HAIR, ANYONE?

First stunned silence. Then boos.

Page 12

Page 13

Much can happen between a storyboard and the home screen. Close supervision of production values every step of the way is essential to insure quality of the final product. Shown here is a behind-the-scene look at the production of a 60 second spot, encouraging donations of organs upon death. Script was specially written for Phyllis Diller.

Page 13

Page 14

Conceptual explorations—that go beyond just making ads.

Why use words to advertise "New York's Picture Newspaper"? No-copy, all-picture posters for The Daily News were the first of that kind. The campaign won three Gold Medals in succession—a feat comparable to, say, hitting 60 homeruns.

"Grandmother's Day" conceived for the Fortunoff Silver & Jewelry Stores was presented to Congress by Congressman Edward Koch—just to make it official.

The idea of platform sneakers—together with radio and print campaign featuring tall basketball players complaining about their lack of height—was exposed to Thom McAn Shoes.

Page 14

Page 15

Oversized layout designed for Smith Corona pioneered a new trend in media buying: The 3 page fold-out magazine cover.

Cremation: Nature beckons.

Many people feel that the scattering of cremains at sea or on land is one of the most telling expressions of oneness with nature. In our plans for cremations — a selection of several plans for ground burials beginning at $275, complete — we include the scattering of ashes at a place of your choice.

Chapel Hill Cremation Service
1649 First Avenue
New York, New York 10028
734-9056

Can divided at center kept Folger Coffee fresher longer.

Trend toward simple burials suggested campaign on cremation for Chapel Hill.

Rocking chair exercise program developed with the University of Pennsylvania proved that it was possible to shed pounds comfortably.

Page 15

Page 16

Publicity through the years, solicited—and unsolicited.

Anny

The New York Times

Page 16

Page 17

Advertising Age

Newsweek

The Wall Street Journal

Page 17

Page 18

SELECT, DON'T SETTLE

Ad Daily

In the picture

Television Age

Page 18

Page 19

Trouble with 'Slice of Life'

Advertising Age

What Does a Picture Tell?

The New York Times Book Review

Page 19

Books authored:

Advertising Layout and Art Direction
Visual Persuasion: Effect of pictures on the subconscious.
How To Live With A Neurotic Dog
How To Play Golf In The Low 120's
How To Live With A Neurotic Wife
How To Live With A Neurotic Husband

Page 20

How To Look Like Somebody In Business Without Being Anybody
How To Be Analyzed By A Neurotic Psychoanalyst!
The Making Of A Television Commercial
The Systematic Approach To Advertising Creativity

Page 21

Case histories (a few):

The tribulations of a nut
Chock Full O'Nuts
Problem: Introduce mixed nuts in supermarkets.
Solution: Absence of peanuts (not genuine nuts) and therefore cheaper) and higher price suggested slogan: "The Difference In Price Is Peanuts." Ads and radio commercials featured psychiatrist (Viennese) and his patient, the Peanut (Deep-South) complaining bitterly about his being rejected all the time. Similar fate awaits him when therapy is refused for his not qualifying as a nut.

Sell wire, sell copper.
Kennecott
Problem: Increase sales.
Solution: Warn homeowners about the dangers of inadequate wiring (the electrical industry is one of the largest consumers of copper). Increase in sales made the client repeat campaign the following year.

12 movies in 6 months.
AT&T
Problem: Prepare a sophisticated presentation for executives on data communication—and meet a close deadline.
Solution: Design and build auditorium on top of a skyscraper in Chicago...provide multi-screen, audio-video facilities...produce a dozen movies...prepare a promotion ...all at the same time. This 3-day seminar is now in its tenth year, always playing to a full house. It is used as a master plan for similar seminars throughout the country.

Putting shelf paper on supermarket shelves.
Athena
Problem: Widen distribution.
Solution: Rename entire line. "Pretty Please." Make all packages look the same to gain visual dominance on the supermarket shelf by virtue of repetition. (6 to 12 facings). Present the program to supermarket buyers. Distribution more than doubled: six states were added in a single month.

Ride bikes, not cars.
(Name withheld on request.)
Problem: Midwestern gasoline company looking for a promotional idea during the energy crisis: one that would generate additional profits to service stations.
Solution: Sell bicycles to credit card holders. Arrange inventory, warehousing, and drop-shipping.

Page 22

Segmenting the money market.
Central National Bank of Chicago
Problem: Attract more customers.
Solution: Focus on young people from 21 to 31 ("Young Chicagoans"). Offer specialized financial assistance. Talk their language in newspapers, television, radio, and special promotions such as fashion shows in the bank's lobby. Campaign was so successful that it was franchised to other banks.

More suit for more money.
Howard Clothes
Problem: Introduce a more expensive line of men's clothing.
Solution: Use a different name: Alton Ames. Feature the mistress (a girl with a slight accent) of the mystery man in print and on television. Increase in sales was as high as 40% in some areas, after a six week saturation campaign.

"Give A Little Of Yourself."
N.Y./N.J. Regional Transplant Program
Problem: Persuade people to donate organs upon death.
Solution: Present an umbrella campaign to all foundations (kidney, eye, etc.) and regional programs throughout the country (more than a dozen), encompassing donation of all organs. Use Sunday magazine section in various areas to explain the program. Prepare print and commercial messages and get extensive free exposure.

Page 23

References (some):

Bueck, Charles
President, US Trust Company, NYC.
Buxton, Ed
Editor, Ad Daily, NYC.
Byrne, Jack
President, Jack Byrne Advertising, NYC.
(Ex-partner)
Chilnick, Lawrence
Director of PR, NY Community Blood Center, NYC.
Cunningham, John
Chairman Of The Board, Cunningham & Walsh, NYC.
Dane, Max
Doyle Dane Bernbach, NYC.
Danzig, Fred
Executive Editor, Advertising Age, NYC.
Dougherty, Philip
Ad Columnist, The New York Times, NYC.
Gosden, Freeman
Dart Industries, Los Angeles, Calif.
Greer, Peter
Greer Du Bois Advertising, NYC.
Johnson, James
President, Griswald Echelman, Cleveland, Ohio
Lois, George
Lois Holland Gallaway Advertising, NYC.
Mack, Ferris
Editor-In-Chief, Doubleday, NYC.
Newman, Samuel
President, Howard Clothes, Brooklyn, NY.
Pressman, Fred
President, Barney Clothes, NYC.
Sheridan, James
President, Monroe, East Orange, NJ.
Stern, Bert
Photographer, NYC.

Page 24

Inside back cover

Back cover

At last! A dieting plan that does not treat weight conscious people like a flock of sheep. "Personalized Diet" gives you an eating schedule that fits your needs, and your needs only.

For years, experts have been prescribing reducing plans that promise slim waists (along with a jubilant, newborn personality) to all participants, regardless of their personal needs. Modern research shows that this is an impossible premise. No two persons have exactly the same food requirements; patterns of overweight are as varied as fingerprints.

Why your dietary needs are unlike anyone else's.

You are a special person. **There is no one quite like you, unless you have an identical twin.**

Look at your image in the mirror. Your anatomy is unique. Nature may have passed on to you a legacy of heavy (or light) bones, a tall (or short) physique. You may have a tendency to put on weight fast (or slow), depending on your metabolism, and other factors.

Examine your body structure. Did you know that if you are a mesomorph (see chart for definition), your body can absorb more calories than your endomorphic or ectomorphic friends—and without the penalty of excess fat?

And that isn't all. Your age, too, has a lot to do with what (and how much) you should eat.

So does your routine of exercise (if any). Some people have a vast reservoir of "nervous energy" and find it impossible to stay put. They are the kind that want to climb mountains just "because it's

these", jump in a pool first chance they get, and enjoy long, long walks. (A 30 minute walk consumes 150 calories. A brisk stroll like that every day for a whole year and puff, there go 15 pounds.) These people are fortunate—the size of their girth does not depend on food intake alone. Others—perhaps you—are not so lucky.

Your health also plays an important part in your choice of the "right" diet. Your stomach does not constitute your entire digestive system. Your liver, kidney, pancreas—and even your glands—all partake in absorbing food. The condition of your skin, hair, and nails tells you about their performance—and most of all, your sense of well-being.

A crash starvation program may show results—but not for long. Worse still, an unbalanced, "desperation diet" may actually jeopardize your health (both emotional and physical). Any doctor will tell you that eating too little can be just as risky as eating too much. The body has no use for surplus fat—but it still must have its dose of vitamins, minerals, proteins, and—yes—even carbohydrates.

The psychodynamics of eating.

Your outlook on life affects your appetite. Are you basically shy? How much do you really care about your appearance? Do you enjoy a few hours in the kitchen more than anywhere else? Did your parents follow the "clean your plate" regime in your home? Does your craving for a meal originate in your stomach—or in your mind?

No two persons have the same mental approach to food. That is why some people have no trouble at all staying on a diet. Others must make an effort. Which type are you?

How "Personalized Diet" makes it possible to devise a diet for you, and you alone.

Only a few years back, the idea of a large-scale Personalized Diet program would have been a technical—and economical–impossibility. Not any more. Thanks to the marvelous capabilities of electronic computers, it is now possible to process complex information through machines in matters of seconds—and come up with the right answer.

For example, our nine computers at Princeton, New Jersey, have the capacity to absorb, "think through", and collate 452,000,000 bits of information per second. (The best part of the operation is that computers do not make mistakes. To err is human.)

What "Personalized Diet" gives you.

Now, electronic technology makes it possible to actually "compute" a personalized dietary program based on your answers (yes, all 140 of them—as computers "see" them on "Your Personalized Diet Inventory". Your total background is the key to the answer. Your height, weight, age, energy output, sleeping habits, exercise routine, metabolism, anatomical structure, attitude about food, family background, and eating habits are all being considered.

Neatly typed and bound in an easy-to-handle folder, "Personalized Diet" will give you a "master guide" to show you how you can lose weight effectively and safely. You keep this guide, it will provide you with such information as:

1. **Your Calorie Requirement** (different with every dieter)
2. **Your Ideal Weight** (depending on your height, age, energy)
3. **Your "Personality Profile"** (and how your present disposition affects your weight problem)
4. **An Exercise Program** (are you active enough? or too active?)
5. **Your Diet Duration** (reasonable time it will take you to shed pounds)
6. **Health Problems to Look Out For**
7. **Your Special Nourishing Needs** (are you depriving yourself from needed nourishments?)
8. **Your Essential Vitamins** (should you take vitamins? and what kind?)
9. **Foods to Eat**
10. **Foods to Avoid**
11. **Recommended Eating Schedule** (how often should you eat?)
12. **Tips to Make You Stay on a Diet** (it takes more than will power)

Years ago, to obtain such a personalized program would have cost hundreds of dollars. (No wonder, it would have taken large groups of people working for months to arrive at the answers.) But through our scientifically automated process, you can now have the same program for $12.50—or about the price of a couple of hard-cover books on diet fads.

Let the experts watch over your diet.

"Personalized Diet" is not some kind of an artifice. It is not a guessing game. To make sure our recommendations are sound and based on the latest information in the field, we have asked a group of eminent authorities to guide us in our task. Represented on the "Personalized Diet" panel are two doctors, a psychologist, a beauty advisor, a dietician, and a nutritionist. Just imagine what it would cost you to go for advice to each and every one of these people! Through "Personalized Diet" program, you can save that huge expense—and your time.

Meet our panel (from left to right): absorb 452,000,000 bits of information per second Our comp and devise an individualized dietary plan for every subscriber. No wis the time for all good and devis men to come to the aid of their party. Fourscore and seven years ago our fathers brought men to co forth on this continent a new nation conceived in liberty and dedicated to the proposition forth on th that all men are created equal. Fourscore and seven years ago our fathers brought forth on that all m that all men are created equal. Fourscore and seven years ago our fathers brought forth on that all m that all men are created equal. Fourscore and seven years ago our fathers brought forth on that all m

The rest is up to you.

The soundness of "Personalized Diet" program should be obvious to you by now. While we do not claim that "Personalized Diet" takes place of a long, day-to-day medically supervised diet regime (no dieting plan ever does), we sincerely believe that it is the next best thing available to dieters today—and one that represents a far more intelligent approach to reducing than any mass-produced diet fad on the market which ignores the individual problems of the participants.

Go to it. Fill out questionnaire on right. Enjoy the experience of losing weight.

See opposite page...

250

How the idea for the "Computerized Diet Program" was sold: this proposed two-page newspaper ad (shown here reduced in size) was set in type for the purpose of explaining the basic concept of a computerized diet plan to potential investors. This was not meant to be the final version—it served only to convey the idea.

Fill out chart. Put both chart and coupon below, in envelope. Enclose check or money order. Send it to Personalized Computer Service, Inc. You will get your computerized answer sheet (checked by our panel of experts) by mail. Please be honest with your answers. Computers cannot tell a lie.

Your Personalized Diet Inventory

Your personality profile
- [ ] Very outgoing
- [ ] Active outdoor enthusiast
- [ ] Prefer caution to confidence
- [ ] Ardent television watcher (more than 2 hours a day)
- [ ] Artistic
- [ ] Read more than a book a week
- [ ] Concerned with appearance only when with others
- [ ] Concerned with appearance all the time

Your sex
- [ ] male
- [ ] female

Your metabolism
- [ ] Tend to put on weight quickly
- [ ] Was fat even as a child
- [ ] Able to lose weight quickly
- [ ] Gain weight only when eating excessively

Your medical history
(for the sake of complete accuracy, only information based on a medical check-up will be accepted. Do see your doctor if you have any of these health problems.)
- [ ] Underactive thyroid
- [ ] Overactive thyroid
- [ ] Low blood sugar (hypoglycemia)
- [ ] Anemia
- [ ] Digestive disturbances
- [ ] Acute skin problems
- [ ] Ulcers
- [ ] Arteriosclerosis
- [ ] Arthritis
- [ ] Brittle bones
- [ ] Asthma
- [ ] Diabetes
- [ ] High blood sugar
- [ ] Gout
- [ ] Gingivitis (bleeding of gums)
- [ ] Had medical checkup in the last 6 months
- [ ] Had medical checkup in the last 12 months

Your weight pattern
- [ ] Used to weigh more
- [ ] Used to weigh less
- [ ] Used to be on a diet but gave it up

Your eating habits
- [ ] Have a large breakfast
- [ ] Have a large lunch
- [ ] Have a large dinner
- [ ] Take snacks often (3 times or more)
- [ ] Take occasional snacks
- [ ] Never take snacks

Your dietary control pattern
- [ ] Count calories
- [ ] Watch carbohydrates
- [ ] Take vitamins
- [ ] Take appetite depressants
- [ ] Follows protein diet
- [ ] Consume more than 2 glasses of alcoholic beverages a day
- [ ] Drinks more than 5 glasses of water a day
- [ ] Weight is under medical supervision

Your calorie consumption
(if you don't know, don't check)
- [ ] 1200
- [ ] 1400
- [ ] 1600
- [ ] 1800
- [ ] 2000
- [ ] 2200
- [ ] 2400
- [ ] 2600
- [ ] 2800
- [ ] 3000
- [ ] 3200
- [ ] 3400
- [ ] 3600
- [ ] 4000

Your family background
- [ ] Father was overweight
- [ ] Mother was overweight
- [ ] Grandfather was overweight
- [ ] Grandmother was overweight
- [ ] Food was important in the family
- [ ] Rather cook than do anything else

Height
- [ ] 5'2"
- [ ] 5'4"
- [ ] 5'6"
- [ ] 5'8"
- [ ] 5'10"
- [ ] 6'

Weight
- [ ] 100 lbs.
- [ ] 120 lbs.
- [ ] 140 lbs.
- [ ] 160 lbs.
- [ ] 180 lbs.
- [ ] 200 lbs.

Your sleeping schedule
(check hours per night)
- [ ] 5
- [ ] 6
- [ ] 7
- [ ] 8
- [ ] 9
- [ ] 10
- [ ] 11 or more
- [ ] take frequent naps

Your age
- [ ] Under twenty
- [ ] Under thirty
- [ ] Under forty
- [ ] Under fifty
- [ ] Under sixty
- [ ] Over sixty

Your favorite exercise
- [ ] Jogging
- [ ] Tennis
- [ ] Skiing
- [ ] Skating
- [ ] Calisthenics
- [ ] Bicycling
- [ ] Swimming
- [ ] Bowling
- [ ] Walking
- [ ] Waterskiing
- [ ] Golf
- [ ] Sailing
- [ ] Table tennis
- [ ] Handball
- [ ] Baseball
- [ ] Football
- [ ] Basketball

Your energy quotient
- [ ] Spends most of the day sitting
- [ ] Spends most of the day standing
- [ ] Spends most of the day moving about

Your favorite food
(check three only)
- [ ] Sweets and desserts
- [ ] Vegetables
- [ ] Salads
- [ ] Fruits
- [ ] Meats
- [ ] Seafood (fish included)
- [ ] Dairy products

Your favorite beverage
(check two only)
- [ ] Coffee (black)
- [ ] Coffee (with cream)
- [ ] Coffee (with cream and sugar)
- [ ] Soft drink (low calorie)
- [ ] Soft drink
- [ ] Beer
- [ ] Liquor
- [ ] Tea

Your anatomical structure

*Ectomorph has a linear, more delicate body structure with long arms and legs. He is "slender".

**Endomorph is characterized by a large body with short arms and legs. He is often referred to as "stocky".

***Mesomorph falls between the two types. He has good muscular physique and, in men at least, represents the ideal, athletically proportioned individual.

Ectomorph*   Endomorph**   Mesomorph***

Send in entire page

Personalized Computer Service, Inc.
444 Park Avenue
New York City, New York 10017

I am interested in finding out about my personal dietary needs. Please send me your detailed findings about me. If not completely satisfied in ten days, you will return enclosed check for $12.50

- [ ] check (for $12.50) enclosed
- [ ] money order (for $12.50) enclosed

NAME

STREET

CITY   STATE   ZIP

Send in entire page

"Personalized Diet" Service. We treat you like an individual.

Making a Formal Presentation

Important new advertising campaigns or new-business solicitations are usually presented formally. Key executives from the corporation and the agency may attend these meetings. Most of the meetings are held in the morning when everyone's mind is still fresh. There is a break for lunch, after which the group may reconvene.

Those who attend such meetings normally expect to spend the better part of their day there.

A typical presentation (formal, but not a new-business solicitation) may go something like this:

Preselling: Definition of the Problem

10 minutes

1. *Making everyone feel at ease.* Writing pads and pencils are furnished. Coffee may be served. Introductions are made, with people's job responsibilities briefly outlined. An attempt is made to break the ice. The general purpose of the meeting (a new campaign, a change in strategy) is stated in a few words, and copies of the agenda are distributed.

10 minutes

2. *Definition of need.* This is where the presenter subtly shifts gear: he or she is now beginning to lay the groundwork for selling an idea. However, the idea is not yet revealed. Building anticipation is part of good salesmanship. (Remember the pyramid? It starts with information, not the idea.)

20 minutes

3. *Definition of the target.* Sales goals are set. These may be long-range (annual) or short-range (for example, $10 worth of merchandise sold for each $1 spent in a local newspaper campaign by a retailer) or defined in terms of market share (percentage of the total industry volume). Qualitative and quantitative audience analysis follows.

10 minutes

4. *The product.* Strengths and weaknesses of the product are evaluated from the consumer's point of view.

Revelation of the Idea

30 minutes

5. *The creative platform.* The presentation of the big idea is the moment of truth: it is what everybody has been waiting for. You can unveil the entire campaign for everyone to take it all in at a single glance, with layouts lined up chronologically. Or, if you want the client to spend more time with each ad, you can hold the layouts up one by one. It may be a good idea to line them all up against the wall

30 minutes (cont)

to show the graphic continuity of the campaign. Ideas for television commercials can be conveyed with the aid of storyboards with or without sound accompaniment. Radio commercials can be presented in the form of written scripts or of taped demonstration recordings.

Revelation of the Idea

15 minutes

6. *Applicability of the campaign.* This is the time to show applications of the advertising theme, not only in the five major media (TV, radio, magazine, newspaper, poster) but also in special advertising vehicles. The broader the uses of the same basic idea, the more appealing it is to the client. Not only are multimedia campaigns effective, but they offer considerable production economies. The same artwork can be used across the board.

20 minutes

7. *Method of execution.* Samples of finished illustrations or photographs will give the client a fairly good idea of what the final product is going to look like. One way to do this is to ask the artist to do speculative sketches at less than his or her regular fee, but with the understanding that if the work is approved, he or she will be assigned to finish it. If such an arrangement proves to be impractical, the next-best thing is to show samples of the artist's past work. Pictures projected on a screen are especially interesting in terms of offering a change of pace.

Try not to enter a detailed financial discussion at this point. Costs may divert the client's attention from the creative material that is being presented. Reassure the client, if need be, that you will cover finances later. First, make sure that your audience goes along with the idea.

10 minutes

8. *The campaign as a solution to the problem.* Describe how the campaign answers the specific needs outlined at the beginning of the meeting.

Lunch

1 to 2 hours

A few words about lunch: It is better to have a short one, not much more than an hour, if you plan to continue the meeting. If possible, keep the lunch dry. Too many cocktails loosen inhibitions and encourage quick off-the-cuff question-and-answer periods which could be handled better around the conference table.

9. *Media schedule.* This covers the rationale of media selection, market coverage, reach, frequency, and costs. Media discussions are both the easiest and the most difficult to handle. Factual material is less exposed to subjective criticism than is a layout or copy. On the other hand, reams of statistics make serious demands on listeners' attention span.

10. *Budget analysis.* Since purchase of time and space takes up the greater part of advertising budgets involving important financial decisions, no media program is complete without a cost breakdown. Written copies of the cost breakdown should be made available. And another thing: avoid tunnel vision. Individual items should always be viewed in the context of the *total* budget so that they can be examined in their right perspective. A typical cost breakdown includes estimates on the following items:

a. Media placement (television, newspaper, magazine, radio, and so on)

b. Production costs (engraving, printing, TV and radio production, talent costs, binding, and so on)

c. Percentage of the total cost of production in relation to total advertising budget (10 percent, 20 percent, 30 percent)

d. Other expenses (research, sales promotion, mailing, shipping, agency commission, various service fees, per diem travel expenses, and so on)

e. Method of payment (first or fifteenth of the month, direct to media, and so on)

f. Advertising/sales ratio (if available)

g. Total advertising budget (for the fiscal year or on a seasonal basis)

Have the client set aside a fund for opportunistic television buys. Earlier in this book, the volatility of television costs was discussed. It is good business sense to be ready to move into "avails" quickly.

11. *Time schedule.* A typical breakdown includes:

a. Time required to prepare the cam-

Implementation — 35 minutes

[Courtesy of Jack Byrne Communications, Inc.]

Page Twenty-Seven (27)
ADVERTISING STRATEGY

RADIO
Roll-Out Area #1

	SEP	OCT	NOV	DEC	JAN	FEB	MAR	APR	MAY	JUN	JUL	AUG
PERIODS (TOTAL – 16-1/2 Weeks)	X TEN DAYS			–		X ONE WEEK		X ONE WEEK		X	X THIRTEEN WEEKS	X
AVERAGE FREQUENCY PER WEEK	40			–		40		40	–	50	50	50
COST/WEEK / COST/MONTH	SEPT. $35,140/week for 10 days or $55,570			JAN. $35,140/week for one week or $35,140				APR. $35,140/week for one week or $35,140		$43,900 per week JUN-4 weeks-$175,600 JUL-5 weeks-$219,500 AUG-4 weeks-$175,600		
COSTS BY QUARTER (TOTAL $696,550)	$55,570 (6.76%)			$35,140 (4.33%)			$35,140 (4.33%)			$570,700 (84.5%)		
COVERAGE	Average: 790 commercials per market 80% of TV homes 80% of radio homes											

Promotional calendar for a new product indicates radio schedule for a 12-month period in test area.

paign (research, copy, art, production, getting approvals, shipping, and so on)

b. Launching date of the campaign

c. Posttesting (audience studies, benchmark research projects, market penetration analysis)

d. Media issue dates (such a schedule can be projected many months or even a full year in advance.

If possible, familiarize the client with media-buying procedures and, in particular, the omnipresence of closing dates. Some magazines require material 2 to 3 months ahead of time. Television commitments made several months in advance usually produce better and less expensive results than do stopgap decisions made at the last minute. Production of advertising can take several weeks or even months, as in the case of a television commercial. An understanding client will take these facts into consideration.

12. *Reaction of the sales force.* There may be resistance from salespeople to the advertising program (for example, they may feel that direct-response advertising competes with them on commissionable sales). Show how the advertiser can cope with this type of situation (for example, a loss of prospects based on mail-in coupons could be turned into sales leads).

13. *Reaction of retailers.* The client may be interested in finding out about the impact that the advertising will have on retailers. Include in the presentation examples of joint retail-manufacturer promotions, cooperative advertising, use of local media (particularly newspapers, broadcasts, and outdoor advertising), new franchise operations, and other retail-oriented programs.

14. *Marketing penetration.* Examine the relationship between marketing and advertising activities, particularly insofar as the advertiser's distribution is concerned. Discuss with the client at this point, if possible, the distribution schedule. Anticipate the problems that go with changing advertising tactics. It is unlikely that competitors will allow their market shares to dwindle without putting up a good fight.

15. *Testing.* If a need for test marketing is indicated, describe the program in detail: specific markets, media coverage, costs, and projectability of results. Explain why you are recommending a roll-out program: it can keep the client from making mistakes on a larger and more expensive scale.

16. *Summation.* This is a critical part of the presentation and the one that is most apt to invite rhetoric. More than ever, the presenter must try not to succumb to such tempting platitudes as:

"This campaign may not win awards, but it will sell."

"You get what you pay for."

"Our cost-per-1000 figures will make your advertising dollars go further."

High-pressure salesmanship impresses some clients some of the time, but there are so many exceptions that it is safer to use a more subtle approach. Most business people resist being pushed into making decisions too quickly. Here is how you can bring the meeting to a graceful close and still encourage immediate action:

a. *Summarize the highlights of the presentation.* Show how the idea covers the problem, how effective it could be, the way it differs from competitors' ideas, why it is a good investment, and what the relationships are between advertising and marketing, between creative and media, and so on.

b. *If the client seems reluctant to approve the total program, present it piecemeal.* To wit:

A single advertisement (TV, print), not the entire campaign
The basic concept, not the implementation
The copy, not the layout
The layout, not the copy
The method of execution, not the concept
The media schedule, not the creative
Part of the media schedule

c. *Secure approval of the advertising budget.* This could prove to be the most formidable hurdle of all. It is at this point that a typical client asks for time out to mull things over at his or her own pace. The delay could hurt your bargaining position with media. So try getting approval on part of the advertising budget, for example, 6 months, a given period (back-to-school promotions, Christmas, and so on), or a given marketing area (one or two cities, regions, and so on).

Demonstrate how the campaign can be tested along the way by means of controlled experiments. A single television commercial run on a few stations (perhaps on cable television) could be an inexpensive way to throw out a feeler. Work out a complete market-to-market program. Introduce the client to the idea of conducting bench-mark studies to gauge progress.

d. *Secure approval on production.* It is usually easier to get the client to commit himself or herself on production costs, which are less substantial than media expenditures. Have the campaign approved in principle at least, so that you will have a basis to negotiate with suppliers at an early stage. As a business executive, the client will appreciate the cost advantages of making advance arrangements.

17. *Question-and-answer period.* The floor is open at this point, particularly to those who for reasons of protocol have not yet had their chance to express an opinion. A time limit put on the discussion will keep it from running over schedule.

Have the experts answer technical questions. Art directors are best qualified to talk about typography, media buyers to explain frequency and reach, production people to compare offset with letterpress reproduction, and so on. The client will appreciate getting information straight from the horse's mouth.

A good way to adjourn a meeting is to let everyone know precisely what is expected of him or her in the way of a decision. *Make sure that the client knows that the next move is his or hers, and that it is to approve the advertising.*

How formal must a layout be at a formal presentation?

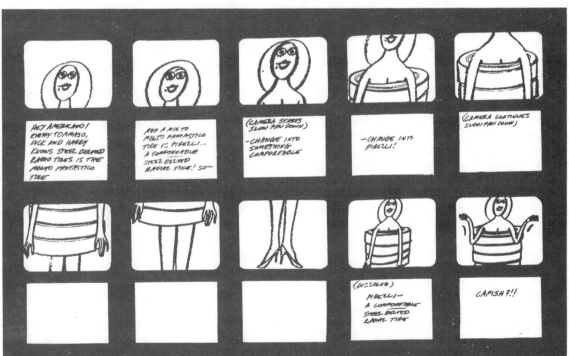

Formal need not mean tight, comprehensive layouts or finished art. This storyboard scribbled on a pad by agency president George Lois is typical of the way he presents his ideas to a client. It was one of the many suggestions he made to Pirelli Tires at a single meeting. Fast and prolific, this celebrated artist-writer has often been able to produce in person nearly all the creative material for as many as fifteen to twenty multimillion-dollar advertisers.

Psychologically, it is often advantageous to let clients in at the early stages; they enjoy the sense of personal involvement.

255

Making an Informal Presentation

By far the majority of meetings between agencies and clients are informal, often with only staff members present. Implementation of an advertising campaign entails a myriad of media, marketing, creative, and production details. It would be much too time-consuming for the top echelon to watch over each and every problem which arises.

It is not uncommon for an agency to have such informal get-togethers more than 100 times a year, not counting contacts over the telephone or by correspondence. Basically, there is little difference between a formal and an informal presentation except in matters of protocol. Usually, everyone is on a first-name basis, and conversation flows easily across the conference table.

Every organization has its own set of rules for the way in which such shirt-sleeve meetings should be conducted. It is interesting to note the differences that exist. As one moves from east to west across the country, an unassuming, "just plain folks" approach becomes increasingly evident, with California and Texas leading the way. Generally speaking, the younger the organization, the less apt are its executives (right up to the president) to stand on ceremony. Members of the entertainment world, fast-moving retail executives, and brash self-made entrepreneurs are most prone to make swift, off-the-cuff decisions even though there are times when a more deliberate approach would be useful. At the opposite end of the spectrum are officers of banks, insurance companies, and other stately institutions who feel more comfortable while operating within the confines of established corporate policies.

A typical agenda of an informal creative presentation may go something like this:

1. *Definition of the problem*. Reasons for the meeting. Discussion of the audience, marketing strategy, distribution problems, changes in public taste and buying patterns, new media developments, competitive activity, sales, and so on. Need for a new advertisement or a campaign.

2. *Presentation of the idea*. At an informal meeting, this is often left to members of copy and art departments, with the account executive present. Many decisions are made on the spot.

3. *Impact of the idea*. Impact on the consumer, corporate sales force, retailers, and other intermediaries and ways to measure effectiveness. Relationship between advertising and marketing. Is the recommendation consistent with corporate policies? (Will top management approve it? If not, why not?)

4. *Discussion of media and production*. Analysis of production costs. Names of outside suppliers (illustrators, photographers, television directors and producers, printers, models, and so on) are submitted for finishing layouts and storyboards. Estimates are examined not only individually but with regard to the total advertising budget.

5. *Schedule*. Closing dates in print and broadcast; time required for production.

6. *Legal problems*. Copy claims examined in the light of current regulations. Possible censorship problems, particularly with the broadcast media.

7. *Uses of the idea elsewhere than in advertising*. Various tie-ins, publicity, collateral and promotional opportunities.

8. *Summary and discussion*. Unless the meeting has been called to review ongoing projects, the client is asked to approve new concepts.

The Importance of Being Informed about the Client

As mentioned before, unfamiliarity with the client's problems concerning the company, corporate policies, products, markets, distribution channels, competition, and past advertising efforts is the most frequently cited reason for presentation failures, especially in new-business solicitations. Typical is the comment made by the chief executive of a truck-leasing company who listened to more than two dozen agencies expressing interest in his account: "Only two knew the distinction between renting and leasing a truck." Or from another advertiser: "Our new agency presented us with an idea we used 3 years ago." An extensive survey conducted by Edward Buxton among high-level executives of major corporations confirms this judgment: 76 percent of clients complained about soliciting agencies "not doing their homework."

In fairness to agencies, it should be said that this situation is often exaggerated in the mind of the advertiser. Knowledge of a client's problems does not automatically ensure creative brilliance. Still, many ideas remain unsold for lack of solid information, with loss of the client's confidence as the inevitable result.

A Whole New Ball Game: The New-Business Presentation

For most advertising agencies, the difference between success and failure lies in their ability to secure new business. Maintaining a status quo is considered an ominous sign in the industry. The inflation rate built into our economy makes it imperative for an advertising agency to show an annual growth of at least 10 percent in gross billing.

Increased billings generated from within (growth in billings and added commissions derived from swelling media costs) may partially cover expanding overhead. But there is also the attrition of clients (a fact of life in the agency business), which must be compensated for. Only a steady influx of new business will cover that loss. This is why advertisers, particularly those who do not require the extensive services of a major agency, often receive more than 100 new-business calls once the news of their availability has been announced in the trade press.

Clearly, long-established, advertising agencies (those in business for at least 10 years) have a distinct advantage over their leaner cousins in making new-business solicitations. They have the staff and the financial resources to put together a more elaborate presentation.

Not all agencies rely on speculative solicitations to attract new business. Quite a few, particularly the larger ones, flatly refuse to present a campaign based on what they consider inadequate information. The AAAA sides with them. Thus, some clients learn not to expect agencies to make specific creative recommendations in their solicitations. They rely on past performance as the basis for making a selection or offer payment for the extra effort. Cases in point are the $10 million National Airlines account, which paid $10,000 for out-of-pocket costs to each of the four agencies invited to make a solicitation; and Datsun, which gave each of the three finalists vying for its $35 million account a sum of $15,000.

Be that as it may, the majority of agencies still feel that speculative presentations, often surprisingly rich and expensive pageantries of layouts and storyboards, are worth the effort. For all one knows, from a practical point of view they may be right. Ideas for a new campaign are hard to resist for business executives always looking for ways to boost their sales.

A typical new-business solicitation is not very different from any other type of presentation. First, the problems are defined; then solutions are offered. Only the third step is unique to a new-business presentation, for it concerns itself with the introduction of the new (or so it is hoped) agency.

The focus is shifted at this point from the client's problems to the qualifications of the agency to handle the client's account in the following way:

Familiarity with the Product or Product Category The specific experience (packaged goods, fashion, automobile) of those assigned to the account is emphasized.

Noncompetitive Account For the sake of protection, most clients prefer an agency which has no competitive account in the house. But there are exceptions. In the absence of *direct* competition, as is the case with theaters (each play is a new product), publishing (books are one-time exclusives), or local banks and retailers (they sell only within their own trading areas), the agency may be asked to handle several "competitive" accounts. In fact, it may become sought after primarily for its expertise in a particular field.

Work Performed for Other Clients The majority of clients learn about an agency through its performance and the trade publicity which follows outstanding work. A series of ads (or even a single one) may catch the attention of an advertiser and induce him or her to pay a visit to the agency.

Account List The size and nature of accounts handled is a fair indication of the agency's experience, talents, and in-depth servicing capability.

Longevity of Accounts A quick turnover of clients may point to a few skeletons in the closet, particularly in the area of in-depth staffing, marketing know-how, and follow-through. However, reasons for client dissatisfaction should be examined for each individual case. Some advertisers are notoriously divorce-oriented in their business dealings, changing agencies periodically in the name of sound business practice (a questionable assumption, to say the least). To cite an instance, a $1.5 million New York–based coffee account came to rest (on occa-

DRAMATIZING THE AGENCY'S PACKAGED-GOODS EXPERIENCE
Lack of product experience did not deter Dancer Fitzgerald Sample from going after the $30 million Toyota account. After talking quietly to some ten agencies, the client narrowed the choice to three. As it happened, Dancer Fitzgerald Sample had built its reputation on campaigns such as those for Bounty paper towels, L'eggs pantyhose, and Bayer aspirin—important accounts but none that had anything to do with cars. So the agency switched tactics and put its emphasis on tough packaged-goods experience. Here is what Barney Brogram, national advertising manager for Toyota, had to say about his company's open-mindedness. "The fact is that automobiles, although they are a different thing, are bought by people who think the same way as those consumers who buy packaged goods." Sales went up by 18 percent during the next year.

257

sion for only a month or so) at no fewer than eleven advertising agencies in about a decade.

It bears mention that in the final analysis, agency-client relations still are directly traceable to the chemistry between people. Reactions to an idea can *never* be predicted with scientific accuracy.

The tenuous nature of the business is perhaps best explained by Charles Moss, vice-chairman of Wells, Rich, Green, Inc.: "It's a people business. . . . Relationships are a combination of many things—the presentation, the people, and basically a lot of instincts that are as much unsaid and unseen as sensed."

Size: Amount of Billing and Number of Personnel A healthy cash flow gives the agency the financial base it needs to service its clients adequately, maintain top professional talent, enjoy a credit rating with media (to contract for time and space without having to pay in advance), and negotiate from strength.

A word of caution, however: modest billings do not necessarily indicate a lack of talent or servicing capability. There are some excellent shops that stay small by choice. In this case, direct contact with principals may in fact improve a client's chances for getting better advertising.

Philosophy Most agencies take pride in their point of view, usually reflecting that of the founder or founders. The agency's orientation may be creative ("The most important part of advertising is the ad itself"), hard-sell ("It does not matter what the ad looks like as long as it sells"), tilted toward marketing ("An advertising agency must also provide marketing services for its clients"), research-conscious ("We like to find out first"), or full-service ("Large enough to accommodate all our advertiser's creative *and* marketing needs").

Stripped of the semantic nuances, two basic philosophical concepts emerge, *creative* and *business*. Even when there is a marriage of the two (always in the case of a successful agency), one tends subtly to dominate the other.

Facing pages (6 by 8 inches) make this handsome brochure a useful new-business tool for Cunningham & Walsh. Each spread represents the work done for a particular client. Photographs are in full color, printed on heavy, glossy white stock. The text is printed on light-brown rough-textured paper.

Members of the creative department discuss their favorite ads in this eighteen-page twenty-fifth–anniversary booklet of the illustrious Doyle Dane Bernbach advertising agency.

The entire twenty-page issue of *Ayernews* is devoted to showing the outstanding work this agency has done, with about 120 people working on the project for a major client, the U.S. Volunteer Army (spending around $50 million annually).

Making a Solicitation: Put It on Paper

Human memory being what it is, verbal comments have a way of sinking into oblivion unless they are reduced to writing.

Notes of paper, if nothing else, at least will give the client something to take back to his or her office and a chance to review it in privacy.

Moreover, writing imposes a mental discipline on the presenter, helping him or her to organize the material.

It should be remembered that most advertisers visit a number of agencies before making a selection. The average is five or six, but often it is many more. (Frank Perdue, the "tough man with the tender chicken," sat through forty-seven presentations in 7 months before deciding to go with Scali, McCabe, Sloves.

Another advertiser, Renault USA, considered sixty agencies before choosing Marsteller.)

Many of these presentations, although given by different people and varied in content, appear to the client to follow a similar *basic* pattern. So things can get pretty confusing. The advertiser may recall certain ads but not the agency that presented them, or the people who made the presentation but not the ads.

Even if the advertiser has taken notes during the meeting (not many clients do), who can blame him if he feels punch-drunk at the end of a very full day?

The structure of a written presentation may best be displayed as follows:

Book One

1. General review of the situation (market analysis, target definition, nature of problem, competition)
2. Market strategy (rationale for the approach)
3. Creative platform (the approach)
4. Campaign recommendation (implementation)

5. Media (type of media, vehicles, reach, time schedule, costs)
6. Research (before-and-after advertising)
7. Budget (Production and media allocations, the total budget, agency compensation, other expenses)

Book Two

8. Agency background (list of clients, tenure, amount of annual billing, product experience, campaigns, sales results, creative awards)
9. Client service organization chart (backup, lines of communication between client and agency)
10. Biographies (backgrounds of key personnel)
11. Brief statement about the agency's qualifications to serve the client

Book Three

12. Agency-client contract (agency functions, terms, starting date, cancellation clause)
13. Methods of compensation (fee or commission system, billing procedure, schedule of payments)

Other subjects may be added to the list.

The structure suggested above is divided into three sections. This is done because not all people present at a meeting are interested in everything. Junior executives or R&D staffers need not participate in making decisions about corporate finances. Nor do art directors or copywriters wish to get involved in the legal ramifications of an advertising contract.

How to Make a Presentation Brochure More Graphic

1. Covering materials, such as binding cloth, buckram, leather, plastics, fabrics, or metal, will give the binder a more finished look. Have the supplier make something special just for you. For example, in making a presentation to a fabric manufacturer, you may want to use the manufacturer's fabric for jacket material, for example.

2. The name of the client on the cover will make the presentation appear custom-made.
3. Large foldout pages bound in the brochure will accommodate oversize ads such as magazine spreads, storyboards, and charts.
4. Have "demos" reproduced on vinyl sheets.
5. Binders come in all sizes and colors today. Many can be made to specifications at a relatively low cost. Pockets can be used to hold full-page newspaper ads folded in halves or quarters.
6. A cardholder inside the plastic-coated binder will hold name cards of the agency or key executives, or both.
7. Insert tabbed index dividers for easy reference. They are available in a variety of colors.
8. Slip loose photographs or other illustrative material into acetate sleeves.
9. Use colored prints made on a color photocopier machine. These can be reproduced directly from slides and transparencies and enlarged.
10. Cutout magazine or newspaper pictures will enliven the message. All you need is a pair of scissors.
11. Standard wallpaper patterns will provide a touch of color.
12. For chart or display headings, use rub-on dry transfer letters and symbols. They provide an exciting change of pace from the body text.
13. Polaroid shots of the advertiser's product will strike a familiar note with the client.
14. Polaroid shots of people provide human interest. Include biographies.
15. The IBM Selectric composer is virtually a one-man composing room. Its fonts offer several dozen different sizes and type specimens. The same is true of VariTyper, another quick and inexpensive form of typesetting.
16. Have more than a single presentation brochure. Classify material by subject; i.e., use a separate folder for legal information, agency background, etc.
17. Offer to send presentation brochure by messenger—if carrying it is an imposition on the client.

CLIENT-SERVICE ORGANIZATION CHART, PREPARED FOR A NEW-BUSINESS PRESENTATION BY A MEDIUM-SIZE ADVERTISING AGENCY

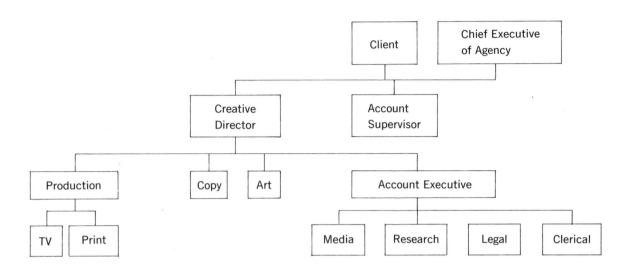

Implicit in this diagram is the fact that the client can touch base not only with the account group but also with other departments in the agency, including the creative. The main purpose of such an organization chart is to demonstrate graphically the range of services the client can expect from his or her advertising agency.

HOW FRIEDLICH, FEARON & STROHMEIER INC. TELLS PROSPECTIVE CLIENTS ABOUT ITS KEY PEOPLE

Bruce Friedlich
Chairman and President

Bruce Friedlich's career in the communications field has included publication, client and agency roles. Immediately prior to founding his own advertising agency in 1960 he was Director of Sales at Bache & Co., where he managed a sales force of 850 people in 65 offices, with parallel responsibilities for advertising and public relations. Earlier he had worked for Fortune Magazine for 10 years and was New York Manager, directing promotion, market research and sales for the magazine.

A graduate of Dartmouth, where he majored in sociology, Bruce Friedlich was elected to Phi Beta Kappa in his junior year. He subsequently earned a Master's Degree from NYU's College of Engineering, and has done additional graduate work at the NYU School of Business, Colgate, and the New York Institute of Finance.

For a number of years he was the president of his Dartmouth class. He currently directs the annual Dartmouth student/alumni career conference and is the Academic Affairs Officer for the Dartmouth Alumni Association of New York City.

Bruce Friedlich is an American Association of Advertising Agencies representative to the National Advertising Review Board, and a member of the 4A's Committee to Improve Advertising.

Martin Rowe
Senior Vice President/ Treasurer

During the growth period of any organization, someone must assume the very large responsibility of holding a tight rein on an oft-threatened galloping expansion. At FF/S, that man is Marty Rowe.

Author and executor of the firm's cost accounting and computerized time record system, he has enabled us to keep an accurate and efficient pricing system for all our clients, on an individual basis, thereby maintaining that delicate balance between service and cost.

Marty's experience spans nineteen years' association with advertising traffic and production. As Production Manager for the L. W. Frohlich Company, he was responsible for guiding ethical and consumer advertising for Helena Rubenstein, Parke-Davis, Johnson & Johnson, Procter & Gamble and Mead Johnson & Co. He has also supervised production on various children's and women's fashion accounts plus a number of industrial accounts.

Marty received his professional training at New York University and the Westinghouse School of Typography and Printing. He is a member of the Production Manager's Club of New York and the N. Y. Credit and Financial Management Association.

Dennis Webster
Vice President/Copy Supervisor

One of the pioneers of the agency, Dennis spent five years turning out creative ideas for Shearson, Newsweek, Fortune, Burns and others before leaving for a three-year hiatus with the Doremus and deGarmo agencies. Happily, he is now back doing business at the old stand. Among his earlier associations were the San Francisco offices of J. Walter Thompson and Fletcher Richards, Calkins & Holden.

His talented typewriter has also turned out copy for such diverse clients as Piper Aircraft, Great Western Wine, Ford, Pan American, Folger's Coffee, U.S. Travel Service, Rollei Cameras, Friden Calculators, National Distillers & Chemical Corp., Greenwood Mills, Shell Chemical and Pitney-Bowes. Dennis has won the recognition of his peers in the form of more than 25 awards for creativity in print, television and collateral.

Holder of a B.S. degree from Muhlenberg and a master's degree from the Columbia University Graduate School of Journalism, he started his writing career as a newsman, editing two weekly newspapers. Dennis commutes from his home in Chappaqua, N.Y., which gives him an opportunity to keep up with his insatiable 150-book-a-year reading habit.

Stephen Fenton
Copywriter

Deciding that a copywriter's life would be more challenging and satisfying than a career in law and politics, Steve left Syracuse University Law School for N. W. Ayer, where he worked on award-winning campaigns for Newsweek and AT&T.

Subsequent stints at BBDO and Young & Rubicam saw him writing for E. I. duPont, United Fund, Campbell's Soup, General Electric, Eastern Airlines, General Foods and the Rums of Puerto Rico.

Steve is a graduate of the School of Government of The American University. While there he was a part of AU's College Bowl Team, and served as a staff member for several Congressmen.

Since coming to FF/S, he's kept one foot in politics, taking his M.A. at City University of New York in political science. He plans to begin his Ph.D. studies in the near future while still writing copy.

Steve was elected to the American Academy of Political and Social Sciences, and serves as a Trustee of The McBurney Fund.

Freestanding profile cards (5 by 13 inches) with biographies and photographs printed on cardboard are part of the agency's new-business presentation kit (a box 14 by 17 inches by 1 inch deep). Ad samples and case histories are included.

ABRIDGED VERSION OF A PROPOSAL ON THE PROMOTION OF SPANISH GREEN OLIVES IN THE UNITED STATES

Prepared by Marsteller Inc. advertising to outline a major marketing and advertising campaign. Information was received in part from the Stanford Research Institute, in Palo Alto. The original document was eighty typewritten pages long.

(Inside page)

TABLE OF CONTENTS

INTRODUCTION

Purpose of the document: to provide a detailed plan for the marketing of Spanish green olives in the United States.

(Pages 3–12)

Review of the market for bottled green olives and canned ripe olives. Sales figures. Green olives outsell ripe olives 3 to 1. Trends. Seasonal aspects. Regionality. Trade margins. Consumer profile. Olive consumption and usage. Foods eaten with olives. Impulse versus planned purchasing. Consumer criteria for judging quality.

(Pages 13–17)

PROBLEMS AND OPPORTUNITIES

Problems Inflation-recession economy and how it makes consumers restrict purchases. Extreme seasonality, leading to uneven sales patterns. Distribution lags in East Central, Southwest, and Pacific regions. Lack of concerted promotion in green olives in the United States. No real Spanish-olive image in the consumer's mind. No ongoing research to provide market information. Consumer attitudes completely unknown.

Opportunities Integrated promotion –advertising –public relations program can increase public awareness and purchases of olives. Seasonal patterns allow concentration of promotional effort. Research will provide many answers.

(Pages 18 –22)

MARKET SELECTION

Market Selection
Criteria used to select four sales development markets: sales per capita, geographical differences, private-label share approximating national average, no more than 10 percent share of any single brand, type of retail trade in the market (large chain, small chain, voluntaries, cooperatives, independents).

On the basis of this analysis, these are the selected markets: New York: East (special reasons given for inclusion of New York); Jacksonville-Tampa: Southeast; Minneapolis–St. Paul: West Central; St. Louis: Central.

Use of control market for sales tracking and comparison with development markets. Philadelphia versus New York; Miami versus Jacksonville–Tampa; Kansas City versus Minneapolis–St. Paul. Comparable criteria applied in all markets.

(Pages 23–25)

CREATIVE STRATEGY

Creative Strategy
Changing eating patterns in the United States. The three-a-day routine is giving way to four-, five, or six-a-day meals. More and more quick meals are eaten on the run. There is more home entertaining rather than eating out. These trends offer a promising opportunity for olives.

1. To continue promoting olives as an ingredient in a wide variety of recipes and as a party food.

2. But also to expand their use to the area of an everyday fun food, requiring no special occasion for their enjoyment.

Olives are to be eaten whole right out of the jar as well as in recipes— for frequent snack occasions, not just for weekend parties. The creative strategy is designed to take olives beyond a limited, specialized status into the category of finger food, which is so popular with people of all ages in contemporary American life.

To accomplish this, the creative approach endows olives with a happy, fun-oriented personality. The association should be pleasurable and exciting, offering a joyous taste experience. It is this kind of image which triggers so much impulse buying. The copy theme itself must depart from conventional food appeals and rapidly create high awareness.

All the above objectives and requirements are met by these three simple words: "Olive it up!"

Like many successful advertising campaigns, this concept is based upon an already-familiar expression, "Live it up." This unexpected variation has a high impact value and lasting memorability. Quick, short, and charged with impact, this theme lends itself to endless interpretation in *all* media.

(Pages 26–38)

MEDIA

Media Objectives To reach segments of the market responsible for grocery purchases; to concentrate advertising during peak selling periods for olives; to select media which can be rolled out to any market and eventually used nationally.

Strategy Major portion of the media dollars to be spent on television. Reasons: the prime purchasers of groceries are women, and 89 percent of all food purchases in supermarkets are made by them.

A national study of olives shows the following usage of olives, based upon women aged 25 to 54 as 100 percent of the total market:

Age	Percent
25–34	27
35–44	38
45–54	35
	100

Therefore, the target audience for the television campaign, against which reach and cost-efficiency measurements are to be made, are women aged 25 to 54. Thirty-second announcements are purchased in all time periods to allow the broadest possible exposure, representing 225 to 250 gross rating points per week, for 4 weeks. It is estimated that each 4-week advertising schedule will deliver approximately 95 percent household reach and 9.68 frequency. Two 3-week thrusts are planned with a 3-week hiatus between flights, for an 8-week total advertising period. Daytime, early-fringe, early-news, prime-time, late-news, and late-night schedule will be used.

Supporting this schedule are newspapers and bus posters. In addition, 400-line ads running once a week for 5 of the 8 weeks on the food page of major dailies will be scheduled. Moreover, for 1 month 100 buses will carry the Spanish-olive message in New York City in the spring. If this addition to the total media mix proves successful in New York, it will be added to other markets.

(A schedule for each development and control market including names of new newspapers, circulation, size and number of ads, costs, time periods, number of spot announcements, type, size, number, and costs of bus posters follows.)

(Page 39)

(Pages 40–47)

FLOW CHART

SALES PROMOTION

Objectives To promote interest on the consumer and trade level, supply all levels of retail trade with sales aids, and gain trade cooperation.

Strategies Test a newspaper-distributed coupon. Merchandise this campaign to the trade to gain active in-store cooperation. Provide a complete package of point-of-sale and selling materials. Conduct meetings in the sales development markets to acquaint private-label trade with the current plan and keep all the importers and distributors apprised.

Detailed description of the 10-cents-off coupon, choice of newspapers (using the St. Louis area as a testing ground), and employment of a coupon clearance house (probably A. C. Nielsen) to handle detailed work for this effort and supply statistical analysis of redemption to check effectiveness. Costs per consumer, retailer, and redemption service house; also cost of redemption based upon two insertions (multiply cost of coupon by 2 percent of the total circulation of the newspaper). If the coupon program proves to be successful, a roll-out program is contemplated.

In-Store Materials Price channel strips, danglers and wobblers, shelf talkers, case curtains (poster design repeated over and over on a roll of paper).

Selling Materials to Equip Those Selling to the Trade or the Store Manager Sales brochure (four-page full-color piece with pockets to hold various plan details and point-of-sale samples), letterheads (colorful reproduction of the campaign theme "Olive It Up!"), TV photoboards (full-color storyboards with a brief selling message), reprints of newspaper ads, reproduction of bus cards, and samples of advertising schedules.

Market Meetings In each market, prior to the advertising start date, two meetings will be held, one for importers and distributors who have branded merchandise on the market and an additional meeting to introduce the Spanish Green Olive campaign to the retailers who have private labels.

Measurement Research will be conducted in the four markets to determine actual usage of promotional materials. In addition, agency personnel will conduct in-person field checks in order to gain firsthand knowledge of the results of the overall plan.

Costs Budget for sales promotion materials and redemptions.

(Pages 48–60)

MARKETING RESEARCH

Consumer-tracking Study To measure the change in consumer usage and attitudes toward Spanish olives in the four sales development markets. The study would track consumer's usage behavior, purchase behavior, advertising awareness, and attitude change during a period running from preadvertising through both major advertising flights. Three phases of interviewing are planned: a preadvertising bench-mark study against which subsequent usage and attitudinal data can be evaluated; and two postwaves, one after each major advertising–promotion flight.

The tracking data will be obtained for all four sales development markets. They will also be obtained for a control market for which no advertising-promotion campaign is being planned.

A total of 250 telephone interviews conducted in each of the five markets per wave will allow a representative sample with a maximum range of statistical variance of 8 percent (plus-and-minus leeway) at the 95 percent confidence level. Usage of 60 percent of past 3 months will be assumed. Schedule of interviews, timing, and costs.

Specifically, the following information will be investigated through research:

Uses of olives by size, color, and type
Frequency of use
Who uses and who uses most
Occasions of use and how used
Purchase and repurchase data
Brand awareness (aided and unaided)
Brand preferences
Advertising awareness
Advertising–point-of-sale recall
Awareness of an attitude toward green
  olive origin and Spanish origin
Coupon redemption
Key demographic data

SAMI (Sales Areas Marketing, Inc.)

(Page 61)

Budget	Recapitulation
Media	$741,860
Production	63,140
Advertising subtotal	$805,000
Sales promotion	35,000
Research	60,000
Total	$900,000 *

*Includes agency commission of 15 percent.

It was agreed that the agency would be paid in ten equal installments during the period March 1–December 31 of this year.

(Page 62)

TIMETABLE

Various start-up activities predicated on approval of the plan.

Activity	Due Date (1975; Week of)
Marketing plan presentation	February 18
Copy test start	February 24
Copy test results; start production	March 10
National survey start	March 17
SAMI (start of monthly research)	March 31
Marketing tracking study; bench mark	April 21
National survey results	April 21
Advertising start	May 12

NOTE: This timetable covers the start-up period. As progress is made, a complete 12-month timetable is readied.

(Pages 63–80)

APPENDIX

Three-column, 135-line newspaper mat ads, one featuring a 10-cents-off offer.

Supermarkets were encouraged to put up display islands, stacking the product.

Shelf talker printed in green, red, and black.

T-shirt, button, and the ever-popular frisbee, each featuring the advertising slogan "Olive It Up."

Pocket folder holds reprints of advertising and promotional material.

Retailers were told about the television campaign featuring Charo, the vivacious "cuchi-cuchi" girl whose Spanish origin made her a natural choice for the role of spokeswoman for this product.

Type of Presentation: To Each His Own

Ideas should be presented in a rational, businesslike manner to a client; this is hardly the time for histrionics. As in everything else, style must never be allowed to get in the way of the substance of the presentation. Having said that, we are now in a position to examine the other side of the coin. Obviously, there is one. A stand-up presentation going on for several hours can try the patience of even the most stoic of audiences.

In that case, almost any change of pace will be welcome.

Before you decide on the type of approach you wish to take, a little soul searching may be in order. Examine these aspects of the presentation:

1. *Length of speech.* Good speakers can hold their own for an hour at the most; 15 to 30 minutes are usually adequate.

2. *Type of delivery.* Individuals as well as corporations have preference as to the type of presentations they like to listen to. Generally speaking, those in the music business use their ears as well as their eyes in evaluating ideas; toy manufacturers are accustomed to dealing with three-dimensional prototypes; bankers and insurance executives are more willing to bear with long-range financial projections than, say, retail executives eager to look for immediate results (AT&T has been known to set marketing directions as far as 10 years ahead); fashion manufacturers are artistically inclined; and people in entertainment appreciate showmanship, even a touch of humor.

3. *Time available.* Many executives plan their appointments far in advance, sometimes on an hourly basis. It is an imposition to ask them to stay at a meeting that runs over the schedule. If time is too short to do justice to the idea, it may be better to set up another meeting.

4. *Subject matter.* Obviously, the presentation of a single ad takes less time than that of an entire campaign. Because of its complexity, the unveiling of a new marketing or media strategy usually requires greater effort than most other parts of a normal advertising presentation.

5. *Individual preferences.* Every speaker has his or her own feelings about making a presentation. Some shun visual aids for fear of losing personal contact with the audience, particularly if there are slides which must be shown in a dark room. Others make lavish use of graphic material. Then there are those who prefer to read their speeches from a script. Others look for spontaneity and, in fact, encourage interruptions from the floor to generate a discussion.

6. *Formal vs. informal.* Subject should not be the only deciding factor in structuring a meeting. People are more important. For reasons best known to themselves, some individuals are averse to rigid, formal presentations; they prefer the easy atmosphere of give and take, making contributions on the spur of the moment. Others listen quietly and form judgments at a more deliberate pace.

How to Liven Up a Presentation

Here are a few good ways to break up the monotony:

1. *Alternate speakers.* Have the experts cover their respective fields. One person, the chief executive or an account supervisor, can make the introductions and act as a master of ceremonies.

2. *Use sound: music, sound effects, taped interviews (with consumers, retailers, and so on), spot announcements (by professionals).* The recorded human voice has a ring of authenticity; comments made by outsiders lend credibility to the presentation. Whenever possible, use demos for voice and music. If they are rough cuts, say so before the client starts wondering about the quality of reproduction. More carefully executed demos will probably create a better impression, but talent and studio rent can be expensive. Still, there are many agencies which in collaboration with a producer take a calculated risk with a nearly finished or finished commercial.

You may want a piano or an organ in the conference room on which to play live music for a client. Look for singers and musicians among your own employees; their presence can add a homey touch to the proceedings.

3. *Hold the meeting in some place outside your regular conference room.* Hotel rooms, theaters, auditoriums, and even nightclubs are available for presentation purposes in all major cities. Many of these places have their own built-in audio-video facilities: screens, microphones, both 16- and 35-millimeter projectors (with a union operator), stereo sound systems, and often elaborate platform arrangements that serve as a stage setting for fairly good-sized casts.

Depending upon your time and budget, you may even want to try your luck at out-of-the-way, exotic places. Airplanes, pullman cars, orchards (used once for a presentation to an association of citrus-fruit growers), country clubs (most are eager to accommodate business groups), beaches, foreign cities, private homes, art galleries, television stations, and boats (a yacht accommodating 250 people to take a 4-hour cruise around Manhattan can be rented for $2000)—all have been used to provide pleasant surroundings for new-business solicitations.

4. *Show; do not tell.* As mentioned before, some speakers, for personal reasons, are wary of graphic aids. However, there is little doubt that the eyes have it over the ears. (The U.S. Department of the Navy reports that in its training programs it uses 20 percent audio and 80 percent video on which to convey the message.) Charts, magnetic boards, blackboards, oversize sketch pads, cork panels to tack drawings), and easels all are useful in providing vi-

sual spice to what could otherwise turn into a humdrum lecture.

It is also relatively inexpensive to have (buy, rent, or lease) a slide projector. Layouts, pictures of agency personnel, and samples of artwork can be thrown on the screen many times enlarged. Also impressive are the newly developed projection *systems* which make possible smooth transitions between each picture (dissolves, fades, and so on) and synchronized sound (using magnetic sound projectors) with up to a 140-slide capacity. In addition to slide projectors, of course, there are a number of easy-to-handle movie projectors that enable the speaker to use highly sophisticated audio-video techniques with a relatively small investment.

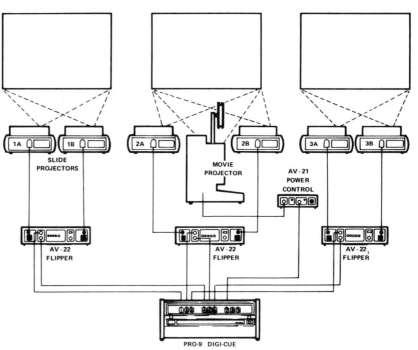

Not every agency can afford, or feels it is necessary, to use multi-image presentations. Some do, however, and with good results. Slide projectors can be programmed so that the images projected on multiscreens offer an illusion of movement. Shown here is a projector-and-screen layout, set up by Wollensak 3M Company. Six projectors and one movie projector, commanded by a single keyboard and cued to an audio track, case images on three screens simultaneously or separately.

Even the roughest storyboard takes on a different hue when projected on a large screen, with music or voice-over used as a bridge between frames. These sketches were part of a presentation made by Young & Rubicam for Travelers Insurance Company.

Elaborate audio-video facilities are used by the McCann-Erickson advertising agency in New York. Multi-image projection systems, some combining four slide projectors and two 16-millimeter movie cameras, are hooked up to remote-control consoles for optical effects, making it possible for the agency to prepare sophisticated audio-video demos. Mixers can handle four-piece musical ensembles (for example, piano, bass, drums, and guitar) plus a vocal arrangement using three separate microphone inputs. The agency's own closed-circuit video system covers several offices in the building as well as clients' headquarters to save time in getting approvals. The agency maintains six miniauditoriums for presentations.

How the "Let Your Fingers Do the Walking" Campaign Was Presented to the American Telephone & Telegraph Company

Setting the Tone

Presentation was made in a large oval-shaped conference room at the New York office of Cunningham & Walsh Inc., with executives from the client and the agency. The meeting began at 9:30 A.M. and lasted, as planned, until noon.

More than seventy comprehensive sketches of magazine ads, posters, store decals, point-of-sale material, direct-mail pieces, television commercials, promotional giveaway items, material for press kits, merchandising aids, napkins (for use in AT&T cafeterias), tent cards (to put on dining tables), and other material were shown. The layouts were tacked to a floor-to-ceiling corkboard wall and divided by categories. During the first part of the meeting, all advertising material was kept hidden behind a black opaque drapery so that there would be no distraction.

The atmosphere was informal; client and agency could look back to a long and satisfying business relationship. Everyone in the room was on a first-name basis; many people had known each other for years. However, it was obvious from the beginning that this conference was scheduled to be all business. The client made no secret of his growing frustration with the member companies of the Bell System that as yet had to approve a single umbrella theme for their local advertising campaigns. The client expressed hope (under the circumstances, "hope" sounded rather commanding) that the agency's proposal for a new campaign would provide him with the means to overcome this obstacle.

The conference opened on a light note with apologies from the agency for the haggard look of some of its people present, brought on, the client was told, by many a sleepless night agonizing over the creative dilemma.

Establishing Credibility

1. Past campaigns were reviewed. Lettered on cardboard was a list of slogans used until now:

Find It Fast
Wolley Segap[2] Says
Smart Shopper Look . . .
Why Are the Yellow Pages Yellow?
Look with Luke
Nine out of Ten People Look . . .
Nine-and-a-half out of Ten People Look . . .

2. Proofs of previous magazine campaigns were exhibited. The agency pointed out that

[2]Yellow Pages spelled backward.

Establishing Credibility

these always fared well in Starch readership studies.

3. However, the agency shared the client's opinion that a national thrust based upon a single and consistent theme would greatly enhance the impact of an advertising campaign for the entire Bell System.

4. The client was informed that the advertising theme about to be shown was copy-tested not only with consumers but also with Yellow Pages advertisers (who spend more than $1 billion a year on display and the ubiquitous one-line ads in this medium). The proposed new campaign (not yet revealed) was compared with the old one by an outside impartial research organization. More than 1000 interviews were conducted and processed. The results appeared to show great promise.

Revealing the Idea

5. Now the black drapery was pulled off the wall. Bursting into sight were the graphic elements of the proposed new advertising campaign: the "Let Your Fingers Do the Walking" slogan. This was a high point of the meeting. The sound of the theme song filled the room. Two attractive girls from the June Taylor Dancers came through the door, passing out "Let Your Fingers Do the Walking" buttons and sixty-page copies outlining the campaign, along with photostatic reproductions of the ads. Both girls wore tight-fitting yellow leotards designed specially for the occasion. A huge cutout black silhouette of a hand reaching from the shoulders down to the heels covered the back of the costumes, illustrating the Walking Fingers concept.

6. There followed a short discussion regarding the various applications of the Walking Fingers theme, in all media.

Implementation

7. Presentation of a full media schedule for a 6-month period followed. A 60 percent of television budget was recommended. An experimental black-and-white commercial (shot for $500 on 16-millimeter film) was shown. Storyboards of subsequent commercials demonstrated the flexibility of the campaign and the ease with which new ads could be created for future use. Written copy of a detailed budget breakdown was passed around the table.

8. The use of a picture of the Walking Fingers was proposed as an emblem to appear in all Yellow Pages advertising for graphic consistency.

9. The agency recommended two bench-mark

studies, to be conducted 6 months apart, to measure the change in public awareness as a result of the campaign.

10. It was suggested that a national conference be held as soon as possible, to be followed by a series of regional conferences, to discuss with the member companies the change in the advertising approach. (As it happened, nineteen of the

twenty-one Bell System members adopted the campaign within a few months, and the other two soon after.)

11. The client approved the ''Let Your Fingers Do the Walking'' campaign on the spot, expressing his appreciation for the effort that was put into it.

Lunch followed.

After 15 years of usage, the Walking Fingers became the official trademark of the Yellow Pages, appearing in all its advertising and promotional material. It ranks between first and second on nationwide unaided-recall tests, and the campaign appears in seven foreign countries.

Shown here are an outdoor poster and logos supplied by the parent company to its members. Today, in the words of AT&T, ''The emblem is meant to be generic to the entire telephone industry.''

Chapter Fifteen
It Pays to Develop a Creative Mind

The reader at this point may ponder and ask: "But is "being creative" worth all the bother?" And bother it is. *The Systematic Approach to Advertising Creativity* makes no false pretenses with regard to the intellectual effort needed to produce workable ideas.

And yet, speaking not only for himself but also for hundreds of others who spend much of their waking (and sometimes sleeping) hours striving to come upon the big idea, this writer can only answer the question, "Is it worth all the bother?" with a resounding "Oh, yes." This chapter briefly tells why.

Creativity Is Money in the Bank

Here is a simple but important by-product of putting one's wits to productive use: *Creativity is well paid.* Very well, indeed. The table on the following page, based upon the findings of one of the largest advertising employment placement agencies in the country, Jerry Fields Associates, tells something of the high premium placed on creativity in ad-

vertising. (The table excludes the usual fringe benefits such as profit sharing, pension plans, and expense accounts.) It is interesting to note that these salaries are close to, and in some cases even surpass, those of people in top management (particularly in small and medium agencies), not excluding the person in the front office, the president.

With high earning power goes prestige; a large paycheck invites authority. Nearly all creative directors in advertising agencies carry the title of vice president on their business cards. And that is only part of the story. Most advertising agencies today are started by creative people, usually art and copy (perhaps with a third party representing management to tie all the loose ends together).

Equally reassuring is the fact that a creative reputation has considerable longevity. On and on lingers this honorific appellation, for many years and sometimes for a lifetime. The author and his or her ads become closely associated, reminding the audience of his or her existence every time they appear on the printed page or the television screen. Thus the creator gets a reward for the same idea not once but many times.

Creativity Has Visibility

Creative advertising people have the best of two worlds: they get paid for what they do, and their work receives maximum exposure where it counts the most, in mass media. Few other occupations offer the same opportunity for an individual to rise to quick fame and fortune.

Moreover, the client foots the bill, sometimes amounting to several millions of dollars, for the exposure. While it is true that few advertisers would want to finance a publicity campaign for art directors, copywriters, or television producers, there is not much they can do about the rub-off effect of a successful advertising campaign—no more than producers can stop their star performers from sharing the limelight with them in hit plays.

Additional celebrity is bound to come from the press. Members of the advertising fraternity have never been known for reticence in getting their names in print. Being in the communications business, they have an instinct for news, and most journalists are only too happy to be presented with ready-to-use press releases prepared by professionals.

Perhaps it is this penchant for self-promotion that makes it possible for several major metropolitan newspapers (including the prestigious *New York Times*) to have sufficient material for carrying an extensive advertising column 5 times a week. Additional space is provided by more than fifty magazines wholly or partly covering communications industry. The most comprehensive of all, *Advertising Age*, with a base circulation of nearly 70,000, has 50 to 150 pages of news packed with people, places, and perspectives and reaches well over 250,000 readers. This publication, defined in the masthead as a "national newspaper of marketing," has stringers in every major city in the United States. *Ad Daily, Anny, The Gallagher Report, Madison Avenue, Media Decisions,* and *Art Direction* are not far behind in coverage. So it is no wonder that most big or even medium-size fish in advertising wittingly or unwittingly find themselves living in the proverbial fishbowl.

Moreover, there are awards to be won; each is presented to delighted recipients amid appropriate fanfare. Members of the trade press keep a close vigil of the proceedings. The work of the winners is hung at shows, carted from city to city all around the nation and the world, and finally reproduced for posterity in handsomely printed annuals with credits given to the source. Since some of these books reach a considerable number of decision makers, it literally pays to be included. The average printing of *"The One Show" Annual of Advertising, Editorial and TV Art & Design,* at $25 a copy, exceeds 20,000. Approximately 700 people attend the annual Art Director's Award night in New York to be inspired and to inspire. Black-tie Clio Award festivities attract nearly 2000 professionals; attendance at New York's Andy Awards festivities is not far behind. Both organizations reprint entries (print, TV, radio, poster, and so on) in their respective manuals.

With so many awards being bestowed on so many, it is entirely possible for a creative person to submit the same advertisement to a number of shows simultaneously and in up to 5 categories out of as many as 100 per event. Thus, a single outstanding ad or campaign can easily pick up two, three, or more citations. Perhaps the all-time record for award-winning performance should go to 2-minute commercial, "Yesterday," produced for the Eastman Kodak Company. After only a few exposures on television, it was graced with no fewer than fifteen important international awards, among them a diploma from the ACC Japan Festival, inclusion in "100 Best TV Commercials" from *Advertising Age,* two finalists places (Andy Awards and International Broadcasting Awards) inclusion in "50 Best TV Commercials" from the American Institute of Graphic Arts, second prize from the American Advertising Federation, series recognition from the American Television Commercials Festival, a Silver Phoenix at the Atlanta International Film Festival, "Grand Prix de Télévision" at the Cork International Film Festival, a finalist place at the International Broadcasting Awards, a Special Gold Award from the International Film and TV Festival of New York, a citation for distinctive merit from the Art Directors Club, and first prize at the American Television Commercials Festival and the Venice Film Festival. This list merely skims the surface; the commercial could have won more awards had there been enough time to submit it to other shows.

Account executives and marketing and media men have fewer opportunities to prove their creative flair as palatably as do their colleagues in art and copy; there are fewer trophies to go around. But word travels just the same. In a business that holds creativity in such high esteem, talent does not go unheeded for very long, regardless of job title.

Current Salary Levels of Creative Personnel in Advertising Agencies*

	LARGE ($50 million+)	MEDIUM ($10 to $50 million)	SMALL ($5 to $10 million)
Creative director	$75,000–125,000	$40,000–65,000	$35,000–50,000
Associate creative director†			
Creative supervisor†	28,000–55,000	30,000–45,000	
Creative group head†			. . .
Executive art director	40,000–60,000	25,000–40,000	15,000–25,000
Group art director	35,000–55,000	30,000–45,000	
Copy supervisor	30,000–60,000	30,000–45,000	. . .
Art supervisor	30,000–50,000	30,000–40,000	. . .
Senior copywriter	20,000–35,000	20,000–30,000	. . .
Art director	16,000–35,000	12,000–30,000	12,000–22,000
Junior copywriter	10,000–15,000	7,000–15,000	7,000–13,000
Assistant art director	10,000–12,000	10,000–14,000	10,000–12,000

*Figures represent high and low averages.
†These are all the same job but with different titles. All usually supervise art, copy, and TV production.

A campaign by Doyle Dane Bernbach for its first account, Ohrbach, soon had other clients joining the agency. The celebrated eye-patch ad made not only David Ogilvy famous, but his agency as well; today, less than 30 years later, it is the fifth largest agency in the world. A series of ads for Braniff pushed Wells, Rich, Greene into the foreground. A few ads for Volvo put Carl Ally on the map within a few months. Years later, when the account followed the principals to Scali, McCabe, Sloves, a new shop, it proved to be a creative calling card of that agency.

The man in the Hathaway shirt

The Volvo 164
A CIVILIZED CAR BUILT FOR AN UNCIVILIZED WORLD.

Creativity Builds Advertising Agencies

Advertising history is replete with success stories of agencies that built instant yet lasting reputations with a single campaign. A few such classics are shown above and on the left-hand page. As with individuals, the creative efforts of advertising agencies, through use of mass media, soon reach the eyes and ears of a large number of prospective clients, many with budgets of several million dollars burning holes in their corporate pockets.

That is why the word *creativity* has such a special ring to it. It has long become a final approbation in the field. One study conducted by the Gallagher Reports among 159 advertising agencies shows that 88 percent of agency presidents consider the performance of their creative departments the most critical in new-business assignments. Once an agency's creative reputation has been firmly established, everything else seems to fall into line. Clients

knock on the door. The agency profits. Referrals come from everywhere, including such unlikely places as competitive advertising agencies that for one reason or another cannot take on an account and are asked for recommendations. There is no doubt that creative agencies dominate the advertising scene today. Some have become large and highly profitable organizations in a relatively short time.

Indirectly, these agencies are most responsible for the unprecedented proliferation of new "hot shop" agencies in the last decade or so. They bring up creative people who then are able to manage advertising agencies of their own. For example, in the last 15 years, Doyle Dane Bernbach alumni have managed to start more than ten new shops, most of them highly successful.

Creativity Is a Way of Life

Perhaps the greatest fulfillment experienced by creative people comes from the knowledge that they are

capable of having ideas. The spirit of creativity—willingness to explore, question, and change things—seeps into every sphere of human activity, business being only one of them. People with active, inquisitive minds make better friends, parents, civic leaders, traveling companions, house guests, and, probably, lovers. Interested in the world around them, they become more interesting to their fellow human beings.

Curiosity kills boredom.

One of the finest rewards of creativity is the sense of independence that it brings. Creative people become known not only for what they are but also for what they do. Their work heralds their arrival and subtly sets the tone for their presence.

They are no longer dependent upon a single job or on the whims of a single employer. Doors everywhere swing open to them. They have the option to walk through any one of them.

In short, they are their own man or woman.

Creative persons have something to sell that everybody wants.

Ideas.

Index

V

Vending-machine advertising, 183
Viacom, 156
Village Voice, The, 151
Virginia Slims cigarettes, 53
Vogue, 150
Volkswagen (cars), 165, 176, 224
Volvo (cars), 36, 147, 213, 273

W

Warner/Levinson (music composers),
   147

Weaver, Bob, 213
Wells, William D., 50
White Shoulders perfume, 53
Williams, Gluyas, 136
Wolf, Henry, 215
Wolf, Jacob, 215
Wollensak 3M Company, 267
Word-of-mouth advertising, 183
Working habits (*see* Creativity,
   working habits and)
Wyeth, N. C., 136

X

Xerox Corp., 29

Y

Yamaha (motorcycles), 66
Yellow Pages, 183, 222, 269

Z

Zaid, Barry, 125
Zieff, Howard, 128, 208–209